BOOK DI
FRANCE

BOOK DIRECT
FRANCE

Catharine Hutton

Robertson McCarta

First published in 1990 by
Robertson McCarta Limited
122 King's Cross Road
London WC1X 9DS
© Robertson McCarta Ltd, 1990

Managing Editor Folly Marland
Designed by Liz Rose
Production by Grahame Griffiths
Typeset by Columns of Reading Ltd
Printed and bound in Great Britain
by Butler & Tanner Limited, Frome

British Library Cataloguing in Publication Data
Hutton, Catharine
    Book direct: France.
    1. France. Visitors' guides
    I. Title
    914.4′04838

ISBN 1–85365–172–9

CONTENTS

ACKNOWLEDGEMENTS

Special thanks are due to:

The French Government Tourist Office and Pauline Hallam in particular.

The staff of the regional and departmental tourist boards in France and those, too, at the many Tourist Offices in the resorts who supplied current information.

George Kerr for his unfailing help and guidance.

My friend and colleague Gill Lloyd, my husband Tony and children Amy and Toby for their support and encouragement.

INTRODUCTION

The object of this book is to encourage you to choose a holiday in France with a difference – one which allows you to be more adventurous than you have already been perhaps. Have you, for example, ever thought of cycling through the Loire valley, learning to canoe on the Ardèche or hang glide in the Alps; of playing golf in the Pyrénées or ballooning in Burgundy? How about crossing the wintry Vercors in dog sleds or learning to bake bread in 200-year-old ovens; or taking a spa holiday where the accent is on elegant relaxation? The chances are that you haven't, but if you're contemplating a change, let us help.

The first part of this book is the **activities** section – amongst which you may find listed your own favourite hobby or pastime, golf, for example, or fishing. Or a particular activity may appeal to you for the first time. If that is the case, let us persuade you to holiday in France, combining summer sun, winter snow or springtime loveliness with an activity holiday which you can arrange for yourself, by writing or picking up the telephone.

The **maps** at the back of the book will help you to pinpoint the area of your interest, while the second part of the book provides an invaluable 'resort guide', with over 400 major French **resorts** listed (by seaside, lakeside, mountain or in rural locations, and also including some city cultural centres), together with detailed regional guides and information, specific to each resort, on whom to contact for sport and leisure activities.

Stages in obtaining information:

1. Decide on the region of interest, and then write to the Comité Régional du Tourisme (CRT) at the address given. This is the equivalent to the British regional tourist board and, provided you have enclosed two or three International Reply Coupons (available from the Post Office), you will receive a fair amount of general information on this part of France.

2. Having studied this French information, plus our guide to the resorts within the region, you may now need more specific details, particularly about direct booking accommodation. This is the point at which you write to the Comité Départemental du Tourisme (CDT) office at the addresses given. Each resort featured in the gazetteer has the name of the *département* it lies within alongside it. Back will come even more information (again you must enclose International Reply Coupons to cover postage).

3. When you require information specific to a particular resort, you can phone or write direct to its Tourist Office. For example, the entry for **Collioure** in the **Languedoc-Roussillon** region lists information 🖅 available from: place du 18 Juin.

Thus, the address to write to would be:
Office de Tourisme de Collioure,
place du 18 Juin,
Languedoc-Roussillon,
FRANCE.

You will now receive on-the-spot details of hotels, self-catering accommodation, restaurants and camp sites as well as entertainments and local transport.

Bon voyage! Bon appetit! Bonnes vacances!

GENERAL INFORMATION
■ *FRENCH TOURIST OFFICES* ■

Austria
Hilton Center 259C, 1030 Vienna
Belgium
21 avenue de la Toison-d'Or, 1060 Bruxelles
Canada
1981 avenue McGill Collège, Tour Esso, Suite 490, Montreal
Denmark
Frederiksberggade 28, 1459 Copenhagen
Italy
via Sant'Andrea 5, 20121 Milan
and
93 via Vittorio Veneto, 00187 Rome
Japan
Landvic No 2, Akasaka Building, 2-10-9 Akasaka-Minato-Ku
Netherlands
Prinsengracht 670, 1017KX Amsterdam
Spain
Gran Via 59, 13 Madrid
and
Gran Via 656, 10 Barcelona

Switzerland
84 rue du Rhône, 1204 Geneva
and
Bahnhofstrasse 16, 8022 Zurich
United Kingdom
178 Piccadilly, London W1V 0AL
United States of America
610 Fifth Avenue, New York, N.Y. 10020
and
6645 North Michigan Avenue, Suite 430, Chicago, Illinois 60611
and
90212 Wilshire Boulevard, Beverly Hills, California 90212
and
World Trade Center, 2050 Stemmons Freeway, Dallas, Texas 75258
West Germany
1 Westendstrasse 47, D6 Frankfurt-Main
and
Berliner Allee 26, D4 Düsseldorf

■ *LOISIRS ACCUEIL* ■

There are currently 49 Loisirs Accueil offices throughout France, which offer a special service to the holidaymaker seeking something out of the ordinary. An organisation created under the patronage of various offices of tourism in France, their aim is to create, promote and develop new types of holiday in rural France.

Their brochures, most of which are in French, list unusual and interesting short break ideas and they offer a direct booking system with accommodation arranged in local *gîtes*, hotels or camp sites. What they offer varies from region to region, but the main themes are leisure and sporting activities. Thus there are, for example, fishing and barging holidays, canoeing trips, white-water rafting, cycling holidays and tennis coaching; crafts and gastronomy weekends; golf tuition holidays and horse riding or horse-drawn caravan holidays. For a fuller list see under Short Breaks (page 51).

The Loisirs Accueil addresses are listed after the regional introductions to each area in the gazetteer section of this book and in the Short Breaks section. A small selection, concentrating on cycling and rambling holidays, is produced in collaboration with the Gîtes de France organisation (Gîtes de France, Loisirs Accueil Department, 178 Piccadilly, London W1V 9DB) and the brochure is in English.

■ EMERGENCIES AND PROBLEMS ■

Emergencies
There are two emergency phone numbers:
Police and Ambulance **17**, Fire **18**

Theft or loss
Of car or personal belongings:
go to the nearest local or national police station (*gendarmerie* or *Commissariat de Police*).
Of passport or identity papers:
go to the nearest local or national police station, consulate or embassy, or administrative police headquarters (*préfecture*).
Of credit cards:
go to the nearest local or national police station or town hall (*mairie*) and immediately notify:
Diner's Club ☎ 47.62.75.00
Carte Bleue (Barclaycard and Visa) ☎ 42.77.11.90
American Express ☎ 47.08.31.21
Eurocard (Mastercard and Access) ☎ 43.23.46.46

Breakdown
In the event of a breakdown or accident on a motorway or toll road, contact the police by using the telephones sited in orange posts and located every 2 km. Place the hazard warning triangle 45 m behind your vehicle.

■ NATIONAL HOLIDAYS ■

Administrative offices and most shops close on public holidays. If any national holiday falls on a Tuesday or a Friday, the day between it and the nearest Sunday is also a holiday:

New Year's Day: January 1
Easter Monday (date varies)
Labour Day: May 1
Ascension Day (date varies, according to Easter)
VE Day: May 8
Whit Monday (date varies, according to Easter)
Bastille Day: July 14
Assumption Day: August 15
All Saints' Day: November 1
Remembrance Day: November 11
Christmas Day: December 25

The French take most of August as their annual leave (*Les Grandes Vacances*) and six out of ten of them go to the seaside for their holidays – the *French* seaside, of course! The traffic jams at the end of August, when the whole of France seems on the move, are therefore best avoided!

■ TELEPHONING ■

Calls can be made from public telephone booths, either with coins or with magnetic *télécartes*. Since most of the phone booths now seem to be converting away from coins, obtaining a phone card is advisable. They are sold in Post Offices and cafés/tabacs (50 units = 40F, 120 units = 96F).

To phone countries outside France
Dial 19, wait for the dial tone, then dial the **country code** followed by the area or city code (if relevant) followed by the number of the person you want to reach.

For the United Kingdom, dial 19, wait for the dial tone, then dial 44 followed by the STD code *minus the first 0*, followed by the number of the person you want to reach. Cheap rates (plus 50 per cent extra time) apply betweeen 10.30 p.m. and 8 a.m. (weekdays) and at weekends (after 2 p.m. on Saturdays).

Country codes

Australia	19 + 61
Austria	19 + 43
Belgium	19 + 32
Denmark	19 + 45
Italy	19 + 39
Japan	19 + 81
Luxembourg	19 + 352
Spain	19 + 34
Sweden	19 + 46
Switzerland	19 + 41
United Kingdom	19 + 44
United States	19 + 1
West Germany	19 + 49

To phone France from the UK
A simplified telephone system means that all French subscribers have an eight-figure number. All Paris numbers should begin with a 4, and with 3 or 6 for the Paris outskirts.
Dial the international access code 010 33, then either (1) plus the eight-figure number for Paris or simply the eight-figure number for the provinces.
To phone Paris from the provinces Dial 16 followed by (1) plus the eight-figure number.
To phone the provinces from Paris
Dial 16 followed by the eight-figure number.
To phone internally
Paris to Paris or province to province, simply dial the eight-figure number.

Operator **13**, Directory Enquiries **12**
Telegrams by phone (in English): (1)42.33.21.11

In an emergency, reverse-charge calls can be made to any foreign country which accepts them. Called *PCV* in French, dial 19 + 33 followed by the country code (as above). No collect calls can be made in France, but calls can be received in a public phone box where a blue bell sign is displayed.

■ *EMBASSIES* ■

The UK Foreign Office publish a leaflet entitled *Get it right before you go,* which tells you the dos and don'ts in France and outlines the services available from the various consulates. This leaflet is available from the FGTO (178 Piccadilly, London W1V 0AL) and from travel agents.

Australia
4 rue Jean Rey, Paris 15 ☎ 40.59.33.00
Austria
12 rue Edmond Valentin, Paris 7 ☎ 47.05.27.17

Belgium
9 rue de Tilsitt, Paris 17 ☎ 43.80.61.00
Canada
35/37 avenue Montaigne, Paris 8 ☎ 47.23.01.01
Denmark
77 avenue Marceau, Paris 16 ☎ 47.23.54.20
Italy
47 rue de Varenne, Paris 7 ☎ 45.44.38.90
Japan
7 avenue Hoche, Paris 8 ☎ 47.66.02.22
Luxembourg
3 avenue Rapp, Paris 7 ☎ 45.55.13.37
Netherlands
7 rue Eblé, Paris 7 ☎ 43.06.61.88
Spain
6 rue Greuze, Paris 16 ☎ 45.53.39.82
Sweden
17 rue Barber du Puy, Paris 7 ☎ 45.55.92.15
Switzerland
142 rue de Grenelle, Paris 7 ☎ 45.50.34.46
United Kingdom
16 rue d'Anjou, Paris 8 ☎ 42.66.38.10
(There are also British consulates in Bordeaux, Boulogne, Calais, Cherbourg,
Dunkerque, Epernay, Le Havre, Lille, Lyon, Marseille, Nantes, Nice, Perpignan,
St Malo/Dinard and Toulouse).
United States of America
2 avenue Gabriel, Paris 8 ☎ 42.96.12.02
West Germany
13 avenue Franklin D. Roosevelt, Paris 8 ☎ 42.99.78.00

TRAVEL INFORMATION
■ *TRAVEL BY CAR* ■

You'll need a valid driving licence, insurance certificate and car registration papers,
plus a distinguishing GB plate. The 'Green Card' international insurance card is
recommended, although no longer compulsory for cars coming from the Common
Market countries or for those from Sweden, Norway, Finland, Austria and
Switzerland. It will, however, give you better cover if you take one and the AA and
RAC can advise you further. British headlamps must be adjusted to dip to the right
(special stick-on strips can be bought), and yellow lamps fitted (or yellow paint
applied). A set of spare bulbs and a hazard warning triangle (for use in the event of
an accident) are also required.
● The international road sign system operates in France. Watch out, though, for the
traffic lights which are often situated high above the road.
● Driving is on the right-hand side of the road and it is important to remember to
yield right-of-way to the right when emerging from a stationary position.
● Speed limits: open road 90 kmph
dual carriageways 110 kmph
towns and cities 60 kmph
motorways 130 kmph
Paris ring roads 80 kmph
● Seat belts must be worn, by law.
● Helmets must be worn on motorcycles and motorbikes.

With over 4,800 km of motorway *(autoroute)*, France has a good network which is well serviced. Toll roads *(autoroutes à péage)* vary in price, the Calais to Menton route costing about 340 FF in total. Roads are classified A for *Autoroute*, N for *Route Nationale* and D for *Route Départementale*.

In winter, even in the mountains, driving is not severely restricted. Road conditions can be checked by phoning the 24-hour Inter Service Route in Paris ☎ 48.58.33.33, and, if required, snow chains can be cheaply purchased from hypermarkets in the winter resort areas.

CAR HIRE

Car hire can be arranged locally by enquiring at the Tourist Office, or in advance by contacting any of the following international agencies:
Avis Rent-a-Car, Hayes Gate House, 27 Uxbridge Road, Hayes, Middx ☎ 01-848 8733
Budget Rent-a-Car International, Marlowes, Hemel Hempstead HP1 1LD
☎ 0800 181181
Godfrey Davis Europcar, Bushey House, High Street, Bushey, Watford ☎ 01-950 5050
Hertz Rent-a-Car, Radnor House, 1272 London Road, Norbury, London SW16 ☎ 01-679 1777

■ *TRAVEL BY AIR* ■

From Paris any destination in France can be reached within an hour, on average, by excellent and frequent internal air connections. Air Inter, the national domestic carrier, flies between Paris and 30 major French towns and resorts. There are three types of flight, depending on the time of day: red (full fare), white (up to 30 per cent reduction), blue (up to 60 per cent reduction). Reduced fares are also offered for children, groups, students and senior citizens.

Airports in the UK offering direct flights to Paris are: Heathrow, Gatwick, Stansted London City (STOLport), Birmingham, Manchester, Bristol, Aberdeen, Edinburgh, Glasgow, Southampton, Jersey, Dublin, Cork and Shannon.

Major French airports served include: Bordeaux, Brest, Clermont-Ferrand, Le Havre, Lille, Lyon, Marseille, Metz, Montpellier, Mulhouse/Basle, Nantes, Nice, Perpignan, Quimper, Rennes, Strasbourg and Toulouse. Paris has two airports, Orly and Charles-de-Gaulle. Corsica is served principally by Ajaccio airport.

CARRIERS OPERATING OUT OF THE UK
Aigle Azur, Air France, 158 New Bond Street, London W1Y 0AY ☎ 01-499 9511
Air Canada, 140/144 Regent Street, London W1R 6AT ☎ 01-759 2636
Air Europe, Galleria, Station Road, Crawley RH10 1HY ☎ 0345 444737
Air France, 158 New Bond Street, London W1Y 0AY ☎ 01-499 9511
Air UK, Norwich Airport, Fifers Lane, Norwich, Norfolk NR6 6ER ☎ 0345 666777
Air Vendée, Air France, 158 New Bond Street, London W1Y 0AY ☎ 01-499 9511
Aurigny Air Services, Town Office, Victoria Street, St. Anne's, Alderney
☎ 048 182 2886
Brit Air, Air France, 158 New Bond Street, London W1Y 0AY ☎ 01-499 9511
British Airways, West London Air Terminal, Cromwell Road, London SW7 4ED
☎ 01-897 4000
British Midland Airways, East Midlands Airport, Castle Donnington, Derbyshire
☎ 0332 810552
Dan Air, Newman House, 71 Victoria Road, Horley, Surrey ☎ 0293 820222
Euro-Express, 227 Shepherds Bush Road, London W6 7AS ☎ 01-748 2607
Jersey European Airways, Jersey Airport, St Peter ☎ 0534 45661
London City Airways, London City Airport, London E16 2QQ ☎ 01-511 4200

Nouvelles Frontières, 1/2 Hanover Street, London W1R 9WD ☎ 01-629 7772
TAT, Air France, 158 New Bond Street, London W1Y 0AY ☎ 01-499 9511

In conjunction with the French Railways (SNCF), the national airline, Air France, offers competitively priced combined air and train travel fares. You can fly in to Paris from one of the UK airports and onward travel is then by rail to any of the 3,000 stations in France.
Contact: Air France, 158 New Bond Street, London W1Y 0AY ☎ 01-499 9511

■ TRAVEL BY SEA ■

Cross-Channel ferries and hovercraft offer quick and cheap car and passenger crossings throughout the year. Brochures detailing crossings (some only operate during the summer months) and fares are available at travel agents nationwide, or contact direct:

Brittany Ferries, The Brittany Centre, Wharf Road, Portsmouth PO2 8RU
☎ 0705 827701
Condor Hydrofoil, The North Pier Steps, St. Peter Port, Guernsey ☎ 0481 26121
Emeraude Ferries, 2 Albert Quay, St Helier, Jersey ☎ 0534 74458
Hoverspeed, Maybrook House, Queens Gardens, Dover CT17 9UQ ☎ 0304 240241
P & O European Ferries, Enterprise House, Channel View Road, Dover
☎ 0304 203388
Sally Line, Argyle Centre, York Street, Ramsgate ☎ 0843 595522
Sealink, Charter House, Park Street, Ashford, Kent ☎ 0233 47033

ROUTES AND OPERATORS

Cork – Roscoff (Brittany Ferries)
Dover – Boulogne (Hoverspeed, P & O, Sealink)
Dover – Calais (Hoverspeed, P & O, Sealink)
Dover – Dunkerque (Sealink)
Folkestone – Boulogne (Sealink)
Jersey – St Malo (Condor Hydrofoil, Emeraude Ferries)
Newhaven – Dieppe (Sealink)
Plymouth – Roscoff (Brittany Ferries)
Poole – Cherbourg (Brittany Ferries)
Portsmouth – Caen (Brittany Ferries)
Portsmouth – Cherbourg (P & O, Sealink)
Portsmouth – Le Havre (P & O)
Portsmouth – St Malo (Brittany Ferries)
Ramsgate – Dunkerque (Sally Line)
Southampton – Le Havre (P & O)
Weymouth – Cherbourg (Sealink)

Once in France, ferry connections to the island of Corsica operate from Marseille, Nice and Toulon, travelling to Ajaccio, Bastia, Calvi, Ile Rousse and Propriano. Early booking is essential in summer.
Contact: SNCM, 179 Piccadilly, London W1V 0BA ☎ 01-409 1224; and in France, SNCM, 12 rue Godot-de-Mauroy, 75009 Paris ☎ 42.66.60.19

■ TRAVEL BY TRAIN ■

The French railway system is run by the Société Nationale des Chemins de fer Français, or SNCF for short, and is the largest rail network in western Europe. Details of fares, routes and special deals and reductions are available from principal British

Rail Travel Centres and continental rail-appointed travel agents. There are, for example, reduced rate tickets for families (*Rail Europ Family*), for senior citizens (*Rail Europ Senior*), for the under 26s (*Carré Jeune/Carte Jeune*), and, for everyone, there is the *France Vacances Pass* and the *Billet Séjour.*

There are two classes, first and second. On certain trains, the TEE *(Trans Europe Express)*, for instance, only first class seats are available. Reservations are recommended to be sure of a seat and are mandatory on the high-speed TGV (*Train à Grande Vitesse*) which, running at 270 kmph, are the fastest trains in the world. To avoid a 20 per cent surcharge, tickets bought in France must be punched and date-stamped at one of the orange automatic machines (*composteur*) before going onto the platform. An English-language train information service operates in Paris, ☎ 45.82.08.41. Many stations offer a car hire service and over 280 of them also offer a cycle hire service.

Long drives can be avoided by using the French Railways' **Motorail** service. A network of special overnight trains carry sleeping passengers and their cars and motorbikes across the length and breadth of the country, towards the summer sun or the winter ski resorts. The service connects direct from the ferry or hovercraft terminals at Boulogne, Calais and Dieppe; there are English-speaking staff on hand to check you and your car on board and a free breakfast is served the next morning. The winter service, with on-board bar and disco, leaves Calais at 8 p.m. and arrives at Moutiers in the French Alps by 8 a.m. the following morning. Special summer holiday services on board trains, such as the *Cévenol, Aubrac* and *Ventadour*, travelling through some of the most picturesque routes in France, the Auvergne, Alps and Périgord, for example, also provide entertainment in the form of live music, mini-theatre, audio-visual presentations and games for children. Contact: SNCF (French Railways), 179 Piccadilly, London W1V 0BA

■ *TRAVEL BY COACH* ■

Regular services in modern, comfortable coaches with long-distance trips broken by frequent stops. Pick-ups are arranged all over the UK, with such destinations offered as:

Aix-en-Provence, Amiens, Annecy, Antibes, Bayonne, Biarritz, Bordeaux, Cannes, Chambéry, Chamonix, Digne, Grasse, Grenoble, Lourdes, Lyon, Marseille, Montpellier, Nice, Paris, Pau, Perpignan and Tours. Several operators can be contacted:

Euroways Express Coaches, 7 York Way, London N1 9UD ☎ 01-730 8235
Hoverspeed, Maybrook House, Queens Gardens, Dover CT17 9UQ ☎ 01-544 7061
National Express Eurolines, 52 Grosvenor Gardens, London SW1 0AU
☎ 01-730 0202 (bookable at National Express offices).
Supabus, Western House, 237/239 Oxford Street, London W1R 1AD ☎ 01-439 9368
(bookable at National Express offices).

WHERE TO STAY IN FRANCE

Before travelling to France, particularly if your visit coincides with the peak holiday period, you should have made reservations for accommodation.

The French *Comité Régional du Tourisme*, equivalent to the British Regional Tourist Boards, as well as the Tourist Boards for the *départements* within the regions (*Comité Départmental du Tourisme*) will supply, on request, specific brochures detailing camping, hotel and self-catering *gîte* accommodation in their area, from which you can make your choice. (The addresses for all these regional and departmental boards are given in the gazetteer section of this book.)

Once in France, the local Tourist Office, which is known either as an *Office de Tourisme* or a *Syndicat d'Initiative,* can provide on-the-spot advice and information on accommodation availability.

Some Tourist Offices belong to the *Accueil de France,* a service whereby personal callers will have hotel reservations made for them by telephone (a small charge will be made) for the same day and up to eight days in advance. These offices are open every day of the year in the following towns:

Aix-les-Bains ● Angers ● Avignon ● La Baule ● Besançon ● Blois ● Bordeaux ● Caen ● Calais ● Cannes ● Dijon ● Evian ● Grenoble ● Le Havre ● Lille ● Limoges ● Lyons ● Marseilles ● Metz ● Nancy ● Nîmes ● Orléans ● Perpignan ● Perros-Guirec ● Quiberon ● Rheims ● La Rochelle ● Rouen ● Strasbourg ● Toulon ● Tours ● Vichy ●

Just as at camp sites, hotel prices must be displayed outside and inside the establishment. Breakfast is not mandatory and you should not be billed for it if you haven't had it! When reserving accommodation, make sure the amount of deposit (*arrhes*) is clearly stated, and ask for a receipt for any sum paid. When making telephone reservations, ensure that you state your arrival time, as hotels may re-allocate rooms after 7 p.m. If you find yourself delayed en route, make a courtesy phone call to the hotel, stating your revised arrival time.

■ *CAMPING* ■

There are probably more camp sites in France than any other country in Europe, and they enjoy an excellent reputation. Living under canvas can be wonderful fun as many of the camp sites are more like holiday camps in their provision of on-site shopping facilities and entertainment, with such activities as riding, tennis, canoeing, etc., all laid on. Amenities do vary, though; there are about 11,000 camp sites in France officially star-graded as follows:

*	basic but adequate amenities
**	good all-round standard of amenities
***	first class standard with emphasis on comfort and privacy
****	very comfortable, low-density and landscaped sites

All sites must display their grading and charges at the site entrance. They must have roads connecting with the public highway, and be laid out so as to respect the environment, with at least 10 per cent of the ground devoted to trees or shrubs. They must also have adequate fire and security arrangements, permanent and covered washing and sanitary facilities, linked to public drainage, and daily refuse collection. The maximum number of people per hectare is 300. However, at peak periods, when all sites are under considerable strain, there may be some relaxation in the regulations.

Sites graded ** and above must have communal buildings lit (and roads for *** and ****), games areas (with equipment for *** and ****), a central meeting place, points for electric razors, surrounding fence with a day guard (night watchman for *** and **** sites). Sites graded *** and **** must also have washing facilities in cubicles, hot showers, safety deposits, telephones and good shops on or close to the site.

Both campers and caravanners will find an International Camping Carnet useful. Although not compulsory, some sites do require that you have one, and its presentation may even result in a discount being offered. The carnet gives evidence of insurance against third-party risks and may be obtained by members from the AA, RAC, Camping and Caravanning Club, the Caravan Club and the Cyclists Touring Club. If you do not belong to any of the above, you may contact the GB Car Club, P.O. Box 11, Romsey, Hants SO5 8XX, who will supply them.

Many books are devoted to this subject, but a good first step might be to obtain the official FFCC (French Federation of Camping and Caravanning) guide from Springdene, Shepherd's Way, Fairlight, Sussex TN35 4BB (price £6.95). This details 11,000 sites in French with a small supplement in English, and will indicate which sites accept advance bookings. You may then write direct to your selected camp site using, if you wish, the following letter and enclosing an International Reply Coupon (available from the Post Office).

Monsieur le Directeur   *Date*
Camping ....
....
(address)

Monsieur le Directeur
Dear Sir

Ayant obtenu votre adresse par l'intermédiaire des Services Officiels du Tourisme Français à Londres, je vous serais obligé de me communiquer, rapidement, vos conditions et tarifs au séjour suivant:

I have selected your address with the help of the French Government Tourist Office in London, and I should be grateful if you would let me know, at your earliest convenience, your conditions for the following stay:

Arrivé le ....   *Départ le* ....
Arriving on ....   Departing on ....

Nous sommes .... *adultes et* .... *enfants agés de* .... *ans*
We are .... adults and .... children aged .... years

Nous désirons   *réserver*   *un emplacement*   *pour une voiture*
We wish   to book   a pitch   for a car

caravane motorisé   *louer une tente/caravane/bungalow*
motor caravan   to hire a tent/caravan/chalet
                                  (delete where applicable)

Veuillez me répondre directement à l'adresse ci-dessous:
Please answer direct to my address below: (BLOCK CAPITALS)

Mr/Mrs ....
....
....

Avec mes remerciements
Yours faithfully

There also exist several camping associations in France with *Select Site Reservations* able to make advance reservations for you. This agency covers the three French chains of **Airôtels** (40 sites *** and ****), **Castels et Camping Caravanning** (47 sites *** and ****), and **Sites et Paysages de France** (35 sites *** and ****).
Select Site Reservations, Travel House, Pandy, Nr Abergavenny, Gwent NP7 8DH
☎ 0873 890770
The following British operators can also make site bookings on your behalf:
The Caravan Club, East Grinstead House, East Grinstead RH19 3HW ☎ 0342 316101
Eurocamp Independent, 22-24 Princess Street, Knutsford, Cheshire WA16 6BG
☎ 0565 55399
Response Reservations, 22 High East Street, Dorchester DT1 1EZ ☎ 0305 67404

For those who prefer all-inclusive packages, however, contact any of the following British operators who offer pre-erected tents on sites throughout France. Brochures from these operators will answer individual queries on needs and destinations.

Canvas Holidays, 9/13 Bull Plain, Hertford SG14 1DY ☎ 0992 553535
Carefree Camping, 126 Hempstead Road, King's Langley, Herts WD3 8AL
☎ 09277 61311
Eurocamp, Edmundson House, Tatton Street, Knutsford WA16 6BG ☎ 0565 3844
Freedom of France, 2–5 Market Place, Ross-on-Wye, Herefordshire HR9 5LD
☎ 0989 768168
French Life, 26 Church Road, Horsforth, Leeds LS18 5LG ☎ 0532 390077
Intasun, 2 Cromwell Avenue, Bromley, Kent BR2 9AQ ☎ 01-290 1900
Keycamp, 92-96 Lind Road, Sutton, Surrey SM1 4PL ☎ 01-661 7334
Sunsites, 22-24 Princess Street, Knutsford, Cheshire WA16 6BN ☎ 0565 55644

■ *CARAVANNING* ■

The following British operators offer caravans on sites in France:

AA Motoring Holidays, P.O. Box 100, Fanum House, Halesowen B63 3BT
☎ 021-550 7401
Air France Holidays, 69 Boston Manor Road, Brentford TW8 9JQ ☎ 01-568 6981
All-Association for Active Learning, 9 Haywra Street, Harrogate HG1 5BJ
☎ 0423 505313
Amigo Leisure, 6 Fairway, Carlyon Bay, St. Austell PL25 3QE ☎ 0726 814476
Angel Travel, 44 High Street, Borough Green, Sevenoaks, Kent TN15 8BJ
☎ 0732 884109
Becks Holidays, Southfields, Shirleys, Ditchling, Hassocks BN6 8UD ☎ 07918 2843
Breakaway Holidays, 14 West Street, Storrington RH20 4EE ☎ 09066 5623
Brittany Caravan Hire, 15 Winchcombe Road, Frampton Cotterell, Bristol BS17 2AG
☎ 0454 772410
Brittany Ferries, The Brittany Centre, Wharf Road, Portsmouth PO2 8RU
☎ 0705 827701

Canvas Holidays, 9/13 Bull Plain, Hertford SG14 1DY ☎ 0992 553535
Carasol Holidays, 6 Hayes Avenue, Bournemouth BH7 7AD ☎ 0202 33398
The Caravan Club, East Grinstead House, East Grinstead RH19 3HW ☎ 0342 316101
Carefree Camping, 126 Hempstead Road, Kings Langley WD4 8AL ☎ 09277 61311
Carisma Holidays, Bethel House, Heronsgate Road, Chorley Wood WD3 5BB
☎ 09278 4235
Chalets de France, Travel House, Pandy, Nr Abergavenny NP7 8DH ☎ 0873 890770
Club Cantabrica Holidays, Holiday House, 146/48 London Road, St Albans AL1 1PQ
☎ 0727 66177
Continental Camping Holidays, 12 Coronation Drive, Penketh, Warrington WA5 2DD
☎ 0925 728975
Cosmos Motoring Holidays, Tourama House, 17 Homesdale Road, Bromley BR2 9LX
☎ 01-464 3121
Cresta Holidays, 32 Victoria Street, Altrincham WA14 1ET ☎ 0345 056511
Dieppe Ferries Holidays, Weymouth Quay, Weymouth DT4 8DY ☎ 0305 777444
Econocamps, 9 Glenton Way, Romford, Essex RM1 4AG ☎ 0708 21837
Esprit, 15 Clifton Hill, Exeter EX1 2DL ☎ 0392 70506
Eurocamp, Edmundson House, Tatton Street, Knutsford, Cheshire WA16 6BG
☎ 0565 3844
Fleur Holidays, 29 North Park Drive, Blackpool FY3 8LR ☎ 0253 301719
Four Seasons, Springfield, Farsley, Pudsey, Leeds LS28 5UT ☎ 0532 564374
France Individuelle, 122 High Street, Billingshurst, West Sussex RH14 8EP
☎ 0404 381 5166
French Life Motoring Holidays, 26 Church Road, Horsforth, Leeds LS18 5LG
☎ 0532 390077
French Riviera Holidays, Regency House, 45 Thornhill Drive, Nuneaton CV11 6TD
☎ 0203 374444
French Travel Service, Georgian House, 69 Boston Manor Road, Brentford TW8 0JQ
☎ 01-568 8442
Haven Abroad, P.O. Box 9, Hayling Island, PO11 0NL ☎ 0705 466111
Holiday Charente, Wardington, Banbury OX17 1SA ☎ 029575 8282
Holimartine (South of France) Ltd, 132 Drake Street, Rochdale DL16 1PP
☎ 0706 353330
Hoseasons Holidays Abroad, Sunway House, Lowestoft NR32 3LT ☎ 0502 500555
Hoverspeed Ltd, Maybrook House, Queens Gardens, Dover CT17 9UQ
☎ 0304 240241
Impact Holidays, Devonshire Chambers, 10 Devonshire Street, Carlisle CA3 8LP
☎ 0228 45252
Intasun France, Intasun House, Cromwell Avenue, Bromley BR2 9AQ
☎ 01-290 1900
International Caravan Holidays, 9 Wentworth Drive, Lichfield WS14 9HN
☎ 0543 252726
Keycamp Holidays, Ellerman House, 92/96 Lind Road, Sutton SM1 4PL
☎ 01-661 1836
Lagrange Vacances, 16/20 New Broadway, London W5 2XA ☎ 01-579 7311
Matthews Holidays, 8 Bishopsmead Parade, East Horsley KT24 6RP ☎ 04865 5213
NAT Holidays, Devonshire House, 29/31 Elmfield Road, Bromley BR1 1LT
☎ 01-466 6660
Newborne Côte d'Azur, 49 Madeira Avenue, Worthing BN11 2AX ☎ 0903 37809
NSS Riviera Holidays, 199 Marlborough Avenue, Hull HU5 3LG ☎ 0482 42240
PGL Adventure, 104 Station Street, Ross on Wye HR9 7AH ☎ 0989 768768
Rendez-Vous France, Holiday House, 146/148 London Road, St Albans AL1 1PQ
☎ 0727 45400
Riviera Sailing Holidays, 45 Bath Road, Emsworth PO10 7ER ☎ 0243 374376
Sally Tours, Argyle Centre, York Street, Ramsgate CT11 9DS ☎ 0843 595566
Sandpiper Holidays, Ivy Cottage, Tilt Road, Stoke d'Abernon, Cobham, Surrey
☎ 0932 68658

Sealink Holidays, Charter House, Park Street, Ashford TN24 8EX ☎ 0233 47033
Selection Holidays, 26 Downsway, Shoreham by Sea BN4 5GN ☎ 0273 461153
Solaire Holidays, 1158 Stratford Road, Hall Green, Birmingham B28 8AF
☎ 021-778 5061
Solmer Travel, 10 Berwyn Road, Richmond TW10 5BS ☎ 01-876 1331
Sparrow Holidays, Fiveacres, Murcott, Oxford OX5 2RE ☎ 086 733 350
Stallard Holidays, Stallard House, 29 Stoke Newington Road, London N16 8BL
☎ 01-254 6444
Sunscene Holidays, 40 Market Place South, Leicester LE1 5HB ☎ 0533 20644
Uniquest Holidays, 97 Northwood End Road, Haynes, Bedford MK45 3QD
☎ 023 066396
Val Rose Holidays, South Lodge, The Village, Petersfield GU31 4AZ ☎ 0730 62955
Venue Camping, 409 Canterbury Road, Kenington, Ashford TN25 4DU
☎ 0233 629950
Welcome Holidays, 18 Kings Drive, Thames Ditton KT7 0TH ☎ 01-398 0355

■ *CHATEAUX* ■

The opportunity to stay in private châteaux homes is offered by the following British operators:

Billington Travel, 2a White Hart Parade, Riverhead, Sevenoaks TN13 2BJ
☎ 0732 460666
La France des Villages, Model Farm, Rattlesden, Bury St Edmunds IP30 0SY
☎ 044 93 7664
France Directe, 2 Church Street, Warwick CV34 4AB ☎ 0926 497989
The French Selection, Chester Close, Chester Street, London SW1X 7BQ
☎ 01-235 0634
Hampton House Travel, 51 Fife Road, Kingston-upon-Thames KT1 1SF
☎ 01-549 2116
North Sea Ferries, King George Dock, Hedon Road, Hull HU9 5QA ☎ 0482 796145
Paris Travel Service, Bridge House, Ware SG12 9DF ☎ 0920 3900
Par-Tee Tours, Riverside House, 53 Uxbridge Road, Rickmansworth WD3 2DH
☎ 0923 721565
Travellers, 277 Oxlow Lane, Dagenham, Essex ☎ 01-985 9679
World Wine Tours, 4 Dorchester Road, Drayton St Leonard OX9 8BH ☎ 0865 891919

■ *GITES* ■

These are Government-sponsored, self-catering rural properties which can be anything from a small cottage or village house to a flat or part of a farm. These are perfect for families travelling by car and offer an economical way to stay in France and meet and mix with the locals. A small membership fee entitles you to a fully illustrated official handbook and free reservation service. Contact *Gîtes de France*, 178 Piccadilly, London W1V 9DB ☎ 01-493 3480.

Other options for self-catering accommodation are detailed in the tourist literature supplied by the 22 regions of France themselves. Addresses for the Comité Régional du Tourisme (regional tourist boards) are listed after every regional introduction in the gazetteer section of this book. More specific details for a particular location can be obtained by writing to the *Relais des Gîtes Ruraux de France et de Tourisme Vert* for each department, whose addresses are listed below.

Many private companies offer *gîte*, villa, chalet or apartment accommodation throughout France. These can be located at the coast or in rural or mountain resorts, and are frequently sold as packages with flights included, but can also be accommodation only. British operators offering this service are listed under each region in the gazetteer section.

Ain (01)
1 place Clemenceau, 01000 Bourg-en-Bresse ☎ 74.23.61.96 (guide costs 25F)
Aisne (02)
1 rue Saint-Martin, B.P.116, 02000 Laon ☎ 23.20.45.54 (guide costs 10F)
Allier (03)
35 rue de Bellecroix, 03402 Yzeure Cedex ☎ 70.44.41.57 (guide costs 16F)
Alpes-de-Hautes-Provence (04)
Rond-Point du 11 Novembre, 04000 Digne ☎ 92.31.52.39 (guide costs 30F)
Hautes-Alpes (05)
5 ter, rue Capitaine-Bresson, B.P.55, 05002 Gap ☎ 92.51.31.45 (guide costs 45F)
Alpes-Maritimes (06)
55 promenade des Anglais, 06000 Nice ☎ 93.44.50.59 (guide costs 30F)
Ardèche (07)
4 avenue de l'Europe-Unie, B.P.221, 07002 Privas Cedex ☎ 75.64.04.66 and
☎ 75.64.70.00 (guide costs 38F)
Ardennes (08)
1 avenue de Petit-Bois, B.P.331, 08105 Charleville-Mézières ☎ 24.33.11.77 and
☎ 24.33.38.66 (enclose International Reply Coupon)
Ariège (09)
14 rue Lazéma, 09000 Foix ☎ 61.02.90.42 (guide costs 20F)
Aube (10)
2 bis, rue Jeanne-d'Arc, 10010 Troyes Cedex ☎ 25.73.25.36 (enclose International
Reply Coupon)
Aude (11)
70 rue Aimé-Ramon, 11000 Carcassonne ☎ 68.47.09.06 (guide costs 25F)
Aveyron (12)
APATAR, 5c, boulevard du 122e R.I., 12006 Rodez Cedex ☎ 65.68.11.38 (guide costs
25F)
Bouches-du-Rhône (13)
Domaine du Vergon, 13370 Mallemort ☎ 90.59.18.05 (guide costs 20F)
Calvados (14)
6 promenade Mme-de-Sévigné, 14039 Caen Cedex ☎ 31.82.71.65 (guide costs 35F)
Cantal (15)
22 rue Guy-de-Veyre, 15019 Aurillac Cedex ☎ 73.93.04.03 (guide costs 17F)
Charente (16)
place Bouillaud, 16021 Angoulême ☎ 45.92.24.43 (guide costs 13F)
Charente-Maritime (17)
2 avenue de Fétilly, B.P.32, 17002 La Rochelle Cedex ☎ 46.67.34.74 (guide costs
35F)
Cher (18)
10 rue de la Chappe, 18000 Bourges ☎ 48.65.31.01 (guide costs 20F)
Corrèze (19)
36 avenue du Général de Gaulle, 19000 Tulle ☎ 55.26.46.88 (guide costs 22F)
Corse (20)
22 boulevard Paoli, 20090 Ajaccio ☎ 95.20.51.34 and ☎ 95.22.70.79 (guide costs
15F)
Côte d'Or (21)
42 rue de Mulhouse, 21000 Dijon ☎ 80.68.38.41 (guide costs 20F)
Côtes-du-Nord (22)
5 rue Baratoux, B.P.556, 22010 Saint-Brieuc Cedex ☎ 96.61.82.79 (guide costs 45F)
Creuse (23)
1 rue Martinet, B.P.89, 23011 Guéret ☎ 55.52.87.50 and ☎ 55.52.89.50 (guide costs
25F)
Dordogne (24)
16 rue Wilson, 24009 Périgueux ☎ 53.53.44.35 (enclose two International Reply
Coupons)

Doubs (25)
Les Eaux Vives, 15 avenue Droz, 25000 Besançon Cedex ☎ 81.80.38.18 (guide costs 20F)
Drôme (26)
avenue Georges-Brassens, 26500 Bourg-lès-Valence ☎ 75.43.01.70 (guide costs 30F)
Eure (27)
5 rue de la Petite Cité, B.P.882, 27008 Evreux Cedex ☎ 32.39.53.38 (guide costs 30F)
Eure-et-Loir (28)
10 rue Dieudonné-Costes, 28024 Chartres ☎ 37.21.37.22 (guide costs 15F)
Finistère (29)
5 allée de Sully, 29322 Quimper Cedex ☎ 98.95.75.30 (guide costs 55F)
Gard (30)
3 place des Arènes, B.P.122, 30011 Nîmes ☎ 66.21.02.51 (guide costs 20F)
Garonne (31)
18 place Dupuy, 31000 Toulouse Cedex ☎ 61.62.442.62 (guide costs 15F)
Gers (32)
route de Tarbes, 32003 Auch Cedex ☎ 62.63.16.55 (guide costs 20F)
Gironde (33)
38 rue Ferrère, 33000 Bordeaux ☎ 56.81.54.23 (guide costs 30F)
Hérault (34)
rue Chaptal, 34076 Montpellier Cedex ☎ 67.92.88.00 (guide costs 35F)
Ille-et-Vilaine (35)
1 rue Martenot, 35000 Rennes ☎ 99.02.97.41 (guide costs 35F)
Indre (36)
Gare routière, rue Bourdillon, 36000 Chateauroux ☎ 54.27.58.61 (guide costs 20F)
Isère (38)
14 rue de la République, B.P.227, 38019 Grenoble Cedex ☎ 76.44.42.28 (guide costs 30F)
Jura (39)
39021 Lons-le-Saunier Cedex ☎ 84.24.57.70 (guide costs 30F)
Landes (40)
Cité Galliane, B.P.279, 40005 Mont-de-Marsan ☎ 58.46.10.45 (guide costs 25F)
Loir-et-Cher (41)
11 place du Château, 41000 Blois ☎ 54.78.55.50 (guide costs 21F)
Loire (42)
43 avenue Albert-Raimond, B.P.50, 42272 Saint-Priest-en-Jarez Cedex ☎ 77.79.15.22 (guide costs 25F)
Haute-Loire (43)
4 avenue Charles-de-Gaulle, 43000 Le Puy-en-Velay ☎ 73.93.04.03 (guide costs 18F)
Loire-Atlantique (44)
46 bis, rue des Hauts-Pavés, B.P.1141, 44024 Nantes Cedex ☎ 40.76.39.90 (guide costs 22F)
Loiret (45)
3 rue de la Bretonnerie, 45000 Orléans ☎ 38.54.83.83 (guide costs 15F)
Lot (46)
430 avenue Jean-Jaurès, 46004 Cahors ☎ 65.22.19.20 (guide costs 25F)
Lot-et-Garonne (47)
rue de Péchabout, 47000 Agen ☎ 53.96.44.99 (guide costs 20F)
Lozère (48)
place Urbain V, B.P.4, 48002 Mende ☎ 66.65.34.55 (guide costs 30F)
Maine-et-Loire (49)
place Kennedy, 49100 Angers ☎ 41.88.23.85 (guide costs 10F)
Manche (50)
rue du Belle, B.P.419, 50009 Saint-Lô Cedex ☎ 33.57.52.80 (guide costs 35F)

Marne (51)
Complexe agricole de Mont-Bernard, route de Suippes, B.P.525, 51009 Châlons-sur-Marne Cedex ☎ 26.64.08.13 (guide costs 10F)
Haute-Marne (52)
Hôtel de Conseil Général, 89 rue Victoire-de-la-Marne, 52011 Chaumont Cedex ☎ 25.32.65.00 (guide costs 10F)
Mayenne (53)
19 rue de l'Ancien-Evêché, 53000 Laval Cedex ☎ 43.53.27.40 (guide costs 25F)
Meurthe-et-Moselle (54)
5 rue de la Vologne, 54524 Laxou ☎ 83.96.49.58 (guide costs 10F)
Meuse (55)
Préfecture, 55012 Bar-le-Duc Cedex ☎ 29.79.48.10 (guide costs 18F)
Morbihan (56)
2 rue du Château, B.P.318, 56403 Auray Cedex ☎ 97.56.48.12 (guide costs 45F)
Moselle (57)
64 avenue André-Malraux, 57045 Metz Cedex ☎ 87.63.13.25 (guide costs 10F)
Nièvre (58)
Nièvre Tourisme, Hôtel du Département, B.P.839, 58019 Nevers ☎ 86.59.14.22 (guide costs 10F)
Nord (59)
14 square Foch, 59800 Lille ☎ 20.57.00.61 (guide costs 20F)
Oise (60)
1 rue Villiers-de-l'Isle-Adam, B.P.222, 60008 Beauvais Cedex ☎ 44.48.16.87 (guide costs 7F)
Orne (61)
60 rue Saint-Blaise, B.P.50, 61002 Alençon Cedex ☎ 33.26.18.71 (guide costs 20F)
Pas-de-Calais (62)
44 Grande-Rue, 62200 Boulogne-sur-Mer ☎ 21.31.66.80 (guide costs 10F)
Puy-de-Dôme (63)
69 boulevard Gergovia, 63038 Clermont-Ferrand ☎ 73.93.04.03 (guide costs 21F)
Pyrénées-Atlantiques (64)
Cité administrative, 124 boulevard Toutasse, 64000 Pau ☎ 59.80.19.13 (guide costs 30F)
Hautes-Pyrénées (65)
22 place du Foirail, 65000 Tarbes ☎ 62.34.52.82 (guide costs 28F)
Pyrénées-Orientales (66)
30 rue Pierre-Bretonneau, B.P.946, 66020 Perpignan Cedex ☎ 68.55.33.55 (guide costs 25F)
Bas-Rhin (67)
7 place des Meuniers, 67000 Strasbourg ☎ 88.75.56.50 (guide costs 35F)
Haut-Rhin (68)
3 place de la Gare, 68000 Colmar ☎ 89.41.41.99 (guide costs 15F)
Rhône (69)
4 place Gensoul, 69287 Lyon Cedex ☎ 78.42.65.92 (guide costs 25F)
Haute-Saône (70)
rue des Bains, B.P.117, 70002 Vesoul ☎ 84.75.43.66 (guide costs 20F)
Saône-et-Loire (71)
boulevard Henri-Dunant, B.P.522, 71010 Macon Cedex ☎ 85.38.50.66 (guide costs 15F)
Sarthe (72)
Hôtel du Département, 21X, 72040 Le Mans Cedex ☎ 43.81.72.72 (enclose an International Reply Coupon)
Savoie (73)
24 boulevard de la Colonne, 73000 Chambéry ☎ 79.85.01.09 (guide costs 55F)
Haute-Savoie (74)
52 avenue des Iles, B.P.327, 74037 Annecy Cedex ☎ 50.67.20.89 (guide costs 55F)

Seine-Maritime (76)
chemin de la Bretèque, B.P.59, 76232 Bois-Guillaume ☎ 35.60.73.34 (guide costs 25F)
Seine-et-Marne (77)
Maison Départementale du Tourisme, Château Soubiran, 77190 Dammarie-les-Lys ☎ 64.37.47.15 (guide costs 10F)
Yvelines (78)
Hôtel du Département, 2 place André-Mignot, 78010 Versailles ☎ 30.21.36.73 (guide free)
Deux-Sèvres (79)
70 rue Alsace-Lorraine, 79000 Niort ☎ 49.24.00.42 (guide costs 37F)
Somme (80)
21 rue Ernest-Cauvin, 80000 Amiens ☎ 22.92.26.39 (enclose International Reply Coupon)
Tarn (81)
B.P.89, 81003 Albi Cedex ☎ 63.54.39.81 (guide costs 25F)
Tarn-et-Garonne (82)
place du Maréchal-Foch, Hôtel des Intendants, 82000 Montauban ☎ 63.63.31.40 (guide free)
Var (83)
1 boulevard Maréchal-Foch, B.P.215, 83006 Draguignan ☎ 94.67.10.40 (guide costs 25F)
Vaucluse (84)
La Balance, B.P.147, 84008 Avignon Cedex ☎ 90.85.45.00 (guide free)
Vendée (85)
124 boulevard Aristide-Briand, 85013 La Roche-sur-Yon Cedex ☎ 51.62.33.10 (guide costs 30F)
Vienne (86)
11 rue Victor-Hugo, B.P.287, 86007 Poitiers ☎ 49.41.58.22 (guide costs 15F)
Haute-Vienne (87)
32 avenue Général-Leclerc, 87100 Limoges ☎ 55.79.04.04 (guide costs 25F)
Vosges (88)
13 rue Aristide-Briand, B.P.405, 88010 Epinal Cedex ☎ 29.35.50.34 (guide costs 25F)
Yonne (89)
14 bis, rue Guynemer, 89000 Auxerre ☎ 86.46.01.39 (guide costs 10F)
Territoire de Belfort (90)
rue de l'Ancian-Théâtre, 90020 Belfort ☎ 84.21.27.95 (guide free)
Essonne (91)
4 rue de l'Arche, 91100 Corbeil-Essonnes ☎ 60.89.31.32 (guide free)
Val d'Oise (95)
2 rue Le Campus, 95031 Cergy-Pontoise Cedex ☎ 34.43.32.57 (guide free)

Not to be confused with a *Gîte de France* is the *Gîte d'Etape.* Specifically designed for groups or individual cyclists, walkers, cross-country skiiers and, where indicated, riders, they are situated along the footpath networks and regularly signposted. Here comfortable overnight accommodation is offered, often in bunk-bed dormitories, and either with the use of a kitchen or with meals prepared by a warden.

■ *HOLIDAY FUN PARK* ■

The name and fame of the Center Parcs villages have grown over the last 20 years or so since their creation in the Netherlands. The newest to be built (1988), and the first in France, is Les Bois-Francs, near Verneuil-sur-Avre in Normandy. Perfect for short weekend breaks for young families, there are numerous indoor and outdoor leisure facilities and a superb swimming area, its constant temperature creating a subtropical environment whatever the weather outside. Open all year round, the accommodation is in self-catering villas and there is a choice of restaurants, full children's entertainments and acres of outdoor space to enjoy. Sealink organise all-inclusive ferry and accommodation packages for three or four nights.

Sealink, Charter House, Park Street, Ashford, Kent ☎ 0233 47033

■ *HOLIDAY VILLAGES* ■

A concept which is particularly popular in France, holiday villages offer self-contained entertainment and leisure facilities and a choice of accommodation types, a style of holiday ideal for the young and for those with families. Several British operators, most famous, perhaps, Club Méditerranée, offer all-inclusive packages in locations throughout France:

Allez France, 27 West Street, Storrington, Pulborough RH20 4DZ ☎ 09066 2345
Club Méditerranée, 106/110 Brompton Road, London SW3 1JJ ☎ 01-581 1161
French Travel Service, Georgian House, 69 Boston Manor Road, Brentford TW8 0JQ ☎ 01-568 8442
Sealink Holidays, Charter House, Park Street, Ashford TN24 8EX ☎ 0233 47033
VVF Holiday Villages, 5 World's End Lane, Green Street Green, Orpington BR6 6AA ☎ 0689 62904
Mark Warner, 20 Kensington Church Street, London W8 ☎ 01-938 1851

■ *HOME EXCHANGE* ■

Home exchange services, featuring many parts of France, are offered by the following companies:

Global Home Exchange and Travel Service, 12 Brookway, Blackheath, London SE3 9BJ ☎ 01-852 1439
Intervac International Home Exchange Service, 6 Siddals Lane, Allestree, Derby DE3 2DY ☎ 0332 558931

■ *HOTELS* ■

The FGTO (French Government Tourist Office, 178 Piccadilly, London W1V 0AL ☎ 01-491 7622) publish a full list of hotel groups with details of booking offices in the UK as well as those French chains with whom you book direct. They can also offer further advice. A selection showing the variety of hotel accommodation on offer throughout France is listed below:

Campanile
Small, modern ** hotels (126 of them) throughout France. Guide provides good street location maps.
Contact: Campanile, 40 rue de Villiers, 92300 Levallois-Perret ☎ 47.57.11.11
Chambres d'Hôte
Bed and breakfast accommodation in private homes, usually in rural France.
Contact: Gîtes de France Ltd, 178 Piccadilly, London W1V 9DB ☎ 01-408 1343 and 01-493 3480
Château Accueil
Stay as a guest in a private château or manor house, with personal welcome and attention by the owners. This organisation represents over 70 such properties often set in magnificent grounds and with facilities for fishing and riding. Multi-lingual booklet.
Contact: World Wine Tours, 4 Dorchester Road, Drayton St Leonard OX9 8BH ☎ 0865 891919

Châteaux, Hôtels, Indépendents et Hostelleries d'atmosphere
Stylish private establishments, such as châteaux, hotels and castles, offering hotel-type accommodation and services, but unaffiliated to any overseeing body. The illustrated guide book is in French and lists 300 (including a section on restaurants).
Contact: Château de Pray, B.P.146, 37401 Amboise Cedex ☎ 47.57.23.67

Climat de France
Chain of 140 ** hotels throughout France.
Contact: Voyages Vacances Ltd, 213 Piccadilly, London W1V 9LT ☎ 01-494 2261

France Accueil
Family-run ** and *** hotels, many with pools. Guide lists 160.
Contact: FA Hotels (UK) Ltd, 15 Stradbrook, Bratton Westbury, Wiltshire BA13 4SF ☎ 0380 830125

Grandes Etapes Françaises
Ten luxury château-hotels, most situated in prime wine regions, perfect for fly-drive holidays.
Contact: Representation Plus, The Business Village, Broomhill Rd, London SW18 4JQ ☎ 01-871 5038

Logis et Auberges de France
Small and medium-sized family-run hotels often with restaurant. Ideal for short breaks or motoring holidays, these * and ** hotels are almost always rurally situated, and provide a very good standard of accommodation. There are over 4,500 listed and a guide to them can be obtained from the French Government Tourist Office (enclose 80p in stamps). Brittany Ferries offer a motoring package (Flexible France), making use of 300 or so of the Logis chain and supplying pre-paid vouchers to travellers. Their brochure is available at travel agents.

Moulin Etape
This is a chain of 36 * to **** hotels with a difference – they are all located within converted mills. Some have restaurants, most are on or near water, all are beautiful. The brochure is in French, detailing the history of each, price guide, exact location and address and the telephone number for bookings.
Contact: FGTO for brochure.

Relais du Silence
This chain of 139 hotels specialises in offering locations of total peace and tranquillity for restful stays. There is a multi-lingual brochure as the chain operates in many European countries.
Contact: Hôtels Relais du Silence, 4 cours de la Libération, 38100 Grenoble ☎ 76.48.10.49 (enclose International Reply Coupon).

Relais et Châteaux
Luxury hotel accommodation in a chain of 150.
Contact: FGTO (178 Piccadilly, London W1V 0AL) for guide (enclosing 80p in stamps).

Relais St-Pierre
This is a chain of 112 hotels which specialise in offering good local fishing possibilities and flexible meal times to those who are on fishing holidays. They will also prepare what you catch for your dinner or freeze it for a later date. Non-fishing members of the party are often catered for, too, with a selection of tours and excursions.
Contact: 41 rue Taitbout, 75009 Paris ☎ 42.81.12.11

■ *MONASTERIES AND CONVENTS* ■

An extensive list can be obtained from the FGTO of locations and addresses of religious institutions offering male and female accommodation.

■ *SELF-CATERING ACCOMMODATION* ■

The local Tourist Office will supply details of apartment rental agencies or rentals with private individuals in the resort of your choice. Before taking on an agreement, you should ensure that a rental contract is supplied, describing the condition of the premises, cost and any agency commission. The Fédération Nationale des Agents Immobiliers (FNAIM), the national real estate agents association, publish a guide to real estate agents.

Contact: Allo Vacances FNAIM, 6 rue de al Pépinière, 75008 Paris ☎ 42.93.04.42

British operators offering self-catering accommodation in France, whether *gîte*, apartment or villa, are listed under each region in the gazetteer section of this book.

■ *YOUTH HOSTELS* ■

With over 300 youth hostels (*auberges de jeunesse)* throughout France, this type of accommodation has always provided the young with a cheap and cheerful means of visiting another country. An International Youth Hostels membership card must first be obtained from the *Youth Hostels Association (YHA),* Trevelyan House, St Albans, Herts ALM1 2DY ☎ 0727 55215. There are youth hostels in Paris and its outskirts and cheap accommodation can also be arranged by contacting *Accueil des Jeunes en France*, 12 rue des Barres, 75004 Paris ☎ 42.72.72.09

ACTIVITY HOLIDAYS

A wide range of sports and activities has been listed within the following themed sections:

● Holidays for Health ● Holidays with Horses ●
● Outdoor Leisure ● Short Breaks ● Special Interest Holidays ●
● Watersports ● Winter Sports ●

Whatever your sporting or special interest, you can be sure that there are firms in France, as well as in Great Britain, eager to match your enthusiasm with a well-planned tour. Thus there are angling holidays to be booked in the Limousin; cruises on the waterways of Poitou-Charentes or Alsace; golfing short breaks; and gourmet cookery courses in Quercy, Périgord and Brittany. You can even hire a gypsy caravan for a breathless week's race round the Dordogne at 6 kmph!

Where applicable, we have listed operators catering for such special interest holidays, organisations with their own programmes and catalogues for the traveller to study.

HOLIDAYS FOR HEALTH

 *SPAS* ■

A lthough all drinking waters contain proportions of certain minerals, according to the soils from which they are derived, they are not classified as 'mineral' waters. This term is confined to waters from those wells and springs which age-long experience has shown to possess particular medicinal value. Mineral springs are widely distributed throughout the world and the therapeutic value of France's mineral springs has been appreciated for over 2,000 years.

'Taking the cure' became a pastime of the rich and famous from the eighteenth century onwards, with resorts growing up to cater for their extended stays. These spas, or 'watering places' as they were affectionately known, became fashionable *rendezvous*. Today, with the increased pressure of modern-day living taking its toll, these charming, latter-day resorts are enjoying renewed popularity.

Not only can you visit for the recommended cure for particular complaints, but many resorts have extensive modern facilities and now offer a range of general health, fitness and beauty treatment packages, frequently in conjunction with sports activities, and very much along the lines of a health farm. Vichy, for example, known worldwide for its water, and which has enjoyed a reputation as a spa town since the time of the Romans, now offers short health and fitness packages individually prescribed after medical consultation, and incorporating such elements as pool gymnastics, jet showers, muscle-strengthening exercises, mud baths and underwater massage. Other spas offer variations on a theme and produce brochures detailing treatments, costs and hotel accommodation options. The combined effects of a choice location, time to relax and take care of yourself, full entertainment (almost always including a casino) and sports facilities has long been popular with the French, but increasingly foreign visitors are also beginning to appreciate what is on offer.

Many spas, in conjunction with major hotels, offer 'health and tourism' packages for one or two weeks, details of some of which are given below. Further information can be obtained by contacting the Tourist Offices at the resorts themselves.

Aix-les-Bains (anti-smoking, anti-stress, keep fit, cellular rehabilitation)
Institut Marlioz, BP 46, 73102 Aix-les-Bains ☎ 79.61.00.91
Capvern-les-Bains (relaxation, slimming, keep fit)
Hotel du Laca, 65130 Capvern-les-Bains ☎ 62.39.02.06
Divonne-les-Bains (keep fit, relaxation)
Les Grands Hotels, F-01220, Divonne-les-Bains
Evian-les-Bains (diet for better living, relaxation)
Royal Club Evian, 74500 Evian ☎ 50.75.14.00
Vittel
Club Méditerranée, Place de la Bourse, 75083 Paris

Spas are listed below according to the region in which they are situated, together with the altitude and an indication of the climate you can expect. In most cases the telephone number given is that of the thermal establishment itself.

ALSACE AND LORRAINE

Bains-les-Bains (*300 m fresh*) circulatory disorders
(16 Apr-12 Oct) ☎ 29.36.32.04
Contrexéville (*350 m fresh*) kidneys/urinary disorders
(15 Apr-15 Oct) ☎ 29.08.03.24
Merkwiller-Pechelbronn (*150 m mild*) rheumatism/bone joint damage (Mar-Dec)
☎ 88.80.70.11
Morsbronn-les-Bains (*183 m sedative*) rheumatism/bone joint damage (open all year)
☎ 88.09.31.91
Niederbronn-les-Bains (*250 m mild*) rheumatism/bone joint damage (open all year)
☎ 88.09.60.55
Plombières-les-Bains (*450 m fresh*) digestive organs (May-Nov)
☎ 29.66.01.58
Vittel (*335 m temperate*) kidneys/urinary disorders
(open all year) ☎ 29.08.00.00

AQUITAINE

Cambo-les-Bains (*60 m mild*) rheumatism/bone joint damage
(1 Feb-22 Dec) ☎ 59.29.78.54
Dax (*12 m fine*) rheumatism/bone joint damage (open all year)
☎ 92.31.06.68
Eaux-Bonnes (Les) (*750 m fresh*) respiratory/lymphatic disorders
(15 May-30 Sep) ☎ 59.05.34.02
Eaux-Chaudes (Les) (*675 m fresh*) respiratory/lymphatic disorders

(open all year) ☎ 59.05.31.55
Eugénie-les-Bains (*90 m temperate*) kidneys/urinary organs
(1 Mar-30 Nov) ☎ 58.51.19.51
Préchacq-les-Bains (*20 m mild*) rheumatism/bone joint disorders
(29 Mar-7 Nov) ☎ 58.57.21.21
Saint-Christau (*320 m mild*) skin diseases (1 Apr-31 Oct)
☎ 59.34.40.04
Salies-de-Béarn (*54 m mild*) gynaecological conditions
(open all year) ☎ 59.38.10.11
Saubusse-les-Bains (*10 m mild*) kidneys/urinary organs
(10 Mar-25 Nov) ☎ 58.57.31.04
Tercis-les-Bains (*45 m mild*) skin diseases (open all year)
☎ 58.57.80.03

AUVERGNE

Bourbon-l'Archambault (*240 m temperate*) rheumatism/bone joint damage (6 Apr-31 Oct)
☎ 70.67.07.88
Bourboule (La) (*850 m mild*) respiratory/lymphatic disorders
(2 May-30 Sep) ☎ 73.81.02.92
Châteauneuf-les-Bains (*390 m sedative*) rheumatism/bone joint damage (2 May-30 Sep)
☎ 73.86.67.49
Châtel-Guyon (*430 m fresh*) digestive organs (25 Apr-5 Oct)
☎ 73.86.00.08
Chaudes-Aigues (*750 m temperate*) rheumatism/bone joint damage (26 Apr-17 Oct)
☎ 71.23.51.06
Mont-Dore (Le) (*1,050 m mild*)

respiratory/lymphatic disorders
(15 May-30 Sep) ☎ 73.65.05.10
Néris-les-Bains (*350 m mild*) nervous system (21 Apr-24 Oct)
☎ 70.03.10.39
Royat-Chamalières (*450 m fine*) circulatory disorders
(1 Apr-28 Oct) ☎ 73.35.80.16
Saint-Nectaire (*700 m dry*) kidneys/urinary organs
(25 May-30 Sep) ☎ 73.88.50.01
Vichy (*260 m temperate*) digestive organs (open all year)
☎ 70.98.95.37

BOURGOGNE

Bourbon-Lancy (*240 m temperate*) rheumatism/bone joint damage
(10 May-10 Oct) ☎ 85.89.18.84
Maizières (*350 m mild*) rheumatism/bone joint damage
(1 Mar-30 Nov) ☎ 80.90.18.33
Saint-Honoré-les-Bains (*300 m temperate*) respiratory/lymphatic disorders (27 Mar-30 Sep)
☎ 86.30.73.27
Santenay-les-Bains (*220 m mild*) metabolic disorders (Apr-Oct)
☎ 80.20.62.32

CHAMPAGNE-ARDENNE

Bourbonne-les-Bains (*270 m temperate*) rheumatism/bone joint damage (1 Mar-30 Nov)
☎ 25.90.07.20

FRANCHE-COMTE

Lons-le-Saunier (*255 m temperate*) respiratory/lymphatic disorders (1 Jun-31 Oct) ☎ 84.24.20 34
Luxeuil-les-Bains (*300 m fresh*) gynaecological conditions (1 Apr-30 Nov) ☎ 84.40.44.22
Salins-les-Bains (*354 m temperate*) respiratory/lymphatic disorders (Feb-Nov) ☎ 84.73.04.63

ILE DE FRANCE

Enghien-les-Bains (*50 m sedative*) respiratory/lymphatic disorders (open all year) ☎ 34.12.70.00

LANGUEDOC-ROUSSILLON

Alet-les-Bains (*206 m temperate*) digestive organs (10 May-30 Sep) ☎ 68.69.90.27
Amélie-les-Bains (*230 m temperate*) rheumatism/bone joint damage (15 Jan-23 Dec) ☎ 68.39.01.00
Avène-les-Bains (*350 m Mediterranean*) skin diseases (15 May-15 Oct) ☎ 67.23.41.87
Bagnols-les-Bains (*910 m invigorating*) circulatory disorders (25 Apr-25 Oct) ☎ 66.47.60.02
Balaruc-les-Bains (*0 m sea air*) rheumatism/bone joint damage (28 Feb-17 Dec) ☎ 67.48.51.02
Boulou (Le) (*90 m temperate*) digestive organs (15 Jan-22 Dec) ☎ 68.83.01.17
Fumades-les-Bains (Les) (*200 m dry*) respiratory/lymphatic disorders (1 Apr-30 Nov) ☎ 66.24.81.19
Lamalou-les-Bains (*200 m Mediterranean*) nervous system disorders (open all year) ☎ 67.95.25.55
Molitg-les-Bains (*450 m Mediterranean*) skin diseases (1 Apr-30 Nov) ☎ 68.05.00.50
Prats-de-Mollo-La-Preste (*740-1,130 m fresh*) kidneys/urinary organs (1 Apr-14 Nov) ☎ 68.39.71.01
Rennes-les-Bains (*310 m temperate*) rheumatism/bone joint damage (15 Apr-15 Nov) ☎ 68.69.87.01
Vernet-les-Bains (*650 m fresh*) rheumatism/bone joint damage (open all year) ☎ 68.05.52.84

LIMOUSIN

Evaux-les-Bains (*460 m dry*) rheumatism/bone joint damage (1 Apr-21 Oct) ☎ 55.65.51.77

MIDI-PYRENEES

Argelès-Gazost (*460 m temperate*) circulatory disorders (1 Jun-30 Sep) ☎ 62.97.03.24
Aulus-les-Bains (*780 m invigorating*) kidneys/urinary disorders (9 Jun-30 Sep) ☎ 61.96.01.46
Aurensan (*250 m temperate*) kidneys/urinary disorders (1 Jun-31 Oct) ☎ 62.09.46.06
Ax-les-Thermes (*720 m Mediterranean*) rheumatism/bone joint damage (4 Feb-31 Dec) ☎ 61.64.24.83
Bagnères-de-Bigorre (*550 m sedative*) nervous system (7 May-20 Oct) ☎ 62.95.00.23
Bagnères-de-Luchon (*630 m temperate*) respiratory/lymphatic disorders (1 Apr-20 Oct) ☎ 61.79.03.88
Barbazan (*450 m temperate*) digestive organs (10 May-30 Sep) ☎ 61.88.38.18
Barbotan-les-Thermes (*130 m temperate*) circulatory disorders (1 Feb-20 Dec) ☎ 62.69.52.09
Barèges (*1,240 m fresh*) rheumatism/bone joint damage (1 Jun-30 Sep) ☎ 62.92.68.02
Beaucens-les-Bains (*480 m temperate*) rheumatism/bone joint damage (1 Jun-30 Oct) ☎ 62.97.04.01
Capvern-les-Bains (*450 m fresh*) kidneys/urinary organs (2 May-15 Oct) ☎ 62.39.00.02
Castéra-Verduzan (*110 m mild*) kidneys/urinary organs (2 May-31 Oct) ☎ 62.68.13.41
Cauterets (*1,000 m sedative*) respiratory/lymphatic disorders (open all year) ☎ 62.92.51.60
Cransac (*292 m sedative*) rheumatism/bone joint damage (1 Apr-31 Oct) ☎ 65.63.09.83
St-Sauveur-les-Bains (*730 m mild*) gynaecological conditions (15 May-30 Sep) ☎ 62.92.81.58
Salies-du-Salat (*300 m mild*) respiratory/lymphatic disorders (2 May-20 Oct) ☎ 61.90.56.41
Ussat-les-Bains (*485 m fine*) nervous system (1 Apr-31 Oct) ☎ 61.05.74.74

NORD-PAS DE CALAIS

Saint-Amand-les-Eaux (*17 m temperate*) rheumatism/bone joint damage (1 Mar-15 Dec) ☎ 27.48.50.37

NORMANDIE

Bagnoles-de-l'Orne (*220 m temperate*) circulatory disorders (1 Apr-30 Sep) ☎ 33.30.82.31
Forges-les-Eaux (*175 m temperate*) circulatory disorders (open all year) ☎ 35.90.52.67

POITOU-CHARENTES

Rochefort-sur-Mer (*5 m sea air*) rheumatism/bone joint damage (all year except Jan) ☎ 46.99.08.64
Roche-Posay (La) (*75 m mild*) skin diseases (open all year) ☎ 49.86.21.03
Saujon (*7 m temperate*) nervous system (open all year) ☎ 46.02.97.55

PROVENCE – ALPES – COTE D'AZUR

Aix-en-Provence (*250 m Mediterranean*) rheumatism/bone joint damage (open all year) ☎ 42.26.01.18
Berthemont-les-Bains (*950 m Mediterranean*) respiratory/lymphatic disorders (May-Oct) ☎ 93.03.47.00
Camoins-les-Bains (*130 m Mediterranean*) respiratory/lymphatic disorders (1 Mar-15 Dec) ☎ 91.43.02.50
Digne-les-Bains (*600 m dry*) rheumatism/bone joint damage (Mar-Dec) ☎ 92.31.06.68
Gréoux-les-Bains (*400 m dry*) rheumatism/bone joint damage (1 Feb-23 Dec) ☎ 92.74.22.22

RHONE-ALPES

Aix-les-Bains (*250 m temperate*) rheumatism/bone joint damage (open all year) ☎ 79.35.38.50
Aix-les-Bains (*280 m temperate*) respiratory/lymphatic disorders Institut Marlioz ☎ 79.61.00.91
Allevard-les-Bains (*475 m*

temperate) respiratory/lymphatic disorders (17 May-24 Sep)
☎ 76.97.56.22
Brides-les-Bains (Salins-les-Thermes) (*600 m mild*) metabolic disorders (15 Apr-31 Oct) ☎ 79.55.23.44
Challes-les-Eaux (*310 m mild*) respiratory/lymphatic disorders (3 May-26 Sep) ☎ 79.85.20.04
Charbonnières-les-Bains (*250 m temperate*) circulatory disorders (open all year) ☎ 78.87.16.26
Divonne-les-Bains (*500 m fresh*) digestive organs (open all year) ☎ 50.20.05.70

Evian-les-Bains (*376 m mild*) kidneys/urinary organs (open all year) ☎ 50.75.02.30
Léchère-les-Bains (La) (*440 m mild*) circulatory disorders (1 Apr-31 Oct) ☎ 79.22.61.61
Montrond-les-Bains (*360 m temperate*) digestive organs (15 May-1 Oct) ☎ 77.54.43.63
Neyrac-les-Bains (*390 m fresh*) skin diseases (29 Apr-31 Oct) ☎ 75.36.42.07
Propiac-les-Bains (*530 m mild*) metabolic disorders (Mar-Nov) ☎ 75.28.09.00
Sail-les-Bains (*300 m sedative*)

skin diseases (15 May-30 Sep) ☎ 77.64.30.81
Saint-Gervais-les-Bains (*850 m fresh*) skin diseases (Apr-Sep) ☎ 50.78.23.47
Saint-Laurent-les-Bains (*750 m dry*) rheumatism/bone joint damage (1 Apr-31 Oct) ☎ 66.46.04.58
Thonon-les-Bains (*430 m fresh*) kidneys/urinary organs (open all year) ☎ 50.26.17.22
Uriage-les-Bains (*410 m temperate*) skin diseases (1 Apr-24 Oct) ☎ 76.89.10.17
Vals-les-Bains (*250 m fresh*) metabolic disorders (open all year) ☎ 75.37.46.68

■ *THALASSOTHERAPY* ■

Seawater treatment is the latest therapy, making full use of the special properties of seawater, seaweed and sea air, together with the most advanced medical techniques. Thalassotherapy, its name deriving from the Greek *thalassa* meaning the sea, tones the muscles and is recommended for sufferers of rheumatism and as a post-operative therapy.

The main area for treatment is in Brittany and listed below are those centres specialising in this form of treatment but, as with spas, also offering general health and fitness packages as well. Further information can be obtained by writing direct to the thalassotherapy establishment or to the Tourist Office of the resort.

AQUITAINE

St-Jean-de-Luz
Hélianthal Thalasso Club
Contact Erna Low Consultants, 9 Reece Mews, London SW7 3HE ☎ 01-584 2841

BRETAGNE

Carnac
Centre de Thalassothérapie, BP 83, 56340 Carnac (1 Jan-20 Nov) ☎ 97.52.04.44
Douarnenez
Centre de Cure Marine de la Baie de Tréboul Douarnenez, 42 bis rue des Professeure Curie, BP 4, 29100 Douarnenez (open all year) ☎ 98.92.30.50 and ☎ 98.72.09.59
Perros-Guirec
Centre de Thalassothérapie de Perros-Guirec, BP 50, Bd Joseph Bihan, Plage de Trestraou, 22700 Perros-Guirec (late Feb-mid Nov) ☎ 96.23.28.97)

Quiberon
Institut de Thalassothérapie de Quiberon , BP 170, 56170 Quiberon (Feb-Dec) ☎ 97.50.20.00
Roscoff
1. Institut Marin Rockroum, Centre de Thalassothérapie, BP 28, 29211 Roscoff (Apr-Oct) ☎ 98.69.72.15
2. Clinique de Rééducation Fonctionelle, Kerlena, BP 13, 29211 Roscoff (open all year) ☎ 98.61.24.15
St-Malo
Les Thermes Marins, Grande Plage, 100 Bd Hébert, BP 32, 35401 St-Malo

LANGUEDOC-ROUSSILLON

Cap d'Agde
Thalacap, Place de la Falaise, 34300 Cap d'Agde ☎ 67.26.14.80
Port Barcarès
Institut Thalassa, BP 30, 66420

Port Barcarès ☎ 68.86.30.90
La Grande Motte
Institut de Thalassathérapie, BP 43, 34280 La Grand Motte ☎ 67.85.39.71

SPECIALIST TOUR OPERATORS

Air France Holidays, 69 Boston Manor Road, Brentford TW8 9JQ ☎ 01-568 6981
Angel Travel, 44 High Street, Borough Green, Sevenoaks, Kent TN15 8BJ ☎ 0732 884109
France Directe, 2 Church Street, Warwick CV34 4AB ☎ 0926 497989
French Travel Service, Georgian House, 69 Boston Manor Road, Brentford TW8 0JQ ☎ 01-568 8442
Erna Low Consultants, 9 Reece Mews, London SW7 3HE ☎ 01-584 2841
Par-Tee Tours, Riverside House, 53 Uxbridge Road, Rickmansworth WD3 2DH ☎ 0923 721565

■ *NATURISM* ■

France's excellent climate lends itself to the practice of naturism and there is a strong naturist movement, with clubs all over the country and over 60 naturist holiday centres. To quote the Fédération Française de Naturisme:

Naturism is a way of living in harmony with nature. Its main feature is the practice of social nudity, the purpose of which is to encourage respect for oneself, for others and for the environment.

If you are put off by these rather high-sounding aims, then remember that many of the naturist holiday resorts, especially in the Cap d'Agde area, are intended more for those seeking an overall tan than indulging in a naturist atmosphere. Nevertheless, naturists contend that in this age of stress and status-awareness a naturist holiday could prove to be an ideal way of escaping from the social attitudes that divide us. Like the friendly, family-orientated movement it is, it provides a marvellous opportunity to meet people from all walks of life, from all countries and in all shapes and sizes. Their simple advice would be: dare to go bare! You'll probably enjoy it as fears, misgivings and butterflies melt away in the sun.

The principal regions of France where naturist holiday resorts are based are listed below, with details of a selection of the centres. Virtually every centre has facilities for camping and visiting caravans, and quite a few have chalets, caravans or tents to hire. Often there are shops and restaurants on site. There are apartments to let in places like Cap d'Agde, Aphrodite Village and the Ile du Levant, and there are now also several naturist hotels.

The Central Council for British Naturism produces an excellent survey of the French centres in the form of regional leaflets which, while not implying official recognition, do provide basic information on the merits of each. The Council can also provide, on request, brochures and price lists for most of the centres. In addition, the French Naturist Federation publishes an illustrated guide to a selection of their centres, in English, under the title *Centres de Vacances Naturistes Français*. This guide comes with the official recommendation of this body, together with prices and booking details. To obtain this guide and the information produced by the Central Council for British Naturism, write to Jim Miller, Overseas Secretary, 8 Palmer Close, Redhill, Surrey RH1 4BX (enclosing three first-class stamps).

A final word of warning. Respect the sun. Use plenty of protective sun-tan cream and take a siesta.

AQUITAINE

Both sites are situated on the Atlantic coast and have every convenience. Euronat is a series of villages set in sandy woodland bordering a fine beach, while La Jenny has chalet accommodation and extremely good facilities, particularly for children.
Euronat, Grayan-l'Hôpital, 33590 St-Vivien-de-Medoc
☎ 56.41.40.81
Village Naturiste de la Jenny, 33680 Le Porge ☎ 56.26.56.90

BRETAGNE

A camping and chalet centre in Morbihan, in the south-east of Brittany, for those who prefer a country-based holiday.
Château du Bois de la Roche, 56820 Neant-sur-Yvel
☎ 97.74.42.11.

CENTRE

As a base for visiting the châteaux of the Loire, this centre would be ideal.
Bois de la Herpinière, Turquant, 49730 Montsoreau
☎ 41.51.74.81

CORSE

There are eight centres in Corsica, all on the east coast. Four are near Bastia in the north, three are near Porto Vecchio in the south, while U Furu is near Bonifacio in the extreme south, and is the only inland centre on the island, although with a riverside setting.
Tropica, 20230 San Nicolao
☎ 95.38.80.71
Bagheera, Bagheera-Giustiniana, 20230 San Nicolao
☎ 95.38.43.87
Club Corsicana, 20230 Linguizetta ☎ 95.38.80.25
Rivabella, 20270 Aleria

☎ 95.38.81.10
La Chiappa, 20137 Porto Vecchio
☎ 95.70.00.31
Club des Amis de Neptune, Cala
Genovese, Testa Ventilegne,
20169 Bonifacio ☎ 95.73.06.29
Villata, 20144 Ste-Lucie-de-Porto-
Vecchio ☎ 95.71.44.72
U Furu, Camping Naturiste U
Furu, Route de Nota, 20137
Porto Vecchio ☎ 95.70.10.83

LANGUEDOC-ROUSSILLON

The Languedoc coast has seen
much recent development. Port-
Leucate is a newly created resort
with two naturist village centres,
Aphrodite and Ulysse, offering
villa and flat accommodation. Cap
d'Agde, in which seven
developments form a complete
naturist town, is the centre most
concentrated on by the specialist
operators. Serralongue is a high,
rugged and fairly remote
mountain site close to the Spanish
frontier. It stipulates no single
men.
Aphrodite-Village, Port-Leucate
☎ 68.40.90.42
Ulysse, Mer Alpes Reservations,
58 rue Maurice Ripoche, 75014
Paris ☎ (1)545.67.00
Cap d'Agde, Agence René Oltra,
Port Ambonne, 34308 Cap
d'Agde ☎ 67.26.33.78
Le Village Naturiste du Bosc,
Zone Gymnique de Ricazouls,
34800 Octon ☎ 67.96.07.37
Serralongue. Village Club
Naturiste de Serralongue, 66230
Prats-de-Mollo ☎ 68.39.60.60

MIDI-PYRENEES

Chaudeau is in the heart of the
Dordogne, a wooded camping
centre with lakeside bathing.
Laulurie is a small rural centre in
the heart of the Périgord region,
close to several tourist sites.
L'Eglantière is a peaceful centre
with the Pyrénées as a backdrop,
and with river bathing.
Domaine Naturiste de Chaudeau,
Les Charmilles, 24700 St-Géraud-
de-Corps ☎ 53.82.49.64
Laulurie, 24330 La Douze
☎ 53.06.74.00
L'Eglantière, Aries-Espenan,
65230 Castelnau-Magnoac
☎ 62.99.83.64

PROVENCE-ALPES-COTE D'AZUR

Not surprisingly, the Provence
area saw the birth of naturism.
The traffic-free Ile du Levant,
lying just off the coast from Le
Lavandou and Hyères, was the
first naturist centre to be created
in 1931, and the well-known,
island-based village of Héliopolis
comprises hotels and other
accommodation amidst typical
Mediterranean scenery. Lauzons
is a hillside site in the Provence
countryside as is Chandelalar,
while Enriou is in a peaceful
location with windsurfing and
other watersports on the nearby
Lac de Verdon. There are also
several mountain centres, unique
amongst them Les Clapières
which offers winter skiing.

Les Lauzons, Centre Naturiste de
Limans, Limans, 14300
Forcalquier ☎ 92.76.00.60
Domaine d'Enriou, 04480
St-Laurent-du-Verdon
☎ 92.74.41.02
Ile du Levant, Union des
Commercants, 83146 Ile du
Levant
Les Clapières, Centre Naturiste
de Montagne, 05100 Briançon
☎ 92.21.15.83
Le Haut Chandelalar,
Briançonnet, St-Auban
☎ 93.60.43.83

RHONE-ALPES

Camping centre at the foot of a
steep slope in a wooded loop of
the spectacular Gorges de
l'Ardèche, with canoeing, fishing
and swimming. Cars have to be
left above and luggage is
transferred down by hoist!
La Plage des Templiers, B.P.22,
07700 Bourg-Saint-Andéol
☎ 75.04.28.58

SPECIALIST TOUR OPERATORS

Club Holidays, 35 Balmoral
Drive, Mansfield, Notts
NG19 7HW ☎ 0623 24177
Eden Holidays, 92 The Avenue,
Sunbury-on-Thames, Middx
TW16 5E ☎ 0932 784041
Emsdale Travel, 5 Rigby Mews,
Cranbrook Road, Ilford, Essex
IG1 4PG
Peng Travel, 86 Station Road,
Gidea Park, Essex RM2 6DB
☎ 04024 71832

HOLIDAYS WITH HORSES

Equestrianism is now the fifth most popular sport in France. The French Tourist
Organisation has ensured that riders wishing to have holidays with horses are
well catered for, and the result is that the holidays on offer are organised to the
last detail in the true French manner, right down to midnight picnics and bivouacs –
the perfect escape. For those riders seeking a holiday of excitement and adventure,
and for whom going abroad means saying a sad adieu to a four-hooved friend, a
holiday spent with a French horse instead might be the answer!
   Where riding centres are located in or close to the resorts in this book, they have
been included, but in addition there is an excellent booklet published by the
Association Nationale pour le Tourisme Equestre (ANTE) 15 rue de Bruxelles, 75009

Paris, and any would-be riders in France would do well to obtain a copy. It gives a contact address for each *département* in France and hundreds of names and addresses of regional centres.

Types of holiday which you will see mentioned are called *randonnées* – rides, trips or excursions. Thus:

Weekend de Randonnée – when the riders are away from base for one night only. These are very popular;

La Randonnée – takes the rider away for two to four days; and

La Grande Randonnée – lasting five days or more.

Accompanied *randonnées* include the price of the guide and you will be taken as a group. Depending on the location chosen, you travel through magnificent countryside, woodland, long stretches of beach or along lake edges, ideal trips for the horse lover as they provide the opportunity for a true bond to develop between rider and horse. Tours usually consist of loops so there is no need to retrace the route. Reservations can be made to suit age requirements and some centres specialise in holidays for young riders, paying careful attention to individual ability.

For those with advanced riding ability it is possible to go out alone (or as a private group of friends) on itineraries with overnight stays, meals, etc., organised by the centre. Most establishments offer special rates, particularly out of season, for groups of six to eight riders, and it is sometimes possible to arrange special 'à la carte' treks outside scheduled itineraries.

Promenades – Many centres accept holidaymakers who are passing through and just wish to have an hour's ride, accompanied or not. You can also go out for a half-day trek, while perhaps the most pleasant excursions are day trips with a break for a picnic lunch (or with your own supply in the saddle bag). It is always wise to telephone in advance to check what is on offer.

Reservations should be made as far in advance as possible and through the Centre Equestre Organisateur. You should state your age, riding ability, weight and your exact requirements. A deposit equivalent to 30 per cent is usually required. Before leaving the centre you should ensure that you know what you have paid for,

such as board and lodging and baths, etc. You may need to hire a tent. If an animal is deemed to have been over-worked or any tack is lost or damaged, the cost will be deducted from the deposit. Accommodation offered on equestrian holidays is often in modest *dortoirs* (dormitories). But there are also trips which lay emphasis on enjoying the gastronomic delights of the region at the end of each day!

Another increasingly popular alternative is that of travelling by means of hand-painted, horse-drawn caravans, Romany-style. Slow and leisurely (travel is at approximately 5 kmph), this type of holiday has immediate and obvious appeal for the horse-lover, and allows plenty of time to enjoy the delights of the countryside. Further details under Short Breaks (page 51) and operators are also mentioned under the resorts in the gazetteer.

SPECIALIST OPERATORS

Cavalry Tours, 14 Cromwell Crescent, London SW5 9QW
☎ 01-602 8433
Equitana Holidays, Oxleaze Farm, Filkins, Lechlade, Glos.
☎ 036785 489
La France des Villages, Model Farm, Rattlesden, Bury St Edmunds IP30 0SY
☎ 044 93 7664
Inntravel, Hovingham, York YO6 4JZ ☎ 065 382742
LSG Theme Holidays, 201 Main Street, Thornton LE6 1AH
☎ 0509 231713
Slipaway Holidays, 90 Newland Road, Worthing BN11 1LB
☎ 0903 821000

OUTDOOR LEISURE
■ *BALLOONING* ■

Hot-air ballooning must be one of the most spectacular ways of seeing the countryside and certain areas of France offer the perfect conditions required. Trips can last anything from one hour to four days, depending on your budget and adventurous inclinations, and locations are mentioned throughout the gazetteer section of this book. One thing is certain though, once you've tried it you'll want to go up again and again!

Burgundy is a popular area for ballooning, with short flights available from Beaune, Chagny and Chalon-sur-Saône; or you can float across vineyards, châteaux, villages and woodland on a magical four-day trip which takes in wine tastings and gourmet dinners, as well as guided tours to famous châteaux and picnics in beauty spots. These trips have been successfully run by Buddy Bombard for over ten years, and operate between May and October with first class accommodation starting and finishing in the beautiful town of Beaune. Details from Abercrombie & Kent Travel.

Or in Franch-Comté glide across the wooded Jura hills and vineyards between June and September. Options for trips vary between introductory flights with two days' accommodation included, to gourmet and champagne flights over a longer period of time, which also take in sightseeing and wine tastings. Flights are based at Château Chalon, north of the spa town of Lons-le-Saunier and details are available from Aerostatic Voyager.

Flights, meals and accommodation can also be arranged by Champagne Air-Show for individuals or groups. In conjunction with visits to the prestigious champagne houses of the Champagne-Ardenne area, tastings and a guided tour of Reims, these trips can be booked for one to three days.

More than likely you may even be tempted to take the next step and actually learn to pilot a balloon yourself. The Balloon Team have a small base near Toulouse where students can prepare for their Private Pilot's Licence (Balloons) over one or two weeks, in predictable weather conditions and amidst glorious countryside.

If your taste is for the ultimate in aerial sightseeing, then take a 'helicopter cruise' with Map Travel. They offer luxury trips with their helicopter packages, including top-level accommodation, gastronomic treats, wine tastings and visits. Tours can last anything from one-day flights over the châteaux of the Loire, to a six-day tour of France, flying between Paris and Monte-Carlo via the Alps.

SPECIALIST OPERATORS

Abercrombie & Kent Travel, Sloane Square House, Holbein Place, London SW1W 8NS ☎ 01-730 9600

Aerostatic Voyager, 483 Green Lanes, London N13 4BS ☎ 01-886 0812

The Balloon Team, 30 Buckingham Road, Chippenham, Wiltshire SN15 3TF ☎ 0249 658157.

Champagne Air-Show, 15 bis, place St-Nicaise, 51100 Reims ☎ 26.82.59.60

Map Travel, 13 rue de Tournon, 75006 Paris ☎ 46.34.16.18

■ CYCLING ■

The French take their cycling very seriously, as you'll observe from the enthusiastic audience the summertime *Tour de France* attracts, both along the route and via the constant television coverage. For the non-competitive, however, a week or two spent on two wheels may well qualify as the 'perfect' French holiday. What could be better than exploring off the beaten track, with picnic lunches bought in quiet villages? Such an adventure can prove both healthy and relaxing; it might also form the basis for a new-found intimacy with the country and its people.

There is no need to be put off by the so-called hazards of continental driving. French motorists treat cyclists with great respect, giving them a wide berth and often sounding their horns to warn of their approach before overtaking. Minor French roads lend themselves to cycling, being generally free from heavy traffic.

This type of holiday can, of course, be geared to all levels of cyclist and all levels of comfort. Some choose to travel totally self-contained, carrying tent and sleeping bag; others travel to any one of the 280 or so SNCF stations which operate the *Train + Vélo* bike-hire service, and take their journey on from there; still others book with one of the specialist holiday operators whose price includes flights, bike hire,

itineraries, hotel accommodation and daily onward transport of your luggage. Explore Worldwide, for example, offers 15-day cycling trips through the Loire valley.

Details of how to transport bicycles on the French rail network, and the stations which operate the cycle-hire scheme can be obtained from SNCF French Railways, 179 Piccadilly, London W1V 0BA ☎ 01-493 9731 and from continental rail-appointed travel agents.

Most Tourist Offices in good cycling areas produce excellent short-circuit routes (which can be requested in advance or on the spot), and the Loisirs Accueil organisation offer all-inclusive cycling tours in half a dozen regions. Write for their brochures at the addresses listed under Short Breaks (page 51). The Cyclists Touring Club also organise tours, and membership entitles you to detailed information sheets on France and a useful glossary of spares.

SPECIALIST TOUR OPERATORS

The Cyclists Touring Club,
Cotterell House, 69 Meadrow,
Godalming, Surrey GU7 3HS

☎ 04868 7217
Explore Worldwide, 1 Frederick Street, Aldershot GU11 1LQ
☎ 0252 319448
Susi Madron's Cycling for Softies, Lloyd's House,

22 Lloyd Street, Manchester M2 5WA ☎ 061-834 6800
Triskell Cycle Tours,
35 Langland Drive, Northway, Sedgley DY3 3TH
☎ 09073 78255

■ *FISHING* ■

France can be conveniently divided into six large fishing areas, representing the vast river basins of the Rhine and Meuse, the Seine, the Loire and the Rhône and the Charente, Adour and Garonne.

Within these areas, the fishing waters – river, lake, reservoir or mountain pool – are either in private ownership or under the control of the State. To fish in private waters, of course, the owner's permission is needed; on State property, an angler, who must be a paid-up member of an angling association, has to obtain a permit and pay the annual fishing tax. A duly stamped tax card, which can be obtained from the nearest fishing tackle shop, should always be carried. The shop will also advise about any local regulations (often to be found posted at the *mairie* (town hall), and help by recommending the best fishing sites.

For fishing purposes, French waters are classified into category 1 (for salmon and trout) and category 2 (for all other fish). For category 1 fishing a supplementary tax is levied.

Salmon and trout fishing have their closed seasons in France from Sep/Oct to Feb/Mar. Category 2 waters in the south and south east of France close on the second Tuesday in March and re-open on the last Friday in April. In other regions, the closure operates between the first Tuesday after 15 April and the first Friday following 8 June.

The Conseil Supérieure de la Pêche (CSP), 134 avenue de Malakoff, 75016 Paris, publish an excellent pamphlet entitled *Fishing in France*, outlining in great detail the regulations governing the sport, including underwater fishing and sea fishing, both from the shore and from a boat. It even lists the size limits pertaining to certain fish, below which the catch must be thrown back. They also produce a first-class fishing map of France, with a list, in English and French, of the commonest types of fish to be found.

The patron saint of fishermen, St Peter, is present at numerous fishing centres throughout France, for the 112 hotels in the Relais St-Pierre chain offer accommodation geared to meeting the special needs of anglers: a place to keep tackle, flexible meal times, facilities for cooking or freezing catches, and other leisure activities for non-fishing members of your family. Contact: Relais St-Pierre, 41 rue Taitbout, 75009 Paris ☎ 42.81.12.11

COARSE FISHING (CATEGORY 2)

In Brittany, there are some 9,600 km of rivers and canals open to the fishing public. In the Astrée region of Forez (in the upper Loire), there are a thousand lakes to be fished. In the Lake Vassivière area of Limousin, and in the surrounding rivers (the Gartempe, the Maulde and the Taurion), category 2 fish abound – carp, roach, tench, pike and perch. The lake itself offers a wealth of coarse fishing, with well-placed centres at Eymoutier and along the 48-km stretch of lake shore.

The Loire and its tributaries (the Cher, Creuse, Sarthe and Loir), the Seine, the Rhône, the Dordogne and Garonne – all of these great river basins teem with coarse fish: carp (*carpe*), grayling (*ombre commun*), pike (*brochet*), roach (*gardon*), tench (*tanche*), bream (*breme*), eel (*anguille*), barbel (*barbeau*), perch (*perche*), pike-perch (*zandre*), cat fish (*poisson-chat*), pollan (*lavaret*) and burbot (*lotte*).

GAME FISHING (CATEGORY 1)

The trout and salmon waters are, for the most part, high in the hills where the mountain streams run fierce and cold. In the Pyrenees, indeed, they are not called streams but *gaves,* mountain torrents. There are fine trout (and char) waters in the Gave d'Osseau, from Oloron up to the Spanish frontier, and in the Gave d'Aspe, with excellent angling centres at Bidarray, St-Jean-Pied-de-Port, Licq-Atherey, Mauleon and Pau in the Pyrénées-Atlantiques; St-Gaudens and St-Girons, as well as Tarbes and Foix in the Hautes-Pyrénées.

Good trout fishing too in Brittany – in the tributaries of the Aulne, and in the Aven and Blavet. In Normandy, in the Dives, the Touques above Lisieux, the upper reaches of the Orne and in the Risle.

In the Auvergne, the River Allier thrashes with trout and the mountain streams of the Dauphiny Alps also offer first-class fishing, as do the Drac and the Bourne and, further south, the Drôme and the Bez. In the Haute-Savoie, fishing enthusiasts head for such centres as Chambéry, Albertville and Bonneville.

In the Loire basin there are fine trout streams in the higher reaches and in the tributaries: the Ance is popular with anglers, and Bas-en-Basset, where it joins the Loire, is a favoured fishing centre. There are trout to be fished at St-Eulalie, at Mesves on the Mazou, at Pouilly-sur-Loire and in the upper reaches of the Loiret, between Olivet and Beaugency.

In the Haute-Vienne, the Gartempe and Vienne rivers offer excellent fishing and within Haute-Vienne itself there are some 1,900 km of river bank offering both trout and salmon possibilities.

There are salmon in the Allier, preferring its faster moving waters to those of its parent, the Loire. Salmon also swim in the Midi-Pyrénées and, above all, in the Pyrénées-Atlantiques where, between April and July each year, in the village of Navarrencz, the World Salmon Fishing Championships are held in that prince of mountain torrents, the Gave d'Oloron.

SPECIALIST TOUR OPERATORS

Association for Active Learning (ALL), 9 Haywra Street, Harrogate HG1 5BJ
☎ (0423) 505313

France Voyages, 145 Oxford Street, London W1R 1TB
☎ 01-494 3155

French Travel Service, Georgian House, 69 Boston Manor Road, Brentford TW8 0JQ ☎ 01-568 8442

Cliff Smart's Angling Holidays, 141 Queensway, Burton Latimer, Northants NN15 5QQ
☎ (0536) 724226

Travellers, 277 Oxlow Road, Dagenham, Essex
☎ 01-985 9679

■ *GOLF* ■

G olf was first played in France in the Pyrénées, on the Basque coast and in Brittany, all places which, over the past hundred years, have been the favoured holiday and retirement retreats of wealthy English families.

Did two Scots officers of Wellington's army 'design' a course at Pau when they were quartered there in 1814 during the Peninsula War? Perhaps. What is certain is that the first golf club in France was opened at Pau in 1856 and that, almost 80 years after that, membership was still almost exclusively British.

Brittany, too, was another great favourite for holidays, and Dinard golf course opened here in 1887 to meet the needs of British residents. A year later, Biarritz, fashionable resort of royalty and high society, had its own course. Compiègne, in Picardy, followed seven years later.

However, there was never the same surge in golf-course construction in France as in Great Britain, and never the same passion for the game. Holiday golf for the British tourist and 'society' golfer was well catered for by Spanish and Portuguese clubs and by the travel organisations and hotels linked with them. Then, it seemed, the centime dropped, and there was a sudden explosion of golf planning in France. New courses were designed and constructed: sports complexes, 18- and 9-hole courses and, in many cases, courses with a clutch of three interchangeable 9-holers. What had for long been chic at St-Cloud, Cannes-Mougins and St-Nom-la-Bretesche was now being played not only by tourists, but by French family groups.

In 1981 there were only 43,000 members of French golf clubs. Six years later the figure had trebled. In every corner of the country there was an annual increase in membership of over 25 per cent. To keep up with this growth there was a flowering of new clubs, in the environs of Paris, naturally, in Normandy and Brittany, the Loire valley, the Basque country and the Pyrénées, the Bouches-du-Rhône, Provence, the Alps and eastern France. Today there are over 200 clubs up and down the country and the number increases by the month. Whereas, for example, there are today a mere dozen courses in the Provence and Côte-d'Azur region, the French Golf Federation predicts there will be almost 100 by the year 1992.

What, then, does French golf have to offer the visitor? There are four championship courses grouped close to Paris: St-Cloud, St-Nom-la-Bretesche, La Boulie and St-Germain. Others are at La Baule (near the mouth of the Loire), at Cognac and at Biarritz. There are courses built around or dominated by magnificent châteaux: La Cordelière (in champagne country), Ozoir-la-Ferrière, Val-de-Cher (in the Auvergne), La Bretesche and Boisgelin (in Brittany) and Chaumont (in Picardy). There are exclusive courses at Cannes-Mougins, Deauville and Le Touquet. There are links courses at Granville (in Normandy) and Sables-d'Or-les-Pins (in Brittany), at Chiberta (near Biarritz), Wimereux (in the Pas-de-Calais) and Dinard (in Brittany). Reflecting the splendid variety of the French countryside, the Golf des Volcans (near Clermont-Ferrand) sits encircled by extinct volcanoes and by the Puy-de-Dôme. Chamonix lies in a valley beneath Mont Blanc. In Savoie, Golf des Arcs, 1,500 m above sea level, has fairways crossed by mountain streams. Annecy overlooks Lake Annecy, as Evian overlooks Lake Geneva. Pruneville lies betwen the Vosges and the Jura mountains. Etretat (in Normandy) is laid out along the cliff tops, and 900 m above Monte-Carlo the Mont-Agel course is carved out of the granite cliffs.

The range is enormous. The green fee rates, generally quoted by the day rather than the round, vary accordingly, but they are, as a rule, much higher than those in Britain. About 150F is an average midweek charge, but at some clubs weekend rates (even when accompanied by a member), can rise to 300F and more. Equipment too is more expensive; balls tend to cost twice as much as in the UK.

Most clubs in France, like most shops, close for one day during the week. It is wise to reserve a tee at least a day in advance and certainly at weekends. Weekend golf in France tends to take place largely in the afternoon and the attitude to the game is far

less serious than in Britain. It is quite often a game for the whole family and tends, therefore, to be slow in playing; five hours a round is not exceptional. But the enthusiasm is there, if not always the strictest observance of the rules of etiquette!

Golf in France can be said to have taken off in fine style. Now is the time to try the flavour of its courses and their locations before they become, in a few years' time, as commercial perhaps as those in Spain. Meanwhile, surely, as the French as a nation learn to love the sport more and more, we can expect the emergence of France's Ballesteros and the full flowering of the country as a golfing nation.

SPECIALIST TOUR OPERATORS

Air France Holidays, 69 Boston Manor Road, Brentford TW8 9JQ ☎ 01-568 6981
Brittany Direct Holidays, 362 Sutton Common Road, Sutton SM3 9PL
☎ 01-641 6060
Brittany Ferries, The Brittany Centre, Wharf Road, Portsmouth PO2 8RU
☎ 0705 827701
Cresta Holidays, 32 Victoria Street, Altrincham WA14 1ET
☎ 0345 056511
Dan-Air Fly-Drive, Norway House, 21/24 Cockspur Street, London SW1Y 5BN
☎ 01-930 5881
Eurogolf Ltd, 3b London Road, St Albans AL1 1LA
☎ 0727 42256
Flaine Information,

128a Hamlet Court Road, Westcliff on Sea SS0 7LN
☎ 0702 343381
France Directe, 2 Church Street, Warwick CV34 4AB
☎ 0926 497989
La France des Villages, Model Farm, Rattlesden, Bury St Edmunds IP30 0SY
☎ 044 93 7664
Francophiles Ltd, Barkers Chambers, Barker Road, Maidstone ME16 8SF
☎ 0622 688165
Freedom in France, Meadows, Poughill, Bude, Cornwall EX23 9EN ☎ 0288 55591
Lagrange Vacances, 16/20 New Broadway, London W5 2XA
☎ 01-579 7311
Longshot Golf Holidays, Meon House, College Street, Petersfield, Hants
☎ 0730 66561
Meridian Holidays,

12/16 Dering Street, London W1R 9AB ☎ 01-493 2777
Par-Tee Tours, King Cedar House, 1 Burfield Road, Chorleywood, Herts
☎ 09278 3544
Sun France, 3 Beaufort Gardens, London SW16 3BP
☎ 01-679 4562
Tourarc UK, 197b Brompton Road, London SW3 1LA
☎ 01-589 1918
Voyages Jules Verne, 21 Dorset Square, London NW1 6QG
☎ 01-724 6624

Useful address: Fédération Française de Golf, 69 avenue Victor Hugo, F-75116 Paris
☎ *15.00.62.20*

Where golf courses are located in or close to the resorts in this book they have been included, but the following is a list of public and private golf courses.

ALSACE

Bas-Rhin
Golf de Strasbourg (18 pri)
route du Rhin, 67400 Illkirch
Graffenstaden ☎ 88.66.17.22
Haute-Rhin
Golf de Bale (18 pri)
rue de Wentzwiller, 68220
Hagenthal le Bas ☎ 89.68.50.91
Golf du Rhin Mulhouse (18 pri)
Ile du Rhin, 68670 Chalampé
☎ 89.26.07.86

AQUITAINE

Dordogne
Golf de Perigueux (9 pub)
Domaine de Saltgourde, 24430
Marsac ☎ 53.53.10.18
Golf de Lolivarie (9 pri)
La Croix Sagelat, 24170 Belves
☎ 53.30.22.69
Gironde
Golf d'Arcachon (18 pri)
35 boulevard d'Arcachon, 33260
La Teste de Buch ☎ 56.54.44.00
Golf Bordelais (18 pri)
Domaine de Kater, avenue
d'Eysines, 33200 Bordeaux
Cauderan ☎ 56.28.56.04
Golf de Bordeaux Cameyrac
(27 pri) 33450 Saint Loubes
☎ 56.72.96.79
Golf de Bordeaux Lac (18 pub)
avenue de Pernon, 33300
Bordeaux ☎ 56.50.92.72
Golf de l'Ardilouse (18 pri)
33680 Lacanau Ocean
☎ 56.03.25.60
Landes
Golf d'Hossegor (18 pri)
avenue du Golf, 40150 Hossegor
☎ 58.43.56.99
Mont de Marsan (9 pri)
40090 Saint Avit ☎ 58.75.63.05
Golf de Moliets (18 pub)
40660 Moliets ☎ 58.48.54.65
Lot-et-Garonne
Golf d'Agen (9 pri)
route de St Ferreol, 47240 Bon
Encontre ☎ 53.96.95.78
Golf d'Albret (9 pri)
Le Pusocq, 47230 Barbaste
☎ 53.65.53.69
Golf de Castelnaud (27 pri)
B.P.186, 47304
Villeneuve-sur-Lot
☎ 53.01.74.64
Pyrénées-Atlantiques
Golf de Biarritz (18 pri)
Le Phare, avenue E. Cavell,

64200 Biarritz ☎ 59.03.71.80
Golf de Chiberta (18 pri)
104 boulevard des Plages, 64600
Anglet ☎ 59.63.83.20
Golf de Chantaco St-Jean-de-Luz
(18 pri) route d'Ascain, 64500
St Jean de Luz ☎ 59.26.14.22
Golf de la Nivelle St-Jean-de-Luz
(18 pri) place William Sharp,
64500 Ciboure ☎ 59.47.18.99
Golf de Pau (18 pri)
64140 Pau Billère ☎ 59.32.02.33
Golf de Pau Artiguelouve (18 pri)
Domaine St Michel, 64230 Lescar
☎ 59.83.09.29

AUVERGNE

Allier
Golf du Val de Cher Montluçon
(18 pri) 03190 Nassigny, Hérisson
☎ 70.06.71.15
Golf de Vichy Sporting Club
(18 pri) allée Baugnies, 03700
Bellerive sur Allier
☎ 70.32.39.11
Golf des Avennelles Moulins
(18 pri) Toulon sur Allier, 03400
Yzeure ☎ 70.20.00.95
Puy-de-Dôme
Golf des Volcans Clermont
Ferrand (18 pri)
La Bruyère des Moines, 63870
Orcines ☎ 73.62.15.51
Golf du Mont-Dore (9 pri)
63240 Le Mont-Dore
☎ 73.65.00.79
Golf de Charade (9 pub)
63130 Royat-Charade
☎ 73.35.73.09

BOURGOGNE

Côte-d'Or
Golf de Dijon Bourgogne (18 pri)
Bois des Norges, 21490 Norges la
Ville ☎ 80.35.71.10
Nièvre
Golf de Nevers (9 pub)
58470 Magny Cours
☎ 86.58.18.30
Saône-et-Loire
Golf Chalon-sur-Saône (18 pub)
Zone de Loisirs de Saint Nicolas,
Chatenoy en Bresse, 71380 Saint
Marcel ☎ 85.48.61.64
Yonne
Golf de Clairis (13 pri)
Domaine de Clairis, 89150
Savigny sur Clairis
☎ 88.86.33.90

BRETAGNE

Côtes-du-Nord
Golf de Pen Guen (18 pri)
22380 Saint Cast Le Guildo
☎ 96.41.91.20
Golf des Sables d'Or Les Pins
(9 pri) 22240 Fréhel
☎ 96.41.42.57
Golf des Ajoncs d'Or (18 pub)
22410 St Quay Portrieux
☎ 96.70.48.13
Golf de Saint Samson (18 pri)
route de Keneroc, 22670
Pleumeur Bodou ☎ 96.23.87.34
Golf du Bois Gelin (9 pri)
Plehedel, 22290 Lanvollon
☎ 96.22.31.24
Finistère
Golf de Brest Iroise (18 pub)
Parc de Lann Rohou, 29220
Landerneau ☎ 98.85.16.17
Golf de Quimper et de
Cornouaille (9 pri)
Manoir de Mesmeur, 29133 La
Forêt Fouesnant ☎ 98.56.97.09
Golf de l'Odet Quimper (18 pub)
Clohars Fouesnant, 29118
Bénodet ☎ 98.57.26.16
Ille-et-Vilaine
Golf de Rennes (9 pri)
35000 St Jacques de la Lande
☎ 99.64.24.18
Golf de Saint Malo le Tronchet
(18 pri)
35540 Miniac Morvan
☎ 99.68.96.69
Golf de Dinard (18 pri)
35800 St Briac sur Mer
☎ 99.88.32.07
Morbihan
Golf de Sauzon (9 pub)
56360 Belle Isle en Mer
☎ 97.31.64.65
Golf de Saint Laurent Ploemel
Carnac (18 pub)
56400 Auray ☎ 97.56.85.18

CENTRE

Eure-et-Loir
Golf du Perche Nogent Le
Rotrou (9 pri)
La Vallée des Aulnes, 28400
Souance au Perche
☎ 37.52.10.33
Indre
Golf des Dryades en Pays de
George Sand (18 pri)
Pouligny Notre Dame, 36160
Ste Sévère sur Indre
☎ 54.30.28.00

Golf de Touraine (18 pri)
Château de la Touche, 37510
Joue les Tours ☎ 47.53.20.28
Loir-et-Cher
Golf de Salbris (9 pri)
Château de Rivaulde, 41300
Salbris ☎ 54.97.21.85
Golf de Chambon-sur-Lignon
(9 pri) Beaujeu, 43400 Le
Chambon ☎ 71.59.28.10
Golf des Bordes (18 pri)
41220 Saint Laurent Nouan
☎ 54.87.72.13
Loiret
Golf du Val de Loire Orléans
(9 pri) Château de la Touche
Donnéry, 45450 Fay aux Loges
☎ 38.59.25.15
Golf de Sully sur Loire (18 pri)
L'Ousseau, 45600 Viglain
☎ 38.36.52.08
Golf de Sologne La Ferté St
Aubin (18 pri) route de Jouy le
Potier, 45160 Ardon
☎ 38.76.57.33
Golf de Vaugouard Montargis
(18 pri) Fontenay sur Loing,
45210 Ferrières ☎ 38.95.81.52
Golf de Marcilly Orléans (18 pri)
Domaine de la Plaine, 45240
Marcilly ☎ 38.76.11.73

CHAMPAGNE-ARDENNE

Ardennes
Golf des Ardennes Charleville
Mézière (9 pri) Les Poursaudes
Villers le Tilleul, 08430 Poix
Terron ☎ 24.37.31.98
Aube
Golf de la Cordelière Troyes
(18 pri) Château de la Cordelière,
10210 Chaource ☎ 25.40.11.05
Marne
Golf de Reims (18 pri)
Château des Dames de France,
51390 Gueux ☎ 26.03.60.14

FRANCHE-COMTE

Doubs
Golf de Besançon (18 pri)
La Chevillotte, 25660 Saône
☎ 81.55.73.54
Golf de Prunevelle Montbéliard
(18 pri) Ferme des Petits Bans,
25420 Dampierre sur le Doubs
☎ 81.98.11.77

ILE-DE-FRANCE

Seine-et-Marne
Golf de Fontainebleau (18 pri)
route d'Orléans,77300
Fontainebleau ☎ 64.22.22.95
Golf de Meaux Boutigny (18 pri)
Le Bordet Boutigny, 77100
Meaux ☎ 60.25.63.98
Golf de la Marsaudière (9 pri)
R.N.371, 77173 Chevry Cossigny
☎ 64.25.44.39
Golf d'Ozoir la Ferrière (27 pri)
Château des Agneaux, 77300
Ozoir la Ferrière ☎ 60.28.20.79
Golf de Crecy la Chapelle (18 pri)
Ferme de Montpichet, 77580
Crecy la Chapelle ☎ 64.04.70.75
Yvelines
Golf de Fourqueux (27 pri)
36, rue de St Nom, 78112
Fourqueux ☎ 34.51.41.47
Golf de la Boulie (45 pri)
78000 Versailles ☎ 39.50.59.41
Golf d'Isabella (9 pri)
Ste Appoline R.N.12, 78370
Plaisir ☎ 30.54.09.62
Golf de la Vaucoulers (18 pri)
78910 Civry la Forêt
☎ 34.87.62.29
Golf du Prieure (36 pri)
78440 Gargenville ☎ 34.76.70.12
Golf de Saint Germain (36 pri)
route de Poissy, 78100
St Germain en Laye
☎ 34.51.75.90
Golf de Saint Nom la Breteche
(36 pri) Hameau de la Tuilerie
Bignon, 78860 St Nom la
Breteche ☎ 34.62.54.00
Golf de St Quentin en Yvelines
(27 pri) Base de Loisirs, R.N. 12,
78190 Trappes ☎ 30.50.86.40
Golf de Rochefort en Yvelines
(18 pri) 78730 Rochefort en
Yvelines ☎ 30.41.31.81
Golf de Villennes sur Seine
(9 pub) route d'Orgeval, 78670
Villennes sur Seine
☎ 39.75.30.00
Essonne
Golf de Chevry (9 pub)
91190 Gif sur Yvette
☎ 60.12.40.33
Golf du Coudray (27 pri)
91830 Le Coudray Montceaux
☎ 64.93.81.76
Golf de Saint Aubin (18 pub)
91190 Saint Aubin
☎ 69.41.25.19
Golf de Saint Pierre du Perray
(18 pub) 91100 Corbeil
☎ 60.75.17.47

Hauts-de-Seine
Golf de Saint Cloud (36 pri)
Parc de Buzenval, 60 rue du 19
janvier, 92380 Garches
☎ 47.01.01.85
Val-de-Marne
Golf d'Ormesson (18 pri)
Belvedere du Parc, 94490
Ormesson sur Marne
☎ 45.76.20.71
Val-d'Oise
Golf de Domont (18 pri)
route de Montmorency, 95330
Domont ☎ 39.91.07.50
Golf de Seraincourt (18 pri)
Gaillonnet, 95450 Vigny
☎ 34.75.47.28
Golf de Villarceaux Chaussy
(18 pri)
95710 Bray et Lu ☎ 34.67.73.83

LANGUEDOC-ROUSSILLON

Aude
Golf de la Pinède (9 pri)
11370 Port Leucate
☎ 68.40.00.62
Gard
Golf Club de Campagne (18 pri)
route de Saint Gilles, 30000
Nimes ☎ 66.70.17.37
Hérault
Golf de Saint Thomas Bèziers
(9 pri) route de Pezenas, 34290
Servian ☎ 67.98.62.01
Golf de Bombequiols (9 pri)
St André de Bueges, 34190
Ganges ☎ 67.73.72.67
Golf de la Grande Motte (18 pub)
34280 La Grande Motte
☎ 67.56.05.00
Golf de Coulondres Montpellier
(9 pri) 4 rue des Erables, 34980
Saint Gely du Fesc
☎ 67.84.13.75
Lozère
Golf du Sabot (9 pri)
48000 La Canourgue
☎ 66.32.81.49
Pyrénées-Orientales
Golf de Font Romeu (9 pub)
avenue Jean Paul, 66120 Font
Romeu ☎ 68.30.21.67
Golf de Saint Cyprien (27 pri)
66750 Saint Cyprien
☎ 68.21.01.71

LIMOUSIN

Corrèze
Golf d'Aubazine (18 pub)

Ass. Corrèzienne de Golf
Complexe Touristique du
Coiroux, 19190 Beynat
☎ 55.27.25.66
Haute-Vienne
Golf de Limoges (18 pub)
Saint Lazare avenue du Golf,
87000 Limoges ☎ 55.30.28.01

LORRAINE

Meurthe-et-Moselle
Golf de Nancy (18 pri)
54460 Liverdun ☎ 83.24.53.87
Meuse
Golf de Combles Bar le Duc
(9 pri) 55000 Combles en Barrois
☎ 29.45.16.03
Golf de Madine (9 pub)
Nonsard, 55210 Vigneules
☎ 29.89.32.50
Moselle
Golf de Metz Cherisey (9 pri)
Château de Cherisey, 57420
Verny ☎ 87.52.70.18
Vosges
Golf d'Epinal (18 pub)
rue du Merle Blanc, 88001 Epinal
☎ 29.34.65.97
Golf de Vittel (18 pri)
88800 Vittel ☎ 29.08.18.80

MIDI-PYRENEES

Ariège
Golf Club de l'Ariège (9 pub)
09240 La Bastide de Serou
☎ 61.64.56.78
Haute-Garonne
Golf de Luchon (9 pri)
route de Montauban, 31110
Luchon ☎ 61.79.03.27
Golf de Toulouse (18 pri)
31000 Vieille Toulouse
☎ 61.73.45.48
Golf de Toulouse Palmola
(18 pri) 31680 Buzet sur Tarn
☎ 61.84.20.50
Gers
Golf de Guinlet (9 pri)
32800 Eauze ☎ 62.09.80.84
Golf Las Martines (9 pri)
route de Ste Livrade, 32600 L'Isle
Jourdain ☎ 62.07.27.12
Lot
Golf du Mas Del Teil (9 pri)
La Chapelle Auzac, 46200
Souillac ☎ 65.37.01.48
Hautes-Pyrénées
Golf de Laloubère Tarbes (9 pub)
65310 Laloubère ☎ 62.96.06.22

Golf de Lannemezan (18 pri)
La Demi Lune, 65300
Lannemezan ☎ 62.98.01.01
Tarn
Golf de la Barouge (9 pri)
Pont de l'Arn, 81660 Mazamet
☎ 63.61.06.72
Golf des Etangs de Fiac (9 pri)
Braziz, 81500 Lavaur
☎ 63.70.64.70
Tarn-et-Garonne
Golf d'Espalais (9 pub)
82400 Valence d'Agen
☎ 63.29.04.56
Golf des Roucous Sauveterre
(9 pri) 82110 Lauzerte
☎ 63.95.83.70

NORD – PAS-DE-CALAIS

Nord
Golf de Thumeries Douai (9 pri)
Bois Lenglart, 59239 Thumeries
☎ 20.86.58.98
Golf de Dunkerque (9 pub)
Coudekerque Village, 59380
Bergues ☎ 28.61.07.43
Golf de Bondues Lille (27 pri)
Château de la Vigne, 59910
Bondues ☎ 20.23.20.62
Golf de Brigode Lille (18 pri)
36 avenue du Golf, 59650
Villeneuve d'Ascq
☎ 20.91.17.86
Golf des Flandres (9 pri)
137 boulevard Clemenceau, 59700
Marcq en Baroeul ☎ 20.72.20.74
Golf du Sart Lille (18 pri)
5 rue Jean Jaures, 59650
Villeneuve d'Ascq
☎ 20.72.02.51
Golf de Valenciennes (9 pri)
chemin Vert, 59770 Marly les
Valenciennes ☎ 27.46.30.10
Pas-de-Calais
Golf d'Hardelot (18 pri)
avenue du Golf, 62152 Neufchâtel
Hardelot ☎ 21.83.73.10
Golf du Touquet (54 pri)
avenue du Golf, 62520 Le
Touquet ☎ 21.05.68.47
Golf de Wimereux (18 pri)
route d'Ambleteuse, 62930
Wimereux ☎ 21.32.43.20

BASSE-NORMANDIE

Calvados
Golf de Cabourg (18 pri)
route de Sallenelles, 14390 Le

Home Varaville ☎ 31.91.25.26
Golf Public de Cabourg (9 pub)
avenue de l'Hippodrome, 14390
Cabourg ☎ 31.91.70.53
Golf de Clécy Cantelou (9 pri)
Manoir de Cantelou, 14570 Clécy
☎ 31.69.72.72
Golf de Deauville (27 pri)
14800 St Arnoult ☎ 31.88.20.53
Golf de Clair Vallon (9 pri)
14510 Houlgate ☎ 31.91.06.97
Golf de Bayeux Omaha Beach
(18 pri) 14520 Port en Bessin
☎ 31.21.72.94
Manche
Golf de Brehal (18 pub)
50290 Brehal ☎ 33.51.58.88
Golf de Cherbourg (9 pri)
Domaines des Roches, Village de
l'Eglise, 50470 La Glacerie
☎ 33.44.45.48
Golf de Coutainville (9 pri)
50230 Agon ☎ 33.47.03.31
Golf de Fontenay en Cotentin
(9 pri) Fontenay sur Mer, 50310
Montebourg ☎ 33.21.44.27
Golf de Granville (18 pri)
Breville, 50290 Brehal
☎ 33.50.23.06
Orne
Golf de Bagnoles de l'Orne
Andaine Golf Club (9 pub)
route de Domfront, 61140
Bagnoles de l'Orne
☎ 33.37.81.42

HAUTE-NORMANDIE

Eure
Golf de Vaudreuil Louviers
(18 pri) 27100 Le Vaudreuil
☎ 32.59.02.60
Seine-Maritime
Golf de Dieppe (18 pri)
route de Pourville, 76200 Dieppe
☎ 35.84.25.05
Golf d'Etretat (18 pri)
route du Havre, 76790 Etretat
☎ 35.27.04.89
Golf du Havre (18 pri)
Hameau Saint Supplix, 76930
Octeville sur Mer ☎ 35.46.36.50
Golf de Rouen (18 pri)
chemin des Communeaux, 76130
Mont St Aignan ☎ 35.76.38.65
Golf de Saint Saens (9 pri)
Domaine de Vaudichon, 76680
Saint Saens ☎ 35.34.25.24

PAYS DE LA LOIRE

Loire-Atlantique

Golf de la Baule (18 pri)
Domaine de St Denac, 44117
St André des Eaux
☎ 40.60.46.18
Golf de la Bretesche Missillac
(18 pri) 44160 Pontchâteau
☎ 40.88.30.03
Golf de Nantes (18 pri)
44360 Vigneux de Bretagne
☎ 40.63.25.82
Golf de Pornic (9 pri)
49 bis boulevard de l'Ocean,
Ste Marie sur Mer, 44210 Pornic
☎ 40.82.06.69
Maine-et-Loire
Golf d'Angers (18 pri)
Moulin de Pistrait, St Jean des
Mauvrets, 49320 Brissac Quince
☎ 41.91.96.56
Mayenne
Golf de Laval (9 pri)
Le Jariel, 53000 Change les Laval
☎ 43.53.16.03
Sarthe
Golf du Mans (18 pri)
route de Tours Mulsanne, 72230
Arnage ☎ 43.42.00.36
Vendée
Golf de St Jean de Monts (9 pub)
Sporting Golf, 85160 St Jean de
Monts ☎ 51.58.13.06

PICARDIE

Aisne
Golf de l'Ailette (9 pub)
02000 Laon ☎ 23.24.83.99
Golf du Val Secret (9 pri)
Ferme de Farsoy, 02400 Brasles
☎ 23.69.01.80
Golf du Mesnil Saint Laurent
(9 pri) 02720 Homblières
☎ 23.68.19.48
Oise
Golf de Chantilly (27 pri)
60500 Vineuil Saint Firmin
☎ 44.57.04.43
Golf de l'Icl Lamorlaye (36 pri)
Rond Point du Gd Cerf Lys-
Chantilly, 60260 Lamorlaye
☎ 44.21.26.00
Golf de Chaumont en Vexin
(18 pri) Château de Bertichère,
60240 Chaumont en Vexin
☎ 44.49.00.81
Golf de Compiègne (18 pri)
avenue Royale, 60200 Compiègne
☎ 44.40.15.73
Golf de Morfontaine (18 pri)
60520 La Chapelle en Serval
☎ 44.54.68.27
Somme
Golf d'Amiens (18 pri)

80115 Querrieu ☎ 22.91.02.04
Golf de Nampont Saint Martin
(18 pri) 80120 Rue
☎ 22.25.00.20

POITOU-CHARENTES

Charente
Golf d'Angoulême l'Hirondelle
(9 pri) Champfleuri, 16000
Angoulême ☎ 45.61.16.94
Golf du Cognac (18 pub)
Saint Brice, 16100 Cognac
☎ 45.32.18.17
Charente-Maritime
Golf de Saintes (9 pub)
Fontcouverte, 17100 Saintes
☎ 46.74.27.61
Golf de Royan (18 pub)
Golf de la Côte de Beauté, 17420
Saint Palais ☎ 46.23.16.24
Deux-Sèvres
Golf de Mazières en Gatine
(18 pub) 79130 Mazières en
Gatine ☎ 49.63.28.33
Vienne
Golf de Poitiers Golf Poitevin
(9 pri) Terrain des Chalons, route
de Bignoux, 86000 Poitiers
☎ 49.61.23.13
Golf du Haut Poitou (9 pub)
Parc de Loisirs de Saint Cyr,
86130 Jaunay Clan
☎ 49.62.57.22
Golf de Chatellerault (18 pri)
Parc du Connetable, 86270 La
Roche Posay ☎ 49.86.20.21
Golf de Saint-Hilaire (18 pub)
Centre des Loisirs Loudun
Roiffé, 86120 Les Trois Moutiers
☎ 49.98.78.06

PROVENCE – ALPES – COTE D'AZUR

Alpes-Maritimes
Golf de Biot (18 pri)
06410 Biot ☎ 93.65.08.48
Golf de Cannes-Mandelieu
(27 pri) route du Golf, 06210
Mandelieu ☎ 93.49.55.39
Golf de Cannes-Mougins (18 pri)
175 route d'Antibes, 06250
Mougins ☎ 93.75.79.13
Golf de Monte Carlo (18 pri)
La Turbie, 06320 Cap d'Ail
☎ 93.41.09.11
Golf de Cannes-Valbonne
(18 pri) 06560 Valbonne
☎ 93.42.00.08
Golf de Tende (9 pri)
06430 Dom de Tende

☎ 93.04.61.02
Golf du Val Martin (9 pri)
Domaine du Val Martin, 06560
Valbonne ☎ 93.42.07.98
Bouches-du-Rhône
Golf de Fuveau Château l'Arc
(18 pri) Rousset sur l'Arc, 13790
Fuveau ☎ 42.53.28.38
Golf d'Aix Marseille (18 pri)
Domaine de Riquetti, 13290 Les
Milles ☎ 42.24.20.41
Golf de l'Ecole de l'Air (9 pri)
13300 Salon de Provence
☎ 90.53.90.90.
Var
Golf de Beauvallon (9 pri)
83120 Ste Maxime
☎ 94.96.16.98
Golf de Valcros Hyères (18 pri)
83250 La Londe les Maures
☎ 94.66.81.02
Golf de Valescure (18 pri)
route du Golf, 83700 St Raphael
☎ 94.82.40.46

RHONE-ALPES

Ain
Golf de Divonne (18 pri)
01220 Divonne les Bains
☎ 50.20.07.19
Golf Club de la Dombe (9 pri)
Mionnay, 01390 Saint André de
Corcy ☎ 78.91.84.84
Golf de la Commanderie Macon
(18 pri) Laumusse Crottet, 01290
Pont de Veyle ☎ 85.30.44.12
Golf de Villars les Dombes (9 pri)
Golf du Clou, 01330 Villars les
Dombes ☎ 74.98.19.65
Drôme
Golf de Valence Saint Didier
(9 pri) St Didier de Charpey,
26300 Bourg de Peage
☎ 75.59.67.01
Golf du Pilhon (9 pub)
Val Maravel, 26310 Luc en Diois
☎ 75.21.46.75
Isère
Golf de l'Ile d'Abeau (9 pub)
38300 Bourgoin Jallieu
☎ 74.43.28.84
Golf de Lyon Villette d'Anthon
(27 pri) 38280 Villette d'Anthon
☎ 78.31.11.33
Golf d'Uriage Grenoble (9 pri)
Les Alberges, Vaulnaveys le
Haut, 38410 Uriage
☎ 76.89.03.47
Golf Club de Grenoble (18 pri)
La Grande Grange, St Quentin
en Isère, B.P. 8, 38210 Tullins
☎ 76.93.67.28

Loire
Golf du Forez (9 pri)
Domaine de Presles Craintilleux, 42210 Montrond les Bains
☎ 77.30.86.85
Golf de Villerest (9 pub)
Domaine de Champlong, 42300 Roanne ☎ 77.69.70.60
Rhône
Golf du Verger Lyon (18 pri)
69360 St Symphorien d'Ozon
☎ 78.02.84.20
Savoie
Golf d'Aix les Bains (18 pri)

avenue du Golf, 73100 Aix les Bains ☎ 79.61.23.35
Golf des Arcs (18 pri)
73700 Bourg St Maurice
☎ 79.07.48.00
Golf de Méribel (9 pri)
73550 Méribel Altiport
☎ 79.08.65.32
Haute-Savoie
Golf d'Annecy (18 pri)
Echarvines, 74290 Talloires
☎ 50.60.12.89
Golf de Bossey (18 pri)
Château de Crevin, 74160

St Julien en Genevois
☎ 50.43.75.25
Golf de Chamonix (18 pri)
74400 Les Praz de Chamonix
☎ 50.53.06.28
Golf d'Evian (18 pri)
Rive Sud du Lac de Genève, 74500 Evian ☎ 50.75.14.00
Golf de Flaine les Carroz (18 pri)
74300 Flaine ☎ 50.90.85.44
Golf de Megève (18 pri)
Le Mont d'Arbois, 74120 Megève
☎ 50.21.29.79

■ *HANG GLIDING* ■

This is a challenging and exciting sport and if you already hold a UK pilot's licence, then the thought of mountain flying in France, in the foothills of the Alps or the Pyrénées, for example, must be very tempting. The British Hang Gliding Association, 1 Cranfield Airfield, Cranfield MK43 0YR (☎ 0234 751688) is worth contacting and, in particular, its National Training Officer, Bob Harrison, since he can provide further advice. Each country has its own licensing scheme and although there is no reciprocal agreement over ratings between the two countries, France does recognise the UK licensing scheme.

The following is a selection of clubs in France recognised by the national organisation, the Fédération Française de Vol Libre (54 bis, rue de la Buffa, 06000 Nice ☎ 93.88.62.89), and offering tuition under qualified instructors using the latest and safest equipment. While actually learning abroad is rare, since an excellent command of the French language would be required, keen British clubs do organise overseas visits in order to enjoy a change of scene and thermals, as well as to compete internationally. The importance of being adequately insured cannot be overstressed.

BRETAGNE

Bretagne Vol Libre,
218 rue de Verdun, 29200 Brest
☎ 98.41.86.15

MIDI-PYRENEES

Les Ailes du Tarn et Garonne,
Danis-St-Martial, 82000 Montauban ☎ 63.66.15.83
Archiplumes,
8 residence Les Badalans, 65510 Loudunvielle ☎ 62.99.64.50
Ecole Pyrénéenne de Vol Libre, 65240 Vielle Louron
☎ 62.99.68.55

PROVENCE

Vol Club 13000,
Le Gardanon, avenue des Vignes de Marius, 13090 Aix-en-Provence ☎ 42.59.03.39
Avolia,
Ecole de Plan du Bourg, Savournon, 05700 Serres
☎ 92.67.12.21
Ecole Française de Vol Libre, Le Grand Chalet, St-Dalmas, 06420 Valdeblore ☎ 93.02.83.50
Thermodynamic Club, 04360 Moustiers-Ste-Marie
☎ 92.74.66.50

RHONE-ALPES

Vol Libre des Belledonnes,
301 route de la Féclaz, 73230 St-Alban-Leysse ☎ 79.75.25.89
Oxygène,
27 rue de Casino, 73100 Aix-les-Bains ☎ 79.88.94.23
Delta Club de Savoie,
Maison des Sports, 6 Mont Valérieux, B.P.624, 73006 Chambéry ☎ 79.33.17.25
Ecole Fantastique,
Les Granges, 74100 Morzine
☎ 50.79.08.19

■ MOUNTAINEERING AND ROCK CLIMBING ■

Many of the winter alpine resorts also double as climbing centres during the summer as part of the range of activities offered. Enquiries at the local Tourist Office will lead to contact with experienced guides (members of the International Union of Mountain Guides) who will either be running their own climbing courses or will accompany groups or individuals on specific climbs. The resorts listed in the gazetteer section of this book reveal several locations of interest to the rock climber.

In the Rhône-Alpes there is Chamonix, of course, a renowned mountaineering resort at the foot of Mont Blanc, and also summer rock climbing at Villard-de-Lans. In Provence there are accompanied climbs at Fontaine de Vaucluse, and in the Hautes-Alpes *département* the Gap-Céüze near Gap is a climber's paradise. Montgenèvre, Serre-Chevalier, Les Orres and Puy-St-Vincent all offer summer rock-climbing opportunities, the latter having the peaks of Les Ecrins (4,102 m) and Pelvoux (3,900 m) as lofty targets.

The Pyrénées also offer superb climbing possibilities, with courses for beginners under the supervision of the Bureau des Guides at Bagnères-de-Bigorre, Cauterets and Luz-St-Sauveur. In Languedoc-Roussillon there is climbing from bases at Font-Romeu and Montpellier, and in the Vosges at La Bresse and Gérardmer.

As preparation for those already experienced in UK climbing, the British Mountaineering Council offers its members weekend pre-alpine mountaineering courses as an introduction to alpine mountaincraft. Designed to help those intending to visit the Alps for the first time, they can be followed up by week-long or longer courses based at Chamonix, where the mountains offer a range of rock, ice and mixed climbing routes. The Council can also arrange special insurance policy cover for overseas (for mountaineers, climbers, hill walkers, ramblers and skiers) and help with planning routes.

Useful addresses:
British Mountaineering Council, Crawford House, Precinct Centre, Booth Street East, Manchester M13 9RZ ☎ 061-273 5835
Club Alpin Français (CAF), 9 rue de la Boétie, 75008 Paris
Fédération Française de la Montagne (FFM), 20 bis, rue de la Boétie, 75008 Paris

■ MULTI-ACTIVITY HOLIDAYS ■

A glance through the winter sports resorts listed in the gazetteer will reveal that most, if not all, of them also double as summer activity centres capitalising on the accommodation and recreation facilities in situ. In the Provence – Alpes – Côte d'Azur region, for example, see Auron, Montgenèvre, Les Orres, Puy-St-Vincent, St-Véran, Serre-Chevalier, Superdévoluy and Valberg. In the Rhône-Alpes region there is Flaine, Megève, Morzine, La Plagne, Tignes (summer skiing), Val d'Isère, Val Thorens and Villard-de-Lans. All these are major skiing resorts in season and can be contacted direct for further details.

Very popular with the French for family holidays, these mountain locations provide some often stunning springtime or summer scenery, with tempting panoramic hikes or pony rides across alpine meadows. There are also excellent golf courses and tennis courts, with tuition, and where there is water, canoeing and white-water rafting figure high in the popularity stakes. There is rock climbing, of course, and mountain parachuting down grassy slopes, a relatively new sport which guarantees thrills without any real danger. Or try hang gliding or mountain-biking, to say nothing of archery, clay-pigeon shooting and fishing in the numerous mountain lakes. Fitness packages are available at some resorts, making good use of the superior swimming pool facilities, and, in Villard-de-Lans, there are even music lessons and astronomy classes.

Several British operators organise such multi-activity holidays at centres such as those listed above, while others are based at coastal locations where the emphasis is naturally on watersports.

SPECIALIST TOUR OPERATORS

Active Pursuits, Crescent House, Angel Hill, Bury-St-Edmunds IP33 1UZ
☎ 0284 750505
Club Méditerranée, 106/110 Brompton Road, London SW3 1JJ ☎ 01-581 1161
Inntravel, Hovingham, York YO6 4JZ ☎ 065 382742
Mark Warner, 20 Kensington Church Street, London W8
☎ 01-938 1851
PGL Family Adventure, 104 Station Street, Ross-on-Wye HR9 7AH
☎ 0989 768768
Ski Val, 91 Wembley Park Drive, Wembley Park HA9 8HF
☎ 01-903 4444
Tourarc, 197b Brompton Road, London SW3 1LA
☎ 01-589 1918
VFB Holidays, 1 St Margaret's Terrace, Cheltenham GL50 4DT
☎ 0242 526338

■ *NATURE STUDY* ■

Wild mountainous areas, flower-filled meadows, secret river valleys, dense forests, volcanoes, wide, windswept marshland . . . France is a land of great contrasts and riches.

Six national and 24 regional parks cover large expanses of the country, forming conserved areas for the flora and fauna and the cultural traditions of the regions. Each has its own information centre (Maison du Parc), addresses for which are given, together with an indication of the sorts of activities which can be enjoyed within them.

NATIONAL PARKS

The Cévennes – wild and captivating country (in the *départements* of Lozère, Gard and Ardèche), access involves much tiring driving along hairpin bends.
Recreation: walking, skiing, watersports and caving
Information: B.P.4, 48400 Florac ☎ 66.45.01.75

The Ecrins – this is the highest mountain mass in the Alps on the French side of the border, perfect for studying the rare flora and fauna of the area (in the Isère and Hautes-Alpes *départements*).
Recreation: climbing, cycling and walking
Information: 7 rue du Colonel Roux, 05000 Gap ☎ 92.51.40.71

Ile de Port-Cros – in the Hyères group of islands and served by regular ferries from the mainland, Port-Cros is an island reserve for the flora and fauna of the Mediterranean seaboard, the mild climate producing magnificent vegetation.
Recreation: walking
Information: 50 avenue Gambetta, 83400 Hyères ☎ 94.65.32.98

The Mercantour – between the Alpes-Maritimes and the Italian frontier, this mountainous region harbours some of the richest flora and fauna of Europe.
Recreation: caving, walking and climbing
Information: 23 rue de l'Italie, 06000 Nice ☎ 93.87.86.10

The Pyrénées Occidentales – over 337,000 hectares of natural parkland, mountain peaks (the Vignemale its highest at 3,298 m) and wooded valleys, the park includes the Néouvielle nature reserve and its many lakes, and lies between the Néouvielle massif and the Aspe valley along the Pyrénées range, adjacent to the Spanish National Park of Ordesa. Natural habitat for brown bears, wild goats, grouse, vultures and ibex amongst others, there are miles of ramblers' footpaths. Museums and places of interest at Arrens-Marsous,

Cauterets, Luz-St-Sauveur and St-Lary. Many of the scenic roads and passes are famous highlights of the *Tour de France* cycling race in July.
Recreation: walking (the GR10 runs east to west through the park), riding, fishing and climbing
Information: B.P.300, 65000 Tarbes ☎ 62.93.30.60

The Vanoise – a rugged mountain area high up in the Alps encompassing country on both sides of the Franco-Italian border, and including a reserve for endangered species and the opportunity to sight creatures such as the ibex and chamoix; a marvellous area for hikers and botanists with a particularly rich flora to discover.
Recreation: climbing, skiing, walking and escorted tours
Information: 135 rue du Docteur Julliand, B.P.705, 73007 Chambéry ☎ 79.62.30.54

REGIONAL PARKS

Armorique (*Finistère*) – conservation area including the isle of Ouessant and the rural area inland from Brest.
Recreation: fishing, cycling and riding
Information: Ménez-Meur Hanvec, 29224 Daoulas ☎ 98.68.81.71

Brière (*Loire-Atlantique*) – pretty marshland and meadow region.
Recreation: travel by punt through the canals, and riding
Information: 180 Ile de Fédrun, 44720 Saint-Joachim ☎ 40.88.42.72

Brotonne (*Eure and Seine-Maritime*) – spanning the Seine between Rouen and Le Havre, and embracing 35 towns and villages and parts of four different types of countryside (Pays de Caux, Seine valley, the Roumois and Marais Vernier areas), this park is attempting to preserve its historical and cultural heritage together with the natural beauty of this heavily wooded area. Follow the *Route des Fruits*

in spring to see the orchards along the meandering course of the Seine, particularly around Jumièges, and visit the Seine River Museum at Caudebec-en-Caux.
Recreation: riding and walking
Information: 2 Rond-Point Marbec, 76580 Le Trait ☎ 35.37.23.16

Camargue (*Bouches-du-Rhône*) – vast expanses of marshland, rice fields and ranches where herds of white Camargue horses and their little black or brown foals roam alongside the young bulls. The bird sanctuary (not open to the public) is world-famous for its flocks of flamingoes, and provides an excellent habitat for a wide range of marshland birds.
Recreation: riding
Information: Le Pont de Rousty, 13200 Arles ☎ 90.97.10.93

Corsica – some of the finest mountain and coastal scenery in the Mediterranean. The park surrounds the highest peak on the island, Monte Cinto (2,710 m).
Recreation: walking and watersports
Information: 4 rue Fiorella, B.P.417, 20184 Ajaccio ☎ 95.21.56.54

Forêt d'Orient (*Aube*) – forested area with lakeside recreation facilities.
Recreation: watersports, riding and fishing
Information: Maison du Parc, 10220 Piney ☎ 25.41.35.57

Haute-Vallée de Chevreuse (*Yvelines*) – historically important region of wooded river valley, villages and châteaux in the Ile de France.
Recreation: walking and excursions
Information: 13 Grande Rue, 78720 Dampierre-en-Yvelines ☎ 30.52.54.65

Haut-Jura (*Jura*) beautiful and dramatic heavily forested area of Franche-Comté, with numerous lakes. See the wood craft centre at Bois d'Amont.
Recreation: winter sports (especially cross-country skiing), fishing, climbing and walking

Information: Maison du Haut-Jura, Lajoux, 39310 Septmoncel ☎ 84.41.20.37
Haut-Languedoc (*Hérault and Tarn*) – 284,500 hectares of beech forest, habitat for birds of prey, wild sheep, weasels and foxes.
Recreation: canoeing and riding
Information: 13 rue du Cloitre, B.P.9, 34220 Saint-Pons ☎ 67.97.02.10
Landes de Gascogne (*Gironde and Landes*) – once marsh and scrubland, now a vast mature area forested with conifers and planted with sea-grass to hold the gritty coastal soil in place.
Recreation: canoeing and riding
Information: 15 place Jean Jaurès, 40000 Mont-de-Marsan ☎ 58.06.24.25
Livradois-Forez (*Loire, Puy-de-Dôme*) – mountainous country embracing the Monts du Forez region (highest peak Pierre-sur-Haute 1,640 m) and the Monts du Livradois, with high passes and fast-rushing streams separated by a succession of plateaux. The lower slopes bear the traces of past industry where the tall, straight tree trunks were used for the manufacture of ships' masts for the navy, while the upper slopes remain covered by beautiful forests of oak, silver birch, beech and conifers. The traditional crafts of the area, wood work and lace-making, are being revived.
Recreation: walking (GR330 crosses this area)
Information: Saint-Gervais-sous-Meymont, 63880 Olliergues ☎ 73.95.54.31
Lorraine (*Meuse, Moselle, and Meurthe-et-Moselle*) – lakes and vast forests covering 1,260,900 hectares.
Recreation: watersports, shooting, fishing and climbing
Information: 10 avenue Camille Cavalier, B.P.35, 54703 Pont-à-Mousson ☎ 83.81.11.91
Lubéron (*Vaucluse, Alpes-de-Haute-Provence*) – a mountain chain under two different climatic influences and a part of Provence still isolated and unspoilt.
Recreation: riding
Information: 1 place Jean Jaurès, B.P.128, 84400 Apt

☎ 90.74.08.55
Marais Poitevin, Val de Sèvre and Vendée (*Charente-Maritime, Deux-Sèvres and Vendée*) – extensive marshland area.
Recreation: travel by punt through the canals
Information: Maison du Parc, La Ronde, 17170 Courcon ☎ 46.27.82.44
Montagne de Reims (*Marne*) – the slow-growing, long-lived and remarkably gnarled and twisted *Faux de Verzy* beech trees are a feature of this hilly area around the outskirts of Reims, indeed only at two sites in the world are the *Faux* to be found (*Fagus* is Latin for beech).
Recreation: walking
Information: Maison du Parc, Pourcy, 51160 Ay ☎ 26.59.44.44
Morvan (*Saône-et-Loire, Côte d'Or, Nièvre and Yonne*) – pleasant country of woods, lakes and streams.
Recreation: walking, riding, canoeing and fishing
Information: Maison du Parc, Saint-Brisson, 58230 Montsauche ☎ 86.78.70.16
Nord – Pas-de-Calais – aiming to aid and encourage economic activities within the natural rural and coastal countryside, this park encompasses three areas: the Plaine de la Scarpe et de l'Escaut (around St-Amand-Raismes), the Audomarois (around St-Omer) and the Boulonnais (around Boulogne).
Recreation: cycling, riding, coastal walking, boat hire
Information: Espace Naturel Régional, 17 rue Jean Roisin, 59800 Lille ☎ 20.60.60.60
Normandie-Maine (*Manche, Mayenne, Orne and Sarthe*) – gently undulating countryside where abundant birdlife inhabits the forests of beech, oak and pine. The park extends over the upper valleys of the Sarthe and Mayenne, the agricultural plains around Alençon and Argentan, and the meadow and copse hill country on both sides of the border with the Pays de la Loire. Over 1,584,350 hectares embrace 150 towns and villages, where traditional craftwork is encouraged, and the four large forests of the Andaines, Ecouves,

Mortain and Perseigne.
Recreation: walking
Information: Maison du Parc, B.P.5, 61320 Carrouges ☎ 33.27.21.15
Pilat (*Loire*) – essentially rural, with wooded hills, the highest being Crêt de la Perdrix (1,432 m), broad green plateaux and valleys of orchards.
Recreation: riding, watersports and canoeing on an artificial river at Saint-Pierre-de-Boeuf, walking and cross-country skiing
Information: Le Moulin de Virieu, 2 rue Benay, 424140 Pelussin ☎ 74.87.65.24
Queyras (*Hautes-Alpes*) – small area containing some of the highest villages in Europe and a network of ramblers' paths.
Recreation: walking, climbing, canoeing and riding
Information: avenue de la Gare, B.P.3, 05600 Guillestre ☎ 92.45.06.23
St-Amand-Raismes (*Nord*) – large forested area and conservation area for wild boar, sheep and deer.
Recreation: walking, watersports and riding
Information: for information centre see Nord – Pas-de-Calais
Vercors (*Isère and Drôme*) – *maquis* country of dense undergrowth.
Recreation: walking
Information: chemin des Fusillés, B.P.14, 38250 Lans-en-Vercors ☎ 76.95.40.33
Volcans d'Auvergne (*Puy-de-Dôme and Cantal*) – the heavily wooded and extinct volcano region of central France.
Recreation: walking, riding, canoeing, climbing and caving
Information: Montlosier près Randanne, Commune d'Aydat, 63210 Rochefort-Montagne ☎ 73.65.67.19
Vosges du Nord (*Bas-Rhin and Moselle*) – forested area rich in flora and fauna.
Recreation: walking and canoeing
Information: La Petite Pierre, 67290 Wingen-sur-Moder ☎ 88.70.44.30

NATURE RESERVES

AQUITAINE
Le Teich ornithological park:

near Arcachon
Banc d'Arguin ornithological
park: near Arcachon
BRETAGNE
Cap Sizun ornithological park:
near Goulien
Cap Fréhol ornithological park:
near Plevenon
Sept-Iles: near Perros-Guirec
Belle-Ile-en-Mer: near Pointe-de-
Nar Hor Morbihan
PAYS DE LA LOIRE
Ile d'Olonne: near Sables
d'Olonne
St-Denis-de-Payrée: Marais
Poitevin
PICARDIE
Marquenterre ornithological
park: near Abbeville
PROVENCE
Camargue: near Arles
RHONE-ALPES
Villars-les-Dombes ornithological
park: near Bourg-en-Bresse

Specialising in offering hotels
located in perfect peace and quiet
is the *Relais du Silence* chain
(Relais du Silence, 38640 Claix

☎ 76.98.35.79), 140 hotels of
two, three and four stars
throughout France.

The Field Studies Council
organise wonderful trips to
regions of France along specific
themes, such as wild flowers and
butterflies of the Dordogne, and
natural history trips to the eastern
Pyrénées. Listed below are other
British operators who offer all-
inclusive tours to particular areas,
with botanical and birdwatching
themes, often in the company of
an expert.

SPECIALIST TOUR OPERATORS

Branta Travel, 11 Uxbridge
Street, London W8 7TQ
☎ 01-229 7231
Canvas Holidays, 9/13 Bull
Plain, Hertford SG14 1DY
☎ 0992 553535
Cox & Kings Travel, St James'
Court, Buckingham Gate
SW1E 6AF ☎ 01-931 9106

Cygnus Wildlife Holidays,
96 Fore Street, Kingsbridge
TQ7 1PY ☎ 0548 6178
Field Studies Council,
Expeditions Overseas,
Montford Bridge, Shrewsbury
SY4 1HW ☎ 0743 850164
HF Holidays, 142 Great North
Way, London NW4 1EG
☎ 01-203 3381
Ornitholidays 1-3 Victoria
Drive, Bognor Regis, Sussex
PO21 2PW ☎ 0243 821230
Ramblers Holidays, Longcroft
House, Fretherne Road,
Welwyn Garden City AL8 6PQ
☎ 0707 331133
SVP France, PO Box 90,
Chichester, West Sussex
PO18 8XJ ☎ 0243 377862
Voyages Jules Verne, 21 Dorset
Square, London NW1 6QG
☎ 01-724 6624

*Useful address: Fédération des
Parcs Naturels de France, 4 rue
de Stockholm, 75008 Paris*
☎ 42.94.90.84

■ *TENNIS* ■

Turn up with a racket at any of the principal resorts in France and you will be able to hire a court and play. Some clubs offer tuition, likely to be in French, but good fun so it is worth making enquiries. The gazetteer provides extensive details of resorts offering tennis facilities and indicates where coaching is available. For those who would like to combine a holiday with some serious coaching, however, several operators can help.

SPECIALIST OPERATORS

Air France Holidays, 69 Boston
Manor Road, Brentford
TW8 9JQ ☎ 01-568 6981
Club Méditerranée,

106-108 Brompton Road,
London SW3 1JJ
☎ 01-581 1161
Freedom in France, Meadows,
Poughill, Bude, Cornwall
EX23 9EN ☎ 0288 55591
Representation Plus, Herontye

House, Stuart Way, East
Grinstead RH19 4QA
☎ 0342 410567
Sophia Country Club, 1 Chouler
Gardens, Granby Road, Old
Stevenage, Herts SG1 4TB
☎ 0438 350274

■ *WALKING IN FRANCE* ■

Whether you are a beginner or a hardened rambler, the idea of a walking holiday abroad is very appealing. Walking holidays are taken very seriously in France: there is considerable back-up organisation to help the traveller and a magnificent variety of landscapes to choose from.

Publications called *topoguides* are available for each region of France, covering recommended walks in each area, and containing local maps based on those of the IGN (Institut Géographique National) scale 1/50,000, the equivalent of the British Ordnance Survey. These *topoguides* include all relevant information: local and general history notes, special features of interest, distances and estimated walking times, as well as eating, lodging and transport facilities, and they enable hikers to plan their tour in convenient long or short stages. They are produced by the Fédération Française de la Randonnée Pédestre (FFRP), Comité National des Sentiers de Grande Randonnée, 9 avenue George V, 75008 Paris ☎ 47.23.62.32, and cover some 37,000 km of long-distance footpaths, known in France as *Grandes Randonnées* (or *GR*). The British representative for this organisation is Robertson McCarta Ltd, 122 King's Cross Road, London WC1X 9DS ☎ 01-278 8276, who publish the Footpaths of Europe series – walking guides based on translations of the *topoguides*, with full colour maps.

The walks are created and maintained by volunteer members of the FFRP and their linear or circular tours aim not to get the ramblers from A to B as quickly as possible, but to help them to discover the essence of France at their own pace. On a GR, accommodation will obviously be needed en route and addresses are given of hotels, *gîtes*, farmhouses, cottages, youth hostels and mountain refuges, on or just off the route, and in some cases also offering meals.

THE GRANDES RANDONNEES OF FRANCE

There are ten main *Grandes Randonnées*: **GR1** circles the environs of Paris, **GR2** follows the course of the Seine, **GR3** that of the Loire. The Mediterranean is linked with the Atlantic coast from Grasse in Provence to Saintes in Poitou-Charentes by **GR4**, and by **GR5** with Holland from Nice. **GR6** runs between Sisteron in the French Alps and Ste-Foy-la-Grande in the Dordogne. The Vosges and the Pyrénées are linked by the **GR7** from Ballon d'Alsace to Montségur. **GR9** joins the Jura mountains at St-Amour to St-Pons-les-Mures on the Côte d'Azur. From Hendaye to Banyuls the **GR10** runs the breadth of the Pyrénées. The **GR65,** the other major route along the pilgrim path to Santiago de Compostela, runs from Le Puy in the Auvergne to the Spanish frontier.

The *Grandes Randonnées* routes are marked by white and red striped signs, prominently displayed on trees, posts, rocks, etc., and are designed to be walked in several stages, allowing time to appreciate the character of the region.

Another variation is the *Grande Randonnée de Pays* whose routes are usually circuits and which aim to provide the rambler with further insight into a particular area. These routes are marked by yellow and red striped signs, similarly located on prominent natural features along the route. There are also *Petites Randonnées*, or short-distance walks (PR), lasting perhaps a day, or just a few hours and these are signposted in single yellow stripes.

At the beginning of every regional introduction in the

gazetteer section of this book, addresses are given for the information offices for the national or regional parks covered by that area. Further information is available from them and also from the individual Tourist Offices. Casual walkers will find that good local itineraries are produced by the Tourist Offices. Along the coast, particularly in Brittany, there are wonderful walks along the old Customs' paths (*Sentiers de Douanier*).

Many package hiking tours are offered by British tour operators, a selection of whom follows.

SPECIALIST TOUR OPERATORS

Ace Study Tours, Babraham, Cambridge CB2 4AP
☎ 0223 835055
Alternative Travel Group, 1-3 George Street, Oxford OX1 2AZ ☎ (0865) 251195
Belle France, Bayham Abbey, Lamberhurst TN3 8BG
☎ 0892 890885
Countrywide Holidays Association, Birch Heys, Cromwell Range, Manchester M14 6HU ☎ 061-225 1000
Esprit, 15 Clifton Hill, Exeter EX1 2DL ☎ 0392 70506
Explore Worldwide, 1 Frederick Street, Aldershot GU11 1LQ
☎ 0252 319448
France Voyages, 145 Oxford Street, London W1R 1TB
☎ 01-494 3155
French Travel Service, Georgian House, 69 Boston Manor Road, Brentford TW8 0JQ ☎ 01-568 8442
Gîtes de France, 178 Piccadilly, London W1V 9DB
☎ 01-493 3480
HF Holidays, 142/144 Great North Way, London NW4 1EG
☎ 01-203 0433
Inntravel, Hovingham, York YO6 4JZ ☎ 065 382742
Ramblers Holidays, Longcroft House, Fretherne Road,
Welwyn Garden City AL8 6PQ
☎ 0707 331133
River Running Holidays, Wee Knochina'am, Portpatrick, Stranraer DG9 9AD
☎ 077 681 473
Sherpa Expeditions, 131a Heston Road, Hounslow TW3 0RD ☎ 01-577 2717
SVP France, PO Box 90, Chichester, West Sussex PO18 8XJ ☎ 0243 377862
Waymark Holidays, 295 Lillie Road, London SW6 7LL
☎ 01-385 5015
YHA Travel, 14 Southampton Street, London WC2E 7HY
☎ 01-836 8541

SHORT BREAKS

Many *départements* in France, roughly equivalent to the English county, put together brochures under the title **Loisirs Accueil** in which are detailed short break packages within their area. Usually along unusual and interesting themes and often with arranged accommodation, these holidays are a charming way to enjoy France, off-season particularly, combined with the opportunity perhaps to attempt a particular sport or activity for the first time, or even perfect one in a new environment.

There are 49 Loisirs Accueil offices currently in operation and their brochures will be sent on request. It should be noted, however, that the majority of them are in French and, where tuition may be involved in the holiday, this too is likely to be given in French. Your enjoyment of this type of holiday is therefore dependent on having a reasonable command of the French language.

A selection of the types of break offered are detailed below, together with the addresses of all the Loisirs Accueil offices, from which further information is available:

● A supervised week spent learning or improving canoe skills in the Ognon river valley. Based on the calm waters of a lake and on the river (class 1-3), the courses consist of spending 20 hours on the activity of your first choice, plus 20 hours on any number of secondary choices. The options range from archery, canoe-kayak, caving, climbing, to riding and water-skiing. The prices quoted are for beginners (1,340F) and improvers (1,540F) and include basic accommodation.
Contact: Loisirs Accueil Haute-Saône – Belfort

● Based at Châteaudun on the Loir, this short break weekend is designed for the fly-fisherman and the price includes fishing rights on a specially selected stretch of water, full board accommodation, picnic lunch and facilities for cooking the catch. All-year-round accommodation is available in either a tourist class hotel (620F) or * hotel (883F).
Contact: Loisirs Accueil Eure-et-Loir (request brochure in English)

● Discover the châteaux of the Loire by air. Leaving from Tours, the trip lasts 1 hr 30 min and covers Villandry, Chinon, Azay le Rideau, Chambord and Cheverny amongst others. Costs per person are 860F (by plane) and 2,160F (by helicopter). Shorter and cheaper flights are also available.
Contact: Loisirs Accueil Indre-et-Loire (request brochure in English)

● Short two-night cycling circuit along the banks of the river Eure from Chartres to the Château de Maintenon and back. Available throughout the year at 405F per person, the price includes half-board in a double room (* or ** star hotel, detailed itinerary, car parking and onward transportation of luggage.
Contact: Loisirs Accueil Eure-et-Loir (request brochure in English)

● Fully-equipped dormobile for four-six people, available for Saturday-Saturday hire, based at Blois.
Contact: Loisirs Accueil Loir-et-Cher (request brochure in English)

● Try canoeing on the Loire, along the stretch between Châteauneuf-sur-Loire and Beaugency, in the company of a qualified instructor. Available throughout the year, costs range from 90F per person per day, rising to 320F per person with ** hotel accommodation arranged, to 1,650F per person for a full five-day course in July and August with accommodation at the centre and with archery an optional activity. Camping is a possible alternative.
Contact: Loisirs Accueil Loiret (request brochure in English)

● Getting back to nature and a slow pace of life in the region of Vendôme. Hire a four-berth gypsy caravan for any period of time from a weekend upwards. The prices range from 700F for a weekend and 2,200F for a week in low season to 1,000-3,000F for the same periods in high season, with additional days charged at 300F or 400F respectively. The circuits will lead you along pleasant country roads with farmland

stops, and local produce can be purchased along the routes. Instruction on caring for the horse will be provided at the departure point, Savigny-sur-Braye.
Contact: Loisirs Accueil Loir-et-Cher (request brochure in English)

● For the roughshooter, enjoy a day's shooting (October to January) with beaters and gun dogs over 300 hectares in the Sologne Forest, with meals taken at the hunting lodge; duck and waterfowl shoots (July to February) and rabbit and pigeon shoots (January and February). Price per day is 1,370F for all except the rabbit shoot, priced at 630F.
Contact: Loisirs Accueil Loir-et-Cher (request brochure in English)

● South of the Loire, in the Touraine, enjoy luxury full-board **** Relais Château accommodation and unlimited access to the golf course on the estate. These breaks operate from Monday to Friday and between November and March the costs are 3,450F per person rising to 3,700F in high season.
Contact: Loisirs Accueil Indre-et-Loire (request brochure in English)

● Pamper yourself with a weekend spent at the Manoir du Palomino, close to Chartres, in an exceptional riverside setting. Available all year round and priced at 1,000F per double room, there is high-class cuisine in the *** hotel and access to the tennis courts, 5-hole golf course, gymnasium, sauna and body care treatments.
Contact: Loisirs Accueil Eure-et-Loir (request brochure in English)

● Six days' drawing and landscape painting in August in the lovely Périgord Vert region of Charente. Small groups, personally supervised by the Parisian painter Jean Chantrier. Tuition and half-board accommodation in a local Logis de France ** hotel is priced at 2,870F per person and courses run from Mondays to Saturdays.
Contact: Loisirs Accueil Charente

● Three days' golf tuition specially designed for beginners at the Saint-Brice course near Cognac, comprising morning lessons and afternoon rounds under a critical eye. Priced at 2,260F per person, accommodation is in a ** hotel and the courses run on certain dates through the year from March onwards.
Contact: Loisirs Accueil Charente

● One-week canoeing trip down the Cher from St-Amand-Montrond to Preuilly for adults and children over 16 years. Price per person of 1,495F is for specific dates in July and August and includes initial training, canoe and life-jackets, camp site accommodation and meals and back-up support vehicle carrying luggage.
Contact: Loisirs Accueil Cher

● One-hour helicopter flights with a choice of circuits based on Bourges and giving wonderful bird's-eye views of the Berry châteaux at any time of the year. Four passengers travelling together costs 1,765F per person. Shorter trips by light aircraft cost 648F and cover the same circuits.
Contact: Loisirs Accueil Cher

● One-way or return trips by canal on boats equipped for two-six people and lasting anything from a weekend to a fortnight, are available from Easter to November, leaving from St-Satur in the Sancerrois countryside. Depending on size of boats and period of travel, prices range from a weekend (1,150-2,990F) to a week (2,080-5,180F).
Contact: Loisirs Accueil Cher

● Stylish château accommodation and two golf courses to try, the price of 1,750F per person includes Friday night to Sunday morning accommodation, lunches in the club house and one *table d'hôte* dinner. Available all year round.
Contact: Loisirs Accueil Cher

● Variations on the theme of combining top-level accommodation in a private château with a leisure pursuit are also possible for the competent rider. Stays of four days offer

horse rides with picnic lunches and two hunting outings. This break costs 6,000F per person and runs from Monday to Thursday throughout the hunting season (unless there is snow on the ground).
Contact: Loisirs Accueil Cher

● Learn the traditional, speciality cuisine of the Quercy region: stuffed, glazed chicken, red wine stew, *confit de porc*, prunes in brandy and cassoulet. This five-day, six-night course consists of morning preparation sessions followed by lunch, with the afternoons free. Accommodation is in a ** hotel in Montauban or a *** one in Moissac with evening meals provided. Running between May and October, the price is 2,690F or 3,380F depending on hotel choice.
Contact: Loisirs Accueil Tarn-et-Garonne

● Drawing and watercolour tuition by a professional artist at St-Antonin-Noble-Val on eight-day courses between June and September. Accommodation can be arranged in camp site, *gîte* or hotel but the costs for the classes (five hours per day) are 1,100F per person.
Contact: Loisirs Accueil Tarn-et-Garonne

● Learn to canoe in the Midi-Pyrénées. Close to the Spanish border, between Comminges and Andorra in the Couserans region, there is the opportunity to spend six days perfecting this watersport in magnificent surroundings. Full-board accommodation is at the Centre d'Accueil de Paletès and is costed on sharing a room between two (1,100F) or between six (1,500F), and there is evening entertainment. English is spoken on these group courses, which run on certain dates between June and October.
Contact: Loisirs Accueil Ariège-Pyrénées

● Spend six days in accompanied riding and camping in the historic and beautiful Cathar region. Full board is provided as is onward daily transportation of luggage, and commentary on the places of interest en route is included in the price (2,280F per person) as is the transfer from Foix or Castelnaudary station at the beginning and end of the holiday. Evening entertainment and meals take place around the camp fire, and it should be noted that English is spoken on this holiday, which runs at any time of the year.
Contact: Loisirs Accueil Ariège-Pyrénées

● Horse-drawn travel in the Limousin. Hire from Saturday to Saturday between April and October, in caravans for four people, at off-season rates of 3,500F per week to 3,800F in July and August. The rates are reduced for extended hire. Assistance and advice are supplied prior to your departure and nights are spent on farmland sites.
Contact: Loisirs Accueil Haute-Vienne

● One of the most beautiful rivers in France, the Vienne is also one of the most exciting for the angler, with salmon, trout and grayling in abundance. Particular dates between June and September are set aside for separate courses for the beginner or improver, but are all of a week's duration and include Logis de France accommodation, tuition in casting and fly-fishing and supervised fishing sessions, particularly popular in the evenings. There is the opportunity for non-fishing companions to book into the same accommodation and to enjoy themselves elsewhere with tennis, cycling, walking and swimming locally available. Costs per person 2,460F (1,165F for accompanying non-participant).
Contact: Loisirs Accueil Haute-Vienne

● Two days' canoeing and camping in the Loire valley region (rivers used are the Eure, Loir, Huisne or Conie). Camping costs 545F (or * hotel 860F) and the trip is supervised by a qualified leader. Longer trips can be made lasting five days and costing 1,270F (no hotel option).
Contact: Loisirs Accueil Eure-et-Loir

● Hot-air balloon trips over Chartres and the château and aqueduct of Maintenon. Drifting for an hour will cost you 1300F per person. Alternatively, go up in a microlight from the base at Dreux and survey the châteaux below. This hour will cost 490F per person.
Contact: Loisirs Accueil Eure-et-Loir

● Learn to hang glide and enjoy the silent world between the sky and the land. From Saturday to Friday between Easter and September, initiation courses are held combining both theory and practice, with full-board and shared accommodation at the centre included in the price of 4,000F per person.
Contact: Loisirs Accueil Eure-et-Loir

● Weekend fishing and village *gîte* accommodation on the edge of a 9-hectare well-stocked pool or *etang*, in the heart of the rural Perche region. The *gîte* costs 500F for the weekend (weekly rates 930F) with fishing rights an extra 50F (180F).
Contact: Loisirs Accueil Eure-et-Loir

● A short gourmet weekend combining the pleasures of gentle woodland walks (routes supplied), comfortable accommodation and good dining in a *** hotel in a lakeside setting. This break operates from either Saturday morning to Sunday night or Sunday morning to Monday night, all year round except February, and is priced at 320F per person. Use can also be made of any of the facilities of the hotel, which include sauna, solarium and tennis courts.
Contact: Loisirs Accueil Mayenne

● In the heart of the Ardennes, a three-day cookery course covering local gastronomic specialities and taught by a master chef in his **** restaurant. Accommodation is in a *** hotel and costs from 1,030F.
Contact: Loisirs Accueil Ardennes (request brochure in English)

LOISIRS ACCUEIL OFFICES

ALSACE/LORRAINE

Loisirs Accueil Haut-Rhin, Hôtel du Département, 68006 COLMAR Cedex ☎ 89.41.41.99
Loisirs Accueil Moselle, Hôtel du Département, B.P.1096, 57036 METZ ☎ 87.37.57.63

AQUITAINE

Loisirs Accueil Dordogne-Périgord, 16 rue Wilson, 24009 PERIGUEUX Cedex ☎ 53.53.44.35
Maison du Périgord, 30 rue Louis-le-Grand, 75002 PARIS ☎ 47.42.09.15
Loisirs Accueil Gironde, 21 cours de l'Intendance, 33000 BORDEAUX ☎ 56.52.61.40

AUVERGNE

Loisirs Accueil Cantal, 22 rue Guy de Veyre, 15000 AURILLAC ☎ 71.48.84.84
Loisirs-Accueil Haute-Loire, 12 boulevard Philippe Jourde, 43000 LE-PUY-EN-VELAY ☎ 71.09.26.05

BOURGOGNE

Loisirs Accueil Yonne, 1-2 quai de la République, 89000 AUXERRE ☎ 86.51.12.05

BRETAGNE

Loisirs Accueil Côtes du Nord, 5 rue Baratoux, 22000 SAINT-BRIEUX ☎ 96.62.12.41
Loisirs Accueil Ille-et-Vilaine, 1 rue Martenot, 35000 RENNES ☎ 99.02.97.41
Loisirs Accueil Morbihan, Hôtel du Département, B.P.400, 56009 VANNES ☎ 97.42.61.60
Maison de la Bretagne, Complexe Maine-Montparnasse, 17 rue de l'Arrivée, 75737 PARIS Cedex 15 ☎ 45.38.73.15

CENTRE

Loisirs Accueil Cher, 10 rue de la Chappe, 18000 BOURGES ☎ 48.70.74.75
Loisirs Accueil Eure-et-Loir, 19 place des Epars, B.P.67, 28002 CHARTRES ☎ 37.21.37.22
Loisirs Accueil Indre, Gare Routière, 36 rue Bourdillon, 36000 CHATEAUROUX ☎ 54.22.91.20
Loisirs Accueil Indre-et-Loire, 38 rue Augustin Fresnel, B.P.139, 37171 CHAMBRAY-LES-TOURS Cedex ☎ 47.48.37.27
Loisirs Accueil Loir-et-Cher, 11 place du Château, 41000 BLOIS ☎ 54.78.55.50
Loisirs Accueil Loiret, 3 rue de la Bretonnerie, 45000 ORLEANS ☎ 38.62.04.88

CHAMPAGNE-ARDENNE

Loisirs Accueil Ardennes, 18 avenue G. Corneau, 08000 CHARLEVILLE-MEZIERES ☎ 24.56.00.63

CORSE

Loisirs Accueil Corse, 24 boulevard Dominique Paoli, 20090 Ajaccio ☎ 95.22.70.79

FRANCHE-COMTE

Loisirs Accueil Doubs, 15 avenue Edouard Droz, 25000 BESANCON ☎ 81.80.38.18
Loisirs Accueil Jura, Hôtel du Département, B.P.652, 39021 LONS-LE-SAUNIER ☎ 84.24.57.70
Loisirs Accueil Haute-Saône – Belfort, 6 rue des Bains, 70000 VESOUL ☎ 84.75.43.66

ILE DE FRANCE

Loisirs Accueil Seine-et-Marne, 170 avenue Hanri Barbusse, 77190 DAMMARIE-LES-LYS ☎ 64.37.19.36
Loisirs Accueil Val d'Oise, Hôtel du Département, 2 Le Campus, 95032 CERGY-PONTOISE Cedex ☎ 34.25.32.52

LANGUEDOC-ROUSSILLON

Loisirs Accueil Aude, 39 boulevard Barbès, 11000 CARCASSONNE ☎ 68.47.09.06
Loisirs Accueil Lozère, Place Urbain V, B.P.4, 48002 MENDE Cedex ☎ 66.65.34.55
Maison de la Lozère, 4 rue Hautefeuille, 75006 PARIS ☎ 43.54.26.64

LIMOUSIN

Loisirs Accueil Corrèze, Maison du Tourisme, Quai Baluze, 19000 TULLE ☎ 55.26.46.88
Loisirs Accueil Creuse, 43 place Bonnyaud, 23000 GUERET ☎ 55.52.87.50
Loisirs Accueil Haute-Vienne, 4 place Denis Dussoubs, 87000 LIMOGES ☎ 55.79.04.04
Maison du Limousin, 18 boulevard Haussmann, 75009 PARIS ☎ 47.70.32.63

MIDI-PYRENEES

Loisirs Accueil Ariège-Pyrénées, 14 rue Lazéma, 09000 FOIX ☎ 61.65.01.15
Loisirs Accueil Haute-Garonne, 70 boulevard Koenigs, 31300 TOULOUSE ☎ 61.31.95.15
Loisirs Accueil Gers, Maison de l'Agriculture, route de Tarbes, 32003 AUCH Cedex ☎ 62.63.16.55
Maison du Gers et de l'Armagnac, 16-18 boulevard Haussmann, 75009 PARIS ☎ 42.46.91.39
Loisirs Acccuel Lot, Maison de l'Agriculture, 430 avenue Jean Jaurès, B.P.199, 46000 CAHORS ☎ 65.22.19.20
Loisirs Accueil Hautes-Pyrénées, 6 rue Eugène Tenot, 65000 TARBES ☎ 62.93.03.30
Maison des Pyrénées, 15 rue Saint-Augustin, 75002 PARIS ☎ 42.61.58.18
Loisirs Accueil Tarn, Hôtel du Département, 81014 ALBI Cedex ☎ 63.47.56.50
Maison du Tarn, 34 avenue de

Villiers, 75017 PARIS
☎ 47.63.06.26
Loisirs Accueil Tarn-et-Garonne,
place du Maréchal Foch, 82000
MONTAUBAN ☎ 63.63.31.40

NORD – PAS-DE-CALAIS

Loisirs Accueil Nord, 15-17 rue du
Nouveau Siècle, B.P.135, 59027
LILLE Cedex ☎ 20.57.00.61
Loisirs Accueil Pas-de-Calais,
44 Grand'Rue, 62200
BOULOGNE-SUR-MER
☎ 21.31.66.80
Maison Nord – Pas-de-Calais,
18 boulevard Haussmann, 75009
PARIS ☎ 47.70.59.62

PAYS DE LA LOIRE

Loisirs Accueil Loire-Atlantique,
Maison du Tourisme, place du
Commerce, 44000 NANTES
☎ 40.89.50.77

Loisirs Accueil Mayenne,
84 avenue R. Buron, B.P.343,
53018 LAVAL Cedex
☎ 43.53.18.18
Loisirs Accueil Vendée, 8 place
Napoléon Bonaparte, 85000 LA
ROCHE-SUR-YONNE
☎ 51.62.65.27

PICARDIE

Loisirs Accueil Aisne, 1 rue Saint-
Martin, B.P.116, 02006 LAON
Cedex ☎ 23.20.45.54
Loisirs Accueil Somme, 21 rue
Ernest Cauvin, 80000 AMIENS
☎ 22.92.26.39

POITOU-CHARENTES

Loisirs Accueil Charente, place
Bouillaud, 16021 ANGOULEME
☎ 45.92.24.43
Loisirs Accueil Vienne, 11 rue
Victor Hugo, B.P.287, 86007
POITIERS Cedex
☎ 49.88.89.79

PROVENCE – ALPES – COTE D'AZUR

Loisirs Accueil Hautes-Alpes,
16 rue Carnot, 05000 GAP
☎ 92.51.73.73
**Loisirs Accueil
Bouches-du-Rhône**, Domaine du
Vergon, 13370 MALLEMORT
☎ 90.59.18.05

RHONE-ALPES

Loisirs Accueil Ardèche, 8 cours
du Palais, 07000 PRIVAS
☎ 75.64.04.66
Loisirs Accueil Loire-Forez,
5 place Jean Jaurès, 42021
SAINT-ETIENNE Cedex
☎ 77.33.15.39
Loisirs Accueil Savoie,
24 boulevard de la Colonne,
73000 CHAMBERY
☎ 79.85.01.09

■ *PARIS* ■

A t any time of year and for whatever reason you plan a visit, Paris has
attractions that are unsurpassable. Her monuments and art galleries are world
famous, as are her elegant streets, luxury shops and colourful and busy
pavement cafés. Above all there is the enchanting Seine, flowing through her heart
and captivating forever those who visit.

Paris is so large that you need to plan your itineraries carefully, or your feet will
refuse to take you any further! It is the easiest thing in the world to try to see too
much of Paris in one short visit. The city is divided into 20 *arrondissements*
(districts) and a good city map will indicate these. The *Métro* (underground) public
transport system is efficient, clean and easy to use and infinitely preferable to trying
to drive and park a car!

Airports: Charles-de-Gaulle
☎ 48.62.22.80 and Orly
☎ 48.84.32.10
Boat trips: travelling by *bateau
mouche*, there are numerous
commentary-only tours or dine
and cruise trips operating from
Pont d'Iéna (left bank), Pont
Neuf (near Notre-Dame).and
Pont d'Alma (near the Eiffel
Tower).
Car hire: personal car hire is
available through Avis Train +
Auto ☎ 46.09.92.12; Europcar
☎ 30.43.82.82; and Hertz
☎ 47.88.51.51 amongst others.

Also available are
chauffeur-driven cars: Executive
Car – Carey Limousine
☎ 42.65.54.20 and London Cab
in Paris ☎ 43.70.18.18
Flights: sightseeing tours by
helicopter are operated by Heli-
France ☎ 45.57.53.67 and Heli-
Promenade ☎ 46.34.16.18 and
are bookable through the Tourist
Office.
Guided tours and illuminations: a
list of guided tours is available
from the Office de Tourisme de
Paris, 127 avenue des Champs-
Elysées, open every day (9 a.m.-

8 p.m.) ☎ 47.23.61.72. The
major monuments, such as the
Arc de Triomphe, Place de la
Concorde, Notre-Dame and the
Hôtel de Ville are illuminated at
night and best seen perhaps by
any of the organised coach
excursions.
Markets: flower markets, book
markets, fresh produce markets,
the unusual bird market (Sunday
on the Ile de la Cité), the
weekend *Marché aux Puces* (flea
markets) at Saint-Quen and
Montreuil, with their interesting
collections of bric-a-brac, are

worth trying to see.

Night life: both the cabaret show at the Moulin Rouge and the famous Bluebell Girls and international artists at the Lido are popular and spectacular.

Parks and gardens: the *Bois de Boulogne* is a vast park area of 6,096 hectares with seven boating lakes, children's play areas and including the Longchamp racecourse; the *Luxembourg Gardens* have tennis courts and a lake where children sail their toy sailing boats; and near the Louvre are the formal gardens known as the *Jardins des Tuileries* designed by the royal landscape gardener Le Nôtre.

Public transport: tickets valid for both bus and Métro can be purchased singly, but for economy it is best to buy a *carnet* of ten tickets (for use on either), one or more tickets being used on each journey depending on the distance travelled. There are two rail networks: the urban Métro for Paris and its outskirts operates between 5.30 a.m. and 1.15 a.m. and connects with the SNCF national railroad system. There is also the RER (Réseau Express Régional) for the outlying suburbs. Tourists can buy the 'Paris Sésame' card, a fixed-price ticket for unlimited travel all over Paris for two-, four-, or seven-day travel periods. This is available at all main Métro stations, the Tourist Office, the SNCF stations and at either of the two airports.

Shopping: luxury shopping (or window-shopping) at the top fashion and perfume houses includes *Balmain*, 44 rue François 1er; *Cardin*, 27 avenue de Marigny; *Carven*, 6 rond-point des Champs-Elysées; *Chanel*, 31 rue Cambon; *Courrèges*, 40 rue François 1er; *Dior*, 30 avenue Montaigne; *Givenchy*, 3 avenue George V; *Saint-Laurent*, 5 avenue Marceau; and *Ungaro*, 2 avenue Montaigne. Large department stores worth noting are the *Galeries Lafayette*, 40 boulevard Haussmann; *Printemps*, 54 boulevard Haussmann; and *La Samaritaine*, 19 rue de la Monnaie

Sites and monuments: (most

tourist literature for the attractions will supply the name of the nearest Métro station). Buy the 'Museum and Monument' card which gives direct entry without queuing, and is available at all main Métro stations. Most Paris museums are closed on Tuesdays. Amongst those not to be missed are:

Arc de Triomphe: with its 12 avenues of busy traffic fanning out in the shape of a star, it offers fine views over Paris and the Bois de Boulogne, and beneath it there is the eternal flame at the Tomb of the Unknown Soldier.

Georges Pompidou Centre: comprising the city's modern art collection and public reference library, this is a buiding of futuristic design. From its top floor there is a superb view over old Paris. Outside, its large square has become an exciting and informal open-air performance arena with jugglers, mime artists and street musicians from all over the world creating an ever-lively atmosphere.

Les Invalides: originally a hospital for wounded veterans, this is an imposing architectural group of buidings with Napoleon's ashes housed in the circular crypt.

Louvre Museum: one of the world's greatest collections of art treasures including the sculpture *Venus de Milo* and da Vinci's *Mona Lisa*.

Notre-Dame: Paris's monumental Gothic cathedral right at its heart; indeed all road distances are measured from this point.

Sacré-Coeur: on the summit of the romantic Montmartre district, made famous by past and present artists, is the enormous white basilica of Sacré-Coeur, with lovely views across Paris.

Tourist Office: the Office de Tourisme is on 127 avenue des Champs-Elysées ☎ 47.23.61.72 and is open every day (9 a.m.- 8 p.m.)

Views: the *Tour Eiffel*, or Eiffel Tower, (307 m) has restaurants, bars and shops on the first two platforms and an extraordinary view from the third stage over the city and up to 72 km. Constructed in 1889 to celebrate the centenary of the French Revolution, the

tower is a masterpiece of metal construction. Views of the city's landmarks are also possible from the fifty-sixth and fifty-ninth floors of the Montparnasse Tower (209 m), 33, avenue du Maine. An audio-visual presentation on the fifty-sixth floor outlines the history of the city, while the open-air spectacle from the roof terrace of the building reduces Paris's landmarks to miniature dimensions. Access is by lift and takes 38 seconds!

What's On: 24-hr service in English ☎ 47.20.88.98

Companies which specialise in offering short-break travel and accommodation packages are listed below:

SPECIALIST TOUR OPERATORS

Air France Holidays, 69 Boston Manor Road, Brentford TW8 9JQ ☎ 01-568 6981

Albany Travel, 190 Deansgate, Manchester M3 3WD ☎ 061-833 0202

Allez France, 27 West Street, Storrington, Pulborough RH20 0AA ☎ 09066 2345

American Express Holidays, Portland House, Stag Place, London SW1E 5BT ☎ 0345 010333

Angel Travel, 47 High Street, Central Chambers, Tonbridge TN9 1SD ☎ 0732 361115

Anglia Holidays, Norwich Airport, Norwich NR12 8DH ☎ 0603 784131

Brittany Ferries, The Brittany Centre, Wharf Road, Portsmouth PO2 8RU ☎ 0705 827701

Caprice Holidays, 31a Queensway, Stevenage SG2 8AA ☎ 0438 316622

City Express, Space House, Albert Road, Bournemouth BH1 1BY ☎ 0202 294444

Cresta Holidays, 32 Victoria Street, Altrincham WA14 1ET ☎ 0345 056511

Excelsior Holidays, 22 Sea Road, Bournemouth BH5 1DD ☎ 0202 309555

Facet Travel, Oakwood House, Eastern Road, Wivelsfield Green, Haywards Heath RH17 7QH ☎ 04484 351

Fairways & Swinford Travel, 20 Upper Ground, London SE1 9PF ☎ 01-261 1744

France Voyages, 145 Oxford Street, London W1R 1TB ☎ 01-494 3155

French Travel Service, Georgia House, 69 Boston Manor Road, Brentford TW8 0JQ ☎ 01-568 8442

Glyn Maddocks Travel, 8 Belmont, Lansdown Road, Bath BA1 5DZ ☎ 0225 315659

Golden Rail Holidays, P.O. Box 12, York YO1 1YX ☎ 0904 28992

Hamilton Travel, 3 Heddon Street, London W1R 7LE ☎ 01-734 9515

Hoverspeed, Maybrook House, Queens Gardens, Dover CT1 9UQ ☎ 0304 240241

Intasun France, Intasun House, Cromwell Avenue, Bromley BR2 9AQ ☎ 01-290 1900

JAC Travel, 15 Albert Mews, London W8 5RV ☎ 01-589 9213

Jubilee Holidays, 391 Honeypot Lane, Stanmore HA7 1JJ

☎ 01-206 2066

Kirker Europe, 29 Dering Street, London W1R 9AA ☎ 01-491 7699

Moswin Tours, P.O. Box 8, 52b London Road, Oadby, Leicester LE2 5WX ☎ 0533 719922

National Holidays, George House, George Street, Wakefield WF1 1LY ☎ 0924 383838

Osprey Holidays, 110 St Stephen Street, Edinburgh EH3 5AQ ☎ 031-226 2467

Paris Travel Service, Bridge House, Ware SG12 9DF ☎ 0920 463900

Patons Travel Service, 5 Crown Street, Aberdeen AB9 1FD ☎ 0224 584281

P & O European Ferries, Channel View Road, Dover CT17 9TJ ☎ 0304 203388

Quo Vadis, 243 Euston Road, London NW1 2BT ☎ 01-583 8383

Sally Tours, Argyle Centre, York Street, Ramsgate

CT11 9DS ☎ 0843 595566

Sealink Holidays, Charter House, Park Street, Ashford TN24 8EX ☎ 0233 47033

Sovereign Cities, Groundstar House, London Road, Crawley RH10 2TB ☎ 0293 561444

Thomson Holidays, Greater London House, Hampstead Road, London NW1 7SD ☎ 01-387 8451

Time Off, 2a Chester Close, London SW1X 7BQ ☎ 01-235 8070

Travelscene, Travelscene House, 11-15 St Ann's Road, Harrow HA1 1AS ☎ 01-427 4445

Trips to France & Dunedin Travel, 6a Caledonian Road, Edinburgh EH11 2DG ☎ 031-337 0950

Vacances, 28 Gold Street, Saffron Walden CB10 1EJ ☎ 0799 25101

VFB Holidays, 1 St Margaret's Terrace, Cheltenham GL50 4DT ☎ 0242 526338

SPECIAL INTEREST HOLIDAYS
■ *ARTS AND CRAFTS* ■

There are tutored ten-day watercolour painting holidays in the small coastal resort of St-Valéry-sur-Somme in Picardy, with Galleon, or oil and watercolour tuition with the Perigord Painting School in the Dordogne. The Association for Active Learning runs a two-week painting and printmaking course in the Dordogne, and Facet Travel runs lace-making and pottery courses in Normandy, pottery in Alsace and porcelain in the Ile de France. LSG Theme Holidays cater for beginners to advanced in patchwork, embroidery and photography holidays.

Individual resorts may offer further facilities, particularly during the summer, and the departmental tourist boards will supply details.

SPECIALIST TOUR OPERATORS

Association for Active Learning (ALL), 9 Haywra Street, Harrogate HG1 5BJ ☎ (0423) 505313

Facet Travel, Oakwood House, Eastern Road, Wivelsfield Green, Haywards Heath RH17 7QH ☎ 044484 351

Galleon Art Holidays, Units 40/41, Temple Farm, Southend-on-Sea SS2 5RZ

☎ 0702 617900

LSG Theme Holidays, 201 Main Street, Thornton LE6 1AH ☎ 0509 231713

Perigord Painting School, 25 Albion Road, Chesterfield, Derbyshire S40 1LJ ☎ 0246 207743

■ COOKERY ■

The Order of Saint-Esprit was an honour, created by Henri III in 1578, for certain members of the royal family, foreign princes of noble lineage, and dukes and gentlemen with at least three generations of 'blue blood'. Known as the *Chevaliers du Saint-Esprit*, these individuals were decorated with a gold cross attached to a blue ribbon, a 'cordon bleu', and were actually referred to by the title *Cordons Bleus*. It then followed that all those meriting distinction, including the country's best chefs, were thus honoured. When the honour was generally abolished in 1830, however, the term was retained only by professional chefs.

France and her cuisine are inseparable. Indeed most visitors go to France with the express intention of making what and where they eat very much a part of their holiday. Some may even be tempted to further their own culinary skills with a short, fun cookery course or a more structured course over several days, and both French and British operators cater for this interest.

Weekend cookery courses, such as the three which follow, are based at hotels and are under the supervision of the chef. They usually involve preliminary shopping at the local market followed by the preparation and tasting of regional dishes.

Aquitaine
Grand Hôtel du Parc, (details from 13 boulevard de la Marine, 47300 Villeneuve-sur-Lot ☎ 53.70.01.68) offers traditional duck-cooking weekends between November and March.

Burgundy
Hôtel de Paris et de la Poste (details from Jovitour, 10 quai Leclerc, 89300 Joigny ☎ 86.62.16.31) runs a combined hunting and gastronomy weekend in Joigny and Sens.

Champagne-Ardenne
Hôtel d'Orfeuil (details from 29 rue d'Orfeuil, 52400 Bourbonne-les-Bains ☎ 25.90.05.71)

Longer courses, such as the following, are also available.

Ile de France
The Association Cuisine Française (details from Ferme du Grand Chemin, 95510 Villers-en-Arthies ☎ 34.78.17.73) is a private establishment catering for a range of preparation and decoration needs. There is professional tuition in traditional French dishes such as *coq au vin*, *boeuf bourguignon*, etc., as well as nouvelle cuisine and pastries, through to table settings, buffet preparation and the art of floral decoration. Situated 60 km west of Paris, in the heart of the Vexin countryside, accommodation is arranged with a French family and there is ample free time for excursions.

Nord – Pas-de-Calais
● Professional chefs create an interesting menu for this four-day all-inclusive break, with cookery demonstrations over four three-hour periods (plus the services of an interpreter) at the four-star Hôtel Westminster, avenue du Verger, B.P.22, 62520 Le Touquet ☎ 21.05.48.48 (min. 10 persons).
● Five-day courses run throughout the year at Chez Mireille near Berck, with motel or studio accommodation and coach transport. Minimum number in a group is 30 and the course deals with regional dishes, sea food preparation, and cheese and wine combinations. Arrival is on Monday with the course starting on Tuesday morning. Afternoons are spent on excursions. Bookable through Chez Mireille, chemin Genty, 62600 Berck-sur-Mer ☎ 21.09.12.22
● Four-day course at Montreuil-sur-Mer, close to Le Touquet, with demonstrations of preparations of typical French dishes and bread and croissant making. Running throughout the autumn, from Monday to Friday, the accommodation is in a manor house, Château de Montreuil, 4 Chaussée des Capucins, 62170 Montreuil-sur-Mer ☎ 21.81.53.04 and is bookable through Crystal Holidays.

There are, of course, several cookery schools in Paris, some of them world-famous institutions for professionals. A couple of them also offer tuition in English:

Ecole de Cuisine la Varenne, 34 rue Saint Dominique, 75007 Paris ☎ 47.05.10.16
This bi-lingual school teaches the preparation of classic dishes as well as regional and new dishes, in both French and English. Tuition consists of watching the chef and working under his supervision.

Ecole de Cuisine de la Princesse Marie-Blanche de Broglie, 18 avenue de la Motte-Piquet, 75007 Paris ☎ 45.51.36.34
The Princess Marie-Blanche de Broglie speaks French, Spanish and English and runs cookery courses for small groups of six people in her own apartment.

Ecole de Cuisine le Pot au Feu, 14 rue Duphot, 75001 Paris ☎ 42.60.00.94
The oldest cookery school in Paris, its principal business is in preparing pupils for their cookery exams, but it does also have a section for the tuition of adults and those working in the profession.

Ecole du Cordon Bleu, 24 rue du Champ de Mars, 75007 Paris ☎ 45.55.02.77; and 40 avenue

Bosquet, 75007 Paris
☎ 47.20.71.21
Founded in 1895, this is probably the most famous Parisian school, whose Cordon Bleu diploma is the most coveted. Small groups of 12 people are taught in full uniform. While courses are given in French, advanced knowledge of the language is not as essential as a good understanding of culinary terms. Request their brochure in English. Regular demonstrations (followed by tasting) are also given, with translation into foreign languages. Very popular. Contact the school for dates and reservation details.

Ecole Le Nôtre, 40 rue Pierre Curie, 78370 Plaisir
☎ 30.55.81.12
The school's famous chef, Gaston Le Nôtre, has put French cuisine on the centre stage in recent years, and his school at Plaisir, near Versailles, is principally concerned with the tuition of French and foreign professionals.

Ecole de Cuisine du Chef Hubert, 48 rue de Sèvres, 75007 Paris
☎ 40.56.91.20
Modern teaching methods complement this school's emphasis on preserving the creative originality and refinement of French cuisine.

The following British operators also run cookery courses in France.

SPECIALIST TOUR OPERATORS

Crystal Holidays, The Courtyard, Arlington Road, Surbiton, London KT6 6BW
☎ 01–390 3335
Inntravel, Hovingham, York YO6 4JZ ☎ 065 382742
LSG Theme Holidays, 201 Main Street, Thornton LE6 1AH
☎ 0509 231713
Page & Moy, 136-140 London Road, Leicester LE2 1EN
☎ 0533 552521

■ *HISTORY AND HERITAGE TOURS* ■

The France of today owes its flavour and attitudes, its traditions and pride, to the France of the past. A glimpse at least at its history over the 2,000 years since the Romans is surely essential for a full appreciation of the country.

The history and heritage of France can be absorbed in comfort while a coach tours the hand-picked centres and stopping-points to demonstrate whatever theme is at hand. The themes almost suggest themselves. You can follow the life, career and death of Joan of Arc through Domrémy-la-Pucelle, Chinon, Loches, Orléans and finally Rouen. A tour of the royal châteaux of the Loire conveniently embraces the magnificent castles of Beaugency, Chambord, Blois, Chenonceau, Amboise, Azay-le-Rideau, Ussé and Loches. There are tours that offer a study of medieval France, both in Burgundy (Auxerre, Tournus, Cluny, Vézelay, Beaune and Dijon) and in Aquitaine (Poitiers, Brantôme, Chalus, Sarlat, Beynac, Castelnaud, Bonaguil, Cahors, Rocamadour, Albi, Conques, Najac and Carcassonne). Or there are tours of the Romanesque churches of France along the pilgrims' route to Santiago de Compostela (Vendôme, Tours, Chinon, Blois, Bourges and Nevers) and in the Pyrénées (St-Cyprien, Perpignan, Collioure, Elne and Serrabonne). There are art tours of Provence and of Paris and tours of the Gothic cathedrals of the north east.

The coaches are comfortable and stops and overnight bookings are automatic and trouble-free. Prices, of course, cover a wide range, as do the durations of the tours, but further details are available from the operators listed below.

SPECIALIST TOUR OPERATORS

Ace Study Tours, Babraham, Cambridge CB2 4AP
☎ 0223 835055
Association for Active Learning (ALL), 9 Haywra Street, Harrogate HG1 5BJ
☎ 0423 505313
Canvas Holidays, 9/13 Bull Plain, Hertford SG14 1DY
☎ 0992 553535

Country Special Holidays, 153b Kidderminster Road, Bewdley DY12 1JE
☎ 0299 403528
Facet Travel, Oakwood House, Eastern Road, Wivelsfield Green, Haywards Heath RH17 7QH ☎ 04484 351
Francophiles Discover France, 66 Great Brockeridge, Bristol BS9 3UA ☎ 0272 621975
Plantagenet Tours, 85 The Grove, Moordown,

Bournemouth BH9 2TY
☎ 0202 521895
Prospect Music and Art Tours, 10 Barley Mow Passage, London W4 4PH
☎ 01-995 2151
Specialtours, 2 Chester Row, London SW1W 9JH
☎ 01-730 2297
Swan Hellenic Art Treasures Tours, 77 New Oxford Street, London WC1A 1PP
☎ 01-831 1616

■ *LIVE AND LEARN* ■

The conditions governing the teaching of the French language to foreign students in France raise as many questions as there are potential students. How long do the courses last? What organisations handle such courses, and in which parts of France? How much time is required of the student in his studies? What standards are catered for, elementary, intermediate, advanced? Are there crash courses for executives, commercial courses for business men and women, courses for children? What approximately are the costs?

At this stage only general answers can be given, but listed below are the addresses of organisations which will answer individual queries. Broadly speaking, courses last for two, three or four weeks (except those all-year-round university courses of 13-week terms). The number of lessons involved per week vary from 15 to 30, and the students are generally aged 18 and over, with class sizes varying between four and 12. There are intensive courses for business executives with limited time to spare, involving full days' study. Costs vary detween 125F per week to 200F+ (tuition and accommodation), with residence arranged in college, in 'digs' or with French families.

SUMMER LANGUAGE COURSES IN UNIVERSITIES

The FGTO in London (178 Piccadilly, London W1V 0AL) can supply a list of universities and language centres offering summer language courses. Some of these are listed below and should be contacted direct for further information.

ALSACE

Centre International d'Etude de Langues, 4 quai Kléber, Batiment F, Le Concorde, F-67056 Strasbourg Cedex ☎ 88.22.02.13

AUVERGNE

Centre Audio-Visuel de Langues Modernes, B.P.164, F-03206 Vichy Cedex ☎ 70.32.25.22

BOURGOGNE

Cours Internationaux d'Eté, 36 rue Chabot-Charny, F-21000 Dijon ☎ 80.66.20.49

BRETAGNE

Cours d'Eté de Quimper, Faculté des Lettres de Brest, B.P.860, F-29279 Brest Cedex ☎ 98.03.06.87

CENTRE

(courses at Amboise)
Centre de Formation et d'Etudes Françaises Pratiques, 2 place H.-Bergson, F-75008 Paris ☎ (1)45.22.04.11

FRANCHE-COMTE

Centre de Linguistique Appliquée, Stages de Français Pratique, 47 rue Mégevand, F-25030 Besançon Cedex ☎ 81.82.25.01

ILE-DE-FRANCE

Université de la Sorbonne Nouvelle, Paris III, Centre Censier, UER Etudes Françaises pour l'Etranger, 13 rue de Santeuil, F-75005 Paris ☎ (1)45.70.12.90

LANGUEDOC-ROUSSILLON

Centre Universitaire de Vacances, Univeristé Paul Valéry, B.P.5043, F-34032 Montpellier Cedex ☎ 67.41.29.75

LORRAINE

Université de Nancy II, Cours de Vacances pour Etudiants Etrangers, 23 boulevard Albert 1er, F-54000 Nancy ☎ 83.96.16.14

MIDI-PYRENEES

Centre Universitaire d'Eté des Pyrénées, Université de Toulouse-Le Mirail, 109 bis, rue Vauquelin, F-31058 Toulouse Cedex ☎ 61.41.11.05

NORD – PAS-DE-CALAIS

Université d'Eté, Université de Lille III, B.P.149, F-59653 Villeneuve d'Ascq Cedex ☎ 20.91.13.00

NORMANDIE

Université de Caen, Cours Internationaux d'Eté, esplanade de la Paix, F-14032 Caen Cedex ☎ 31.93.26.76

PAYS DE LA LOIRE

Université de Nantes, Université d'Eté, B.P.1025, F-44036 Nantes Cedex ☎ 40.74.74.01

POITOU-CHARENTES

Université de Poitiers, Faculté des Lettres et Langues, Section de Français pour Etrangers, 95 avenue du Recteur-Pineau, F-86022 Poitiers ☎ 49.46.01.28

PROVENCE

Université de Provence, Cours d'Eté pour Etudiants Etrangers, 29 avenue Robert-Schumann, F-13621 Aix-en-Provence ☎ 42.59.22.71

RHONE-ALPES

Centre Universitaire d'Etudes Françaises, B.P.25X, F-38040 Grenoble Cedex ☎ 76.42.48.37

Of course, Paris itself offers a range of language schools and courses of varying lengths and intensities, and enquiries should be made to ascertain just what they provide in the way of accommodation as well. *Prolingua*, for example, offer an '*à la carte*' course especially designed for companies, and also fun learning programmes for children.

ELFE (Ecole de Langue Française pour Etrangers), 10 rue Saint-Marc, 75002 Paris ☎ (1)42.36.64.00
France Langue, 2 rue de Sfax, 75116 Paris ☎ (1)45.00.40.15
Inlingua Ecole de Langues, 109 ruc dc l'Université, 75007 Paris ☎ (1)45.51.46.60
Institut de Langue Française, 15 rue Arsène-Houssaye, 75008 Paris ☎ (1)42.27.14.77
Language Studies International, 350 rue Saint Honoré, 75001 Paris ☎ 42.60.53.70
Prolingua, 11 rue de la Grande Fontaine, 78100 St-Germain-en-Laye ☎ 39.73.90.60

In addition there are numerous language centres and institutes throughout France, often in some of the most popular holiday locations, offering study holidays with recreation and entertainment combined. A specialist advice service plus guide to these language schools, together with details of the types of courses and accommodation they offer, is available from: *Cultural and Educational Services Abroad (CESA)*, 44 Sydney Street, Brighton, Sussex BN1 4EP ☎ (0273) 683304. In London, The French Centre (Chepstow Lodge, 61/69 Chepstow Place, London W2 4TR ☎ 01-221 8134) also arranges language courses in France for all ages (nine years upwards) and stages.

Private operators, such as *Accents, Langues et Loisirs*, for example, offer a programme (seven or 14 nights, Apr-Oct) of language holidays for adults in groups. Accommodation is in the students' residence, attached to the village home of the couple who run this company. In the Rhône-Alpes close to Geneva, and with plenty of free time for visits, these courses are not for absolute beginners, but are fun and practical. The *Association for Active Learning (ALL)* is a non-profit-making company closely associated with the French charitable institution Renouveau, promoting language and other study courses at Renouveau centres throughout France. Catering specially for children is the centre at Cap d'Ail, close to Monte-Carlo, where boys and girls, aged between 13 and 17 years, can attend two-, four-, six-and eight-week courses. Enquiries should be made to the Ligue Française de l'Enseignement et de l'Education Permanente Service National Vacances, B.P.313, 75989 PARIS Cedex.

SPECIALIST TOUR OPERATORS

Accents, Langues et Loisirs, Artemare, 01510 Vivieu-le-Grand ☎ 79.87.33.96 or telephone by direct transfer to France by calling ☎ 061-798 0388
Association for Active Learning (ALL), 9 Haywra Street, Harrogate HG1 5BJ ☎ (0423) 505313
En Famille Overseas, The Old Stables, 60b Maltravers Street, Arundel BN18 9BG ☎ 0903 883266
Euro Academy, 77a George Street, Croydon CR0 1LD ☎ 01-686 2363
Freedom in France, Meadows, Poughill, Bude, Cornwall EX23 9EN ☎ 0288 55591
LSG Theme Holidays, 201 Main Street, Thornton LE6 1AH ☎ 0509 231713
VFB Holidays, 1 St Margaret's Terrace, Cheltenham GL50 4DT ☎ 0242 526338

■ *PILGRIMAGES* ■

T he religious centre of Lourdes attracts three million pilgrims annually who gather in a spiritual atmosphere to attend the ceremonies and processions in this holy city, the chief point of pilgrimage being the grotto where the Virgin Mary appeared 18 times to Bernadette Soubirous. The following operators provide accommodation and travel packages.

SPECIALIST TOUR OPERATORS

Interchurch Travel, The Saga Building, Middleburg Square, Folkestone CT20 1AZ ☎ 0800 300 444
Kestours, Travel House, Elmers End, Beckenham BR3 3QY ☎ 01-658 7316

Pilgrims Way, 56 Tooting High Street, London SW17 0RN ☎ 01-767 7825
Tangney Tours, 73 Crayford High Street, Crayford, Kent DA1 4EJ ☎ 0322 59511

■ *SPORTING EVENTS* ■

Rugby internationals, the Monaco Grand Prix, the Le Mans 24-hour race, tennis championships, the Tour de France cycle race, the Prix de l'Arc de Triomphe horse race . . . the French calendar is marked by a number of internationally famous sporting events for which several British operators arrange travel, accommodation and tickets. Exact dates vary from year to year and the FGTO in London should be contacted for details:

Paris-Dakar Car Rally (Dec/Jan)
Monte Carlo Rally (Jan)
Le Touquet Enduro Motorcycle Race (Feb)
Le Mans 24-hour Motorcycle Race (Apr)
Paris Marathon (Apr)
Monaco Grand Prix (May)
Paris International Tennis (May/Jun)
Le Mans 24-hour Endurance Race (Jun)
Tour de France Cycle Race (Jul)
Le Castellet, Grand Prix de France (cars) (Jul)
Le Castellet, Bol d'Or (motorcycles) (Sep)
Paris, Prix de l'Arc de Triomphe (Oct)
Paris, 6-hour Motorboat Race (Oct)

SPECIALIST OPERATORS

Chequers Travel, Newbridge House, Newbridge, Dover CT16 1YS ☎ 0304 204515
Liz Fenner Worldwide Yachting Holidays, 35 Fairfax Place, London NW6 4EJ ☎ 01-328 1033
Gullivers Travel, 10 High Street, Tewkesbury ☎ 0684 293175

Just Tickets, Lincoln Oaks, Ranelagh Grove, Broadstairs CT10 2TE ☎ 0843 65160
Glyn Maddocks Travel, 8 Belmont, Lansdown Road, Bath BA1 5DZ ☎ 0225 315659
Keith Prowse Supersports, Banda House, Cambridge Grove, Hammersmith, London W6 0LE ☎ 01-741 8989
Paris Travel Service, Bridge House, Ware SG12 9DF ☎ 0920 463900

Sports Abroad, The Travel Centre, Wix Hill House, West Horsley, Surrey KT24 6DZ ☎ 0483 225000
Tee Mill Tours, 56 Tooting High Street, London SW17 0RN ☎ 01-767 8737
Travellers, 277 Oxlow Lane, Dagenham, Essex ☎ 01-985 9679

■ *FESTIVALS, CARNIVALS AND OTHER EVENTS* ■

Again exact dates vary from year to year (check with the FGTO in London), but jazz festivals, such as those at Nice and Montauban, the Pablo Casals festival in Lubéron and the music festival in Aix-en-Provence are catered for by several British operators. Alternatively, you can write direct to the Tourist Office of the town concerned for further booking and accommodation details:

Feast of St-Vincent, Burgundy (Jan)
Menton Lemon Festival (Feb)
Paris Fashion Shows (Feb and Sep)
Nice Carnival (Feb)
Cannes International Bridge and Chess Festival (Feb)
Dunkerque Carnival (Feb)
Paris Agricultural Show (Mar)
Foire de Paris (Apr/May)
Cannes Film Festival (May)

Bordeaux, Musical May Concerts (May)
Stes-Maries-de-la-Mer Gypsy Festival (May)
Strasbourg Musical Festival (Jun)
Bastille Day (July 14), celebrated throughout France
Nice, Grande Parade du Jazz (Jul)
Quimper, Fêtes des Cornouailles (Jul)
Avignon Festival (Jul)
Aix-en-Provence Festival (Jul)
Orange Chorégies Music Festival (Jul/Aug)
Paris Festival Estival (Jul/Sep)
Antibes Jazz Festival (Jul)
Lorient, Celtic Festival (Aug)
Lyons, Berlioz Festival (Sep)
Dijon, Fêtes de la Vigne (Sep)
Paris Dance Festival (Oct/Nov)
Paris Fair of Contemporary Art (Oct)
Beaujolais Nouveau Release (Nov)
Beaune Wine Auction (Nov)
Paris International Boat Show (Dec)

SPECIALIST OPERATORS

David Balfry Jazz Tours,
37 Wood Street,
Stratford-upon-Avon CV37 6ES
☎ 0789 67532
Country Special Holidays,
153b Kidderminster Road,

Bewdley DY12 1JE
☎ 0299 403528
GW Henebery, Kareol, Islip,
Oxford OX5 2SU
☎ 08675 6341

There is no direct booking agency in Great Britain for opera, theatre or cinema seats.

The Paris Opéra season runs from the end of September to mid-July and bookings must be made direct by writing to: Théâtre de l'Opéra, Service Location par Correspondence, 8 rue Scribe, 75009 Paris ☎ (1)47.42.53.71 (Mon-Sat 12.00-6 p.m.)

■ *WAR GRAVES AND BATTLEFIELDS* ■

Few of us do not have a relative or forefather who either experienced the hardships and deprivations of trench warfare in the fields of northern France during World War I, or witnessed the bitter struggles on the beaches and in the *bocage*, the river valleys and hedgerows that dominate the landscape of Normandy, in the summer of 1944. Today we pass through these areas en route to warmer climes without, perhaps, a moment's thought, and yet not only do visits to the battlefields and war graves provide an insight into the extraordinary fortitude and sacrifice of individuals caught up in the epic conflicts of modern Europe, but we can also enjoy the peace and solitude of attractive rural France. Either as a break from a long journey, or during a long weekend's golf, a morning spent at one of the sites will prove an unforgettable and awe-inspiring experience.

WORLD WAR I

The battlefields and war graves of 'the war to end all wars' are largely confined to the Franco-Belgian border. It was in the area of the Pas-de-Calais, Picardy and the Somme that for four years, from 1914, the Allies slogged it out with the Kaiser's army in a series of battles where the victors often gained little more than a few hundred metres. Villages,

towns and huge tracts of countryside, including one third of the *département* of the Somme, were razed to the ground in the defensive shelling which characterised this trench warfare.

Many memorials to the dead remain today, and the war graves of the fallen Allied troops are scrupulously maintained by the War Graves Commission. In the spring, before the crops grow, the outline of the trenches and dug-

outs shows clearly through the flat, open fields.

Specialist tour operators are listed below, while for those who wish to travel independently and perhaps visit the grave of a relative, the War Graves Commission address is also given. Supplied with adequate details, they will attempt to locate the cemetery for you.

Amiens is a good base for exploration of the numerous

memorials, cemeteries and museums of the Somme and of the battlefield sites over the nearby frontier of Belgium. Notable memorials include the huge Thiepval memorial that dominates the valley of the River Ancre, and the preserved trenchworks at Camp Terre Neuve. For information on individual battlefields and locations, contact the Office de Tourisme de la Somme, 51 Mail Albert 1er, 80 Amiens ☎ 22.92.26.39.

In Lorraine, the Memorial Museum of the Battle of Verdun and the Citadel of Verdun are a fascinating museum and monument to the titanic struggle between the French and German armies during the 1914-18 war, with over one million casualties. There is an audio-visual account of the siege of this French city and a museum displaying uniforms, weapons and documents of the period.

WORLD WAR II

The Normandy landing beaches of 'Operation Overlord' are enjoyed during the summer by holidaymakers, but the designated landing zones remain: Juno, Sword and Gold beaches for the British and Canadian forces, and Utah and Omaha for the American assaults. Because of the intense interest in this, the greatest military seaborne invasion, the Bayeux-based Comité du Débarquement (CD) have erected directional signs throughout the region and information plaques at places of interest. These enable the visitor to locate the landing areas, cemeteries and museums which proliferate the area, between the Orne estuary in the east to the dunes of Varreville in the west. As a result, the Normandy battlefields are the best-marked and the most easily accessible of all World War II battlefields. Again, the specialist tour operators are listed below and the

War Graves Commission will help locate a specific grave on request.

Museums in Normandy
Some of the best museums are listed below, while there are also several private museums along the Normandy coast, with collections of D-Day memorabilia.

Arromanches-les-Bains: Exposition Permanente du Débarquement is located near the sea wall in this small port. A diorama of the landings, with commentary, explains the events leading up to D-Day and tells how the operations developed. There is a film of the construction of the floating Mulberry harbour and a model of Mulberry B. The remains of the real Mulberry can be seen from the panoramic window which runs the length of the museum.

Bayeux: Musée Memorial de la Bataille de Normandie is located on the boulevard Général Fabian Ware near the British Cemetery.

Bénouville: Musée des Troupes Aéroportées adjacent to the Pegasus bridge.

Caen: Musée Memorial de la Bataille.

Merville: Musée de la Bataille de Merville is east of the Orne river just outside the town of Merville-Franceville.

Ouistreham-Riva-Bella: Musée du Commando No 4 on the boulevard du 6 Juin near the Riva-Bella beach.

Ste-Marie-du-Mont-la-Madeleine is located in a converted German bunker on Utah beach (closed January).

Ste-Mère-Eglise: A small town immortalised in the film *The Longest Day*, the Musée des Troupes Aéroportées is situated nearby.

Other war memorials of special interest

Limousin
Oradour-sur-Glane: the scene of a horrific SS massacre, this village is preserved as it was found after the Germans had annihilated the entire population and set the buildings ablaze. A poignant and moving reminder of man's inhumanity to man and a gruesome memorial to war's innocent victims. Visitors walk amongst the ruins in total silence (13 km north east of St-Junien).

Lorraine
Maginot Line: bypassed by the German blitzkreig in 1940, the huge defence works have recently been restored and provide a fascinating insight into the military thinking of the French High Command after World War I. Visit the Gros Ouvrage de Fermont between Longuyon and Longwy, 50 km from Verdun.

SPECIALIST TOUR OPERATORS

Major and Mrs Holt's Battlefield Tours, Golden Key Building, 15 Market Street, Sandwich, Kent CT13 9DA ☎ 0304 612248
Martin Middlebrook's Battlefield Tours, 48 Linden Way, Boston, Lincs PE21 9DS ☎ 0205 64555
Milestone Tours, 37a Outram Street, Sutton-in-Ashfield, Notts NG17 4BA ☎ 0623 517275
Oldroyd Tours, Moorlands, Hutton, Weston-super-Mare, Avon BS24 9QU ☎ 0934 812283
Pennine Euro-Travel, 6/10 Green Road, Meanwood, Leeds L56 5JP ☎ 0532 785597

For the location of a particular grave, contact the War Graves Commission well in advance of an anticipated trip:
Commonwealth War Graves Commission, 2 Marlow Road, Maidenhead, Berks SL6 7DX

■ WINE TOURS ■

The French are not shy about extolling their wines. There are road signs featuring a bunch of grapes to remind tourists that they are approaching a sensational wine region. There are *Routes du Vin* in Alsace and Champagne, Burgundy and Bordeaux. Wayside billboards boast the proximity of some magnificent château or domaine, and every wine-growing group of villages has its *cave coopérative*.

In Anjou and Touraine, many of the homes are built from the local limestone, or *tufa*, dug from the riverbeds of the great Loire valley. As a visitor, you may well find yourself in just such a cool, cave-like shelter tasting the precious local product, a dry Vouvray perhaps or a glass of red Chinon. What better way to sample the wines of the country? Then buy bottles for your journey and an *al fresco* meal, crowned at the end by fresh strawberries drenched in red Bourgeuil.

ALSACE

Between the Rhine and the Vosges mountains lies the Alsatian wine region producing, mainly, white wines, and named in many cases after the grape rather than the place of origin. Its most famous wines are the Riesling (fruity), Muscat (dry), Gewurztraminer (*Gewurz* means spice in German), and Sylvaner. Along the *Route du Vin*, 100 km from Mulhouse to Strasbourg, are the pretty flowered villages of Riquewihr, Kaiserberg and Ribeauvillé, famed for both its Riesling and its Gewurztraminer, and for its wine fair held in July each year.

CHAMPAGNE

By contrast, in the Champagne country, the focus is on the deep cellars of Reims and Epernay rather than on the vineyards. Here the processes of fermentation, *cuvée* and *tirage* take place prior to the wine's storage in 192 km of underground galleries beneath the great wine houses of Veuve Cliquot, Pommery and Mumms, Pol Roger and Möet et Chandon.

RHONE VALLEY

To the south of the great Burgundy wine region, flanking the Rhône from Lyon to Avignon, lie the Côtes du Rhône vineyards of the velvety Côte Rôtie, Hermitage and Cornas in the north around Tournon and, close to Orange, the great red wine of Châteauneuf du Pape and the rosé of Tavel. Roussillon and Languedoc to the west and Provence to the east of the Rhône valley all boast their own excellent wines: the Côte de Roussillon from the wild hill country overlooked by the Pyrénées, the full-bodied Corbières from the land between Narbonne and Carcassonne, and the red Minervois of Languedoc, strong and dry.

LOIRE VALLEY

The Loire is a river virtually bordered by vineyards along its 1,600 km from the high Auvergne down to the sea at Nantes. Sancerre in Berry is a dry white wine, Blanc Fumé a white of Pouilly-sur-Loire. Downriver, beyond Orléans, the Touraine yields white Vouvray, Anjou its sweet white wine and rosé, and, around Nantes, the white Muscadet.

BORDEAUX

The red wines or clarets of Bordeaux are probably the best known in the world. Two rivers feed the Bordeaux region, the Garonne and the Dordogne, coming together 16 km north of Bordeaux itself to form the Gironde. The Medoc wine area, producing the finest claret, is to the north west, flanking the Gironde, with the great names of its châteaux: Margaux, d'Issan, Beychevelle and, in the Pauillac area, Château Latour, Château Lafite and Château Mouton-Rothschild. The Graves district of gravelly soil is to the south and produces, for the most part, dry white wine. The Château la Brède is a superb moated building in the Graves wine district which surrounds the Sauternes area producing the famous Sauternes sweet white wines, the most famous of them Château d'Yquem and Barsac. Between the junction of the Dordogne and the Garonnes, the district called Entre-Deux-Mers produces mostly white wines of great distinction. To the north of the Dordogne are the great claret districts of the rich velvety St-Emilion and Pomerol wines.

BURGUNDY

The sources of the three great river systems, the Seine, the Rhône and the Loire, and the baking inland sun, go to make Burgundy the other great vineyard of France. Red, white, still or sparkling, the range is complete. Dry Chablis country comes first in the long, thin trail of vineyards running south between Dijon and Lyon, the *Route des Grands Crus*. The Côte d'Or region with its two great vineyards, Côte de Nuits and Côte de Beaune, where the village names leap straight from the wine list on to the road signs: Gevrey-Chambertin, Vougeot, Vosne-Romanée, Nuits-St-Georges, Pommard, Volnay, and for their world-famous white wines Meursault and Montrachet. South again and the visitor is in Mâcon and Beaujolais country.

British and French tour operators have not been slow to spot a powerful motive for holiday travel, and the main wine areas are well served by coach, by river and canal cruisers, even by balloon flights. The following tour operators specialise in wine tours and holidays:

SPECIALIST TOUR OPERATORS

Air France Holidays, 69 Boston Manor Road, Brentford TW8 9JQ ☎ 01-568 6981
Association for Active Learning (ALL), 9 Haywra Street, Harrogate HG1 5BJ ☎ 0423 505313
Allez France, 27 West Street, Storrington, Pulborough RH20 4DZ ☎ 09066 2345
Arblaster & Clarke Boo's Breaks, 104 Church Road,

Steep, Petersfield GU32 2DD ☎ 0730 66883
Blackheath Wine Trails, 13 Blackheath Village, London SE3 9LD ☎ 01-463 0012
Club Francais, 83 Victoria Road, Chislehurst BR7 6DE ☎ 01-468 7049
Country Special Holidays, 153b Kidderminster Road, Bewdley DY12 1JE ☎ 0299 403528
Facet Travel, Oakwood House, Eastern Road, Wivelsfield Green, Haywards Heath RH17 7QH ☎ 044484 351
Farthing Holidays, 36 High Street, Kibworth LE8 0HQ ☎ 0537 533883
Francophiles Discover France, 66 Great Brockeridge, Bristol BS9 3UA ☎ 0272 621975
Glyn Maddocks Travel, 8 Belmont, Lansdown Road, Bath BA1 5DZ ☎ 0225 315659
Inntravel, Hovingham, York YO6 4JZ ☎ 065 382742
Moswin Tours, P.O. Box 8, 52b London Road, Oadby, Leicester LE2 5WX ☎ 0533 719922
Renaissance Tours, P.O. Box 67, Folkestone CT20 1AZ ☎ 0303 47931
Slipaway Holidays, 90 Newland Road, Worthing BN11 1LB ☎ 0903 821000

Sport Abroad, The Travel Centre, Wix Hill House, West Horsley, Surrey KT24 6DZ ☎ 0483 225000
Travellers, 277 Oxlow Lane, Dagenham, Essex ☎ 01-985 9679
Voyages Vacances, 213 Piccadilly, London W1V 9LT ☎ 01-494 2261
World Wine Tours, 4 Dorchester Road, Drayton St. Leonard OX9 8BH ☎ 0865 891919

Those who wish to learn the fine art of wine-tasting should write to the Comités Interprofessionels des Vins de Bourgogne, wine growers' and trade associations which organise complete courses (English spoken) on vineyard techniques and wine-tasting. They also issue specialised brochures:

CIB (Comité Interprofessionel de la Côte d'Or et de l'Yonne pour les vins d'appellation contrôlée de Bourgogne), rue Henri Dunant, 21200 Beaune ☎ 80.22.21.35

CIBM (Comité Interprofessionel des vins de Bourgogne et du Mâconnais), 389 avenue de Lattre de Tassigny, 71000 Mâcon ☎ 85.38.20.15

■ *WORKING IN FRANCE* ■

Working abroad is the subject of the excellent guide published by the Central Bureau for Educational Visits and Exchanges, *Working Holidays*. An invaluable aid, it is updated annually and lists a wide range of paid and voluntary work opportunities throughout the world. Its section on France is popular and early application is advised. The guide is available from major bookshops or direct from the Bureau (address below). As a rule, a good knowledge of French and relevant skills/qualifications are required for most types of work. Some of the many opportunities offered in *Working Holidays* are:

Archaeological digs
Various types of excavation work are available all over France. To be accepted on a dig you are often expected to have studied the classics or history, but beginners are welcome. You will receive board and lodging, instruction and, occasionally, a small amount of money.

Community work
For people interested in community work there are various schemes and projects throughout France, including such activities as running playschemes for children and helping the disadvantaged, homeless and handicapped. Volunteers generally receive board and

lodging and may also be given pocket money and travel expenses.

Couriers
Couriers on camp sites are often required to look after the welfare of holidaymakers. They may be expected to put up and take down tents at the beginning and end of

the season as well as clean and maintain the camping equipment. Hard, physical work, it is generally well paid and some knowledge of French is usually required.

Domestic and catering staff
Hotel jobs are available for chambermaids, cleaners, kitchen assistants and waiters during the summer, and at ski resorts during the winter. Opportunities also exist for au pair and nanny positions throughout France.

Grape-picking and farm work
Seasonal employment is available on farms, mainly grape-picking and maize-topping. The work is hard and the hours long and this includes working at weekends and in all weathers. Basic board and lodging are usually provided by the farmer. The grape harvest (*vendange*) takes place between 20 September and 30 October in Beaujolais, Aquitaine, central France, Burgundy, Midi-Pyrénées and Champagne. The type of work can be divided into three categories: picking the grapes, collecting the baskets and emptying them. Remember that this type of work is sought by French students as well as the regular army of seasonal workers and the unemployed, and can therefore be very hard to find. The topping of maize takes place between 10 July and 15 August in south-west France and the Auvergne.

Be warned of firms advertising in the national press offering opportunities for grape-picking. They are only offering cheap one-way coach travel to the grape-picking areas, not a job. In the past, many young people have been stranded this way, without money or the means of returning home. It is important to obtain a job before travelling; you may do this by applying to ANPE, the local public employment agencies in France. Further information in *Working Holidays*.

Teachers and instructors
Experienced sports instructors are needed by holiday companies for a variety of sports (tennis, sailing, skiing, windsurfing and canoeing), to coach holidaymakers. Arts and crafts teachers are also sometimes required. Young people are also required as monitors in French holiday camps to look after children and supervise sports activities. Full board and pocket money are provided and a good knowledge of French is usually needed.

Workcamps
These provide short-term voluntary service opportunities for young people to work and live with people from different racial and cultural backgrounds. Projects have included helping farmers with cheese and bread-making, renovation and painting of various community buildings, marking out cross-country ski runs, tree-felling and fencing. Board and lodging are provided but volunteers usually pay their own travel expenses.

The Central Bureau was established in 1948 by the British Government and is wholly funded by the Department of Education and Science. In addition to the *Working Holidays* guide, it also publishes *Study Holidays* which is another useful source of information and opportunities for those students planning to take a year off between school and university, particularly those wishing for posts as assistants in French schools. An excellent range of leaflets is produced and further information is available from:
The Central Bureau for Educational Visits and Exchanges, Seymour Mews House, Seymour Mews, London W1H 9PE ☎ 01-486 5101.

The French Embassy (58 Knightsbridge, London SW1X 7JT ☎ 01-235 8080) issues a leaflet entitled *Employment in France for British nationals and nationals of other EC countries*. If you do decide to work in France, you are also advised to obtain the Department of Employment leaflet with the similarly catchy title: *Working in Europe – How to get a job in another EEC member state, and what you should know before you accept it*. EEC nationals may stay in France for up to three months (on a full passport) to find a job. If you do find one, a residence permit must be applied for. Application forms are available from the *Préfecture de Police* in Paris and from local police stations (*gendarmerie*) elsewhere. If you wish to work for more than six months, you should register for a job through the local ANPE office (Agence Nationale pour l'Emploi), equivalent to the British Jobcentre.

The organisations listed below publish information sheets for young people and students wishing to live or work in France:

The French Centre, 61/69 Chepstow Place, London W2 4TR ☎ 01-221 8134
Accueil des Jeunes en France, 12 rue des Barres, 75004 Paris (for correspondence) or 16 rue du Pont Philippe and 119 rue Saint Martin (for personal callers)
Centre d'Information et de Documentation Jeunesse (CIDJ), 101 quai Branly, 75740 Paris

WATERSPORTS
■ *CANOE-KAYAK* ■

This is a very popular sport in France, practised at both championship and Olympic level with enormous success. While the term canoë-kayak is used, there are, in fact, two distinct disciplines. Canoeing, with its origins in Canada, is performed kneeling and with a single bladed paddle, while a kayak is paddled Eskimo-style, from a seated position, and with a double bladed paddle.

There are over 600 competitive clubs within the Fedération Française de Canoë-Kayak (FFCK) which, in turn, has created the Ecole Française de Canoë-Kayak, welcoming tourists and holidaymakers to some of its best locations by the sea or on the rivers, where non-competitive courses and trips are organised for both children and adults during the holiday season. These can vary from hourly lessons to full-blown trips, or descents, lasting several days, with accommodation included. It is worth noting that an especial welcome is given here to those with a handicap.

With 250,000 km of navigable rivers, France is a paradise for canoeists, and frequent mention is made, throughout the resort gazetteer, of facilities available to the holidaymaker. Rivers are divided into six categories of difficulty: classes 1 and 2 suitable for beginners, classes 3 and 4 requiring skill to manoeuvre round obstacles, and classes 5 and 6 dangerous, if not impassable. As far as starting the sport is concerned, though, no particular physical qualities are necessary.

The FFCK is a highly professional body and can supply maps and guides to specific areas, addresses of clothing and equipment suppliers, films and videos on the sport, as well as the invaluable guide, *Vacances canoë-kayak en France*, published annually.

The French *Loisirs Accueil* brochures (see under Short Breaks) are full of suggestions for this type of holiday and their organisation offers various short break ideas including the following. In the Eure-et-Loire: accompanied two-day trip with hotel accommodation (May-Oct). In the Dordogne: trips on the River Vézère. No guide but first-morning tuition plus two to six days with accommodation in a hotel (May-Oct). In the Dordogne valley: 120-km trip lasting five or six days with camping accommodation and your gear transferred on for you (July-Sept). Contact Loisirs Acceuil Dordogne-Périgord, 16 rue Wilson, 24009 Périgueux Cedex ☎ 53.53.44.35, for further details. There is also a kayak beginners'/improvers' week on the River Vézère (class 3) with an all-inclusive price for tuition and camping accommodation (1300F). Contact Loisirs Accueil, Quai Baluze, 19000 Tulle ☎ 55.26.46.88.

Several British-based operators offer canoeing holidays too. *PGL Young Adventure* have their own centre at Le Mas de Serret on the Ardèche, which is the base for supervised holidays of one or two weeks' duration for children of seven years and over. Accommodation is in tents, with tuition culminating in an unforgettable three-day descent.

While a selection of locations and courses in the Auvergne and Limousin is listed below, facilities are also available at many centres on the River Dordogne, where the river is clean and the beaches safe for bathing. For specific information on clubs nearest to your planned destination, contact the FFCK direct (17 route de Vienne, 69007 Lyon ☎ 78.61.32.74).

AUVERGNE

(on the Allier and Loire rivers)
Useful address: Ligue Auvergne de Canoë-Kayak, 32, rue Charles Péguy, 63800 Cournon d'Auvergne.

Aurec-sur-Loire *(Haute-Loire)*
Parc de Loisirs, 43110 Aurec-sur-Loire ☎ 77.35.21.51 (eight years to adults + handicapped – hourly and daily hire plus courses with accommodation July/Aug).
Aydat *(Puy-de-Dôme)*

Club des Sports de Clermont-Aydat, 27 rue des Salins, 63000 Clermont-Ferrand ☎ 73.93.93.59 (eight-18 years + accompanied handicapped – five-day courses with/without accommodation July/Aug).

Brioude *(Haute-Loire)*
Club Omnisport Brivadois, Base
du Pont de Lamothe, 43100
Brioude ☎ 71.50.43.82 and Le
Gray-Vieille-Brioude, 43100
Brioude ☎ 71.50.14.18 (ten
years to adults + handicapped –
daily hire plus two-, three- or six-
day courses July/Aug).
Brives Charensac *(Haute-Loire)*
Sports Loisirs Brivois, La Roche-
Rouge, St Germain Laprade,
43700 Brives Charensac
☎ 71.02.29.13 or ☎ 71.05.54.34
(eight years to adults – hourly and
daily hire July/Aug).
Chilhac *(Haute-Loire)*
Cap'Vacances 25, rue
Saint-Pierre, B.P.85 43100
Brioude ☎ 71.50.00.70 (ten
years to adults + handicapped –
half-day and daily hire plus week-
long courses all year round).
Cournon *(Puy-de-Dôme)*
Direction Départementale de la
Jeunesse et des Sports, 34 rue
Albert Thomas, 63000 Clermont-
Ferrand ☎ 73.35.54.51 (ten
years to adults – series of half-day
courses July/Aug).
Ebreuil *(Allier)*
Club Nautique de Sioule et
Bouble, 03450 Ebreuil (eight
years to adults + handicapped –
hourly and daily hire July/Aug
with other periods on request).
Issoire *(Puy-de-Dôme)*
Union Sportive Issoirienne, Stade
Nautique, 63500 Issoire and
M. Sursin, Place de Vieux
Marché, 63114 Coudes (seven
years to adults – hourly and daily
hire plus three or five-day courses
July/Aug).
Les Fades-Besserve
(Puy-de-Dôme)
Centre Nautique des
Fades-Besserve, Base de
Confolant-Miremont, 63380
Pontaumur ☎ 73.79.92.75 and
M. Brun 11, avenue Jean Jaurès,
63510 Aulnat ☎ 73.61.04.97
(eight years to adults – hourly and
daily hire plus six-day or half-day
courses July/Aug. Weekends only
May, June and September).
Langeac *(Haute-Loire)*
Club de Kayak Langeadois,
Reilhac, 43300 Langeac
☎ 71.77.18.87 (eight years to
adults – hourly and daily hire plus
courses July/Aug).
Langeac to Issoire

Seven-day trips with
accommodation for 16 years
upwards (1,970F)
July-September. Contact Ligue
d'Auvergne de Canoë-Kayak Plan
d'Eau, 63800 Cournon ☎
73.84.30.06 or M. Gaime (C.T.R.
Canoë-Kayak), Lotissement le
Laire – Le Broc 63500 Issoire
☎ 73.55.03.66
Langeac to Saint-Yorre
Nine days on the Allier with tent
accommodation for 17 years
upwards (2,120-2,440F)
June-September. Contact
Association Sylva Vieux-Fraisses-
Rocles, 48300 Langogne
☎ 66.69.50.28
Lavoute-Chilhac *(Haute-Loire)*
Base du Chambon de Cerzat,
43380 Lavoute-Chilhac
☎ 71.77.25.90 and Action
Loisirs, 43390 Auzon
☎ 71.76.16.17 (seven years to
adults – hourly and daily hire plus
two-six-day courses with/without
accommodation; weekends from
Easter onwards).
Monistrol d'Allier *(Haute-Loire)*
Club de Canoë-Kayak du Haut
Allier, Base de Plein Air, 43580
Monistrol d'Allier ☎ 71.57.23.90
(in season) or ☎ 71.57.21.86
(ten years to adults +
handicapped – half-day and daily
hire plus courses. River descent
May-Sept).
Moulins *(Allier)*
Club Omnisports Populaire de
l'Agglomération Moulinoise 8 rue
de Potiers, 03000 Moulins
☎ 70.20.24.57 (adults half-day
and daily hire July/Aug).
Néris-les-Bains *(Allier)*
Base de Canoë-Kayak, Lavault
Ste-Anne, 03310 Néris-les-Bains
☎ 70.07.20.73 (eight years to
adults + handicapped – hourly
and daily hire plus eight-day
training courses July/Aug).
Plan d'eau de Vieure *(Allier)*
Association de Gestion du Plan
d'Eau de Vieure, 03430 Cosne
d'Allier ☎ 70.07.20.82 (eight-15
years July/Aug, week-long
training with or without
accommodation).
Pont-du-Château *(Puy-de-Dôme)*
Club Nautique Castelpontin,
20 chemin de Chantagret, 63430
Pont-du-Château ☎ 73.83.02.76
and 4 rue Pont-du-Château,
63360 Saint-Beauzire

☎ 73.33.95.59 (ten years to
adults – hourly and daily hire.
River descent May-Sept).
Retournac *(Haute-Loire)*
Base de Plein Air, 43130
Retournac ☎ 71.59.44.72
(July/Aug) and 1 rue de Daveyne
– Retournaguet, 43130 Retournac
☎ 71.59.42.70 (all ages – hourly
hire plus three- or six-day courses
with/without accommodation,
May-Oct).
Saint-Flour *(Cantal)*
La Sanfloraine Sports Loisirs,
avenue de Besserette, 15100
Saint-Flour ☎ 71.60.13.60 (12
years to adults – daily hire
July/Aug).
Vichy *(Allier)*
Centre Omnisports Passeport
Sportif, B.P. 161, 03206 Vichy,
Cédex ☎ 70.32.04.68 (ten years
to adults – one- to three-week
courses July/Aug).

LIMOUSIN

(on the Vézère, Corrèze, Diège
and Dordogne rivers)
Useful addresses: Comité
Départemental de Canoë-Kayak,
Centre Culturel et Sportif, 19000
Tulle, Limousin.
Maison du Canoë-kayak, 2 rue
Noël Ballay, 75020 Paris
☎ 43.72.16.97

The international rally of canoë-
kayak takes place at Argentat-
sur-Dordogne on the first Sunday
in July and the rally on the
Vézère takes place at Le Saillant
on the first Sunday in August.

Anzême *(La Creuse)*
Association sportive et culturelle
d'Anzême, 23000 Anzême
☎ 55.52.67.83 (hire and tuition
July/Aug).
La Celle-Dunoise *(La Creuse)*
Creuse Randonnée, 43, Place
Bonnyaud, B.P.243, 23005
Guéret ☎ 55.52.33.00 (two-day
courses for beginners May/June.
Also kayak trips from here to
Crozant in July/Aug on demand –
contact Kayak Club Marchois,
Maison des Jeunes de Guéret,
avenue Fayolle, 23000 Guéret
☎ 55.52.37.22)
Vassivière (Lac de)
Fédération des Oeuvres Laïques,
rue Ingres, 23000 Guéret

☎ 55.52.06.32 (1,000-hectare lake ideal for all watersports enthusiasts).

SPECIALIST TOUR OPERATORS

Headwater Holidays, 62a Beach Road, Hartford CW8 3AB
☎ 0606 782011
Holiday Charente, Wardington, Banbury OX17 1SA

☎ 029575 8282
LSG Theme Holidays, 201 Main Street, Thornton LE6 1AH
☎ 0509 231713
PGL Young Adventure Ltd, 104 Station Street, Ross-on-Wye HR9 7AH
☎ 0989 768768

OPERATORS SPECIALISING IN RAFTING

Explore Worldwide, 1 Frederick Street, Aldershot GU11 1LQ
☎ 0252 319448
Road Runner Holidays, Unit 42, Canal Bridge, Enterprise Centre, Meadow Lane, Ellesmere Port L65 4EH
☎ 051-356 4440

■ CANAL AND RIVER CRUISING ■

The great rivers of France were originally linked up for commercial purposes by a network of canals. Raw materials and goods could be despatched between the Mediterranean and the Atlantic by way of the Canal du Midi. A watery trade route ran down the length of the country from the Channel to the Mediterranean, from Le Havre to Marseille.

This commercial usage has virtually disappeared now, and instead France is opened up to pleasure cruising along almost 8,000 km of navigable waterways, through some of its most beautiful country – Brittany, the Loire, Aquitaine, the Midi, the Rhône, Burgundy, the Seine and Alsace-Lorraine.

The craft plying these waters range from the modest single cabin two-berth motor launch, through larger models for four or six passengers, up to the adapted continental barge (*peniche*) and the frankly luxurious barge, catering for as many as 20 passengers in state rooms with their own facilities, gourmet meals in the dining saloon and a crew of eight. Along the routes there are ports of call from which excursions reach into the hinterland, by road or even balloon trips from a field close to the barge's moorings, from there to rise and drift low over vineyards, châteaux and market towns in the soft breeze and the sinking sun of early dusk, the ideal ballooning hour.

In Brittany there are some 640 km of navigable waterways, and many boat-hiring firms dotted along the Nantes-Brest Canal which passes through the Muscadet vineyards and links the lower reaches of the Loire to Angers and Le Mans with the Rivers Vilaine and Blavet.

There are 160 km of navigable water between Rochefort and Angoulême on the Charente, running through cognac country at Cognac, and offering visits to the amphitheatre at Saintes, ancient capital of western Gaul.

Construction of the Canal du Midi was begun in 1681 and took 14 years in the building – pick and shovel work by a labour force of 12,000 men. It runs for 240 km from Toulouse to Agde on the Mediterranean, linking with the Canal Laterale à la Garonne and the Garonne itself to reach back to Bordeaux on the Atlantic coast. Cruisers sail from Toulouse for Carcassonne, Narbonne and Sète, thence by canal junction to the lower Rhône for Beaucaire and Avignon.

The waters of Burgundy, the Rivers Yonne, Upper Saône and Ouche and the Canal du Centre, the Loing Canal, the Canal du Bourgogne and the Canal du Nivernais, all 960 km of them, offer perhaps the richest cruising country of all. Several operators offer a great variety of tours of the Burgundy vineyards – Beaune, Côtes de Nuit and Chablis – and visits to the châteaux of Rochepot, Ancy-le-Franc and Tanlay, to Fontenay Abbey, the monastery of Flavigny and Auxerre cathedral. Embarkation points include Dôle, Pouillenay Tonnerre, Dijon, Joigny and Auxerre, passing en route Briare, Nemours, Langres, Montargis (excursion point for the châteaux of the Loire).

On the Rhône, departure points for river cruises are at Valence and Lyons. Further north, the Rhône links with the Burgundy complex of waterways, and to the north east, through Epinal, with the waters of Alsace-Lorraine.

From Strasbourg, cruiser hire companies operate boats on the River Ill and the Canal du Marne au Rhin to Toul and Nancy, and between Verdun, Charleville and Bar-le-Duc on the Canal de l'Est.

In the Ile de France, the Upper Seine links the River Yonne with the interlacing canals between Fontainebleu, Courlon, Nemours, Joigny, Vézelay and Sens, Corbigny, Briare and Dijon. The River Oise, running from Conflans to Compiègne, passes through Pontoise where Pissarro and Cézanne often painted.

There are, of course, strict rules of river and canal etiquette, and all of these can be obtained from the SNLBP (Syndicat National des Loueurs de Bateaux de Plaisance) Port de la Bourdonnais, 75007 Paris ☎ 45.55.10.49. Amongst other items worth remembering are the speed limits of 10 kmph on canals and 5 kmph on rivers. But who would want to pass through such lovely countryside any faster? Most canal locks are closed on public holidays; on working days many of them also close for a brief lunch break. Where better for travellers to break their fast and sip a glass of wine?

UK-BASED COMPANIES ENGAGED IN CRUISING FACILITIES IN FRANCE

Abercrombie and Kent, Sloane Square House, Holbein Place, London SW1W 8NS
☎ 01-730 9600
Angel Travel, 47 High Street, Central Chambers, Tonbridge TN9 1SD ☎ 0732 361115
Blakes Holidays, Wroxham, Norwich NR12 8DH
☎ 0603 3224
Blue Line France, P.O. Box 9, Northney Marina, Hayling Island, Hants. PO11 ONL
☎ 0705 468011
Brittany Ferries, The Brittany Centre, Wharf Road, Portsmouth PO2 8RU ☎ 0705 827701
Crown Cruisers, 8 Ber Street, Norwich NR1 3EJ

☎ 0603 630513
European Canal Cruisers, 79 Winchester Road, Romsey SO51 8JB ☎ 0794 514412
La France des Villages, Model Farm, Rattlesden, Bury St Edmunds IP30 0SY
☎ 044 93 7664
French Country Cruises, Andrew Brock Travel Ltd, 10 Barley Mow Passage, London W4 4PH
☎ 01-995 3642
French Life Motoring Holidays, 26 Church Road, Horsforth, Leeds LS18 5LG ☎ 0532 390077
Headwater Holidays, 62a Beach Road, Hartford, Cheshire CW8 3AB ☎ 0606 782011
Heron Cruisers, Stanton House, Romford Road, Pembury TN2 4AY ☎ 089282 5454
Holiday Charente, Wardington, Banbury OX17 1SA
☎ 029575 8282
Hoseasons Holidays Abroad,

Sunway House, Lowestoft, Suffolk ☎ 0502 501 501
SFV Holidays, Summer House, 68 Hernes Road, Summertown, Oxford OX2 7QL ☎ 0865 57738
Slipaway Holidays, 90 Newland Road, Worthing, West Sussex BN11 1LB ☎ 0903 821000
Travel Solutions, 93 Trafalgar Road, London SE10 9TS
☎ 01-853 1980
VFB Holidays, 1 St Margaret's Terrace, Cheltenham GL50 4DT
☎ 0242 526338

The French Government Tourist Office can provide a list of French boat hire companies (cabin cruisers and yachts) belonging to the Syndicat National des Loueurs de Bateaux de Plaisance. Contact FGTO, 178 Piccadilly, London W1V 0AL. They can also supply a list detailing annual closures (*chômages*) of canals for repairs and other purposes.

■ SAILING AND YACHT CHARTER ■

For those travelling to France to learn to sail, details of sailing schools can be obtained from the Comité Régional du Tourisme (CRT) offices, addresses for all of which are given after each regional introduction in the gazetteer section of this book. The resorts detailed in the gazetteer indicate the prime locations and availability of courses for either the novice sailor or those seeking more advanced coaching. An ideal starting point might be in Brittany where the wind is almost always blowing, mildly or strongly but never treacherously, and the Breton coves, creeks and sheltered estuaries provide perfect learning areas. Most resorts have their own sailing schools, open to pupils of all ages, and offering coaching either to an elementary standard for beginners or more advanced tuition for improvers.

British yachtsmen and enthusiasts will find visiting France with their own craft not only a delightful experience but also one requiring very few formalities as long as the visit is as a tourist and for a period of less than six months. It is very important, however, to ensure that your craft is properly registered. Pleasure craft, with inboard motors or without engines, benefit from a simplified arrangement provided that the purpose of the journey is a legitimate, non-immigrant one and that all relevant Customs' regulations are observed.

For all pleasure craft, whether propelled by sails or an engine, and whether made of rigid materials or inflatable, entering French waters temporarily, the French authorities will accept a Certificate of Registration, Official Ship's Papers or, for small yachts and motor boats under 24 m in length, the new Small Ships Register (SSR) issued by the Royal Yachting Association (Victoria Way, Woking, Surrey GU21 1EQ ☎ 0703 629962). However, ships owned by companies must continue to have Official Ship's Papers. Neither *permis de circulation* nor a certificate of competence is required (unless required in the country of origin).

You are permitted to sail and moor along the French coast and inland waterways for a duration of six months, either in one or several visits, during a period of 12 consecutive months. Great Britain being covered by convention, British yachtsmen are exempt from *droit d'escale* (port of call charge), and yachts from the UK sailing between France (including Corsica), Belgium and Holland require no maritime health declaration.

Mooring charges are reasonable but vary from one port to another. For information and to reserve a mooring, contact the Capitainerie du Port of each harbour.

For those who like the idea of yacht charter but who have no previous experience, the option of flotilla sailing makes an attractive alternative. Cruising in company, you require only basic sailing experience as you follow the lead yacht which has a qualified skipper aboard.

Listed below are British operators from whom yachts, either bareboat or crewed, can be chartered. Crewed yachts are very much the luxury end of the market, but with a large party sharing the costs can soon appear more reasonable, and the waters of the Mediterranean ideal. The range of what is on offer varies, but such yachts generally carry watersports equipment, stereo, TV and video cameras as standard; with such extras as four-wheel drive cars and motorbikes also available on board.

SPECIALIST OPERATORS

Camper & Nicholsons (Mayfair) Ltd, 31 Berkeley Street, London W1X 5FA ☎ 01–491 2950
Clearwater Holidays, 17 Heath Terrace, Leamington Spa CV32 5NA ☎ 0926 450002
Island Sailing, The Port House, Port Solent, Portsmouth PO6 4TH ☎ 0705 219844
Liz Fenner (Worldwide Yachting) Holidays, 35 Fairfax Place, London NW6 4EJ ☎ 01–328 1033
Marine Share Ltd, 50a Pall Mall, London SW1Y 5JQ ☎ 01–930 0871
Riviera Sailing Holidays, 45 Bath Road, Emsworth PO10 7ER ☎ 0243 374376
Sundown Yacht Charters, Sundown House, Rectory Lane, Woodmansterne, Surrey SM7 3PP ☎ 07375 51271
Templecraft Yacht Charters, 33 Grand Parade, Brighton BN2 2QA ☎ 0273 695094

■ *SAND YACHTING* ■

Sand yachting, or *char à voile*, is popular on the hard, flat sandy expanses of beach in Picardy, Nord – Pas-de-Calais and parts of Brittany, beaches where there are stretches long enough to attain speed and yet leave areas safe and free for other users. Looking like a kind of beach ballet, this is a competition sport with great visual appeal. Equipment can be hired at locations such as Fort-Mahon-Plage and Quend-Plage-les-Pins, and Dunkerque, for example, offers weekend courses for beginners aged 16 and over.

Beaches where the sport is practised:

Calais – Sangatte, Hardelot, Berck, Le Touquet, Fort-Mahon, Le Crotoy, Ault-Onival, Trouville, Cabourg, Ver-sur-Mer, Saint-Marie-du-Mont, Vauville, Donville, Cherrueix-Saint-Malo, Saint-Efflam, Ploudalmézeau, Saint-Nic-Pentrez, Lorient, Quiberon, Notre-Dame-de-Monts and Saint-Gilles-Croix-de-Vie

Useful address:
Fédération Française de Char à Voile, 62 avenue Bosquet, 75007 Paris

■ *SURFING* ■

Though it has been practised on the Basque coast since the war, surfing is not a local sport at all. The earliest mention of it is from the eleventh century, when surfing was a religious rite for New Zealand Maoris, performed as proof of worthiness for high office.

The best surfing conditions in France are offered all along the Atlantic beaches of the Golfe de Gascogne on the Aquitaine coast, virtually a straight line of resorts north from the Spanish border (Hendaye) to the Basin of Arcachon (Cap Ferret).

Resorts (and beaches) where the sport is practised:

Hendaye, St-Jean-de-Luz (beaches of Ste-Barbe, Acotz, Senix, Lafitenia), Guéthary (Les Alcyons), Bidart (Parlementia), Biarritz (Cote des Basques and main beach), Anglet (Chambre d'Amour), Le Boucau, Capbreton, Hossegor, Seignosse, Vieux Boucau (Port d'Albret), Mimizan, Biscarosse and Cap Ferret

Useful address:
Fédération Française de Surf: 45 avenue du Penon, 40150 Seignosse ☎ 58.43.31.22

■ *UNDERWATER DIVING* ■

The exciting world under the sea opens up for the underwater diver.

The British Sub Aqua Club has just one recognised school in France, Club Equipe in the Port Grimaud area, which welcomes complete beginners, who may wish to prepare for their Novice Diver certificate, as well as those seeking their Sports Diver qualifications. Thorough training is given for both over a two-week period and a considerable amount of written work is involved. Write for details to Club Equipe (France). This is a good area for experienced divers too, with both reef and wreck dives possible off the coast at Cavalaire.

Despite the fact that the sea off Brittany is not that warm, and a diver's movements are affected by currents and tides, the Breton continental shelf offers a luxuriant submarine flora and a varied and abundant fauna as well as several underwater archaeological sites, the Er Lannic cromlech in the Golfe de Morbihan, for example. There are numerous clubs, almost all of them with their own compressor or facilities for filling tanks.

The considerably warmer waters of the Mediterranean offer inexhaustible possiblities and there are diving schools literally all along the coast. For the Riviera write to the Comité Départemental, Fort Carré, 06600 Antibes. Corsica, too, is a very popular area, with diving offered at all the major resorts.

Useful addresses:

British Sub Aqua Club, 16 Upper Woburn Place, London WC1H 0QW ☎ 01-387 9302

Club Equipe (France), 25 Kenilworth Crescent, Parkfield, Wolverhampton WV4 6TA ☎ 0902 336234.

Fédération Française d'Etudes et de Sports Sous-Marins, 24 quai de Rive Neuve, 13007 Marseille ☎ 91.33.99.31

■ *WATERSKIING* ■

The inland lakes and marvellous coastline of France are responsible for the development of the thrilling sport of waterskiing; in fact, France was the first European country to take up this pastime. There are many clubs at coastal resorts and on the island of Corsica, offering hire of equipment and lessons. A perfect holiday activity, relatively easy to learn and safe; the local Tourist Office can advise on operators.

Useful address:
Fédération Française de Ski Nautique, 16 rue Clement Morot, 75008 Paris

■ *WINDSURFING* ■

Large inland lakes and the extensive facilities of the coastal resorts mean that windsurfing is now practised virtually everywhere. Boards can often be hired at the beaches and tuition may be offered on an hourly basis, or longer. A relatively easy sport to master quickly, with balance achievable within a couple of hours' practice, continuous pleasure is to be had from learning to master the various techniques.

Taking your own board abroad should present no problems. You will need to check with your insurance company for cover while abroad, and you also need to take proof of purchase (receipt or similar) to present at Customs when returning. Travel with the board strapped safely upside down to a car roof rack (the two-ladder racks are the most popular), and with the sail off the mast, everything should be secured with straps rather than rubber cords which are dangerous at high speeds. Ensure, too, that when the board is left unattended, you have made it as secure as possible against theft.

Once in France, be aware of the tides and the rapidly changing wind and sea conditions on the coast. For the safety of others in the water (bathers often underestimate the difficulties of controlling and directing a board), speeds are restricted to less than 10 kmph within 300 m of the beach. For the safety of the windsurfer, it is forbidden to sail further than 1,850 m out to sea and it is recommended that you sail in the company of others and remain visible at all times to those on the shore. Buoyancy aids, although not compulsory, are a recommended precaution since it is easy to overestimate your strength.

Useful address:
Windsurfing Information Centre, c/o RYA, Victoria Way, Woking, Surrey GU21 1EQ
☎ 0703 629962

WINTER SPORTS

■ *SKIING* ■

Approximately 20 per cent of France is covered by mountainous regions – the Vosges, Jura, Alps, Massif Central and the Pyrénées. With more than 50 major ski resorts and over 200 other ski centres within these areas, France offers a wealth of choice for both the first-time and experienced skier. In 1992 the town of

Albertville, and the Savoie region as a whole, will host the Winter Olympics, official recognition of France's leading role in winter sports.

The flourishing winter holiday business has meant also that many new purpose-built resorts have grown up in response to the phenomenal increase in demand for facilities since the end of the last war. Some are better than others; some more attractively and carefully planned. Many early mistakes have since been corrected, so that resorts like Valmorel, built in the 1980s, show modern design theory in practice and offer both attractive and traditional wood- and stone-built accommodation close to the slopes.

To obtain official classification as a skiing resort, various standards have to be met following specific guidelines: minimum 1,500 bed availability (50 per cent of which must be self-catering and 20 per cent hotel accommodation); regular shuttle access to the resort from the nearest rail station; medical service provision on site, including ambulances; other organisational considerations such as children's play areas, permanent tourist office facilities and a professional ski school and instructors. The altitude of the resort is another factor, with minimums stated as being 800 m for the Alps, Jura and Vosges; 1,000 m for the Massif Central and Corsica; and 1,200 m for the Pyrénées. Ski centres have no such set of standards to meet and what they offer, therefore, varies greatly.

The means of travelling to the resort of your choice needs careful thought. Charter flights offer a wide range of departure airports and fast service, although there are luggage restrictions, and shuttle transport to and from the resort is often lengthy with frustrating delays. Once at the resort, and without your own car, you may feel restricted. On the other hand, driving out can be a long and tiring experience, often in wintry conditions. The roads and autoroutes are likely to be emptier though, and the ferry crossings cheaper. Similarly coach trips mean a long drive, but they go direct to the resort. The French Railways (SNCF) offer a Motorail service, leaving Calais at 8 p.m. and arriving at Moutiers in the Alps at 8 a.m. the following morning. This way, both you and your car can arrive refreshed and ready to continue the last leg of the journey.

You can book direct by writing to the resort tourist offices themselves, and details will be forthcoming on accommodation options. The popularity of many of the better-known resorts with the British market means that a lot of their brochures are in English. For many, however, the all-inclusive flight and accommodation packages offered by the specialist British operators are hard to beat, when saving time and effort in driving all the way is a consideration. The operators listed below will supply brochures on request. Many of them are small firms specialising in a handful of resorts; others are major package tour operators and their brochures can be found in every high street travel agent.

Useful addresses:
Ski Club of Great Britain, 118 Eaton Square, London SW1W 9AF ☎ 01-245 1033
Association des Maires des Stations Françaises de Sports d'Hiver, 61 boulevard Haussmann, 75008 Paris ☎ 47.42.23.32
Fédération Française de Ski, 50 rue des Marquisats, B.P.451, 74009 Annecy Cedex ☎ 50.51.40.34

Listed below are the main winter sports regions and resorts, more information on which can be found in the gazetteer section of the book (information in brackets indicates in which region they are to be found):

VOSGES

Despite lack of great height (Ballon d'Alsace is 1,250 m), the Vosges range offers a selection of winter sports resorts which, although perfect for cross country (*ski de fond*), can never hope to rival the alpine skiing potential of the Alps.
Airport serving the area: Mulhouse.

La Bresse (see Alsace Lorraine)
Gérardmer (see Alsace Lorraine)

JURA

The deep valleys of this region offer excellent cross country as well as alpine skiing.
Airport serving the area: Geneva.

Les Rousses (see Franche-Comté)

HAUTE-SAVOIE & SAVOIE

(Northern Alps)
This is the principal winter sports region in France, with many of the most famous and popular resorts linked. Less sunny than its southerly counterpart, the pistes

here run from 800-4,000 m.
Airports serving the area:
Chambéry and Geneva.

Les Arcs (see Rhône-Alpes)
Avoriaz-Morzine (see
Rhône-Alpes)
Chamonix (see Rhône-Alpes)
Châtel (see Rhône-Alpes)
La Clusaz (see Rhône-Alpes)
Courchevel (see Rhône-Alpes)
Flaine (see Rhône-Alpes)
Megève (see Rhône-Alpes)
Les Ménuires (see Rhône-Alpes)
Méribel (see Rhône-Alpes)
La Plagne (see Rhône-Alpes)
Samoëns (see Rhône-Alpes)
Tignes (see Rhône-Alpes)
Val d'Isère (see Rhône-Alpes)
Val Thorens (see Rhône-Alpes)

DAUPHINE

The Vercors range near Grenoble
traditionally has good snow and
some large and popular resorts.
Airports serving the area:
Grenoble and Lyon.

L'Alpe d'Huez (see
Rhône-Alpes)
Les Deux Alpes (see
Rhône-Alpes)
Serre-Chevalier (see Provence –
Alpes – Côte d'Azur)
Villard-de-Lans (see
Rhône-Alpes)

MASSIF CENTRAL

Fairly low-altitude alpine and
cross-country resorts, based
around traditional mountain
villages or spas.
Airports serving the area:
Clermont-Ferrand, Geneva or
Lyon.

Le Mont-Dore (see Auvergne)
Super-Besse (see Auvergne)
Super-Lioran (see Auvergne)

ALPES DU SUD

(Southern Alps)
Close to the Mediterranean coast,
this is the sunniest of all the skiing
regions, where crowds are
attracted by sure winter tans and
excellent skiing.
Airports serving the area: Nice,
Marseille, Grenoble and Turin (in
Italy).

Auron (see Provence – Alpes –
Côte d'Azur)
Isola 2000 (see Provence – Alpes
– Côte d'Azur)
Montgenèvre (see Provence –
Alpes – Côte d'Azur)
Superdévoluy (see Provence –
Alpes – Côte d'Azur)
Valberg (see Provence – Alpes -
Côte d'Azur)

PYRENEES

Less developed than the Alps and
correspondingly less crowded, the
resorts here offer gentler slopes,
perfect for beginners and
children. The snow conditions are
more variable on account of the
sunny aspect of the pistes, but the
centres are traditional in nature,
often based on permanent
mountain communities.
Airports serving the area:
Toulouse, Lourdes, Tarbes, Pau,
Perpignan and Barcelona (in
Spain).

Aragnouet-Piau-Engaly (see
Midi-Pyrénées)
Les Angles (see
Languedoc-Roussillon)
Ax-les-Thermes (see
Midi-Pyrénées)
Barèges (see Midi-Pyrénées)
Cauterets (see Midi-Pyrénées)
Font-Romeu (see
Languedoc-Roussillon)
La Mongie (see Midi-Pyrénées)
St-Lary-Soulan (see
Midi-Pyrénées)
Superbagnères (see
Midi-Pyrénées)

SPECIALIST TOUR OPERATORS

Activity Travel, 19 Castle
Street, Edinburgh EH2 3AH
☎ 031-225 9457
Air France Holidays, 69 Boston
Manor Road, Brentford, Middx
☎ 01-568 6981
Alpfit, 19 South End, London
W8 9JQ ☎ 01-938 3755
Alpine Life Ski Chalets, The
Chestnuts, Dunston, Lincoln
LN4 2ET ☎ 0526 20632
Barrett-Boyce Ski Tours,
14 Hawthorn Road, Wallington,
Surrey SM6 0SX
☎ 01-647 8620
Bladon Lines, 56/58 Putney
High Street, London SW15 1SF

☎ 01-785 3131
Blue Sky Ski, Broadway,
Edgbaston Fiveways,
Birmingham B15 1BB
☎ 021-643 2727
Brittany Ferries, The Brittany
Centre, Wharf Road,
Portsmouth PO2 8RU
☎ 0705 827701
Chalet Morzine, 20 Caithness
Road, London W14 0JA
☎ 01-602 1145
Club 18-30, Academic House,
24/28 Oval Road, Camden
Town, London NW1 7DA
☎ 01-485 4141
Club Méditerranée, 106/11
Brompton Road, London
SW3 1JJ ☎ 01-581 1161
Collineige Ski, 30/32 High
Street, Frimley, Surrey
☎ 0276 691996
Crystal Holidays, The
Courtyard, Arlington Road,
Surbiton, Surrey KT6 6BW
☎ 01-399 5144
Enfants Cordiales, 511/513
Upper Elmers, End Road,
Beckenham, Kent BR3 3DD
☎ 01-650 4932
Good Company Holidays,
19 The Parade, Colchester
Road, Romford, Essex
☎ 04023 70663
Go-Ski, Redwing Holidays,
Groundstar House, London
Road, Crawley RH10 2TB
☎ 0293 517733
Horizon Ski, Broadway,
Edgbaston Fiveways,
Birmingham B15 1BB
☎ 021-643 8041
Hourmont Total Ski, Brunel
House, Newfoundland Road,
Bristol BS2 9LU
☎ 0272 426961
Hoverspeed Skiing Holidays,
Maybrook House, Queens
Gardens, Dover CT17 9UQ
☎ 0304 240202
Inghams, Gemini House, 10/18
Putney Hill, London SW15 6AX
☎ 01-785 7777
Just Ski, Travel House,
10 Suffolk Road, Lowestoft
NR32 1DZ ☎ 0502 589187
Erna Low Consultants, 9 Reece
Mews, London SW7 3HE
☎ 01-584 2841
Mogul Ski, Royal Chambers,
Station Parade, Harrogate,
North Yorks ☎ 0423 69512
John Morgan Travel, 22 Hans
Place, London SW1X 0EP

☎ 01-584 6323
Neilson, Holiday House, Domestic Road, Leeds LS12 6HR ☎ 0532 420420
Red Guide Holidays, 18/20 Clifton Street, Blackpool FY1 1JP ☎ 0253 23939
Silver Ski, Conifers House, Grove Green Lane, Maidstone ME14 5JW ☎ 0622 35544
Le Ski, 65 Ashbrow Road, Huddersfield HD2 1DX ☎ 0484 548996
Ski Beach Villas, 8 Market Passage, Cambridge CB2 3QR ☎ 0223 311113
Ski Beat, Greaves Travel, 40/41 Marylebone High Street, London W1M 3AD ☎ 01-487 5687
Skibound Holidays, Blenheim House, 120 Church Street, Brighton BN1 1WD ☎ 0273 676123
Ski Chamois, 18 Lawn Road, Doncaster DN1 2JF ☎ 0302 69006
Ski Choice, 27 High Street, Benson, Oxon OX9 6RP ☎ 0491 37607
Ski Corniche, Knoll House, High Cross, Near Ware, Herts SG11 1BP ☎ 0920 4261
Ski Enterprise, Groundstar House, London Road, Crawley RH10 2TB ☎ 0293 517733
Ski Esprit, Austen House, Fleet GU13 9PE ☎ 0252 616789
Ski Falcon, 33 Notting Hill Gate, London W11 3JQ ☎ 01-229 9484
Ski Fun, 32 Alexander House, Milkern Close, Bletchley, Milton Keynes MK2 2UT ☎ 0908 368332
Ski Global, 26 Elmfield Road, Bromley BR1 1LR ☎ 01-464 6666
Ski Lovers, 11 Liston Court, High Street, Marlow SL7 1ER ☎ 06284 76991

Ski Nat, Holiday House, Leeds LS12 6HR ☎ 0532 422333
Ski Red Fox, Homelea, Portsmouth Road, Esher KT10 9PH ☎ 0372 67643
Ski Sally, Argyle Centre, York Street, Ramsgate, Kent CT11 9DS ☎ 0843 595522
Ski Thomson, Greater London House, Hampstead Road, London NW1 7SD
☎ 01-387 8484
Ski Tonic, 6 Davis Street, Hurst, Berks RG10 0TG
☎ 0734 320042
Ski Total, 10 Hill Street, Richmond TW9 1TN
☎ 01-948 6922
Ski Trax, Henry Bell House, Gilesgate, Hexham, Northumberland NE46 3NJ
☎ 0434 606488
Ski Val, 91 Wembley Park Drive, Wembley Park, Middx HA9 8HF ☎ 01-903 4444
Ski West, 1 Belmont, Lansdown Road, Bath BA1 5DZ
☎ 0225 444516
Ski World, 41 North End Road, West Kensington, London W14 8SZ ☎ 01-602 4826
Ski Worthy, Jordangate House, Jordangate, Macclesfield SK10 1EQ ☎ 0625 511088
Ski Young World, P.O. Box 99, 29 Queens Road, Brighton BN1 3YN ☎ 0273 202391
Skiscene/Intasun, 2 Cromwell Avenue, Bromley, Kent BR2 9AQ ☎ 01-851 3321
Skiscope, Bolnore Road, Haywards Heath, West Sussex RH16 4BX ☎ 0444 441000
Snow Place Chalets, Wicham House, 10 Cleveland Way, London E1 4TR
☎ 01-444 9959
Snow World, 34/36 South Street, Lancing BN15 8AG
☎ 0903 765581
Snowbird Holidays, Grosvenor Hall, Bolnore Road, Haywards

Heath, West Sussex RH16 4BX
☎ 0444 441000
Snowtime, 23 Denmark Street, London WC2H 8NA
☎ 01-836 3237
Jean Stanford Ski Holidays, Ridge House, Chilmark, Salisbury SP3 5BS
☎ 0747 870708
Supertravel, 22 Hans Place, London SW1X 0EP
☎ 01-584 5060
Take-Off Travel, Olivier House, 18 Marine Parade, Brighton, East Sussex ☎ 0273 697215
Tourarc UK, 197b Brompton Road, London SW3 1LA
☎ 01-589 1918
Tracer Ltd, 5 St Andrews Road, West Kensington, London W14 9SX ☎ 01-385 6146
Vacations, 60 Charles Street, Leicester LE1 1FB
☎ 0533 539100
Susie Ward Travel, 11 Cross Keys Close, London W1M 5FY
☎ 01-935 9312
Mark Warner, 20 Kensington Church Street, London W8 4EP
☎ 01-938 1851
Waymark Holidays, 295 Lillie Road, London SW6 7LL
☎ 01-385 5015
White Roc Ski, 755 Fulham Road, London SW6 7LL
☎ 01-731 7842

CROSS-COUNTRY SPECIALISTS

Across-Country, Hovingham, York YO6 4JZ ☎ 065 383741
Ramblers Holidays, Longcroft House, Fretherne Road, Welwyn Garden City AL8 6PQ
☎ 0707 331133
SVP France, 122 High Street, Billingshurst RH14 8EP
☎ 040 381 5165
Waymark Holidays, 295 Lillie Road, London SW6 7LL
☎ 01-385 5015

■ *GLOSSARY OF USEFUL ADDRESSES* ■

Canoeing
Fédération Française de Canoë-kayak,
17 route de Vienne, 69007 Lyon
☎ 78.72.75.81

Climbing
Club Alpin Français, 9 rue la Boétie,
75008 Paris

Cycling
Fédération Française de Cyclotourisme,
8 rue Jean-Marie Jego, 75013 Paris
☎ 45.80.30.21

Fishing
Conseil Supérieur de la Pêche,
Domaine du Paraclet, Fouencamps,
B.P.5, Boves ☎ 22.09.37.47

Gliding
Fédération Française de Vol à Voile,
29 rue du Sèvres, 75006 Paris

Golf
Fédération Française de Golf,
69 avenue Victor Hugo, 75783 Paris
☎ 45.02.13.55

Hang-gliding
Fédération Française de Vol Libre,
54 bis, rue de la Buffa, 06000 Nice
☎ 93.88.62.89

Parachuting
Fédération Française de Parachutisme,
35 rue Saint-Georges, 75009 Paris

Riding
Association Nationale pour la Tourisme
Equestre,
15 rue de Bruxelles, 75009 Paris
☎ 42.81.42.82

River and canal cruising
Syndicat National des Loueurs de
Bateaux de Plaisance,
Port de la Bourdonnais, 75007 Paris
☎ 45.55.10.49

Sailing
Fédération Française de Voile,
55 avenue Kléber, 75784 Paris
☎ 45.53.68.00

Sand-yachting
Fédération Française de Char à Voile,
62 avenue Bosquet, 75007 Paris

Shooting
Office National de la Chasse,
5 rue de Saint-Thibaut, Saint Benoist,
78610 Le Perray en Yvelines
☎ 30.41.80.11

Skiing
Association des Maires des Stations
Françaises,
61 boulevard Haussmann, 75008 Paris
Fédération Française de Ski,
50 rue des Marquisats, B.P.491, 74009
Annecy ☎ 50.51.40.34
Maison de la Neige,
81 avenue des Ternes, 75017 Paris
☎ 45.72.64.40

Walking
Fédération Française de la Randonnée
Pédestre,
9 avenue George V, 75008 Paris
☎ 47.23.62.32

GAZETTEER OF RESORTS

The gazetteer has been written with the general holidaymaker in mind and gives information designed to enable him or her to assess a particular resort according to certain guidelines, specifically holiday and leisure-orientated pursuits. Historical and architectural detail has, therefore, been omitted for the most part, and has been replaced by short descriptions concentrating on the attractions and sporting amenities of each resort. Thus, the following elements have been included: golf courses, riding schools, tennis courts, spa treatment centres, boat trips and hire facilities, watersports facilities, fishing and walks, etc.

Additionally, this information has been highlighted by the use of specially designed symbols, positioned alongside the name of the resort, which give an at-a-glance indication of its environment in terms of a seaside, mountain, rural or lakeside location.

seaside   lakeside

mountain   urban

rural

No single element dominated the choice of resorts for this book. Think of France and a jumble of images presents itself – skiing in the Alps; promenading in Cannes or Nice; baking on vast expanses of beach; sipping wine in a quiet village café; fishing along a shady bank; touring the galleries or museums of Paris; walking in the rugged Provence countryside to the sound of cicadas; staring in wonder at one Loire valley château after another; watching the men of the village playing *boules;* stopping for fresh bread and fruit in yet another charming small town. The list is endless; indeed there are as many different experiences as there are places.

If anything then, this book is an attempt to include all these ingredients and was governed, therefore, by mixing the following elements:

Stations Vertes (*green resorts*)

This is a French concept. At the last count, there were 535 rurally located towns and villages which qualified for the *Station Verte* title. This indicates that they have made attempts to offer recreation facilities, both to their own citizens and to the visiting holidaymaker. Like skiing resorts, *Stations Vertes* have to qualify by satisfying certain criteria, as outlined in their charter. In this case that consists of being able to offer an attractive natural environment (which might include a river, forest, historic or picturesque features, etc.); accommodation in the form of camp site and hotels as well as self-catering; leisure facilities (such as river bathing or swimming pool, tennis courts, riding, fishing, canoeing, sports ground, etc.); and other organisational considerations, such as a Tourist Office and shops offering the basic essentials.

In other words, although perhaps the word 'resort' is not technically true in the sense we traditionally understand it, these *Stations Vertes* are country holiday locations where visiting tourists and holidaymakers are made to feel welcome, and where they may merge with the local life and people while enjoying parts of France which are generally off the beaten track.

This organisation publishes its own official guide (in French) available on request from: La Fédération Française des Stations Vertes de Vacances et des Villages de Neige, Hôtel du Département de la Sarthe, 72040 Le Mans ☎ 43.81.72.72 (please enclose two International Reply Coupons).

Stations Balnéaires (*seaside resorts*)
Some will be familiar places which you may remember from your own early childhood holidays and where, in their turn, you may take your own children. Or they may be the newly created resorts of the Languedoc-Roussillon, where action-packed sporting and activity holidays encourage the young to push their energies to the limits.

Stations d'Hiver (*winter sports resorts*)
Many of the principal skiing resorts have been included, France being the major European destination for alpine and cross-country skiing. The difference between a ski resort and a ski centre is outlined in the Winter Sports section (page 76).

In addition several cities feature out of cultural interest, where stops may be made to see whatever particular treasure is to be found there, be it the stained glass of a cathedral; the ancient tombs of kings and queens; a Roman amphitheatre; or the works of Monet, Sisley or Toulouse-Lautrec. Paris is detailed separately in the Short Breaks section (page 55).

France is divided into 22 metropolitan regions. Since tourist information is dealt with according to these official administrative divisions, this guide has retained them, only combining Alsace and Lorraine, and merging Haute-Normandie (Upper Normandy) and Basse-Normandie (Lower Normandy) into one.
   A general introduction has been written for each of these 20 regions of France, designed to give a flavour of the region, both historically and currently.
   After the introduction, there follow details of the CRT (Comité Régional du Tourisme) and CDT (Comité Départemental du Tourisme) regional and department tourist board offices, to whom the holidaymaker can apply direct (by phone or in writing) for tourist and accommodation literature. In addition, the addresses of the French Loisirs Accueil offices are given (who offer both accommodation and special interest holiday packages), followed by extensive lists of the names and addresses of the specialist UK operators offering self-catering *gîte*, villa or apartment accommodation within the region.

There are 95 *départements* in France (the rough equivalent to a British county), and these are both numbered and named:

01 Ain	22 Côtes-du-Nord	45 Loiret
02 Aisne	23 Creuse	46 Lot
03 Allier	24 Dordogne	47 Lot-et-Garonne
04 Alpes-de-Haute-Provence	25 Doubs	48 Lozère
	26 Drôme	49 Maine-et-Loire
05 Hautes-Alpes	27 Eure	50 Manche
06 Alpes-Maritimes	28 Eure-et-Loir	51 Marne
07 Ardéche	29 Finistère	52 Haute-Marne
08 Ardennes	30 Gard	53 Mayenne
09 Ariège	31 Haute-Garonne	54 Meurthe-et-Moselle
10 Aube	32 Gers	55 Meuse
11 Aude	33 Gironde	56 Morbihan
12 Aveyron	34 Hérault	57 Moselle
13 Bouches-du-Rhône	35 Ille-et-Vilaine	58 Nièvre
14 Calvados	36 Indre	59 Nord
15 Cantal	37 Indre-et-Loire	60 Oise
16 Charente	38 Isère	61 Orne
17 Charente-Maritime	39 Jura	62 Pas-de-Calais
18 Cher	40 Landes	63 Puy-de-Dôme
19 Corrèze	41 Loir-et-Cher	64 Pyrénées-Atlantiques
20A Corse-du-Sud	42 Loire	65 Hautes-Pyrénées
20B Haute-Corse	43 Haute-Loire	66 Pyrénées-Orientales
21 Côte d'Or	44 Loire-Atlantique	67 Bas-Rhin

68 Haut-Rhin
69 Rhône
70 Haute-Saône
71 Saône-et-Loire
72 Sarthe
73 Savoie
74 Haute-Savoie
75 Ville de Paris
76 Seine-Maritime

77 Seine-et-Marne
78 Yvelines
79 Deux-Sèvres
80 Somme
81 Tarn
82 Tarn-et-Garonne
83 Var
84 Vaucluse
85 Vendée

86 Vienne
87 Haute-Vienne
88 Vosges
89 Yonne
90 Territoire de Belfort
91 Essonne
92 Hauts-de-Seine
93 Seine-St-Denis
94 Val-de-Marne
95 Val d'Oise

The region to which each *département* belongs is indicated at the top of every regional introduction.

ALSACE AND LORRAINE

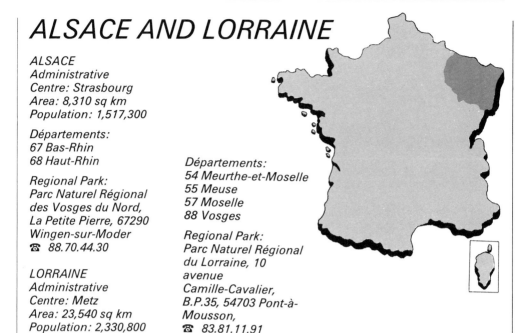

ALSACE
Administrative
Centre: Strasbourg
Area: 8,310 sq km
Population: 1,517,300

Départements:
67 Bas-Rhin
68 Haut-Rhin

Regional Park:
Parc Naturel Régional
des Vosges du Nord,
La Petite Pierre, 67290
Wingen-sur-Moder
☎ 88.70.44.30

LORRAINE
Administrative
Centre: Metz
Area: 23,540 sq km
Population: 2,330,800

Départements:
54 Meurthe-et-Moselle
55 Meuse
57 Moselle
88 Vosges

Regional Park:
Parc Naturel Régional
du Lorraine, 10
avenue
Camille-Cavalier,
B.P.35, 54703 Pont-à-
Mousson,
☎ 83.81.11.91

Alsace and Lorraine are steeped in the history of France and Germany, sandwiched as they are between these two countries. The village of Domrémy in Lorraine was the birthplace of Joan of Arc. The double-barrelled cross of Lorraine was taken by General de Gaulle as the symbol of soon-to-be-freed France. At Strasbourg, Rouget de Lisle composed the song that was to become, during the years of the Revolution, the French national anthem, the *Marseillaise*. In the past hundred years alone, German armies have crossed the Alsace frontier three times (in the Franco-Prussian war of 1870 and in both world wars). Conquest and occupation have followed.

In World War I, Lorraine was the scene of the most appalling carnage, and Verdun, reduced to rubble in 1914-18, is now encircled by silent battlefields, military graveyards and disused forts. The Ossuaire de Douaumont, a mausoleum, houses the bones of 130,000 slain soldiers. Lorraine continues to mourn a nation's and a generation's dead.

Although Alsace, subject to German rule for a greater part of the previous century, remains French at heart, its architecture is half-timbered in style and reminiscent of southern Germany, and the traveller can converse in either German or French. Strasbourg, its capital city, is now the seat of the Council of Europe. Here the memory of ancient and recent wars has finally faded, and sessions of the European Parliament are held at the Palais de l'Europe.

Between Alsace and the Vosges mountains to the west, lie the world-famous wine valleys watered by the upper Rhine. The 140-km *Route du Vin* curls along the foot of the Vosges slopes, linking vineyards with enchanting flower-filled villages like Riquewihr and Kayserberg (where Albert Schweitzer was born), and sending hikers on winding trails up into the hills of the fruity Sylvaner and perfumed Riesling country.

War and industrial activity have, for centuries, scarred the face of much of Lorraine. With today's sense of permanent peace come at last, Nancy, with its eighteenth-century place Stanislas, emerges as one of France's most beautiful cities, and in Metz, the golden sandstone of the thirteenth-century cathedral of St-Etienne matches Strasbourg's pretty canalside quays of La Petite France and the pink sandstone Gothic façade of the cathedral of Notre-Dame.

Strasbourg's watery heart

Suggested tourist routes within the Vosges and following various themes take the motorist to sites of great natural beauty or places of interest:

Route des Lacs: a heart-stopping route through the mountains in the shadow of deep forests with the great lakes as your target.
(Lac de Gérardmer, Lac de Longemer, Lac de Retournemer, Lac des Corbeaux)

Route des Forts: again in the mountains, but following an ancient stategic route which served as the frontier between Lorraine and Franche-Comté. Now, in more peaceful times, the route marks the boundary between the *départements* of Vosges and Haute-Saône. Little frequented, the wild beauty is impressive.
(Remiremont, La Croisette, Fort de Rupt, Col de Mont de Fourche, Col des Croix, Ballon de Servance)

Route des Crêtes et des Chamois: complementing the previous route, this is one of the most beautiful itineraries along the summits of the Vosges and into the natural habitat of the chamois which may still be seen running along the mountainsides. Also including a tour of the lakes on the Alsace slopes, Lac Noir, Lac Blanc and Lac Vert.
(Col du Bonhomme on the N415 then right on the D748, N430, N431 as far as Cernay)

Route de Charme: a short circuit full of rural charm starting from Epinal and following the course of the Moselle.
(Epinal, Girmont, Châtel-sur-Moselle, Portieux, Charmes, Bainville-aux-Miroirs, Haroué, Tantonville, Sion, Diarville, Poussay, Mirecourt, Gugney-aux-Aulx, D39A, Epinal)

Route Thermale: away from the mountains and proceeding ever westward towards the plains, this is a relaxing drive through undulating countryside to taste the waters at Vittel, Contrexéville, Bains-les-Bains and Plombières-les-Bains.
(Remiremont, Plombières-les-Bains, Xertigny, Bains-les-Bains, Hennezel, Darney, Thuillières, Vittel, Contrexéville)

In Alsace, the most famous wine-producing villages can be visited by travelling along the *Route du Vin*:
Route du Vin d'Alsace: running north between Thann and Marlenheim, this motoring itinerary covers many of the prettiest wine-producing villages, and offers the opportunity for tastings and purchases as well as the chance to enjoy the traditional hospitality of the *winstub*.

PRACTICAL TOURIST INFORMATION

Information on Alsace can be obtained by telephoning or writing to either of the tourist board offices listed below, who will supply general information on the region as well as specific booklets detailing camping and hotel accommodation:

Bas-Rhin (67): Office Départemental du Tourisme, Maison du Tourisme, 9 rue de Dôme, B.P.53, 67061 STRASBOURG Cedex ☎ 88.22.01.02
Haut-Rhin (68): Association Départementale du Tourisme (ADT), Hôtel du Département, 68006 COLMAR Cedex ☎ 89.23.21.11

General information on Lorraine can be obtained by writing to the Comité Régional du Tourisme (CRT) office. Specific booklets are produced, detailing camping and hotel accommodation. These can be obtained by writing to the tourist board office of the département *of your choice:*

Regional Tourist Board
Comité Régional du Tourisme (CRT), 1 place St-Clément, B.P.1004, 57036 METZ Cedex
☎ 87.33.60.00

Départements
Meurthe-et-Moselle (54): Association Départementale du Tourisme, 1 rue Mably, B.P.65, 54002 NANCY Cedex ☎ 83.35.56.56
Meuse (55): Comité Départemental du Tourisme (CDT), Hôtel du Département, 55012 BAR-LE-DUC Cedex ☎ 29.79.00.02
Moselle (57): Office Départemental du Tourisme, Hôtel du Département, B.P.1096, 57036 METZ Cedex ☎ 87.32.11.11
Vosges (88): Comité Départemental du Tourisme (CDT), 7 rue Gilbert, B.P.332, 88008 EPINAL Cedex ☎ 29.82.49.93

SELF-CATERING ACCOMMODATION

The following British operators offer self-catering accommodation in the area:

Blakes Holidays, Wroxham, Norwich NR12 8DH ☎ 0603 784131
Chalets de France, Travel House, Pandy, Nr Abergavenny NP7 8DH ☎ 0873 890770
Gîtes de France, 178 Piccadilly, London W1V 9DB ☎ 01-493 3480
Interhome, 383 Richmond Road, Twickenham TW1 2EF ☎ 01-891 1294
Rendez-vous France, Holiday House, 146/148 London Road, St Albans AL1 1PQ ☎ 0727 45400
Slipaway Holidays, 90 Newland Road, Worthing BN1 1LB ☎ 0903 821000
Vacances en Campagne, Bignor, Pulborough RH20 1QD ☎ 07987 433
VFB Holidays, 1 St Margaret's Terrace, Cheltenham GL50 4DT ☎ 0242 526338

SPORTS AND ACTIVITIES

For unusual and interesting holiday ideas, contact the Loisirs Accueil office for the area of your choice:

ALSACE
Loisirs Accueil Haut-Rhin, Hôtel du Département, 68006 COLMAR Cedex ☎ 89.41.41.99
LORRAINE
Loisirs Accueil Moselle, Hôtel du Département, B.P.1096, 57036 METZ Cedex ☎ 87.32.11.11

RESORTS

 Bains-les-Bains *(Vosges)*
Pop: 2,000
Epinal 30 km, Paris 380 km
🛈 place du Bain-Romain ☎ 29.36.31.75

Long-established spa resort situated at the centre of a forested region offering gentle and pleasant theme walks, as well as archery, river and canal fishing, riding and cycling trips.

● Ballooning: ballooning club based here with flights available from Hôtel Les Ombrées ☎ 29.36.31.85
● Boat Hire: the Canal de l'Est offers 97 km of navigable waterways as far as Nancy to the north. Operating from Fontenoy-le-Château, very close by, boats can be hired from S.A. Navigu'est, Fontenoy-le-Château, 88240 Bains-les-Bains ☎ 29.36.31.47
● Camping: Les Pins ☎ 29.36.33.51
● Casino: place de l'Hôtel de Ville.
● Spa: circulatory disorders (16 Apr-12 Oct) ☎ 29.36.32.04 alt: 300 m, climate: fresh.

 La Bresse *(Vosges)*
Pop: 6,000
Alt: 630-1,366 m
Epinal 55 km, Paris 413 km
🛈 21 quai des Iranées ☎ 29.25.41.29

Main winter sports resort in eastern France, La Bresse boasts 70 per cent artificial snow-cover on the Vologne-Chitelet runs, with skiing pistes for all levels of ability and cross-country runs.

● Camping: Belle Hutte ☎ 29.25.49.75
● Climbing: several local peaks include Col de la Grosse Pierre, Crête du Hohneck et de la Martinswand, Les Roches Betty and La Verbruche. Details are available from the Tourist Office.
● Riding: Pré de la Seille ☎ 29.25.44.57

🏛 **Colmar** *(Haut-Rhin)*
Pop: 65,000
Strasbourg 71 km, Paris 440 km
🛈 4 rue des Unterlinden ☎ 89.41.02.29

Large and busy commercial city with a charming old centre of typical Alsatian architecture. Situated at the heart of the plain of Alsace, close to the foothills of the Vosges, Colmar is ideal as a base for excursions. It is, for example, at the start of the *Route du Vin* which meanders through some of the prettiest wine-producing villages in the area. The birthplace of sculptor Bartholdi, creator of the world-famous Statue of Liberty, Colmar is also the home for the fifteenth-century Issenheim altar piece by Grünewald, in the Unterlinden museum.

- Ballooning: and helicopter and light aircraft trips available from Colmar Aerodrome on Saturday afternoons in summer. Bookable through the Tourist Office.
- Camping: Camping de l'Ill ☎ 89.41.15.94
- Cycling: cycles for hire from the SNCF station.

 Contrexéville *(Vosges)*
Pop: 6,000
Epinal 48 km, Paris 339 km
☐ Galeries Thermales ☎ 29.08.08.68

Large and highly organised health and spa resort adjacent to Vittel, set in a wooded valley and offering regular cultural events, as well as many sporting activities, including tennis, riding and cycling trips. Casino.

- Camping: Municipal ☎ 29.08.15.06
- Cycling: cycles for hire from the SNCF station.
- Fishing: and boating on the large lake.
- Golf: see Vittel.
- Riding: Cheval Vert, route de Vittel ☎ 29.08.08.68
- Spa: kidneys/urinary disorders (15 Apr-15 Oct) ☎ 29.08.03.24 alt: 350 m, climate: fresh.
- Walking: accompanied theme walks are available. Enquire at the Tourist Office.

Gérardmer *(Vosges)*
Pop: 10,000
Alt: 666-1,113 m
Epinal 40 km, Paris 400 km
☐ place des Déportés ☎ 29.63.08.74

Heavily damaged in 1944, this town, in the heart of the Vosges mountains, has now become a lively winter and summer resort with exceptional sports and entertainment facilities. Downhill and cross-country skiing in winter, while in summer the lush, green Vallée des Lacs, both here and at neighbouring Xonrupt-Longemer, offers extensive watersports and fishing. For those who visit in April, a mass of yellow carpets the meadows as the daffodils appear. Millions are picked by the local children in preparation for the Fête des Jonquilles on the Sunday closest to 20 April – a floral spectacular.

- Camping: Ramberchamp ☎ 29.63.03.82 on the lakeside.
- Casino: rue d'Epinal ☎ 29.63.14.45
- Climbing: there is a climbing school here and further information is available from the Town Hall (La Mairie) ☎ 29.63.32.23
- Cycling: cycles for hire from the SNCF station

- Golf: (at 40 km) 18h flat, treeless public course, ideal for beginners at Golf d'Epinal, rue du Merle Blanc, 88001 Epinal ☎ 29.34.65.97
- Riding: Centre de Ramberchamp, route de Sapois ☎ 29.55.22.82

 Heudicourt *(Meuse)*
Metz 60 km, Paris 290 km
☐ place des Halles ☎ 29.89.31.71

The enormous Lake Madine (7,448 hectares) near Nonsard has room enough for everyone, whatever their interest. Birdlife is well protected here, with a large nature reserve away from the shores where there is a busy sailing club. Good bathing, as well as riding, archery, tennis, fishing, canoe and pedalo-hire, ensures the popularity of this outdoor leisure base set in the middle of open countryside.

- Camping: at Nonsard, Camping des Aires ☎ 29.89.56.76 and at Heudicourt, Camping des Passons ☎ 29.89.36.08
- Golf: 9h public course at Golf de Madine, Nonsard, 55210 Vigneulles ☎ 29.89.32.50
- Riding: Complexe Equestre de Madine at Heudicourt ☎ 29.89.57.81 and at Vigneulles-les-Hattonchâtel ☎ 29.89.34.55. Trips in horse-drawn caravans are available at Les Eparges from Cheval en Meuse ☎ 29.87.35.69

Le Hohwald *(Bas-Rhin)*
Pop: 400
Alt: 600-1,100 m
Strasbourg 50 km, Paris 430 km
☐ SI ☎ 88.08.30.90

Health and winter sports resort high in the mountains, with wonderful signposted hikes amidst beech and fir tree forests and a spectacular 30-m waterfall an easy walk away.

- Camping: Municipal ☎ 88.08.30.90
- Walking: over 70 km of signposted paths with panorama points at Champ du Feu (6 km), Grande Belle Vue (3 km) and Grande Ceinture (3.5 km).

 Lunéville *(Meurthe-et-Moselle)*
Pop: 24,000
Nancy 30 km, Paris 335 km
☐ Aile Sud du Château ☎ 83.74.06.55

Stroll around the old town, enjoy the summer events in the parks and, between June and September, the late night *son-et-lumière* at the eighteenth-century château. Inspired in design by Versailles and, indeed, preferred to the original by Voltaire, it is set amid lovely formal gardens (les Bosquets).

- Golf: see Nancy.
- Riding: Centre Equestre de Lunéville, la Petite Fourasse ☎ 83.73.11.26 and Relais Equestre de la Vigne, Cirey-sur-Vézouze ☎ 83.42.52.66

Metz *(Moselle)*
Pop: 120,000
Nancy 56 km, Paris 330 km
🇫 place d'Armes ☎ 87.75.65.21

Metz's splendid golden sandstone cathedral of St-Etienne, famous for its brilliant stained glass and its vaulted ceilings, dominates the city and the Moselle valley. A university town and commercial centre, the flower-filled city spreads its colour through attractive gardens beside the river.

● Camping: Camping de Metz ☎ 87.32.42.49
● Golf: 9h private parkland course at Golf de Metz Cherisey, Château de Cherisey, 57420 Verny ☎ 87.52.70.18

 Molsheim *(Bas-Rhin)*
Pop: 7,000
Saverne 28 km, Paris 475 km
🇫 17 place de l'Hôtel de Ville ☎ 88.38.11.61

A picturesque town lying along the *Route du Vin*, on the River Bruche at the foot of the Vosges. An ancient university town, first mentioned in the eighth century, Molsheim is set amongst vineyards, its old ramparts enclosing very old streets. At its heart there is the central square, the Renaissance La Metzig building with its clock tower, fountains and old houses with storks nesting in their rooftops. Molsheim once housed the Bugatti factory which is now a museum in the Cours de Chartreux and can be visited. The *Parc à Cigognes* (storks) is also worth a trip.

● Camping: Camping Municipal ☎ 88.38.11.67

 Munster (Haut-Rhin)
Pop: 5,000
Strasbourg 83 km, Paris 520 km
🇫 place de la Salle des Fêtes ☎ 88.77.31.80

To the east of the *Route des Crêtes* (the Ridge Road), the Munster valley is watered by the River Fecht, with Munster an ideal centre for excursions to the Vosges mountains or for walking and riding in the Lorraine nature park of forests and lakes. The Ridge Road used to service the front line in World War I, today it is a popular tourist route, sending roads and trails into the upper Vosges with little farm inns along the way. Nearby at Gunsbach, on the left bank of the Fecht, is the house of Albert Schweitzer.

● Ballooning: Ballons d'Alsace, 4 rue Hohrod, 68140 Munster ☎ 89.77.22.81 offer unforgettable half-day flights (with certificate).
● Camping: Camping Municipal ☎ 89.77.31.08

 Nancy *(Meurthe-et-Moselle)*
Pop: 100,000
Metz 57 km, Paris 294 km
🇫 place Stanislas ☎ 83.35.22.41

The elegant city of Nancy owes its renown to the place Stanislas, a magnificent eighteenth-century square linked to the place de la Carrière by a triumphal archway. The historic capital of Lorraine, on the River Meurthe, Nancy has a lovely centre with baroque fountains, ornate gateways, grilles and decorated lanterns, the whole magically lit by night, including the old quarter with its ancient Grande Rue.

● Art: the Musée des Beaux Arts houses a fine collection of French paintings.
● Camping: Municipal, Villers-lès-Nancy ☎ 83.27.18.28
● Canoeing: Ligue Lorraine ☎ 83.33.15.57
● Golf: attractive woodland 18h private course at Golf de Nancy, 54460 Liverdun ☎ 83.24.53.87 (closed Mon)
● Riding: Centre Equestre de l'Esch, Jezainville ☎ 83.82.15.14

 Niederbronn-les-Bains *(Bas-Rhin)*
Pop: 5,000
Strasbourg 45 km, Paris 458 km
🇫 place de l'Hôtel de Ville ☎ 88.09.17.00

Health resort in an idyllic setting of lush, rolling countryside at the heart of the Northern Vosges Regional Park and at the foot of Grand Wintersberg, the highest summit in the range. Founded by the Romans, who discovered the mineral springs here, Niederbronn is a residential town which has developed into a well-known health resort, its *curistes* attracted by this picturesque and historic region close to Germany. Casino.

● Camping: Camping Heidenkopf ☎ 88.09.08.46
● Riding: Relais Equestre des Vosges du Nord ☎ 88.72.85.73
● Spa: rheumatism/bone joint damage (open all year) ☎ 88.09.60.55
alt: 250 m climate: mild. Two other smaller spas close by, and also specialising in rheumatism/bone joint damage, are Merkwiller-Pechelbronn (Mar-Dec) ☎ 88.80.70.11 and Morsbronn-les-Bains (open all year) ☎ 88.09.31.91
● Walking: trails through the wooded range (GR53 crosses).
● War Graves: German Cemetery (1939-45) located on a hill east of the town, has 15,148 graves of German soldiers who fell in the region during World War II.

 Obernai *(Bas-Rhin)*
Pop: 10,000
Strasbourg 30 km, Paris 485 km
🇫 Chapelle du Beffroi ☎ 88.95.64.13

Picturesque old town on the *Route du Vin*, with narrow streets and pretty half-timbered houses, their window boxes overflowing with flowers. The birthplace of Ste-Odile, patron saint of Alsace, the Mont-Ste-Odile monastery, with its magnificent site and panorama, is also something of a pilgrimage site. Cycling, riding and walking are

Storks' nest

popular pursuits in this area of vine-covered hillsides, with the complementary pleasures of sauerkraut, pastries and white wine promised for the evenings.

● Camping: Camping Municipal ☎ 88.95.38.48
● Vineyards: follow the signed paths through the heart of the vineyards. These describe the work of the grower and allow the visitor to experience the colours and fragrance of the world of the grape.
● Winter Sports: resorts at Le Champ du Feu and Le Hohwald.

 Orbey *(Haut-Rhin)*
Pop: 3,000
Alt: 500-1,300 m
Colmar 25 km, Paris 500 km
🚩 OTSI du Canton de Lapoutroie-Val d'Orbey
☎ 89.71.33.11

Small tourist town and winter cross-country skiing centre, close to the Col du Bonhomme peak. An excellent walking base in an area of deep forests and beautiful lakes, and perfect for excursions along the *Route des Crêtes*.

● Camping: Camping Municipal ☎ 89.71.27.69
● War Graves: cemetery of Mountain Light Infantry (2,146 French dead). The ridges and trenches of Le Linge (or Lingkopf) battlefield (1914-18).

 La Petite Pierre *(Bas-Rhin)*
Pop: 800
Strasbourg 60 km, Paris 430 km
🚩 22 rue Principale ☎ 88.70.42.30

This tiny village, perched on a rocky promontory, is situated in the midst of the Regional Park, a beautiful forested area of beech, pine and oak where deer and wild boar roam. It is a perfect base for those seeking magnificent panoramas, rural tranquillity and traditional hospitality.

● Camping: Camping Imsterfeld.
● Cuisine: 1 hr 30 min demonstration on the theme of cooking with Alsace wines using a family recipe for Coq au Riesling d'Alsace, passed down through three generations at the Hôtel/Restaurant des Vosges, 30 rue Principale ☎ 88.70.45.05. A three-day (2 hrs per day) traditional Alsace cooking course is offered by the Hôtel/Restaurant Lion d'Or, 15 rue Principale ☎ 88.70.45.06 (Feb-Mar).
● Riding: La Cavalcade, Sparsbach ☎ 88.89.67.81
● Walking: the rambling club, Club Vosgien, has marked walks throughout this area, and there are accompanied walks if required.

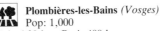 **Plombières-les-Bains** *(Vosges)*
Pop: 1,000
Epinal 30 km, Paris 400 km
🚩 16 rue Stanislas ☎ 29.66.01.30

Mineral springs have been in use here since Roman times. In the last two centuries this pretty town, attractively situated deep in the peaceful wooded valley, became a fashionable resort frequented by figures of French nobility and literary society. Today, with its elegant buildings and full calendar of sporting and cultural events, the town still attracts a large clientele. Leisure facilities include archery, tennis, riding and fishing.

● Boat Trips: 3-hr canal trips leave on Friday and Saturday afternoons from the port of Fontenay-le-Château (7 km).
● Camping: Camping Municipal ☎ 29.66.00.71
● Casino: promenade du Casino.
● Golf: see Epinal.
● Riding: Relais Equestre, route d'Aillevillers ☎ 29.66.00.24
● Spa: digestive organs (May-Sep) ☎ 29.66.01.58 alt: 450 m, climate: fresh.

Remiremont *(Vosges)*
Pop: 12,000
Epinal 27 km, Paris 386 km
✆ 2 place Henri-Utard ☎ 29.62.23.70

Situated on the Moselle river, Remiremont is a pleasant small town typical of the region, although the unusual arcaded shopping area and fountains are a feature. Surrounded by the fir-covered Vosges mountains, this is a land of peaceful villages and fast-running streams.

● Camping: La Demoiselle ☎ 29.62.23.60
● Fishing: category 2 fishing on the Moselle river.
● Riding: La Grange Puton, route d'Hérival ☎ 29.62.52.73
● Walking: an excellent walking area with easy access to the main summits of the Vosges range.

Ribeauvillé *(Haut-Rhin)*
Pop: 5,000
Colmar 15 km, Paris 430 km
✆ 1 Grand'rue ☎ 89.73.62.22

One of the prettiest towns on the *Route du Vin*, famed for its Riesling and Gewurztraminer wines, Ribeauvillé sits at the feet of the three ruined châteaux of Giersberg, St-Ulrich and Le Ht-Ribeau-Pierre. With interesting old houses and fountains to catch the eye, this is very much a tourist centre, with a wine fair held on the penultimate weekend in July.

● Camping: Camping Pierre de Courbetin ☎ 89.73.66.71 and Camping des Trois Châteaux ☎ 89.73.60.26

Riquewihr *(Haut-Rhin)*
Pop: 1,000
Colmar 13 km, Paris 431 km
✆ 2 rue de la 1ère Armée ☎ 89.47.80.80 (Apr-Nov)

In the foothills of the Vosges, this is one of the prettiest and best preserved medieval villages, with interesting houses and courtyards, and surrounded by some of the best vineyards.

● Camping: Camping Intercommunal ☎ 89.47.90.08
● Vineyards: enquire at the Tourist Office about tastings and follow the *Route du Vin* for the Muscat, Riesling, Tokay and Gewurztraminer varieties.
● Walking: in the pine and chestnut forests nearby.

St-Dié *(Vosges)*
Pop: 25,000
Epinal 50 km, Paris 460 km
✆ 32 rue Thiers ☎ 29.56.17.62

St-Dié, like Gérardmer nearby, was burned down in 1944 during the war. Reconstruction of the town and of its characteristic red sandstone buildings has created a large town surrounded by pretty hills with magnificent views from the wooded mountains. A very good centre for motoring or walking trips into the surrounding country and well positioned, too, for winter sports at Gérardmer and Le Hohwald.

● Camping: La Vanne-de-Pierre ☎ 29.56.23.56
● Caving: and potholing with the Spéléo Club de la Haute Meurthe, 17 rue d'Helliueule.
● Cycling: cycles for hire from the SNCF station.
● Fishing: category 1 fishing on the Meurthe river.
● Riding: Ferme de la Ballone ☎ 29.52.22.82
● Walking: and climbing with Club Alpin, chemin de l'Orme ☎ 29.56.13.17

Saverne *(Bas-Rhin)*
Pop: 10,000
Strasbourg 40 km, Paris 450 km
✆ Château des Rohan ☎ 88.91.80.47

Tranquil town of old timbered houses typical of the region. The majestically beautiful eighteenth-century Château des Rohan, known as the 'Alsatian Versailles', sits on a bend in the canal de la Marne au Rhin which cuts through the town. Numerous excursions are possible from Saverne, including a visit to the ruins of the fortress Château du Haut-Barr situated high on a rocky crag and commanding a magnificent panoramic view over the northern Vosges mountains and the plain of Alsace. Nearby Dabo is a popular small resort, set in woodlands and perfect for walks.

● Boat Trips: day cruises outward by boat, return by coach; bookable through the Tourist Office.
● Camping: Camping Municipal ☎ 88.91.35.65
● Cycling: cycles for hire from the SNCF station.
● Fishing: in the Ramsthal pool (Apr-Sep)
● Riding: Club Hippique ☎ 88.91.18.93

Strasbourg *(Bas-Rhin)*
Pop: 254,000
Paris 488 km
❶ 9 rue du Dôme ☎ 88.22.01.02 and place de la Gare ☎ 88.32.51.49

Seat of the Council of Europe and major commercial centre, Strasbourg is a marvellously conserved medieval city, with paths winding through La Petite France, an attractive area of canals and bridges with old half-timbered houses and flowered balconies. The massive cathedral of red sandstone towers over Alsace and features *son-et-lumière* performances, with quays, bridges and public buildings floodlit by night.

- Boat Hire: cruises lasting three or six days can take you along the Rhine into Germany and Holland. Details from Alsace Croisières ☎ 88.32.44.55
- Boat Trips: guided trips along River Ill.
- Camping: Camping Baggersee ☎ 88.39.03.40
- Cycling: cycles for hire from the SNCF station.
- Golf: fine woodland 18h private course at Golf de Strasbourg, route du Rhin, 67400 Illkirch Graffenstaden ☎ 88.66.17.22 (closed Tues).

 Les Trois Epis *(Haut-Rhin)*
Colmar 12 km, Paris 440 km
❶ SI ☎ 89.49.80.56

Situated high amongst the pine trees, this is a summer resort primarily for those who want to enjoy the impressive countryside in an atmosphere of calm. There are picturesque paths to walk. A religious site, it is here that the Virgin Mary is reputed to have appeared in 1491 to some local men.

- Walking: 50 km of marked paths.

 Ventron *(Vosges)*
Pop: 1,000
Alt: 600-1,200 m
Epinal 57 km, Paris 415 km
❶ SI ☎ 29.24.07.02

Small family winter sports resort at the heart of the Vosges mountains, close to the Alsace border and to Bussang, a similar small resort popular as a base in the spring and autumn for walkers who can hike up to the rounded mountain top of the Ballon d'Alsace.

- Camping: (at Bussang) Les Deux Rivières ☎ 29.61.50.36
- Theatre: the People's Theatre at Bussang, Le Théâtre du Peuple, seats 1,200 and is made entirely of wood. As its stage backdrop, it has the mountains! Performances every Sunday in August ☎ 29.61.50.48

 Verdun *(Meuse)*
Pop: 25,000
Metz 66 km, Paris 260 km
❶ place de la Nation ☎ 29.84.18.85

As a memorial to those who fell in World War I, Verdun has become one of the most famous tourist sites in the world; a place of quiet meditation. At the entrance to the Regional Park of North Vosges, there is also the unspoilt countryside to explore by foot, boat or along cycling paths.

- Boat Hire: barges can be hired to depart from Verdun for one-way canal cruises to Bar-le-Duc, Charleville-Mézières or Lutzelbourg and are bookable through Navilor Plaisance, 102 rue du Canal, Lutzelbourg ☎ 87.25.37.07
- Battlefields and Memorials: many group guided tours are available; bookable through the Tourist Office.
- Cycling: cycles can be hired from the SNCF station.
- Golf: (approx 40 km distant at Bar-le-Duc) 9h private course at Golf de Combles Bar-le-Duc, 55000 Combles-en-Barrois ☎ 29.45.16.03
- Walking: GR14 through the Verdun forest.

 Vittel *(Vosges)*
Pop: 7,000
Epinal 42 km, Paris 344 km
❶ place Badenweiller ☎ 29.08.12.72

Such is the international renown of the springs that feed this health resort that the bottling plant here now produces over 800 million bottles of mineral water annually for world-wide consumption. Surrounded by vast areas of landscaped park, on some of which polo is played, this is an all-year rest and recuperation centre in the loveliest of locations, with facilities so good that they are used by those in training for the Olympics.

- Camping: Municipal ☎ 29.08.02.71
- Casino: avenue Bouloumié.
- Golf: 18h private course set in the hills at Golf de Vittel, 88800 Vittel ☎ 29.08.18.80 (closed Nov-Mar and vulnerable to flooding).
- Riding: Centre Equestre du Club Méditerranée ☎ 29.08.18.80
- Spa: kidneys/urinary disorders (open all year) ☎ 29.08.00.00 alt: 335 m, climate: temperate.

AQUITAINE

Administrative
Centre: Bordeaux
Area: 41,407 sq km
Population: 2,550,300

Départements:
24 Dordogne
33 Gironde
40 Landes
47 Lot-et-Garonne
64 Pyrénées-
    Atlantiques

Regional Park:
Parc Naturel Régional
des Landes de
Gascogne, 15 place
Jean-Jaurès, 40000
Mont-de-Marsan
☎ 58.06.24.25

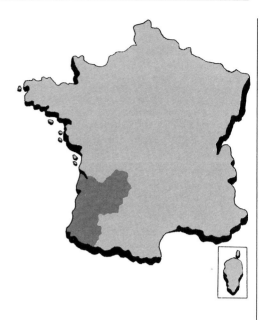

The rain falls on the French slopes of the Pyrénées making them green and lush. By contrast, the rocky Spanish flanks are scorched brown by the sun and wind. The range, running east and west, is pierced by high cols and mountain passes, some snowed up for three months of the year.

The mountains rise modestly at first from the Atlantic coast, a comfortable blue backdrop in the distance viewed from the surf beaches of Biarritz and St-Jean-de-Luz or from the graceful Basque capital Bayonne. This is the country where the game of *pelote* is played, and also of the Basque *corridas,* bullfights in which the bull survives to go through it all again another day.

To the east, the peaks begin to tower on high. At La Rhune the lookout point takes in the wooded sweep of forest, the ocean in the background and beyond, to the north, the far sands of Les Landes.

At St-Jean-Pied-de-Port, on the old pilgrim route to Santiago de Compostela in Spain, the Forêt d'Iraty offers the sheerest rocks for climbing, a wealth of hiking trails in summer (*sentiers de pays*) and cross-country ski routes in winter.

From the Spanish border north to the point of the Gironde estuary in Medoc, there are some 250 km of sandy coast – claimed by some to be the longest beach in the world. Les Landes de Gascogne (the moors of Gascony) were once marsh and scrubland, poor country with poor people scratching a livelihood from it. Then there came the afforestation of the area, with conifers and sea-grasses to hold the gritty coast in place. The protective trees became seven million hectares of timber forests and a new industry was born. The moors, no longer wind-blasted, became gentler territory. Beaches developed. The wealthy from Paris and Bordeaux built holiday homes here, a Bordeaux playground in a new and piquant environment. Today there are family resorts like Pyla-sur-Mer, or the more fashionable resorts of Arcachon and Hossegor.

Aquitaine has always had a strong historical link with England since the dynastic marriage of Eleanor of Aquitaine to Henry II. Before that there were strong trade links. Bordeaux, on the swiftest route to Rome, was a convenient port for the import of English and Welsh gold, tin and iron and for the export of Aquitaine's own treasure, wine. Richard Coeur de Lion was created Duke of Aquitaine, and by the time that the child who was to be Richard II was born in Bordeaux, it was Bordeaux rather than Poitiers that had become the capital of the country. When, finally, the

English were driven from France, Aquitaine, or Gascony (or 'Guienne' as the English called it), was the last English territory held in France.

The English link survives to this day. There are English wine firms operating in Bordeaux. A trace still remains of a 'special relationship'. Bordeaux wine ('clairet' as the English knew it), is world-renowned. The names of small villages in the Medoc are familiar to diners across the world from their wine lists. Medoc, St-Emilion, Graves, St-Julien, Entre-Deux-Mers and Sauternes, relatively small geographical locations around the Gironde estuary, bear the proud names of Bordeaux wine itself.

Bordeaux, the natural heart of this great industry, speaks with authority on all matters connected with the grape. It is situated 96 km inland, up the Gironde estuary, and its Quai des Chartrons and Quai de Bacalon are the bases for the *négociants*, the men and firms who buy and sell, grade and store the wine and maintain the Bordeaux name and reputation in the wine world.

The Medoc is a thin stretch of stony ground, 64 km long by 8 km broad, to the north of Bordeaux and between the Gironde banks and the sea. From this unpromising but pine-sheltered terrain great wines have come over the centuries. The châteaux of the Medoc are not always the impressive buildings found in the upper valley of the Loire; often they are ancient strongholds or no more than country houses, farm buildings, even barns. In the context of wine-making, however, the word château honours the yield of the vineyard rather than its buildings. The names on any wine list speak for themselves: Château Margaux, Château Beychevelle (a beautiful fifteenth-century building), Château d'Issan (one of the oldest châteaux in the Medoc) and, in the famous vineyard area of Pauillac, the three splendid names of Château Latour, Château Lafite and Château Mouton-Rothschild.

The vineyards of St-Emilion, near the junction of the Rivers Isle and Dordogne and the ancient fortified town of Libourne, produce as much wine as Burgundy itself, a rich velvety wine of great quality. St-Emilion is a small cluster of pink houses tumbled together on a hill rising above the vineyards, with cobbled streets threading through a charming and unspoilt township. The wines of Entre-Deux-Mers come from vineyards set in the rolling hills and dales between the Dordogne and the Garonne, with *bastide* towns here as in the Dordogne to the east, Sauveterre and Creon being the best known. The region of Graves is as well known for its red wines (Château Haut-Brion) as for its white (Château La Brède – a modest enough wine but a superb moated château). The lush uplands of the Sauternais, further to the south, in the small communes of Barsac, Bommes and Sauternes, produce those exquisite, golden sweet Sauternes wines, the greatest of them that of the twelfth-century Château d'Yquem. The wine of Lot-et-Garonne is less distinguished than that of its neighbours. The speciality here is not the grape but the prune.

The countryside here attracts many visitors: canoeists at Temple-sur-Lot; walkers along the *sentiers du pays* between Granges-sur-Lot and Ste-Livrade; to the medieval flowered villages of Montpezat, Pujols and Penne and the Château de Bonaguil; to the *bastide* towns of Damazan, Vianne and Bazas and the city of Nerac, capital of the Kingdom of Navarre, its mannered court the setting for Shakespeare's *Love's Labour's Lost*.

The cave dwellings in the valley of the Vézère, tributary of the Dordogne, are often regarded as the 'cradle of European man', for the Cro-Magnon period of Lascaux reaches back some 30,000 years into pre-history. Between the Dordogne and the Lot, the *bastides*, fortified walled towns, some English-built, some French, mark the rivalries and conflicts of the Hundred Years War between France and England, as do the châteaux and churches of the Dordogne valley itself. Unlike the châteaux of the Loire, those of the Dordogne were little touched by the elegant Renaissance hand; they remain rugged strongholds, sometimes partly ruined, not royal palaces or even museums of decorative furniture and tapestries, but essentially relics of the bloody sieges of the Middle Ages. The medieval feel of the region is most vividly preserved in the towns and villages of the river valleys, Sarlat, Domme and Monpazier being outstanding examples. Without the history or the pre-history of the Dordogne region, however, visitors would still be drawn to these river verges by the sheer beauty of the country, its winding rivers, its lofty wooded hills and by the tranquillity of life here.

PRACTICAL TOURIST INFORMATION

General information on the region can be obtained by telephoning or writing to the Comité Régional du Tourisme (CRT) office, while specific booklets are produced detailing camping, hotel and self-catering gîte *accommodation. These can be obtained by writing to the tourist board office for the* département *(CDT) of your choice:*

Regional Tourist Board
Comité Régional du Tourisme (CRT), 24 allées de Tourny, 33000 BORDEAUX ☎ 56.44.48.02

Départements
Dordogne (24): Comité Départemental du Tourisme (CDT), 16 rue du Président-Wilson, 24000 PERIGUEUX ☎ 53.53.44.35
Gironde (33): Comité Départemental du Tourisme (CDT), 21 cours de l'Intendance, 33000 BORDEAUX Cedex ☎ 56.52.61.40
Landes (40): Comité Départemental du Tourisme (CDT), B.P.407, 22 rue Victor-Hugo, 40012 MONT-DE-MARSAN Cedex ☎ 58.46.40.40
Lot-et-Garonne (47): Comité Départemental du Tourisme (CDT), 4 rue André-Chénier, B.P.158, 47005 AGEN ☎ 53.66.14.14
Pyrénées-Atlantiques (64): Comité Départemental du Tourisme (CDT), Maison de Tourisme, rue Jean-Jacques de Monnaix, 64000 PAU ☎ 59.31.01.30

SELF-CATERING ACCOMMODATION

The following British operators offer self-catering accommodation in the area:

Agencefrance Holidays, Lansdowne Place, 17 Holdenhurst Road, Bournemouth BH8 8EH ☎ 0202 299534
Air France Holidays, 69 Boston Manor Road, Brentford TW8 9JQ ☎ 01-568 6981
Allez France, 27 West Street, Storrington, Pulborough RH20 4DZ ☎ 09066 2345
Angel Travel, 47 High Street, Central Chambers, Tonbridge TN9 1SD ☎ 0732 361115
Aquitaine Holidays, 19 Bossiney Place, Fishermead, Milton Keynes MK6 2EF ☎ 0908 606921
AA Motoring Holidays, P.O. Box 100, Fanum House, Halesowen B63 3BT ☎ 021-550 7401
Avon Europe, Lower Quinton, Stratford-on-Avon, Warks CV37 8SG ☎ 0789 720130
Beach Villas, 8 Market Passage, Cambridge CB2 3QR ☎ 0223 311113
Blakes Holidays, Wroxham, Norwich NR12 8DH ☎ 0603 784131

Bowhills Ltd, Swanmore, Southampton SO3 2QW ☎ 0489 877627
Brittany Ferries, The Brittany Centre, Wharf Road, Portsmouth PO2 8RU ☎ 0705 827701
C'est la Vie en France, 16 Seaside Place, Aberdour, Fife KY3 0TX ☎ 0383 860180
Carasol Holidays, 6 Hayes Avenue, Bournemouth BH7 7AD ☎ 0202 33398
Chalets de France, Travel House, Pandy, Nr Abergavenny NP7 8DH ☎ 0873 890770
Cresta Holidays, 32 Victoria Street, Altrincham WA14 1ET ☎ 0345 056511
Crystal Holiday Villas, The Courtyard, Arlington Road, Surbiton KT6 6BW ☎ 01-399 5144
Dominique's Villas, 2 Peterborough Mews, London SW6 3BL ☎ 01-736 1664
Eurovillas, 36 East Street, Coggleshall, Colchester CO6 1SH ☎ 0376 61156
Four Seasons, Springield, Farsley, Pudsey LS28 5UT ☎ 0532 564374
La France des Villages, Model Farm, Rattlesden, Bury St Edmunds IP30 0SY ☎ 044 93 7664
France Directe, 2 Church Street, Warwick CV34 4AB ☎ 0926 497989
France Voyages, 145 Oxford Street, London W1R 1TB ☎ 01-494 3155
Francophile Holidays, 9 Sheaf Street, Daventry NN1 4AA ☎ 0327 78103
Freedom in France, Meadows, Poughill, Bude, Cornwall EX23 9EN ☎ 0288 55591
French Affair, 34 Lillie Road, London SW6 1TU ☎ 01-799 1077
French Life Motoring Holidays, 26 Church Road, Horsforth, Leeds LS18 5LG ☎ 0532 390077
French Travel Service, Georgian House, 69 Boston Manor Road, Brentford TW8 0JQ ☎ 01-568 8442
French Villa Centre, 175 Selsdon Park Road, Croydon CR2 8JJ ☎ 01-651 1231
Gîtes de France, 178 Piccadilly, London W1V 9DB ☎ 01-493 3480
Hoseasons, Sunway House, Lowestoft NR32 3LT ☎ 0502 500555
Hoverspeed, Maybrook House, Queens Gardens, Dover CT17 9UQ ☎ 0304 240241
Intasun France, Intasun House, Cromwell Avenue, Bromley BR2 9AQ ☎ 01-290 1900
Interhome, 383 Richmond Road, Twickenham TW1 2EF ☎ 01-891 1294
Just France, 1 Belmont, Lansdown Road, Bath BA1 5DZ ☎ 0225 446328
Kingsland Holidays, 1 Pounds Park Road, Plymouth PL3 4QP ☎ 0752 766822
Meon Villas, Meon House, College Street, Petersfield GU32 3JN ☎ 0730 68411
Miss France Holidays, 132 Anson Road, London NW2 6AP ☎ 01-452 7409
David Newman's French Collection, P.O. Box 333, 40 Upperton Road, Eastbourne BN21 4AW

☎ 0323 410347
Par-Tee Tours, Riverside House, 53 Uxbridge Road, Rickmansworth WD3 2DH ☎ 0923 721565
Pleasurewood Holidays,Somerset House, Gordon Road, Lowestoft NR32 1PZ ☎ 0502 517271
La Première Quality Villas, Solva, Haverfordwest SA62 6YE ☎ 03483 7871
Prime Time Holidays, 5a Market Square, Northampton NN1 2DL ☎ 0604 20996
Les Propriétaires de l'Ouest, Malton House, 24 Hampshire Terrace, Portsmouth PO1 2QE ☎ 0705 755715
Quo Vadis, 243 Euston Road, London NW1 2BT ☎ 01-583 8383
Rendez-Vous France, Holiday House, 146/148 London Road, St Albans AL1 1PQ ☎ 0727 45400
Rentavilla, 27 High Street, Chesterton, Cambridge CB4 1NB ☎ 0223 323414
Sally Tours, Argyle Centre, York Street, Ramsgate CT11 9DS ☎ 0843 595566
SFV Holidays, Summer House, 68 Hernes Road, Summertown, Oxford OX2 7QL ☎ 0865 57738
Slipaway Holidays, 90 Newland Road, Worthing BN11 1LB ☎ 0903 821000
Starvillas, 25 High Street, Chesterton, Cambridge CB4 1ND ☎ 0223 311990
Sturge, Martin, 3 Lower Camden Place, Bath BA1 5JJ ☎ 0225 310623
Sun France, 3 Beaufort Gardens, London SW16 3BP ☎ 01-679 4562
Sunvista Holidays, 5a George Street, Warminster BA12 8QA ☎ 0985 217444
Tourarc UK, 197b Brompton Road, London SW3 1LA ☎ 01-589 1918
Vacances, 28 Gold Street, Saffron Walden CB10 1EJ ☎ 0799 25101
Vacances en Campagne, Bignor, Pulborough RH20 1QD ☎ 07987 433
Vacances France, 14 Bowthorpe Road, Wisbech PE13 2DX ☎ 0945 587830
Vacations, 60 Charles Street, Leicester LE1 1FB ☎ 0533 537758
VFB Holidays, 1 St Margaret's Terrace, Cheltenham GL50 4DT ☎ 0242 526338
Villa France, 15 Winchcombe Road, Frampton Cotterel, Bristol BS17 2AG ☎ 0454 772410

SPORTS AND ACTIVITIES

For unusual and interesting holiday ideas, contact the Loisirs Accueil office for the area of your choice:

Loisirs Accueil Dordogne-Périgord, 16 rue Président-Wilson, 24009 PERIGUEUX ☎ 53.53.44.35
Maison du Périgord, 30 rue Louis-le-Grand, 75002 PARIS ☎ 47.02.09.15
Loisirs Accueil Gironde, 21 cours de l'Intendance, 33000 BORDEAUX ☎ 56.52.61.40
Loisirs Accueil Landes, B.P.407, 22 rue Victor-Hugo, 40012 MONT-DE-MARSAN Cedex ☎ 58.46.40.40

RESORTS

 Andernos-les-Bains *(Gironde)*
Pop: 6,000
Arcachon 40 km, Paris 627 km
🄳 33 avenue Général-de-Gaulle ☎ 56.82.02.95

Popular resort, second only in importance to nearby Arcachon, lying within the Bassin d'Arcachon amidst pine forests and oyster farms. Casino.

● Beach: 4 km of sandy gently sloping beach.
● Camping: Camping Confort ☎ 56.82.03.27 and Camping Fontainevieille ☎ 56.82.01.67
● Canoeing: on the Eyre (between the basin and Saugnac).
● Cycling: cycles can be hired from the SNCF station.
● Riding: Equitation Mini Ranch ☎ 56.82.01.82

 Arcachon *(Gironde)*
Pop: 15,000
Bordeaux 65 km, Paris 652 km
🄳 place Roosevelt ☎ 56.83.01.69

Dating from the mid-nineteenth century when the wealthy of Bordeaux established villas here, Arcachon remains a very popular and lively pine-backed seaside and health resort situated in the Bassin d'Arcachon, virtually the only kink in an otherwise straight 240 km of coastline. The tidal bay offers perfect conditions for the oyster which is well exploited in numerous farms, and a marina with over 1,000 berths where regattas provide regular and colourful distractions.

● Beach: supervised and sandy while the basin itself is subject to retreating tides twice daily. Try Pilat-Plage (nestling beneath the highest dune in Europe and still advancing on the forest) and Pyla-sur-Mer (at the entrance to the Arcachon basin).
● Camping: Camping les Abatilles ☎ 56.83.24.15
● Casino: boulevard de la Plage ☎ 56.83.41.44
● Cycling: cycles can be hired from the SNCF station.
● Golf: tree-lined 18h private and friendly course at Golf d'Arcachon, 35 boulevard d'Arcachon, 33260 La Teste-de-Buch ☎ 56.54.44.00
● Riding: at l'Etrier d'Arcachon, rue Pierre Frondaie.
● Sailing: numerous schools for sailing and windsurfing.
● Thalassotherapy: (Apr-Oct) Source des Abatilles, 157 boulevard de la Côte d'Argent ☎ 56.83.32.28

 Bayonne *(Pyrénées-Atlantiques)*
Pop: 43,000
Bordeaux 180 km, Paris 770 km
🄳 place de la Liberté ☎ 59.59.31.31

At the confluence of the Nive and Adour rivers, the historic fortified city of Bayonne is now a busy commercial and leisure port. The city's fine Gothic cathedral, medieval quarters with typical Basque and Gascon architecture, museums and traditional summer fêtes and bullfights attract visitors and there's great surfing at nearby Anglet, plus excellent fishing and walking.

- Beach: the nearby seaside town of Anglet-sur-Mer offers good sandy bathing with watersports facilities.
- Camping: Camping de la Chêneraie ☎ 59.55.01.31
- Cycling: cycles can be hired form the SNCF station.
- Golf: 18h private course at Golf de Chiberta, 104 boulevard des Plages, 64600 Anglet ☎ 59.63.83.20 (part-forest part-links course with many memorable holes).
- Thalassotherapy: also based at Anglet-sur-Mer, l'Institut de Thalassothérapie Atlanthal ☎ 59.42.08.09 is situated right on the ocean front and offers combined fitness and seawater therapy treatment.

 **Biarritz** *(Pyrénées-Atlantiques)*
Pop: 28,000
Bayonne 7 km, Paris 780 km
🏢 square d'Ixelles ☎ 59.24.20.24

Of international renown as a *rendezvous* for the wealthy and fashionable, Biarritz now attracts the younger, less-affluent surfing fraternity. A former whaling port, watchmen used to light up fires on the hills nearby to advise the fishermen of their approach. In the course of the seventeenth century, however, the whales retreated from the area, which forced the decline of the port. There followed a period when Biarritz became the favoured resort of Napoleon III, his Empress Eugénie and court, and subsequently of other European royalty and nobility. Nicknamed the 'Queen of resorts and the resort of Kings', it is still a popular retirement choice with a certain old-fashioned elegance and charm. For the modern tourists, though, who, each summer, swell the town's population to over 60,000, it is the beaches which provide the chief attraction.

- Beach: superb sandy beaches which, when the surf is high, are spectacular – Grande Plage, the enormous Plage des Basques (heavy surf) and Plage du Port Vieux (sheltered). There are numerous indoor heated pools.
- Camping: Biarritz ☎ 59.23.00.12 and Splendid Camping ☎ 59.23.01.29
- Casino: Municipal (open all year) and Casino d'Eté.
- Golf: hundred-year-old elegant parkland 18h private course with lovely views of sea and town at Golf de Biarritz, le Phare, avenue E.-Cavell, 64200 Biarritz ☎ 59.03.71.80
- Riding: Biarritz Equitation, allée Gabrielle Dorziat ☎ 59.23.73.00
- Surfing: Surf Club, 25 rue Mazagran ☎ 59.24.22.09; US de Biarritz, 26 avenue

Beausoleil ☎ 59.24.33.85; and Waïkiki, 20 place Clemenceau ☎ 59.24.13.09
- Tennis: 12 outdoor and two indoor courts for hire at Biarritz Olympique, Parc des Sports Aguiléra ☎ 59.23.93.24
- Thalassotherapy: Institut Louison Bobet, avenue de l'Impératrice ☎ 59.24.20.80 and Thermes Marins, 80 rue de Madrid ☎ 59.23.01.22
- Waterskiing: Association Nautique de Biarritz, 17 avenue de l'Impératrice
- Windsurfing: RN 10, Guéthary ☎ 59.54.83.19

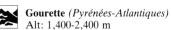 **Carcans-Maubuisson** *(Gironde)*
Lacanau-Océan 14 km, Paris 584 km
🏢 Office de Tourisme ☎ 56.03.34.94

Standing on the banks of France's largest lake (Lake Hourtin-Carcans), and close to the Atlantic, this is a sport and activity resort at the heart of the vast Landes pine forest. A complex of villages, with all types of accommodation, has been created here by those concerned for the careful development of the Aquitaine coast. Tuition on a short or long-term basis in all the principal watersports is offered, plus tennis, archery, cycling and a gym. Cultural activities are organised throughout the season and special emphasis is laid on the benefits obtained from combining physical and mental effort.

- Camping: Camping de Maubuisson ☎ 56.03.36.00

Gourette *(Pyrénées-Atlantiques)*
Alt: 1,400-2,400 m
Pau 50 km, Paris 827 km
🏢 place du Sarrière ☎ 59.05.12.17

Winter sports and health resort situated amidst breath-taking scenery of steep forested valleys and clear mountain waters. Good skiing in winter and invigorating walks in spring or autumn reveal the beauties of this area. Holiday accommodation is provided for 7,500.

- Camping: Camping de Ley ☎ 59.05.11.47 (Jun-Sep)
- Spa: close by at Les Eaux-Bonnes – respiratory/lymphatic disorders (15 May-30 Sep) ☎ 59.05.34.02 alt: 750 m, climate: fresh.

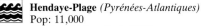 **Hendaye-Plage** *(Pyrénées-Atlantiques)*
Pop: 11,000
St-Jean-de-Luz 14 km, Paris 820 km
🏢 12 rue des Aubépines ☎ 59.20.00.34

Attractively situated with rolling green hills behind the blue waters of the large bay, Hendaye-Plage is a modern resort offering full watersports and recreation facilities, popular with families. With part of the coastline here a protected area, there are many beautiful walks along the tops of steep cliff faces where the Pyrénées meet the sea. Casino.

- Beach: long, sandy and safe, popular with surfers.
- Camping: les Acacias ☎ 59.20.78.76 and Camping Alturan ☎ 59.20.04.55
- Cycling: cycles for hire from Parc des Sports ☎ 59.20.00.18
- Fishing: morning sea-fishing trips, cruising along the Spanish coast and short trips around the bay aboard the *L'Hendayais*. All bookable through the Tourist Office.
- Golf: see St-Jean-de-Luz.
- Sailing: Centre Nautique d'Hendaye Itsasoko Aicea offers individual and group tuition on a weekly basis for children and adults ☎ 59.20.52.52
- Tennis: 12 courts to hire at Parc des Sports ☎ 59.20.02.73

 Hossegor *(Landes)*
Pop: 8,000
Dax 35 km, Paris 757 km
🛈 place Pasteur ☎ 58.43.72.35

Fashionable resort attractively, though curiously set in the pine forest between lagoon and sea. Spanish-style villas nestling amongst the dunes date from the end of the last century and indeed Hossegor has all the right ingredients – forest, lake, dunes and ocean, together with large conservation areas to be discovered only by those on foot. There is a large marina at nearby Capbreton. Casino.

- Beach: sandy and safe on the lakeside.
- Camping: Le Lac ☎ 58.43.53.14 and Le Rey ☎ 58.43.52.00
- Golf: 18h private (and rather exclusive) course at Golf d'Hossegor, avenue du Golf, 40150 Hossegor ☎ 58.43.56.99 (booking essential and handicap certificate required).
- Sailing: also windsurfing.
- Surfing: Atlantique Surf Club ☎ 58.72.03.46
- Walking: through the Landes forest.

 Hourtin-Port *(Gironde)*
Pop: 4,000
Bordeaux 60 km, Paris 555 km
🛈 SI ☎ 56.09.15.57

While the great Atlantic rollers beat the shore at Hourtin Plage 11 km away, the huge inland lake, the Etang d'Hourtin, provides safe and sheltered bathing, sailing and fishing fun and is a young sports-based resort geared particularly towards children. Pine forests reveal cycle tracks which run between the coast and the lake and the little village of Hourtin itself slightly inland.

- Camping: Camping la Côte d'Argent ☎ 56.41.60.25
- Riding: Centre Equestre ☎ 56.09.20.75
- Sailing: UCPA Centre Nautique ☎ 56.09.20.69

 Lacanau-Océan *(Gironde)*
Arcachon 83 km, Paris 592 km
🛈 place de l'Europe ☎ 56.03.21.01

Literally miles of sandy ocean beaches and the warm and sheltered waters of the enormous inland lakes nearby attract the sports-orientated – this is a favourite training location for France's national athletics and football teams.

- Beach: the crashing Atlantic rollers mean that surfing is only safe at specific supervised areas and the best swimming is from the banks of the huge lakes which are more like inland seas – Lake Carcans (at Montaud and Maubuisson) and along the west edge of Lake Lacanau (at Moutchic, Carreyre, L'Escourette, La Grande-Escourre and Langarisse).
- Camping: Airotel de l'Océan ☎ 56.03.24.45 and Camping de Talaris ☎ 56.03.04.15
- Cycling: on paths through the forest.
- Golf: 18h private course at Golf de l'Ardilouse, 33680 Lacanau-Océan ☎ 56.03.25.60
- Sailing: also windsurfing and water skiing on the lakes.
- Tennis: 14 outdoor and two covered courts for hire.

 Lanton *(Gironde)*
Pop: 4,000
Andernos-les-Bains 10 km, Paris 630 km
🛈 Port de Cassy ☎ 56.82.94.46

Sheltered seaside resort midway between Andernos-les-Bains and Arcachon on the Arcachon basin, close to a huge forest of pines and oaks. Three small ports (Cassy, Taussat and Fontanevieille) provide safe harbour for small sailing boats, a popular sport here, and specially created cycling paths hug the coastline from Lanton north via Andernos-les-Bains.

- Camping: le Roumingue ☎ 56.82.97.48
- Sailing: Club Nautique at Taussat ☎ 56.82.57.22
- Tennis: Tennis Club Lantonnais ☎ 56.26.03.65
- Walking: follow the coastal walk trails.

 Laruns *(Pyrénées-Atlantiques)*
Pop: 1,500
Pau 40 km, Paris 810 km
🛈 place de la Mairie ☎ 59.05.31.41

Close to the Spanish frontier (27 km) and nestling in the pretty Ossau mountain valley, Laruns is a small and attractive village, an ideal base for walking and fishing holidays and close to the ski resort of Gourette. An excursion on the little open-topped tourist train, which runs round the mountains from Artouste, is a perfect way to view the surrounding countryside.

- Camping: Camping des Gaves ☎ 59.05.332.37 and Camping Desmé-Barthèque ☎ 59.05.38.88
- Spa: nearby at Les Eaux-Chaudes – respiratory/lymphatic disorders (open all year) ☎ 59.05.31.55 alt: 675 m, climate: fresh.

Libourne *(Gironde)*
Pop: 23,000
Bordeaux 30 km, Paris 575 km
🛈 place de l'Hôtel de Ville ☎ 57.51.15.04

Ancient fortified town at the confluence of the Isle and Dordogne rivers, Libourne was built during the Hundred Years War and is of historical interest and importance. Noted red wines of the region include St-Emilion, Pomerol and Fronsac and these can be enjoyed at any of the good restaurants, while steam-train trips operate on Saturdays between May and October from nearby Guîtres, providing a pleasant excursion for enthusiasts into this famous wine area.

● Art: collection of contemporary art.
● Boat Trips: cruise and dine trips operate from Bordeaux. Enquire at the Tourist Office.
● Camping: Municipal le Ruste ☎ 57.51.01.54
● Cycling: cycles can be hired from the SNCF station.

 Mimizan-Plage *(Landes)*
Pop: 8,000
Arcachon 65 km, Paris 698 km
🛈 avenue Maurice-Martin ☎ 58.09.11.20

Always at the whim of the wind-swept dunes, the original town was long ago an important coastal port. Mimizan today is several kilometres inland, one of the Atlantic resorts termed the 'French Far-West', its houses spread between the woods and the sands.

● Camping: Marina ☎ 58.09.12.66
● Casino: ☎ 58.09.05.02
● Riding: Le Marina, Mimizan-Plage ☎ 58.09.34.25
● Sailing: Club Nautique ☎ 58.09.02.87
● Tennis: eight courts to hire at Tennis-Club, avenue de Leslurgues ☎ 58.09.07.67

 Monflanquin *(Lot-et-Garonne)*
Pop: 2,500
Agen 47 km, Paris 615 km
🛈 place des Arcades ☎ 53.36.40.19

As a reminder of the bitter conflicts waged between England and France, several *bastide* towns dot the Agenais region, typical amongst them being thirteenth-century Monflanquin. On a hill surrounded by attractive countryside, this is an historic small town, ideal for 'getting away from it all', and where fishing, walking and taking life as it comes are very much the order of the day.

● Camping: Municipal de Coulon ☎ 53.36.47.36
● Fishing: category 1 and 2 fishing on the Lède river.

Mussidan *(Dordogne)*
Pop: 4,000
Périgueux 35 km, Paris 535 km
🛈 9 rue de la Libération ☎ 53.81.04.77

Canoeing on the Dordogne

Charming little riverside town surrounded by the vast forests of the Double and the Landais. Well situated for enjoying the natural beauties of the Périgord area. There is good fishing, walking, canoeing, tennis, cycling and pedalo hire.

● Camping: Municipal ☎ 53.81.04.07
● Canoeing: from April onwards canoes for hire on Saturday afternoons and in July and August every day (except weekends), with tuition for beginners.
● Riding: Centre Equestre de Beaupérier ☎ 53.81.71.31 arranges treks into the Double Forest. A pleasurable way of exploring the countryside is by horse-drawn caravan. Details from Régie Départementale de la Dordogne, 24000 Périgueux ☎ 53.53.44.35

 Nontron *(Dordogne)*
Pop: 4,000
Périgueux 49 km, Paris 487 km
🛈 rue de Verdun ☎ 53.56.25.50 (Jun-Sep)

Old houses flank the narrow streets of this steep little town set into the side of a rock face. Below, in the deep, wooded valley, runs the fast-flowing River Bandiat. It is an attractive area with numerous pleasant walks.

● Camping: Municipal de Masvicontaux ☎ 53.56.02.04
● Fishing: category 1 fishing on the Bandiat river.
● Riding: Centre Equestre de Périgord Vert at Milhac-de-Nontron (14 km).

Pau *(Pyrénées-Atlantiques)*
Pop: 90,000
Bayonne 108 km, Paris 770 km
place Royale ☎ 59.27.27.08

Capital of the Pyrénées-Atlantiques *département*, and of the Béarn, Pau is an attractive city, its name deriving from the palissade, or *paua*, which used to protect the château's commanding position over the mountain torrent, the Gave. Popular in the nineteenth century as an over-wintering spot, particularly for Scots and Irish officers retired after the Napoleonic Wars. With the creation of the golf course here and the attractions of its climate, Pau was established as an all-year health resort, and saw the construction of the 'boulevard des Pyrénées', planned to rival the seaside 'promenade des Anglais' at Nice, and giving balcony views, in clear conditions, of the highest summits of the Pyrénées. A busy university town and commercial centre, there is much to attract the visitor to the area.

● Art: the Musée des Beaux Arts contains representative works of European schools.
● Camping: Municipal de la Plaine ☎ 59.02.30.49
● Casino: Municipal.
● Golf: charming 18h private course at Golf de Pau, 64140 Pau Billère ☎ 59.32.02.33 (oldest club in Europe created during Napoleonic Wars); and new 18h private course at Golf de Pau Artiguelove, Domaine-St-Michel, 64230 Lescar ☎ 59.83.09.29

 St-Emilion *(Gironde)*
Pop: 3,000
Bordeaux 35 km, Paris 580 km
place des Créneaux ☎ 57.24.72.03

A name familiar to wine lovers, this little village of medieval streets, perched on the northern slopes of the Dordogne valley, looks down upon its vineyards, whence come the famous vines of the Bordelais region. The gourmet tourist is offered a choice of superb restaurants where local figs, peaches and St-Emilion macaroons are featured. Less than two hours' drive away is the coast at Arcachon, though the wine-tasting *caves* may detain you longer than anticipated!

● Camping: Camping la Barbanne ☎ 57.24.75.80

 St-Etienne-de-Baïgorri *(Pyrénées-Atlantiques)*
Pop: 2,000
Cambo-les-Bains 30 km, Paris 820 km
SI ☎ 59.37.47.28

At the heart of the Basque country, this little valley village is perfectly situated for fishing and walking holidays in magnificent countryside very close to St-Jean-Pied-de-Port.

● Camping: Municipal ☎ 59.37.43.96
● Fishing: category 1 fishing on the Nive.

 St-Jean-de-Luz *(Pyrénées-Atlantiques)*
Pop: 13,000
Biarritz 13 km, Paris 792 km
place Maréchal-Foch ☎ 59.26.03.16

Miles of fine sandy beaches and a pretty location in a sheltered bay beneath the foothills of the Pyrénées make this tuna-fishing port, together with the neighbouring yachting port of Ciboure, both popular and lively. The Spanish influence (10 km from the frontier) is strongly felt, with summer carnivals, dances and bull-fighting, while the town's colourful and animated lifestyle makes it a favourite with artists too. Casino.

● Beach: swimming is sheltered and safe within the bay while the four northern beaches are ideal for surfing. The seaside resort of Guéthary is also close by.
● Camping: Camping Municipal Chibaoa-Berria ☎ 59.26.11.94 and Camping Bord de Mer ☎ 59.26.24.61
● Cycling: cycles for hire at the SNCF station.
● Fishing: sea fishing trips available.
● Golf: 18h private course at Golf de la Nivelle St-Jean-de-Luz, place William-Sharp, 64500 Ciboure ☎ 59.47.19.72 (high-level course with magnificent mountain views); and 18h private course at Golf de Chantaco St-Jean-de-Luz, route d'Ascain, 64500 St-Jean-de-Luz ☎ 59.26.14.22 (parkland).
● Sailing: and windsurfing classes YCB ☎ 59.47.18.31 and UCPA ☎ 59.47.18.17
● Spa: close by at Cambo-les-Bains – rheumatism/bone joint damage (Feb-Dec) ☎ 59.29.78.54 alt: 60 m, climate: mild
● Surfing: classes offered by Ur Kirola Surf Club ☎ 59.51.03.71
● Tennis: 24 courts to hire.

 Ste-Foy-la-Grande *(Gironde)*
Pop: 3,000
Bordeaux 75 km, Paris 550 km
102 rue de la République ☎ 57.46.03.00

Pretty medieval town on the banks of the Dordogne river surrounded by farmland and vineyards and providing an ideal location to enjoy the rural tranquillity of the Gironde.

● Camping: avenue Clemenceau ☎ 57.46.13.84
● Canoeing: canoe hire and descent of the Dordogne with the Club Nautique at Port-Ste-Foy ☎ 53.24.86.12
● Fishing: category 2 fishing on the Dordogne.
● Painting: courses on demand from Francisco Sole-Carnice, La Beauze, Les Leves ☎ 57.41.28.31
● Riding: Les Laurent, St-Antoine de Breuilh ☎ 53.24.80.36
● Tennis: Cléret, Port-Ste-Foy ☎ 53.24.70.47

Sarlat *(Dordogne)*
Pop: 11,000
Périgueux 66 km, Paris 538 km
🛈 place de la Liberté ☎ 53.59.27.67

One of the most attractive small towns in France, Sarlat is world-renowned as a living monument to the artistic and architectural styles of France, ranging from the Middle Ages right up to the eighteenth century. As such it has often provided a natural period setting for film-makers and lends itself to outdoor theatrical performances (Theatre Festival in July and August). The beautiful Dordogne river is nearby, providing the opportunity for fishing, canoeing and swimming from small beaches at such places as Carsac (8 km), La Roque-Gageac (6 km) and at Montfort (6 km) from where, incidentally, the views from the fortress along the Dordogne valley are magnificent.

● Camping: Les Perrières ☎ 53.59.05.84
● Cycling: cycles for hire at the SNCF station.

Seignosse-le-Penon *(Landes)*
Pop: 2,000
Bayonne 28 km, Paris 750 km
🛈 avenue des Lacs ☎ 58.43.32.15

Stretching for 5 km along the seafront, this is a modern seaside resort created in 1964 to offer the best combination of natural beauty with facilities for sports and activities. There are large sea-filled swimming pools, ponds for fishing and walks in the shade of the forest and, for those who require noisier entertainment, a nightclub and evening shows. A climate 'particularly good for children and strained people' as the resort's brochure amusingly claims.

● Beach: four supervised beaches.

● Camping: Penon ☎ 58.43.30.30
● Tennis: 17 courts for hire.

Soulac-sur-Mer *(Gironde)*
Pop: 3,000
Royan 9 km, Paris 515 km
🛈 rue de la Plage ☎ 56.09.86.61

An attractive and predominantly modern seaside resort with an enormous pine-fringed sandy beach draws those with young families in large numbers. Every type of activity is catered for, from archery to parachuting, and there are regular crossings to lively Royan on the opposite side of the estuary.

● Beach: safe for children.
● Camping: Camping Palace ☎ 56.09.80.22 and Camping l'Amélie-Plage ☎ 56.09.87.27
● Casino: Casino de la Plage.
● Cycling: cycles for hire from the SNCF station.
● Tennis: 21 courts for hire.

 Villeneuve-sur-Lot *(Lot-et-Garonne)*
Pop: 24,000
Agen 29 km, Paris 625 km
🛈 Théâtre Georges-Leygues ☎ 53.70.31.37

A *bastide* town like Monflanquin, this is a good rural excursion base attractively set on the banks of the Lot river.

● Camping: Municipal du Rooy ☎ 53.70.24.18
● Cuisine: the Grand Hotel du Parc, 13 boulevard de la Marine, 47300 Villeneuve-sur-Lot ☎ 53.70.01.68 runs traditional duck-cooking weekends, inclusive of accommodation and meals (Nov-Mar)
● Golf: new 27h private course at Golf de Castelnaud, B.P.186, 47304 Villeneuve-sur-Lot ☎ 53.01.74.64
● Riding: Poney Club de la Marsale, Courbiac ☎ 53.70.68.75

AUVERGNE

Administrative
Centre:
Clermont-Ferrand
Area:
25,988 sq km
Population: 1,330,500

Départements:
03 Allier
15 Cantal
43 Haute-Loire
63 Puy-de-Dôme

Regional Parks:
Parc Naturel Régional
des Volcans
d'Auvergne,
Montlosier près
Randanne, Commune
d'Aydat, 63210
Rochefort-Montagne
☎ 73.65.67.19

Parc Naturel Régional
du Livradois-Forez,
Saint-Gervais-sous-
Meymont, 63880
Olliergues
☎ 73.95.54.31

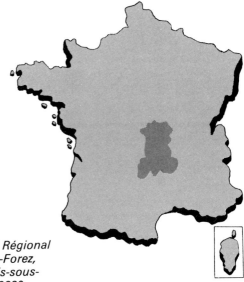

Over a period of 30 million years, since the formation of the Alps, there took place the enormous volcanic convulsions that created the Massif Central. The *département* of Cantal in the Auvergne was the first to be shaped, forming a huge volcanic cone 80 km in circumference, 3,000 m high. There followed the Velay and Dore peaks and, more recently (that is 50,000 years ago), as lava bubbled over and cooled, came the formation of the domed shapes or *puys*, the range of extinct volcanoes within the Puy-de-Dôme. The cones are capped now, or hold mountain lakes, but beneath the feet of grazing cattle the cauldron boils on, as attested to by the wealth of hot springs, healing waters and fashionable spas. Indeed the riches of its earth make the Auvergne one of the main regions in Europe for spas.

While from 1940 de Gaulle's Free France continued its defiance of Hitler from London, Pétain's France chose Vichy for its capital, an elegant spa city of parks and flowered walks. From the Source des Celestins, some 204,570 litres of Vichy water are bottled daily in the interests of better health for visitors drawn by its curative powers, as well as by the sophistication of the city itself with its smart centre of Le Vieux Parc.

There are pre-Roman spas at Royat, Châtel-Guyon and at Le Mont-Dore, at La Bourboule, which boasts the highest arsenic content of any of Europe's spa waters, and at Vic-sur-Cère, once a very fashionable spa, today a pretty village developing into a contemporary holiday resort.

The mountain chain of the Massif Central has tended to isolate Auvergne from the rest of France. Almost entirely rural, the region has bred a sturdy, self-sufficient, religious people. Their livestock graze the mountain slopes. From the milk of cows and goats they make their cheeses in *burons* and *jasseries*: Cantal, the blue Fourme d'Ambert, St-Nectaire, the pungent Gaperon, Chevreton and Bleu d'Auvergne. From the long roots of the gentian and from the bilberry and other berries they make apéritifs and bitter-sweet liqueurs: Crème de Myrtilles, Vervaine de Puys (from verbena), Gentiane and Framboise de Bort.

Being mountainous, isolated and well watered by fast-flowing rivers, the Auvergne is ideal for a variety of outdoor pursuits, including skiing, canoeing, fishing and hiking. For skiers there are three classified downhill ski resorts in the

Lac Pavin

Auvergne (Super-Lioran, Le Mont-Dore and Super-Besse) whose pistes and facilities compare favourably with alpine resorts at the same altitude. Auvergne is also excellent for cross-country skiing, with 3,000 km of paths strewn with refuges, and a dozen areas where marked paths connect cross-country ski centres with mountain villages through woodlands, ridges and valleys.

The Loire and the Dordogne are lively mountain rivers as they tumble through the Haute-Loire, their waters ideal for canoeing. For fishing the mountain streams, rivers and other stretches of water provide salmon and trout amongst other possibilities.

There is good trout fishing on the Sioule river at Châteauneuf-les-Bains, and fine salmon sport at St-Julien in the Haute-Loire.

This magnificent countryside can be overflown by hang glider or hot-air balloon; explored on horseback, bicycle or, perhaps ideally, on foot.

Thirteen main hiking routes cover over 1,000 km of the most picturesque spots – GR4 crosses the Parc des Volcans and GR3 follows the Loire. Shorter PR (*Petite Randonnée*) routes are also signed and maintained. *Relais* and *gîtes* allow for overnight stays. The Parc des Volcans d'Auvergne is the largest Regional Park in France and this protected area offers an exceptional range of flora and fauna, as well as the Chaine des Dômes, a hundred or so dormant volcanoes forming a line from north to south over an area of some 30 km, with Puy-de-Dôme as its highest point. The Monts Dore, grouped over an area of 600 sq km, are interspersed with valleys, waterfalls and lakes, with the Puy-de-Sancy as the highest point at 1,886 m. It is an extraordinary and unforgettable landscape.

Cantal is regarded as the best walking country in all France. The *Grandes Randonnées* routes 3 and 4 run through the centre of France as does the GR65, the Santiago de Compostela pilgrim way to Spain. The *Petites Randonnées* in all four *départements* lead through individual beauty spots, by breathless views, gorges and jagged volcanic peaks, waterside villages and medieval town streets – Montluçon and the narrow cobbled streets of Moulins in Allier; Besse-en-Chandesse in Puy-de-Dôme; Laroquebrou, Thiézac, Puy Mary, the Lander gorges and Salers in Cantal; and, in Haute-Loire, pretty Lavaudieu and the superbly positioned Château Polignac.

The highest peak of the Puys chain, Puy-de-Dôme rises to 1,465 m, its reward for the walker being the ruins of the Gallo-Roman temple of Mercury at its summit, and an unforgettable view, on the clearest days, over 11 *départements*.

Finally, for the motorist who wishes to sample the area in a more leisurely fashion (not forgetting the tight mountain bends), there are the five *Routes des Châteaux* circuits which cover this region: the Circuit en Bourbonnais, the Circuit de Duché d'Auvergne, the Circuit du Dauphiné d'Auvergne, the Circuit du Comté d'Auvergne and the Circuit des Montagnes Cantaliennes. Some, like the twelfth-century Château Murol near St-Nectaire, are impressive ruins while others, like the riverside La Batisse, with gardens designed by Le Nôtre, are sumptuous family homes rich in antique furniture and tapestries.

PRACTICAL TOURIST INFORMATION

General information on the region can be obtained by telephoning or writing to the Comité Régional du Tourisme (CRT) office, while specific booklets are produced detailing camping, hotel and self-catering gîte accommodation. These can be obtained by writing to the tourist board office for the département *(CDT) of your choice:*

Regional Tourist Board
Comité Régional du Tourisme (CRT), 45 avenue Julien, B.P.395, 63011 CLERMONT-FERRAND Cedex ☎ 73.93.04.03

Départements
Allier (03): Comité Départemental du Tourisme (CDT), 35 rue de Bellecroix, B.P.50, 03402 YZEURE Cedex ☎ 70.44.41.57
Cantal (15): Comité Départemental du Tourisme (CDT), 22 rue Guy-de-Veyre, B.P.8, 15018 AURILLAC Cedex ☎ 71.48.53.54
Haute-Loire (43): Comité Départemental du Tourisme (CDT), 4 avenue du Général-de-Gaulle, B.P.4, 43000 LE PUY-EN-VELAY ☎ 71.09.26.05
Puy-de-Dôme (63): Comité Départemental du Tourisme (CDT), 17 place Delille, 63038 CLERMONT-FERRAND Cedex ☎ 73.91.14.40

SELF-CATERING ACCOMMODATION

The following British operators offer self-catering accommodation in the area:

Allez France, 27 West Street, Storrington, Pulborough RH20 4DZ ☎ 09066 2345
Angel Travel, 34 High Street, Borough Green, Sevenoaks, Kent TN15 8BJ ☎ 0732 884109
Bowhills Ltd, Swanmore, Southampton SO3 2QW ☎ 0489 877627
Brittany Ferries, The Brittany Centre, Wharf Road, Portsmouth PO2 8RU ☎ 0705 827701
Chapter Travel, 126 St John's Wood High Street, London NW8 7ST ☎ 01-586 9451
La France des Villages, Model Farm, Rattlesden, Bury St Edmunds IP30 0SY ☎ 044 93 7664
French Travel Service, Georgian House, 69 Boston Manor Road, Brentford TW8 0JQ ☎ 01-568 8442
Gîtes de France, 178 Piccadilly, London W1V 9DB

☎ 01-493 3480
David Newman's French Collection, P.O. Box 733,
40 Upperton Road, Eastbourne BN21 4AW
☎ 0323 410347
SVP France, PO Box 90, Chichester, West Sussex
PO18 8XJ ☎ 0243 377 862
Vacances, 28 Gold Street, Saffron Walden
CB10 1EJ ☎ 0799 25101
Vacances en Campagne, Bignor, Pulborough
RH20 1QD ☎ 07987 433
Vacations, 60 Charles Street, Leicester LE1 1FB
☎ 0533 537758
VFB Holidays, 1 St Margaret's Terrace,
Cheltenham GL50 4DT ☎ 0242 526338

SPORTS AND ACTIVITIES

*For unusual and interesting holiday ideas, contact
the Loisirs Accueil office for the area of your
choice:*

Loisirs Accueil Cantal:
22 rue Guy-de-Veyre, 15000 AURILLAC
☎ 71.48.84.84
Loisirs Accueil Haute-Loire:
12 boulevard Philippe-Jourde, 43000 PUY-EN-
VELAY ☎ 71.09.26.05

RESORTS

Bourbon-l'Archambault *(Allier)*
Pop: 3,000
Montluçon 50 km, Paris 283 km
🄸 place des Thermes ☎ 70.67.09.79

The ruins of Bourbon's fortress dominate this rural
health resort set in an area surrounded by small
valleys grazed by Charolais cattle. A Roman spa,
its name deriving from Borvo, the god of spring
water, it lies at the heart of the Bourbonnais, the
area owned by the Dukes of Bourbon, one of the
most famous branches of French royalty. A region
of historic interest with good fishing and walking.

● Camping: Le Bourbon ☎ 70.67.08.83
● Canoeing: also bathing, pedalo hire and sailing
   on the Etang de Vieure 20 km away.
● Casino: place de Verdun ☎ 70.67.02.73
● Cycling: bicycles to hire at Dagouret, place de
   l'Eglise.
● Spa: rheumatism/bone joint damage (6 Apr-
   31 Oct) ☎ 70.67.07.88 alt: 240 m, climate:
   temperate.
● Walking: Forêt de Tronçais, Vallée de la
   Sioule and Civray.

La Bourboule *(Puy-de-Dôme)*
Pop: 3,000
Clermont-Ferrand 53 km, Paris 440 km
🄸 place Hotel de Ville ☎ 73.81.07.99

Charming small health resort in the
Haute-Dordogne valley amid the Volcans
d'Auvergne Regional Park. Despite the
notoriously high content of arsenic in the waters,
this is the spa capital for children and its sheltered

location, pretty and numerous bridges over the
Dordogne, and summer programme of events
make this a popular rural retreat. Casino.

● Archery: hourly tuition is available from the
   Hôtel de Charlannes ☎ 73.81.01.60 (eight
   years upwards).
● Cycling: cycles for hire from the SNCF station.
● Fishing: category 1 fishing on the Dordogne.
● Golf: see Le Mont-Dore.
   Riding: Centre Equestre de Mont-sans-Souci
   ☎ 73.81.07.59
● Spa: respiratory/lymphatic disorders (2 May-
   30 Sep) ☎ 73.81.02.92 alt: 850 m, climate:
   mild.
● Tennis: semi-intensive courses (July/Aug) at
   boulevard Georges-Clemenceau
   ☎ 73.81.06.09 plus three courts to hire at
   avenue Agis-Ledru ☎ 73.81.11.62
● Walking: for extensive views, climb, drive or
   take the cable car up to the Plateau de
   Charlannes (1,250 m).
● Winter sports: cross-country skiing centre.

Chambon *(Puy-de-Dôme)*
Pop: 400
Le Mont-Dore 18 km, Paris 425 km
🄸 SI ☎ 73.88.62.62

Peaceful lakeside recreation area with the
encircling mountains reflected in its still waters. A
crater lake, formed by volcanic activity 10,000
years ago, now proves a paradise for summer
fishermen and windsurfers.

● Camping: Les Bombes and Le Pré-Bas.
● Fishing: category 1 fishing on the Surains,
   Dyane, Couze de Chaudefour rivers and on
   the lake.
● Golf: see Le Mont-Dore.
● Hang Gliding: five-day courses (16 years
   upwards) from Envogue, chemin de la Plage,
   Murol ☎ 73.88.67.74 (Apr-Sep); also
   ballooning from the same location and
   weekend courses in mountain-biking.
● Sailing: and windsurfing six-day courses
   (July/Aug) for all ages ☎ 73.88.60.49

Châteauneuf-les-Bains *(Puy-de-Dôme)*
Pop: 500
Clermont-Ferrand 48 km, Paris 373 km
🄸 Office de Tourisme ☎ 73.86.67.86

Set in a natural amphitheatre of wooded hills and
along the banks of the River Sioule, this is a
pleasant and relaxing spot for a health resort. Lots
of water-based activities take place here between
May and October, including sailing and
windsurfing.

● Canoeing: tuition and hire on the large stretch
   of water at les Fades-Besserve from Base de
   Confolant ☎ 73.79.92.75.
● Fishing: category 1 fishing on the Sioule river
   and numerous streams.

● Spa: rheumatism/bone joint damage (2 May-30 Sep) ☎ 73.86.67.49 alt: 390 m, climate: mild.
● Walking: numerous signposted circuits.

Châtel-Guyon (Puy-de-Dôme)
Pop: 4,000
Clermont-Ferrand 20 km, Paris 375 km
🎫 parc E.-Clementel ☎ 73.86.01.17

Popular and elegant spa town on the banks of the Sardon and set in an attractive landscape of woods and rocks. Wonderful views of the *puys* attract walkers, while a programme of summer events and the proximity of Riom offer pleasant diversions. Not far away is Volvic from where the famous mineral waters originate. Visits can be made to the bottling plant there and also to the deep subterranean galleries where the dark volcanic stone is cut for many uses, not least that of paving the streets of Paris! Casino.

● Fishing: on the Lac des Prades.
● Riding: Club Hippique ☎ 73.86.15.67
● Spa: digestive organs (25 Apr-5 Oct) ☎ 73.86.00.08 alt: 430 m, climate: fresh.
● Tennis: seven courts to hire at rue Victor-Hugo ☎ 73.86.07.27

Chaudes-Aigues (Cantal)
Pop: 2,000
Espalion 56 km, Paris 524 km
🎫 1 avenue Georges-Pompidou ☎ 71.23.52.75

In the hollow of a sheltered and pretty valley, this little spa town has strongly maintained its rural traditions and remains quite unspoilt and quiet. As its name implies, the waters here are spectacular for the fact that they emerge at 82°C, the hottest in Europe, as a result of subterranean volcanic activity. They have been used since Roman times for central heating. This is the most southerly of the Auvergne spas.

● Camping: Du Couffour.
● Fishing: category 1 fishing on the Remontalou, Truyère, Bès, Levandès and Lebon rivers.
● Spa: rheumatism/bone joint damage (1 May-15 Oct) ☎ 71.23.51.06 alt: 750 m, climate: temperate.
● Tennis: two courts to hire.
● Walking: numerous signposted circuits.

Langeac (Haute-Loire)
Pop: 5,000
Le Puy 45 km, Paris 480 km
🎫 place de l'Hôtel de Ville ☎ 71.77.05.41

At the heart of the wooded river valley, this is an attractive spacious town, a good base for numerous walking and sightseeing excursions on foot, cycle or on horseback.

● Camping: Le Prado ☎ 71.77.08.01

● Canoeing: in the Gorges de l'Allier during July and August, week-long trips with accommodation bookable from Auberge de l'Ile d'Amour ☎ 71.77.00.11
● Cycling: weekend or week-long trips with accommodation (cycles and routes supplied) bookable from Auberge de l'Ile d'Amour ☎ 71.77.00.11. Cycles can also be hired from the SNCF station.
● Fishing: category 1 fishing on the Allier river.
● Tennis: four courts to hire.

Mauriac (Cantal)
Pop: 5,000
Tulle 80 km, Paris 485 km
🎫 place Georges-Pompidou ☎ 71.67.30.26

Enjoying a particularly healthy and fresh climate (alt: 720 m), and located close to the western edge of the Volcans Regional Park, this is an ancient and peaceful town of medieval buildings surrounded by pasture land and an ideal base for walking and exploring the pretty Auze, Mars and Dordogne valleys.

● Camping: La Roussilhe ☎ 71.68.01.85

 ### Le Mont-Dore (Puy-de-Dôme)
Pop: 3,000
Alt: 1,050-1,840 m
Clermont-Ferrand 44 km, Paris 436 km
🎫 avenue Général-Leclerc ☎ 73.65.20.21

Large well-built town and winter sports resort for cross-country skiing. Attractively set within the encircling mountains where the Dordogne river has its source, and dominated in particular by the Puy-de-Sancy (1,886 m), the highest summit of the Massif Central range. Cultural events and summer concerts enliven the already busy atmosphere, with the spa attracting both *curistes* and tourists. A particular attraction for children is the long artificial toboggan run. Casino.

● Climbing: learn the basics – route de Sancy ☎ 73.65.05.22 (May/Jun/Sep/Oct).
● Cycling: cycles can be hired from the SNCF station.
● Fishing: and windsurfing at Lac de Guéry.
● Golf: 9h private course at Golf du Rigolet, 63240 Le Mont-Dore ☎ 73.65.00.79
● Riding: three-day treks during July and August from Club Hippique, chemin des Montagnes ☎ 73.65.04.12
● Spa: respiratory/lymphatic disorders (15 May-30 Sep) ☎ 73.65.05.10 alt: 1,050 m climate: mild.
● Tennis: eight courts (some floodlit) to hire at avenue Réné-Cassin.
● Walking: lovely valley walks with, between June and September, seven-day hikes around the volcanoes or lakes, bookable from the Auberge de Jeunesse (Youth Hostel), route de Sancy ☎ 73.65.03.53

Néris-les-Bains (*Allier*)
Pop: 3,000
Clermont-Ferrand 83 km, Paris 337 km
🛈 carrefour des Arènes ☎ 70.03.11.03

Totally unpolluted and quiet spa town, situated on
the plateau above the Cher valley, with a pleasant
and relaxing climate and atmosphere. Popular as
an excursion base, the town offers visitors a
programme of summer events and concerts and, as
a spa dating back to the Roman era, the
archaeological finds from digs in progress are on
display.

- Camping: Camping du Pavillon du Lac
  ☎ 70.03.17.59
- Canoeing: weekly courses (eight years
  upwards) at Base de Canoë-kayak, Lavault-
  Ste-Anne ☎ 70.07.20.73 (July/Aug)
- Casino: Municipal ☎ 70.03.10.01
- Fishing: category 2 fishing on the Ruisseau du
  Cournauron stream and in numerous pools.
- Golf: (8 km distant) 18h private course with a
  fourteenth-century château as focal point at
  Golf du Val-de-Cher Montluçon, 03190
  Nassigny, Hérisson ☎ 70.06.71.15
- Riding: Domaine de Menevaux
  ☎ 70.03.24.60 and Poney-Club de Larequille
  ☎ 70.51.05.15
- Spa: nervous system (21 Apr-24 Oct)
  ☎ 70.03.10.39 alt: 350 m, climate: mild.
- Tennis: Centre de Win-Tennis offers children
  and adults tuition during the summer
  ☎ 70.64.73.45
- Walking: Forêt de Tronçais and the beautiful
  gorges in the Vallée de la Sioule.

 Le Puy-en-Velay (*Haute-Loire*)
Pop: 27,000
Clermont-Ferrand 130 km, Paris 514 km
🛈 place du Breuil ☎ 71.09.38.41

In an extraordinary volcanic setting, Le Puy is a
town rich in architecture and history and of great
religious significance. As such it is one of the
principal tourist sites of the region. For a week in
mid-September the town travels back in time
recreating the atmosphere (and even the currency)
of the sixteenth century, with street entertainment,
concerts and archery contests.

- Camping: Bouthezard ☎ 71.09.55.09
- Cycling: cycles can be hired from the SNCF
  station.
- Golf: 9h private course at Golf de Chambon-
  sur-Lignon, Beaujeu, 43400 Le Chambon
  ☎ 71.59.28.10

 Royat-Chamalières (*Puy-de-Dôme*)
Pop: 4,000
Clermont-Ferrand 3 km, Paris 391 km
🛈 place Allard ☎ 75.35.81.87

Dotted with grand hotels and tree-lined boulevards
in a wooded valley on the outskirts of Clermont-
Ferrand, Chamalières is noted for the fact that it

prints all the Bank of France currency, and for its
former mayor, Giscard d'Estaing, who became
President of France. There are numerous
excursions to the lakes and volcanoes, a casino and
spa and excellent golf on a course located at an
altitude of over 900 m.

- Camping: Camping de l'Oclède.
- Fishing: category 1 fishing on the Tiretaine
  river.
- Golf: 18h private course where purple heather
  lines the beautiful fairways, at Golf des
  Volcans Clermont-Ferrand, La Bruyère des
  Moines, 63870 Orcines ☎ 73.62.15.51; and 9h
  course at Golf de Charade, 63130 Royat-
  Charade ☎ 73.35.73.09
- Spa: circulatory disorders (1 Apr-28 Oct)
  ☎ 73.35.80.16 alt: 450 m, climate: fine.
- Tennis: beginners and improvers' courses from
  Tennis de Colombier, voie Romaine
  ☎ 73.36.00.69 (July/Aug)

 St-Bonnet-Tronçais (*Allier*)
Pop: 1,000
Bourges 50 km, Paris 280 km
🛈 SI ☎ 70.06.11.30

One of the major attractions of this region is,
without doubt, the magnificent oak groves of the
Forêt de Tronçais. The little town of St-Bonnet is
situated on the edge of a large crater lake in the
heart of the forest, and offers bathing, sailing and
fishing in addition to the joys of the forest's birds
and wildlife.

- Golf: see Néris-les-Bains. Also (approx 40 km
  distant) 18h private course at Golf des Dryades
  en Pays de Georges Sand, Pouligny Notre-
  Dame, 36160 Ste-Sévère-sur-Indre
  ☎ 54.30.28.00
- Riding: Centre Equestre du Bien Aller at
  Cérilly ☎ 70.67.52.69
- Walking: excellent walking base for Massif.

St-Nectaire (*Puy-de-Dôme*)
Pop: 1,000
Clermont-Ferrand 43 km, Paris 431 km
🛈 Anciens Thermes ☎ 73.88.50.86

Peaceful spa village encircled by mountainous
countryside at the heart of the Auvergne, with
numerous châteaux and Romanesque churches to
discover. Casino.

- Camping: L'Oasis.
- Fishing: category 1 fishing on the Courançon,
  Couze-Chambon and Monne rivers.
- Golf: see Le Mont-Dore.
- Riding: Equitation St-Nectaire ☎ 73.88.41.50
- Spa: kidneys/urinary organs (25 May-30 Sep)
  ☎ 73.88.50.01 alt: 700 m, climate: dry.
- Windsurfing: and sailing at Chambon.

Super-Besse (*Puy-de-Dôme*)
Alt: 1,350-1,850 m
Issoire 35 km, Paris 420 km
🛈 Office de Tourisme ☎ 73.79.60.29

Close to the reasonably high and attractive walking base of Besse-en-Chandesse, Super-Besse is a winter sports resort created in 1963. In summer the Lac des Hermines offers bathing, sailing and pedalo hire and there's an artificial toboggan run. Close by is the small and popular crater lake, Lac Pavin, with similar recreation facilities.

● Sailing: and windsurfing – Club Nautique des Hermines offers seven-day courses (eight years upwards) ☎ 73.79.60.49
● Tennis: four-day courses (July/Aug) ☎ 73.79.48.79

 Super-Lioran (*Cantal*)
Alt: 1,250-1,850 m
Clermont-Ferrand 120 km, Paris 515 km
🛈 Office de Tourisme ☎ 71.49.50.08

Modern winter sports resort comprising 60 km of alpine pistes for skiers of all abilities, and 25 km of cross-country routes. As this is the principal winter resort in the Auvergne the facilities are good and, between June and September, the pleasures of its sunny, forested location, at an ideal altitude, attract those who wish to combine walking and exploring the flora and fauna of the region with such sporting pursuits as tennis, archery, ice skating and tobogganing on concrete simulated runs across the fields.

 Vichy (*Allier*)
Pop: 32,000
Clermont-Ferrand 54 km, Paris 340 km
🛈 19 rue du Parc ☎ 70.98.71.94

Surrounded by greenery and water, Vichy is a world-renowned health resort of spacious parks and elegant buildings. Good shopping, summer concerts and events, art galleries and well-equipped water sports facilities on the shores of Lake Allier, as well as its excellent salmon fishing, add to its popular appeal.

● Casinos: Grand Casino ☎ 70.31.68.88 and Elysée Palace ☎ 70.98.25.17

● Cycling: cycles can be hired from the SNCF station.
● Golf: 18h private course and pleasant clubhouse at Golf de Vichy Sporting Club, allée Baugnies, 03700 Bellerive-sur-Allier ☎ 70.32.39.11 (closed Tues).
● Languages: Vichy Centre Audio-Visuel de Langues Modernes ☎ 70.32.2.22 offers French language study courses.
● Parascending: flights for all ages from Yacht Club de Vichy, boulevard de Lattre-de-Tassigny ☎ 70.98.73.55
● Riding: Centre Equestre de Vichy, le Vernet ☎ 70.98.24.76
● Spa: digestive organs (open all year) ☎ 70.98.95.37 alt: 260 m, climate: temperate.
● Sailing: Base Municipale de Voile ☎ 70.32.04.68 and at Mayet-de-Montagne ☎ 70.56.40.59
● Tennis: courts and tuition available at Sporting Club ☎ 70.32.25.20

Vic-sur-Cère (*Cantal*)
Pop: 2,000
Aurillac 21 km, Paris 527 km
🛈 avenue Mercier ☎ 71.47.50.68

Small hydro-mineral spa town in the Cère river valley in a pretty and peaceful setting of green hills. Facilities for riding, tennis, fishing and hang-gliding as well as summer festivals, entertainments (including a casino), excursions and lovely walks in the Massifs du Cantal make this a pleasant country resort.

● Camping: Les Tilleuls ☎ 71.47.51.75
● Riding: Centre Equestre La Cravache ☎ 71.47.55.19 and the Association Cheval Aventur, Las Courtines, Polminhac, 15800 Vic-sur-Cère ☎ 71.47.41.23 organise treks by the day, weekend or longer into the countryside.
● Walking: discover the waterfalls in the picturesque Cère river valley.
● Winter Sports: cross-country skiing trails from here with downhill skiing at Super-Lioran.

BOURGOGNE

Administrative
Centre: Dijon
Population: 1,571,200
Area: 31,592 sq km

Départements:
21 Côte d'Or
58 Nièvre
71 Saône-et-Loire
89 Yonne

Regional Park:
Parc du Morvan,
Maison du Parc, Saint-
Brisson, 58230
Montsauche
☎ 86.78.70.16

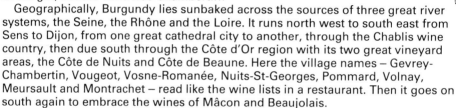

Hilaire Belloc ended a speech at the Vintner's Hall in London: 'When that this too, too solid flesh shall melt, and I am called before my Heavenly Father, I shall say to Him: "Sir, I don't remember the name of the village, and I don't remember the name of the girl, but the wine was Chambertin!" '

Geographically, Burgundy lies sunbaked across the sources of three great river systems, the Seine, the Rhône and the Loire. It runs north west to south east from Sens to Dijon, from one great cathedral city to another, through the Chablis wine country, then due south through the Côte d'Or region with its two great vineyard areas, the Côte de Nuits and Côte de Beaune. Here the village names – Gevrey-Chambertin, Vougeot, Vosne-Romanée, Nuits-St-Georges, Pommard, Volnay, Meursault and Montrachet – read like the wine lists in a restaurant. Then it goes on south again to embrace the wines of Mâcon and Beaujolais.

The heart of Burgundy, the Côte d'Or, is a narrow strip of land 60 km long running south from Dijon, and is divided into two geographical areas, the Côte de Nuits (and Hautes Côtes de Nuits) and the Côte de Beaune (and Hautes Côtes de Beaune). Few large estates exist but instead there is a multitude of individual parcels of vineyards producing wines of varying styles and in limited quantities. The hillier part of the Côte d'Or, known as the Hautes Côtes, is an exposed chalky, rugged landscape, harsher than the sunny slopes of the Côtes. The growers (*vignerons*) sell their wines to dealers (*négociants*) who blend, bottle and market them. It is their selection which ensures the continued reputation of Burgundy wines.

Today, the N6 races south to the Côte d'Azur but, between Dijon and Beaune, an alternative side road, a mere 50 km in length, the *Routes du Vin*, wanders past the greatest vineyards in the world, their fortunes depending on two grapes, the Pinot Noir (red) and the Chardonnay (white). By following the motoring *Routes du Vin* yourself, you will encounter the two regions of vineyards. The Côte de Nuits, lying between Dijon and Nuits-St-Georges, is an area which produces the outstanding red wines for which Burgundy is renowned: Fixin, Gevrey-Chambertin, Chambolle-Mussigny, Vougeot, Vosne-Romanée, Nuits-St-Georges. The Côte de Beaune white wines are the greatest in the world. The reds are also magnificent, with a style more vigorous than their counterparts in the Côte de Nuits. Vineyards are divided into many communes, and each commune has a great number of hamlets (still today called *climats* by the Burgundian vintners), which give them their authentic personality: Nuits-St-Georges, Aloxe-Corton, Beaune, Pommard, Volnay, Meursault, Puligny-Montrachet, Chassagne-Montrachet.

Long known for its culinary delights, Burgundy can even rival the fame of its wines with that of its cooking and its wealth of luxury restaurants means it has become an ever-popular area with weekend Parisian gourmets. The Charolais cattle are now part of the Burgundy landscape and the Burgundians live to eat, it is said, not the other way round! Most dishes are either cooked with wine or designed to bring out the best qualities of the wine. Try *boeuf bourguignon* and *queue de boeuf des vignerons* (oxtail in red wine sauce); *pochouse* (fish stew), *oeufs en meurette* (eggs in red wine) and, of course, *coq au vin*. There are some lovely goat and cow cheeses to discover too (try *epoisses*); *jambon persillé* (ham in a parsley sauce) and, in Dijon, the unusually shaped *pain d'épices* (spiced bread).

In the Middle Ages, the dynastic line of the Dukes of Burgundy amassed vast territories to become more powerful than even the kings of France, but the true prosperity of the area stemmed from the work, during the eleventh century, of the large religious foundations, such as the monasteries of Vézelay and Cluny, in the development of agriculture and the vine.

For the modern, active gourmet, the present lies in boating on the River Yonne, fishing and canoeing in the gorges of the Morvan Regional Park, walking its wooded hills or exploring by barge the sleepy villages and hilltop châteaux flanking the Burgundy canal.

Essentially, the heart of Burgundy still lies in some small village with its vineyards, somewhere in the Côte d'Or. Fifty years ago Gabriel Chevallier, in his novel *Clochemerle*, wrote of just such a village. Its appeal today is as great as ever. Whether the fictional Clochemerle is based on the real village of Vaux-en-Beaujolais cannot be certain, but it breathes of Burgundy, its sun, laughter, work and wine.

PRACTICAL TOURIST INFORMATION

General information on the region can be obtained by telephoning or writing to the Comité Régional du Tourisme (CRT) office, while specific booklets are produced detailing camping, hotel and self-catering gîte accommodation. These can be obtained by writing to the tourist board office for the département (CDT) of your choice:

Regional Tourist Board
Comité Régional du Tourisme (CRT), 53 rue de la Préfecture, 21041 DIJON Cedex ☎ 80.55.24.10

Départements
Côte d'Or (21): Comité Départemental du Tourisme (CDT), Hôtel du Département, B.P.1601, 21035 DIJON Cedex ☎ 80.73.81.81
Nièvre (58): Comité Départemental du Tourisme (CDT), 64 rue de la Préfecture, 58019 NEVERS ☎ 86.57.80.90
Saône-et-Loire (71): Comité Départemental du Tourisme (CDT), 389 avenue de Lattre-de-Tassigny, 71025 MACON ☎ 85.39.47.47
Yonne (89): Association Départementale de Tourisme (ADT), 1-2 quai de la République, 89000 AUXERRE ☎ 86.52.26.27

SELF-CATERING ACCOMMODATION

The following British operators offer self-catering accommodation in the area:

Brittany Ferries, The Brittany Centre, Wharf Road, Portsmouth PO2 8RU ☎ 0705 827701
Chalets de France, Travel House, Pandy, Nr Abergavenny NP7 8DH ☎ 0873 890770
Chapter Travel, 126 St John's Wood High Street, London NW8 7ST ☎ 01-586 9451
La France des Villages, Model Farm, Rattlesden,
Bury St Edmunds IP30 0SY ☎ 044 93 7664
Gîtes de France, 178 Piccadilly, London W1V 9DB ☎ 01-493 3480
Vacances en Campagne, Bignor, Pulborough RH20 1QD ☎ 07987 433
VFB Holidays, 1 St Margaret's Terrace, Cheltenham GL50 4DT ☎ 0242 526338

SPORTS AND ACTIVITIES

For unusual and interesting holiday ideas, contact the Loisirs Accueil office:

Loisirs Accueil Yonne
1-2 quai de la République, 89000 AUXERRE ☎ 86.51.12.05

RESORTS

Avallon *(Yonne)*
Pop: 9,000
Auxerre 52 km, Paris 215 km
🛈 6 rue Bocquillot ☎ 86.34.14.19

To the north of the Morvan lakes area, Avallon is an attractive old town perched on a granite outcrop between two ravines overlooking the valley of the Cousin river, where allotments fall in tiers down towards the valley road. Behind its ramparts, the narrow and ancient cobbled streets are happily distanced from the new town. The Morvan Regional Park, a varied landscape of green slopes, gentle streams, swift rivers for canoeing and fishing and lakes for water skiing and sailing, is ideal country for exploring on foot, horseback or cycle. The *Petite Randonnée* Avallonais, that covering the route from Avallon to Vézelay, is invaluable in travelling this fine nature reserve. There are also pony treks throughout. The nature lover will be as taken by the foxgloves, broom and bog-myrtle which grow in abundance here, as by the gardens of the Avallon township itself.

● Camping: Sous-Roche ☎ 86.34.13.50

- Fishing: category 1 fishing on the Cousin, Cure and Trinquelin rivers. Follow the Vézelay route via the Vallée du Cousin along a charming wooded valley road close to the river.
- Cycling: cycles can be hired from the SNCF station.
- Golf: 13h private course at Golf de Clairis, Domaine de Clairis, 89150 Savigny-sur-Clairis ☎ 88.86.33.90 (closed Wed).
- Tennis: six courts to hire.
- Walking: the *Tour de Morvan* route visits all the lakes.

 Beaune *(Côte d'Or)*
Pop: 20,000
Dijon 45 km, Paris 316 km
🛈 rue de l'Hôtel-Dieu ☎ 80.22.24.51

At the heart of the Côte d'Or wine-producing region, Beaune is the headquarters for most of the major wine merchants. A beautiful and historic town, there is much of architectural and artistic interest, as well as plenty of opportunities for free wine tasting (*dégustation gratuite*). Various dates are important in the wine-world's calendar, chief amongst them perhaps the third Sunday in November when a public auction of wines, *Les Trois Glorieuses*, sets the trend for Burgundy prices.

- Ballooning: one-hour flights over the vineyards (May-Oct) depart from the Château La Borde at Meursanges – Société Bombard ☎ 80.26.63.30
- Camping: Les Cents Vignes ☎ 88.22.03.91
- Cycling: cycles can be hired from the SNCF station.
- Flights: in a Cessna 172 light aircraft, flights over the Loire valley and vineyards are a memorable way to sightsee. Nevair Services ☎ 86.38.85.76
- Golf: see Chalon-sur-Saône.
- Riding: explore the area on small, white Camargue horses during weekend trips with Ferme du Cavalier, Villers-La-Faye, 21700 Nuits-St-Georges ☎ 80.62.91.08
- Spa: at Santenay-les-Bains – metabolic disorders (Apr-Oct) ☎ 80.20.62.32 alt: 220 m, climate: mild.
- Vineyards: for local vineyards open to visitors, contact the Tourist Office or follow the motoring signs *Routes du Vin*. The area around Beaune is known as the Côte de Beaune and is where the white Burgundies originate. North of the town, in the direction of Dijon, is the Côte de Nuits region renowned for the world's greatest red wines. There are numerous outlets offering tastings, whilst all-inclusive three-day programmes, in the company of an expert, incorporating tours, tastings and gastronomic feasts are also available. Contact L'Ambassade du Vin,

23 rue des Tonneliers, 21200 Beaune ☎ 80.21.53.72

 Bourbon-Lancy *(Saône-et-Loire)*
Pop: 6,500
Nevers 73 km, Paris 311 km
🛈 place d'Aligre ☎ 85.89.18.27

The quiet rural setting of this pleasant spa town offers relaxation combined with walking and excursions into the beautiful Loire valley region. Casino.

- Camping: Camping de Saint-Prix.
- Fishing: category 2 fishing on the Loire and the Somme rivers.
- Spa: rheumatism/bone joint damage (10 May-30 Sep) ☎ 85.89.18.84 alt: 240 m, climate: temperate.

 Chagny *(Saône-et-Loire)*
Pop: 5,000
Beaune 16 km, Paris 330 km
🛈 2 rue des Halles ☎ 85.87.25.95

A small, rural town at the heart of the wine-producing country, an ideal base for exploring, by car or on foot, the attractions of this lovely sunny countryside of gently sloping vine valleys.

- Ballooning: one-hour flights (Apr-Nov) with Air Escargot, Remigny ☎ 85.87.12.30, low over the vineyards.
- Camping: Municipal du Pâquier-Fané ☎ 85.87.21.42
- Fishing: category 2 fishing on the Dheune river.

🏛 **Chalon-sur-Saône** *(Saône-et-Loire)*
Pop: 58,000
Mâcon 58 km, Paris 338 km
🛈 square Chabas, boulevard de la République ☎ 85.48.37.97

They say that the two most important liquids in Burgundy are wine and water – *l'un pour boire, l'autre pour voir* (the one to drink, the other to look at). Thus, as a centre for water-borne holidays (this was once the most active port and commercial centre on the Saône), and as a base for exploring this famous wine region, Chalon-sur-Saône is well suited. On Fridays and Sundays the colourful market is set up beside the St-Vincent cathedral and, for those who have been up all night, a couple of all-night bakeries (rue Porte de Lyon and rue des Tonneliers) tempt with their fresh croissants. The old and quiet quarter of place St-Vincent near the river reveals some half-timbered houses, sharply in contrast with the many smart shops, pedestrianised shopping areas and lively street cafés of this large commercial and industrial city.

- Ballooning: book through the Tourist Office for hot-air balloon trips with Chalon's flying club.

- Boat Hire: from the Port de Plaisance ☎ 85.48.83.38, with pleasure trips along the river bookable from Chalon Tourisme, place de Beaune ☎ 85.57.26.39
- Camping: Camping de la Butte, St-Marcel ☎ 85.48.26.86
- Cycling: cycles for hire from Flour, rue Michelet ☎ 80.48.14.81 and from the SNCF station.
- Golf: 18h public course situated by the river and ideal for beginners at Golf Chalon-sur-Saône, Zone des Loisirs de St-Nicholas, Chatenoy-en-Bresse, 71380 Saint Marcel ☎ 85.48.61.64
- Riding: Horse-Club, Lessard-le-National ☎ 85.45.72.27 and, at Sennecey-le-Grand, Poney-Plaisir du Moulin de Vavière ☎ 85.44.70.43

Charolles *(Saône-et-Loire)*
Pop: 4,000
Mâcon 53 km, Paris 370 km
🛈 Couvent des Clarisses ☎ 85.24.05.95

This pleasant little town is dominated by the ruins of the Château des Comtes du Charollais, whose ancient capital this once was. Circled by the Arconce (tributary of the Loire), and Semence rivers, a small canal runs through the town, the old houses reflected in its still waters. Lying prettily amidst a countryside of lush meadows and beautiful forests, this is a region famed for producing the strong white Charolais cattle. They can be seen, very early on Thursday mornings, arriving at the huge market in nearby St-Christophe-en-Brionnais, and you can join the local farmers in enjoying the specialist meat dishes served at village inns throughout the proceedings.

- Camping: Municipal, route de Viry ☎ 85.24.04.90
- Fishing: category 2 fishing on the Arconce and Semence rivers.

Digoin *(Saône-et-Loire)*
Pop: 12,000
Maçon 80 km, Paris 336 km
🛈 6 rue Guilleminot ☎ 85.53.00.81

Situated on the banks of the Loire and at the confluence of several smaller rivers, with an unusual water bridge carrying the Canal du Centre over the Loire, Digoin is a cheerful, bustling town offering a wide range of watersports, excellent fishing and a major boating centre.

- Boat Hire: enquire at the Port de Plaisance ☎ 85.88.51.34 for hire on a weekend or weekly basis.
- Camping: Municipal de la Chevrette ☎ 85.53.11.49
- Riding: Vivre à Cheval, St-Agnan ☎ 85.53.81.39

Dijon *(Côte d'Or)*
Pop: 147,000
Besancon 100 km, Paris 320 km
🛈 34 rue des Forges ☎ 80.30.35.39

A great university and business centre, Dijon is the capital of Burgundy, with artistic and architectural treasures spanning the centuries. Museums, art galleries, medieval streets and churches, vineyards producing wines of international repute and, of course, its famous spicy mustard, all combine to make Dijon one of the most memorable towns in Europe. During the summer there's the annual musical event, *Estivade*, in addition to the regular cultural diet of concerts, opera and the theatre. Lakeside watersports are available at Lake Kir just outside the town's perimeters, in addition to the many pleasant parks, gardens and walks along the banks of the River Ouche.

- Boat Hire: apart from gastronomic cruises lasting a full day, there are holiday barges for hire from Locaboat Plaisance, 14 avenue Jean-Jaurès, 21000 Dijon ☎ 80.41.74.30
- Camping: Camping du Lac ☎ 80.43.54.72
- Cuisine: the celebrated chef of the Hôtel de la Cloche makes his early morning purchases at the market then demonstrates some culinary secrets in the hotel's kitchens. Observing then changes to tasting as lunch is served. Every Tuesday and Friday morning (min eight – max 20) bookable from Bourgogne Tour, 11 rue de la Liberté, 21000 Dijon ☎ 80.30.49.49
- Cycling: cycles for hire from Cycles Pouilly, rue de Tivoli ☎ 80.66.61.75 and from the SNCF station.
- Fishing: peaceful spots along the south bank of Lake Kir.
- Golf: 18h private course at Golf de Bourgogne, Bois des Norges, 21490 Norges-la-Ville ☎ 80.35.71.10. Part-owned by racing drivers Jacques Lafitte and Alain Prost, this is one of the best courses in the north-east.
- Vineyards: see Beaune.

Mâcon *(Saône-et-Loire)*
Pop: 40,000
Lyon 69 km, Paris 396 km
🛈 187 rue Carnot ☎ 85.39.71.37

Almost 300 m wide at this point, the River Saône, its banks lined with footpaths, its waters stroked by the oarsman's blades, threads its way past this elegant city, birthplace of the poet Lamartine. A flourishing centre for the wine trade, this is also an excellent base for exploring the Mâconnais Romanesque churches and the extraordinary prehistoric site at Solutré, where excavations have revealed the skeletons of thousands of horses, thought to have been driven over the cliff in some ancient ritual. Today, this steep limestone cliff provides a challenge for rock climbers. On Saturday mornings come alive with stall-holders' calls at the fruit and vegetable market.

The vendange *(grape harvest)*

- Boat Trips: sightseeing day cruises (some including meals) bookable from Les Grands Bateaux de la Saône, cour de la Gare ☎ 85.38.48.61
- Camping: Municipal les Varennes, Sancé ☎ 85.38.16.22
- Cycling: cycles can be hired from the SNCF station.
- Golf: pleasant 18h private course at Golf de la Commanderie Mâcon, Lamusse Crottet, 01290 Pont de Veyle ☎ 85.30.44.12
- Riding: Poney-Club de Laize, Hurigny ☎ 85.36.91.64
- Vineyards: *Suivez la Grappe* signs guide towards wine-tasting cellars plus Romanesque churches, museums and châteaux. Information from Solutré-Pouilly ☎ 85.35.80.81 and the Tourist Office.

Paray-le-Monial *(Saône-et-Loire)*
Pop: 12,000
Mâcon 67 km, Paris 372 km
🛈 avenue Jean-Paul II ☎ 85.81.10.92

A major centre for pilgrimages, attracting hundreds of thousands of visitors annually to honour the Sacred Heart, and with a rich historical past, this town is a good excursion base for visiting the Brionnais Romanesque churches, particularly that of Anzy-le-Duc. The *Magnificat*, a festival of Christian art (July 8-12), brings together the faithful at a unique cultural event. A delightful rural area of rolling Burgundian meadows and shady, riverside paths, the town was honoured by a visit from Pope John Paul in 1986.

- Camping: Municipal le Pré Barré ☎ 85.81.05.05

- Cycling: cycles can be hired from the SNCF station.
- Fishing: in the Bourbince, Oudrache and Arconce rivers.
- Riding: Centre de Tourisme du Charolais, Le Moulin de Vaux, Nochize.

St-Honoré-les-Bains *(Nièvre)*
Pop: 900
Nevers 67 km, Paris 288 km
🛈 place du Marché ☎ 86.30.71.70

Situated in wonderful countryside, this area is a delight for those who enjoy fishing, walking and riding and is on the edge of the Morvan Regional Park, an area of great beauty. The Romans first established a spa here 50 years before the coming of Christ, and today the well-equipped establishment offers short breaks of two, five or seven days for health, rest and leisure, comprising sports activities, entertainment and revitalising thermal treatments. Casino.

- Camping: Camping Bonneau ☎ 86.30.76.00
- Golf: close to Nevers, 9h public course at Golf de Nevers, 58470 Magny-Cours ☎ 86.58.18.30 (closed Tues).
- Spa: respiratory/lymphatic disorders (27 Mar-30 Sep) ☎ 86.30.73.27 alt: 300 m, climate: temperate.

Sens *(Yonne)*
Pop: 27,000
Troyes 65 km, Paris 118 km
🛈 place Jean-Jaurès ☎ 86.65.19.49

St-Etienne is claimed to be the first Gothic cathedral in the country. Sens was known to the Romans and stands now where the boundaries of the Champagne country, Ile de France and Burgundy, meet. A cluster of sixteenth-century houses on the banks of the Yonne, surrounded by later buildings, are linked by boulevards and promenades of some elegance, where once the old ramparts ran. From Sens, the Ile de France opens up its lovely forests, gardens, châteaux and riverside landscapes, all within easy reach. Walking, cycling and riding tours.

- Camping: Municipal Entre-deux-Vannes
  ☎ 86.65.64.71
- Canoeing: canoes can be hired from the Canoe and Kayak Club ☎ 86.95.34.10
- Cuisine: weekend of cookery and shooting with Hôtel de Paris et de la Poste. Details from Jovitour, 10 quai Leclerc, 89300 Joigny
  ☎ 86.62.16.31
- Cycling: cycles can be hired from MBK Motobecane, rue Victor Guichard
  ☎ 80.56.11.27
- Riding: Centre Equestre et Poney-Club de Saligny, 30 Grande-Rue ☎ 86.97.83.27

Tournus (*Saône-et-Loire*)
Pop: 7,000
Mâcon 31 km, Paris 360 km
🄴 place Carnot ☎ 85.51.13.10

Ancient and historic town situated on the Saône river, whose bridges command serene views. The river here divides two quite different regions. To the east lie the gently rolling river valleys, paradise for anglers. To the west, by contrast, is the Tournugeois, an uneven land of sudden escarpments and vine-covered slopes.

- Camping: Municipal Le Pas Fleury

☎ 85.51.16.58
- Riding: Centre Equestre de Corlay.

Vézelay (*Yonne*)
Pop: 600
Avallon 15 km, Paris 215 km
🄴 rue Saint-Pierre ☎ 86.33.23.69

At Vézelay, Roman and Gothic styles unite in harmony. Classified by UNESCO as a monument on the world heritage list, it was thought incomparable, a perfection of Romanesque architecture, not only the abbey with its splendid pink ochre basilica, but the terraces, houses and ramparts of the village itself. The abbey was founded in the ninth century, and its sacred relics of Mary Magdalene made it a place of pilgrimage and an important stopping point on the pilgrim route to Santiago de Compostela in Spain. Restored in the nineteenth century, the little town now hosts important concerts, and each year, on 22 July, the Pilgrimage of Ste-Madeleine takes place. From bases at Beaune and Nevers, air trips over Vézelay can be made, while below the slow, unhurried pace of life of horse-drawn travel is a popular feature and matches the rural tranquillity of the area.

- Camping: Camping Croix-Ste-Marthe
  ☎ 86.33.24.18
- Horse-drawn travel: holidays in covered wagons and gypsy caravans bookable through Roulottes en Morvan, la Tour Gaillon, Vézelay ☎ 86.33.25.74
- Riding: ALCV (Arts, Loisirs, Campagne Vacances), Moulin de Soeuvres
  ☎ 86.33.31.07

BRETAGNE

Administrative
Centre: Rennes
Population: 2,595,400
Area: 27,184 sq km

Départements:
22 Côtes-du-Nord
29 Finistère
35 Ille-et-Vilaine
56 Morbihan

Regional Parks:
Parc Naturel Régional
d'Armorique,
Ménez-Meur Hanvec,
29224 Daoulas
☎ 98.68.81.71

Parc Naturel Régional
de Brière, 180 Ile de
Fédrun, 44720
Saint-Joachim
☎ 40.88.42.72

The thick granite promontory of Brittany separates the Channel from the Atlantic, jutting west in a wriggling 3,200-km coastline of long beaches, coves, cliff faces and busy little fishing ports. Brittany is sea country, an ideal holiday world for a young family: sunny sands, rock pools to be explored and headlands scrambled, with sailing and windsurfing.

It is the only Celtic region in France. Some of the place names might be in Cornwall. Indeed the graceful old town of Quimper is the capital of France's *Cornouaille*. The Breton country shares King Arthur with Britain's West Country. Here, in La Forêt de Paimpont, the Knights of the Round Table adventured in Merlin's legendary Broceliande and, in the Ile d'Aval, a megalith stands, reputedly marking Arthur's tomb.

Old occupations have all but vanished and once-busy ports have dwindled in activity. The canal system linking the Rivers Sarthe, Mayenne and Vilaine bridges the big waters of the Channel and the Atlantic, and once brought water-borne trade between St-Malo, Redon and Arzal, and between Nantes, Redon, Pontivy and Lorient. It now forms a 640-km inland waterway network for pleasure craft, with several companies, both in the UK and in France, offering cabin cruisers and narrow boats for hire.

The coast, from ancient Dinard to the east, even a hundred years ago a fashionable resort for wealthy English travellers, down to the modern La Baule in the south, offers resorts of all varieties: fishing ports, marinas and yachting basins, secluded coves, creeks, estuaries and wild windsurfing stretches. Indeed windsurfing has become a recent speciality with holidaymakers, and the stretch of coast between Audierne and Concarneau is ideal both for the expert and the novice with windsurfing championships held each year at Pointe de la Torche near Pont l'Abbé.

Many happy family holidays have also been spent at St-Malo, the ancient walled port, in its nearby resorts of Dinard and Dinan, or, not far away, Jugon-les-Lacs, a charming village of old houses on the banks of a big swimming and boating lake. There are also splendid family holidays to be spent on the beaches of Le Val-André, St-Jacut, Ploumanach, Le Conquet, Bénodet and on the vast Erquy beach.

The retired, and perhaps wealthier tourists may wend their way towards the smart and popular Perros-Guirec, to Beg-Meil or St-Cast-le-Guildo, to the marinas of Bénodet and Concarneau or the fashionable yachting centre of L'Aber Wrac'h.

At Pont Aven and Le Pouldu, Gauguin lived and painted for some years,

Concarneau

establishing there the Pont Aven School of Painting. The area continues to attract artists today.

Canal and river cruising takes the visitor through the lovely meadowland and forest of Huelgoat and Paimpont, with boats to hire from Redon and Port Comblant. The Château des Rohan is perched high above the River Oust at Josselin; the moated Château de Fougères squats massively on the River Nancon.

Fishing remains the life-blood of the country. In place of the weather cock atop one village steeple, a tuna fish marks the direction of the prevailing wind. Audierne is still a lobster port, Cancale and Belon are famous for their oysters, Camaret for crayfish, Concarneau for tuna fishing, Douarnenez for sardines.

Inland there are lakes for boating holidays and for fishing. The countryside, broken up by small farms, is ideal for walking and, like Cornwall, there is a profusion of prehistoric remains to be visited. Dolmen (burial chambers) lie throughout the area and, at Carnac, nearly 3,000 menhirs (standing stones) dating back to 4500 BC, punctuate the landscape. Very ancient, too, are the forests of Lanouée, Paimpont and Huelgoat, in a region which was once all forest.

Traditionally, the Bretons recognise hundreds of local saints, many of them not acknowledged by Rome but celebrated in every village by the annual *pardons*, feast days with bannered marches. At lonely points along the coast stone crucifixes have been erected to those who have lost their lives in the surrounding, often cruel, seas of Brittany. Off the coast a spatter of rocky islands stand, many of them, like the Ile d'Ouessant and the beautiful Ile de Bréhat, bird sanctuaries.

At St-Lunaire, on the Côte d'Emeraude, a succession of inlets and cliff faces, rocks, small islands and sudden beaches open up against the many greens of the sea. It was here that Claude Debussy, commemorating Brittany in music, wrote *La Mer*.

PRACTICAL TOURIST INFORMATION

General information on the region can be obtained by telephoning or writing to the Comité Régional du Tourisme (CRT) office, while specific booklets are produced detailing camping, hotel and self-catering gîte accommodation. These can be obtained by writing to the tourist board office for the département (CDT) of your choice:

Regional Tourist Board
Comité Régional du Tourisme (CRT), 3 rue
d'Espagne, B.P. 4175, 35041 RENNES Cedex
☎ 99.50.11.15

Départements
Côtes-du-Nord (22): Comité Départemental du
Tourisme (CDT), 1 rue Chateaubriand, 22000
SAINT-BRIEUC ☎ 96.61.66.70
Finistère (29): Comité Départemental du Tourisme
(CDT), 6 rue Réné-Madec, 29000 QUIMPER
☎ 98.95.28.86
Ille-et-Vilaine (35): Comité Départemental du
Tourisme (CDT), 1 rue Martenot, 35032 RENNES
Cedex ☎ 99.02.97.43
Morbihan (56): Comité Départemental du
Tourisme (CDT), B.P.400, 56009 VANNES Cedex
☎ 97.42.61.60

SELF-CATERING ACCOMMODATION

*The following British operators offer self-catering
accommodation in the area:*

AA Motoring Holidays, P.O. Box 100, Fanum
House, Halesowen B63 3BT ☎ 021-550 7401
Agencefrance Holidays, Lansdowne Place,
17 Holdenhurst Road, Bournemouth BH8 8EH
☎ 0202 299534
Allez France, 27 West Street, Storrington,
Pulborough RH20 4DZ ☎ 09066 2345
Angel Travel, 47 High Street, Central Chambers,
Tonbridge TN9 1SD ☎ 0732 361115
Avon Europe, Lower Quinton, Stratford-upon-
Avon, Warks CV37 8SG ☎ 0789 720130
Beach Villas, 8 Market Passage, Cambridge
CB2 3QR ☎ 0223 311113
Blakes Holidays, Wroxham, Norwich NR12 8DH
☎ 0603 784131
Bowhills Ltd, Swanmore, Southampton SO3 2QW
☎ 0489 877627
Brittany Direct Holidays, 362 Sutton Common
Road, Sutton SM3 9PL ☎ 01-641 6060
Brittany Ferries, The Brittany Centre, Wharf
Road, Portsmouth PO2 8RU ☎ 0705 827701
Brittany Villas, Holiday House, 2 Monson Road,
Tunbridge Wells TN1 1NN ☎ 0892 36616
Carasol Holidays, 6 Hayes Avenue, Bournemouth
BH7 7AD ☎ 0202 33398
Chalets de France, Travel House, Pandy,
Nr Abergavenny NP7 8DH ☎ 0873 890770
Clearwater Holidays, 17 Heath Terrace,
Leamington Spa CV32 5NA ☎ 0926 450002
Cosmos Motoring Holidays, Tourama House,
17 Homesdale Road, Bromley BR2 9LX
☎ 01-464 3121
Cresta Holidays, 32 Victoria Street, Altrincham
WA14 1ET ☎ 0345 056511
Crystal Holiday Villas, The Courtyard, Arlington
Road, Surbiton KT6 6BW ☎ 01-399 5144
Dieppe Ferries Holidays, Weymouth Quay,
Weymouth DT4 8DY ☎ 0305 777444
Eurovillas, 36 East Street, Coggleshall, Colchester

CO6 1SH ☎ 0376 561156
France Directe, 2 Church Street, Warwick
CV34 4AB ☎ 0926 497989
France Voyages, 145 Oxford Street, London
W1R 1TB ☎ 01-494 3155
Freedom in France, Meadows, Poughill, Bude,
Cornwall EX23 9EN ☎ 0288 55591
French Life Motoring Holidays, 26 Church Road,
Horsforth, Leeds LS18 5LG ☎ 0532 390077
French Travel Service, Georgian House, 69 Boston
Manor Road, Brentford TW8 0JQ ☎ 01-568 8442
French Villa Centre, 175 Selsdon Park Road,
Croydon CR2 8JJ ☎ 01-651 1231
Gîtes de France, 178 Piccadilly, London W1V 9DB
☎ 01-493 3480
Hoseasons Holidays Abroad, Sunway House,
Lowestoft NR32 3LT ☎ 0502 500555
Hoverspeed, Maybrook House, Queens Gardens,
Dover CT17 9UQ ☎ 0304 240241
Intasun France, Intasun House, Cromwell Avenue,
Bromley BR2 9AQ ☎ 01-290 1900
Interhome, 383 Richmond Road, Twickenham
TW1 2EF ☎ 01-891 1294
Just France, 1 Belmont, Lansdown Road, Bath
BA1 5DZ ☎ 0225 446328
Lagrange Vacances, 16/20 New Broadway, London
W5 2XA ☎ 01-579 7311
Meon Villas, Meon House, College Street,
Petersfield GU32 3JN ☎ 0730 68411
David Newman's French Collection, P.O. Box 733,
40 Upperton Road, Eastbourne BN21 4AW
☎ 0323 410347
Par-Tee Tours, Riverside House, 53 Uxbridge
Road, Rickmansworth WD3 2DH ☎ 0923 721565
Pleasurewood Holidays, Somerset House, Gordon
Road, Lowestoft NR32 1PZ ☎ 0502 517271
La Première Quality Holidays, Solva,
Haverfordwest SA62 6YE ☎ 03483 7871
Les Propriétaires de l'Ouest, Malton House,
24 Hampshire Terrace, Portsmouth PO1 2QE
☎ 0705 755715
Quo Vadis, 243 Euston Road, London NW1 2BT
☎ 01-583 8383
Rendez-Vous France, Holiday House,
146/148 London Road, St Albans AL1 1PQ
☎ 0727 45400
Rentavilla, 27 High Street, Chesterton, Cambridge
CB4 1NB ☎ 0223 323414
Sealink Holidays, Charter House, Park Street,
Ashford TN24 8EX ☎ 0233 47033
SFV Holidays, Summer House, 68 Hernes Road,
Summertown, Oxford OX2 7QL ☎ 0865 57738
Slipaway Holidays, 90 Newland Road, Worthing
BN11 1LB ☎ 0903 821000
Starvillas, 25 High Street, Chesterton, Cambridge
CB4 1ND ☎ 0223 311990
Sturge, Martin, 3 Lower Camden Place, Bath
BA1 5JJ ☎ 0225 310623
Sun France, 3 Beaufort Gardens, London
SW16 3BP ☎ 01-679 4562
Sunselect Villas, 60 Crow Hill North, Middleton,
Manchester M24 1FB ☎ 061-655 3055
Sunvista Holidays, 5a George Street, Warminster

BA12 8QA ☎ 0985 217444
Tourarc UK, 197b Brompton Road, London
SW3 1LA ☎ 01-589 1918
Eric Turrell Travel, Moore House, Moore Road,
Bourton-on-the-Water, Cheltenham GL54 2AZ
☎ 0451 20927
Vacances, 28 Gold Street, Saffron Walden
CB10 1EJ ☎ 0799 25101
Vacances en Campagne, Bignor, Pulborough
RH20 1QD ☎ 07987 433
Vacances France, 14 Bowthorpe Road, Wisbech
PE13 2DX ☎ 0945 587830
Vacations, 60 Charles Street, Leicester LE1 1FB
☎ 0533 537758
VFB Holidays, 1 St Margaret's Terrace,
Cheltenham GL50 4DT ☎ 0242 526338
Villa France, 15 Winchcombe Road, Frampton
Cotterell, Bristol BS17 2AG ☎ 0454 772410

SPORTS AND ACTIVITIES

*For unusual and interesting holiday ideas, contact
the Loisirs Accueil office for the area of your
choice:*

Loisirs Accueil Côtes-du-Nord,
5 rue Baratoux, B.P. 556, 22010 SAINT-BRIEUC
Cedex ☎ 96.62.12.40
Loisirs Accueil Ille-et-Vilaine,
1 rue Martenot, 35000 RENNES ☎ 99.02.97.41
Loisirs Accueil Morbihan,
Hôtel du Département, B.P.400, 56009 VANNES
Cedex ☎ 97.42.61.60
Maison de la Bretagne,
17 rue de l'Arrivée, B.P.1006, 75737 PARIS Cedex
☎ 45.38.73.15

RESORTS

 Audierne (*Finistère*)
Pop: 3,000
Quimper 35 km, Paris 590 km
🛈 place de la Liberté ☎ 98.70.12.20

Towards the westernmost tip of Europe, Audierne
is essentially a lobster and crayfishing port, with a
good beach nearby. It also caters for pleasure trips,
with daily sailings out to the Ile de Sein, a rocky,
windswept island. For ornithologists, there is an
important bird reserve at nearby Cap Sizun, where
colonies of nesting and migratory seabirds can be
observed.

● Bird Reserve: on Mondays and Thursdays
   between 9 and 12 a.m. (in July and August)
   accompanied walks are offered by the Réserve
   de Cap Sizun at Goulien ☎ 98.70.13.53
● Camping: Kerhuon ☎ 98.70.10.91
● Canoeing: lessons from Club Nautique du
   Goyen ☎ 98.70.86.27
● Fishing: sea fishing trips ☎ 98.70.03.90
● Windsurfing: CNPA offers lessons
   ☎ 98.70.21.69

 Beg-Meil (*Finistère*)
Pop: 1,000
Quimper 20 km, Paris 552 km
🛈 SI ☎ 98.94.97.47 (Jun-Sep)

Modest little harbour resort in unspoilt Brittany,
with a good selection of shops and cafés. Beautiful
views look back over the Baie de la Forêt and
towards Concarneau to which there is a regular
boat service (30-min crossing). Sandy bays and
little rocky coves are good for bathing.

● Camping: La Piscine ☎ 98.56.04.23 and La
   Roche Percée ☎ 98.94.94.15
● Boating: trips to the Iles de Glénan and up the
   Odet river estuary.
● Golf: see Concarneau.
● Riding: Poney-Club at Ferme de
   Kérancoréden, 29118 Gouesnac'h
   ☎ 98.54.67.07; Poney-Club also at
   Renouveau ☎ 98.94.98.47
● Sailing: and deep-sea diving schools.
● Tennis: five hard courts for hire at Kerlosquen
   ☎ 98.56.00.93 (Jun-Sep); and three at
   Renouveau ☎ 98.94.98.47

 Bénodet (*Finistère*)
Pop: 3,000
Fouesnant 9 km, Paris 555 km
🛈 51 avenue Plage ☎ 98.57.00.14

The traditional charms of promenade cafés and
restaurants, sandy beaches, secluded coves and
pine forests ensure the continued popularity of this
delightful little town. Today it acts as a magnet,
particularly for the British, as a windsurfing and
yachting centre and there are boat trips across to
the Iles de Glénan and river trips up the pretty
wooded Odet estuary as well as good river fishing.
Casino.

● Beach: choice of sandy beaches plus numerous
   secluded coves.
● Boat Trips: between April and October cruises
   up the Odet river estuary to Quimper operate
   several times a day. These can be combined
   with a delicious lunchtime or evening meal.
   Vedettes de l'Odet ☎ 98.57.00.58
● Camping: Camping du Port de Plaisance
   ☎ 98.57.02.38
● Golf: new 18h public course at Golf de l'Odet
   Quimper, Clohars Fouesnant, 29118 Bénodet
   ☎ 98.57.26.16
● Riding: Club de Lasso. Enquire at the Tourist
   Office.
● Sailing: and windsurfing school at Yacht Club
   de l'Odet ☎ 98.57.26.09; also UCPA
   ☎ 98.57.03.26

 Cancale (*Ille-et-Vilaine*)
Pop: 5,000
Dinan 34 km, Paris 360 km
🛈 44 rue du Port ☎ 99.89.63.72

Cancale is an important fish-processing rather than

fishing port, specialising in shellfish factories, but the little port, with its sand and shingle beach, has great charm. Cruises embrace the bay of Cancale and the bay of Mont-St-Michel and there are opportunities for sailing, water skiing and scuba diving.

- Boat Trips: from the Gare Maritime at Vivier-sur-Mer ☎ 99.48.82.30
- Camping: Port Mer ☎ 99.89.63.17

 Carnac (*Morbihan*)
Pop: 4,000
Vannes 31 km, Paris 487 km
🖼 74 avenue Druides ☎ 97.52.13.52

Smart seaside resort set amidst pine forests with wide, sheltered, south-facing beaches, a yacht marina and plenty of watersports. Within walking distance are the 3,000 standing stones (menhirs) which are as old and mysterious as those at Stonehenge. Night life is lively in this popular resort and there are sheltered and gently shelving wide, sandy beaches.

- Boat Trips: cruises tour the Golfe du Morbihan and are bookable from quai Franklin, Auray ☎ 97.56.27.64
- Camping: Grande Metairie ☎ 97.55.71.47
- Golf: pleasant and busy parkland 18h public course at Golf de St-Laurent Ploemel Carnac, 56400 Auray ☎ 97.56.85.18
- Thalassotherapy: (open 1 Jan-20 Nov) Centre de Thalassothérapie, B.P.83, 56340 Carnac ☎ 97.52.04.44

 Concarneau (*Finistère*)
Pop: 19,000
Quimper 24 km, Paris 540 km
🖼 quai d'Aiguillon ☎ 98.97.01.44

An important fishing port, Concarneau is also a pleasant seaside resort with an old walled town (La Ville Close) within the colourful harbour, good shopping and a large sailing centre. Boat trips from here to the Iles de Glénan take only 25 minutes and there are several safe and sandy beaches. At low tide they are liable to be very seaweedy.

- Camping: Camping des Prés-Verts ☎ 98.97.09.74 and Camping du Dorlett ☎ 98.97.16.44
- Cycling: cycles can be hired from the SNCF station.
- Fishing: good river and sea fishing.
- Golf: mature and well-maintained 9h private course at Golf de Quimper et de Cornouaille, Manoir de Mesmeur, 29133 La Forêt Fouesnant ☎ 98.56.97.09
- Sailing: Société Nautique de la Baie ☎ 98.97.34.84
- Waterskiing: Locabellou ☎ 98.97.41.03
- Windsurfing: rue des Iles ☎ 98.50.67.83

 Crozon-Morgat (*Finistère*)
Pop: 9,000
Douarnenez 46 km, Paris 588 km
🖼 boulevard de la Plage (at Morgat)
☎ 98.27.07.92

Although the Finistère coast is wild, there are sheltered inlets and, shielded by high cliffs, beaches of marvellous sand, such as that at Crozon-Morgat. The port of Morgat specialises in sardine fishing, but the resort caters for family holidays. The yachting harbour has moorings for 600 and there are sea-fishing trips along the coast.

- Beach: beautiful sheltered beaches.
- Canoeing: lessons available from ULAMIR ☎ 98.27.01.68
- Fishing: sea-fishing trips organised by Vedettes Sirènes ☎ 98.27.29.90
- Riding: Centre Equestre de Trébéron ☎ 98.27.15.06
- Sailing: Centre Nautique de Crozon-Morgat ☎ 98.27.01.98

 Dinard (*Ille-et-Vilaine*)
Pop: 10,000
Rennes 72 km, Paris 417 km
🖼 2 boulevard Féart ☎ 99.46.94.12

Popular for over a century, evidenced by the luxury villas and gardens, the fashionable Côte d'Emeraude (Emerald Coast) resort of Dinard is attractively situated at the mouth of the River Rance opposite St-Malo. Its mild climate encourages year-round family holidaymakers to this, the largest resort on the north coast, with a choice of sandy beaches in attractive rocky bays. Casino.

- Camping: La Ville Mauny ☎ 99.46.94.73 and La Prieure ☎ 99.46.20.04
- Cycling: cycles can be hired from the SNCF station.
- Golf: 18h private links course at Golf de Dinard, 35800 St-Briac-sur-Mer ☎ 99.88.32.07 (founded in 1887, this is the second oldest course in the country).

 Douarnenez (*Finistère*)
Pop: 18,000
Quimper 22 km, Paris 575 km
🖼 2 rue Dr-Mével ☎ 98.92.13.35

Life here revolves around the sea and its associated industries, while holidaymakers and tourists are attracted by its picturesque setting, the pleasant beaches, both here and at Tréboul close by, and the good watersports. They are often to be rewarded, too, by the sight of Breton women going about their business in traditional dress.

- Beach: most facilities offered at the beach Les Sables Blancs at Tréboul.
- Camping: Camping de Kerleyou ☎ 98.74.03.52 and Camping de Trézulien ☎ 98.74.03.76

- Cycling: cycles can be hired from the SNCF station.
- Fishing: sea fishing trips on the Vedette Rosmeur ☎ 98.27.10.71
- Sailing: also canoeing and windsurfing lessons from Centre Nautique ☎ 98.74.13.79; also Voile d'Iroise ☎ 98.92.36.94
- Thalassotherapy: (open all year) Centre de Cure Marine de la Baie de Tréboul-Douarnenez, 42 bis rue des Professeurs Curie, B.P.4, 29100 Douarnenez ☎ 98.74.09.59. The centre specialises in the treatment of sports injuries.

 Erdeven *(Morbihan)*
Pop: 3,000
Carnac 8 km, Paris 492 km
🗗 7 rue Abbé le Barh ☎ 97.55.64.60

Small unspoilt town amidst pretty countryside of pines and gorse, within easy reach of the coastal resorts, where the long stretches of wet sand lend themselves to the sport of sand yachting. As at Carnac, there are menhirs to be seen here amidst a lovely area for riding and walking.

- Beach: nearby plage de Kerhillio has an 8 km safe, sandy beach.
- Camping: Les Sept Saints ☎ 97.55.52.65
- Fishing: on the Etel river and sea fishing.
- Golf: see Carnac.

Erquy *(Côtes-du-Nord)*
Pop: 4,000
Dinard 40 km, Paris 455 km
🗗 boulevard Mer ☎ 96.72.30.12

Small and busy scallop-fishing port and family seaside resort situated within a sheltered bay, with three harbours offering mooring for 400 pleasure boats. There are good beaches at Sables-d'Or-les-Pins (8 km) and at Val-André (11 km) and fine camp sites amongst the typically Breton cottage landscape.

- Camping: les Pins ☎ 96.72.31.12
- Golf: at Sables-d'Or-les-Pins (8 km) ☎ 96.41.42.57
- Riding: ☎ 96.72.19.05

Jugon-les-Lacs *(Côtes-du-Nord)*
Pop: 1,500
Dinan 22 km, Paris 380 km
🗗 SI ☎ 96.31.68.27

Lake Jugon is situated a few kilometres west of Dinan, in a river and *etang* (pool) region rich in fish. The old houses of Jugon-les-Lacs are set between lake and reservoir, an ideal centre for riding, walking and watersports generally. The seaside resorts of St-Malo, Paramé and Dinard are within 30 km.

- Camping: Le Bocage ☎ 96.31.60.16
- Fishing: category 2 fishing on the Arguenon and Rosette rivers.

 Loctudy *(Finistère)*
Pop: 4,000
Douarnenez 39 km, Paris 570 km
🗗 place de la Mairie ☎ 98.87.53.78 (Jun-Sep)

Pretty port on the estuary of the Pont l'Abbé river, popular as a family seaside resort and set amidst the beautiful countryside of the Pays Bigouden area. The rhythm of life is marked by the comings and goings of the fishing boats and there is a fish auction at 5.30 p.m. every day.

- Beach: sandy on the open sea.
- Boat Trips: Vedettes de l'Odet operate trips to the Iles de Glénan and up the Odet estuary (see Bénodet).
- Fishing: good river and sea fishing.
- Sailing: Renouveau ☎ 98.87.40.22
- Windsurfing: Cercle Nautique ☎ 98.87.42.84

Paimpol *(Côtes-du-Nord)*
Pop: 9,000
St-Brieuc 45 km, Paris 495 km
🗗 place République ☎ 96.20.83.16

The seas off Paimpol are full of reefs and the small town, once noted for its cod-fishing fleet, now concentrates on oysters. Boats leave for the Ile du Bréhat, a sunny and fertile little island in the bay of St-Brieuc.

- Camping: Cruckin ☎ 96.20.78.47
- Fishing: sea fishing trips available from Loc'Ocean ☎ 96.20.17.76
- Golf: ideal family 9h private course set in château grounds at Golf du Bois Gelin, Pléhédel, 22290 Lanvollon ☎ 96.22.31.24
- Riding: Coat Bruc, Plourivo ☎ 96.55.93.16
- Sailing: and sea kayaking are popular here, in fact this is the largest kayaking centre in France. Enquire at the Youth Hostel (Auberge de la Jeunesse) ☎ 96.20.83.60

 Penmarc'h *(Finistère)*
Pop: 1,000
Quimper 30 km, Paris 600 km
🗗 SI ☎ 98.58.81.44

Treeless landscape with squat white cottages standing square-set against the weather, for this is a wild and windswept coastline where the invigorating, salty air lends itself to such pursuits as sand yachting, windsurfing and riding along the beach. The enormous, crashing seas are very impressive in rough weather.

- Beach: 12-km sandy beach.
- Camping: Grand Camping de la Plage ☎ 98.58.61.90
- Riding: Centre Equestre de la Joie ☎ 98.58.79.60
- Sailing: Cercle de Voile ☎ 98.58.60.19

Perros-Guirec *(Côtes-du-Nord)*
Pop: 8,000
St-Brieuc 74 km, Paris 526 km
🛈 21 place Hôtel de Ville ☎ 96.23.21.15

An attractive and very popular resort on a coast famed for its rose-red granite rock formations. Good shopping, beaches and lively night life attract the crowds and boats leave daily for trips around the Sept Iles (nature reserve and bird sanctuary).

● Beach: soft sandy beaches at Trestraou and Trestrignel. At Ploumanac'h low tide reveals extraordinarily shaped rocks on the beach.
● Camping: Camping le Ranolien, Ploumanac'h ☎ 96.23.21.13; Trestraou Camping ☎ 96.23.08.11 and Camping Claire Fontaine ☎ 96.23.21.37
● Casino: Casino de la Côte de Granit Rose, plage de Trestraou ☎ 96.23.20.51 (Apr-Sep).
● Golf: see Trébeurden.
● Sailing: open all year, Le Centre Nautique de Perros-Guirec on Trestraou beach offers sailing tuition to children as well as classes in windsurfing and boat hire ☎ 96.23.25.62
● Thalassotherapy: (Feb-Nov) Centre de Thalassothérapie de Perros-Guirec, B.P.50, boulevard Joseph Bihan, Plage de Trestraou, 22700 Perros-Guirec ☎ 96.23.28.97
● Tennis: five courts at Tennis Club de Trestraou ☎ 96.23.22.30
● Walking: follow the old *sentiers de Douanier* (Customs' paths) to Ploumanac'h.

 Pléneuf-Val-André *(Côtes-du-Nord)*
Pop: 4,000
St-Malo 54 km, Paris 450 km
🛈 1 rue Winston-Churchill ☎ 96.72.20.55

Great family resort, particularly popular with the British as it has one of the finest sandy beaches in Brittany and good watersports facilities for such a small town.

● Beach: 3-km curving sandy beach ideal for small children and, at low tide, an enormous play area.
● Camping: Les Monts Colleux ☎ 96.72.95.10
● Casino: (Jul-Sep) La Rotonde ☎ 96.72.85.06
● Golf: see St-Cast-le-Guildo.
● Riding: lessons and treks with Club Hippique de Nantois ☎ 96.72.25.27 and La Jeannette ☎ 96.72.95.79
● Sailing: Centre Nautique offers sailing, kayaking and windsurfing lessons from its bases at the ports of Dahouet and Piegu ☎ 96.72.95.28 (open all year).
● Tennis: 12 courts to hire at Tennis l'Amirauté ☎ 96.72.23.25
● Walking: follow the *sentiers de Douanier* (Customs' paths) along the coast for panoramic views of the Baie de St-Brieuc.

 Quiberon *(Morbihan)*
Pop: 7,000

Vannes 46 km, Paris 502 km
🛈 7 rue Verdun ☎ 97.50.07.84

One of the most beautiful parts of Brittany, Quiberon is a popular and interesting town situated on the very tip of the narrow Côte Sauvage peninsula, the west coast of which is wildly buffeted by the Atlantic. Boat excursions to the accurately named Belle-Ile, plus the smaller islands of Houat and Hoëdic, reward those seeking more good bathing possibilities. Night life is lively and there is a casino, but traffic congestion at weekends can be horrific.

● Beach: numerous safe and sheltered beaches on the east coast *but it is positively dangerous to swim around the rocks or caves on the west even if the sea appears calm.*
● Cycling: cycles can be hired from the SNCF station.
● Thalassotherapy: (open Feb-Dec) Institut de Thalassothérapie de Quiberon, B.P.170, 56170 Quiberon ☎ 97.50.20.00

 Roscoff *(Finistère)*
Pop: 4,000
Brest 64 km, Paris 564 km
🛈 square J.-P. le Jeune ☎ 98.69.70.70

A little fishing port remarkable for being the richest place in Europe for seaweed, hence the popularity of the marine therapy treatment centre here. Not unattractive, the austere old stone houses line the busy port area, another major cross-Channel ferry route. Boat trips to the Ile du Batz sail every hour, its mild climate and good beaches making this a popular excursion.

● Beach: sand and shingle on the nearby estuaries.
● Camping: Camping Municipal ☎ 98.69.70.86 and Camping de Kerestat ☎ 98.69.71.92
● Cycling: cycles can be hired from the SNCF station.
● Fishing: sea fishing trips on Vedettes Blanches ☎ 98.61.77.75
● Thalassotherapy: (open all year) Clinique de Rééducation Fonctionelle Ker-Lena, B.P.13, 29211 Roscoff ☎ 98.61.24.11; also Institut Marin Rockroum Centre de Thalassothérapie, B.P.28, 29211 Roscoff (Apr-Oct) ☎ 98.69.72.15

St-Cast-le-Guildo *(Côtes-du-Nord)*
Pop: 4,000
St-Malo 34 km, Paris 432 km
🛈 place Charles-de-Gaulle ☎ 96.41.81.52

A popular seaside resort which extends the length of a peninsula with seven well-sheltered beaches of fine sand edged by rocky cliffs. There are good watersports facilities and river and sea fishing trips are available.

● Camping: Le Chatelet ☎ 96.41.96.33 and Le Château de Galinée ☎ 96.41.10.56
● Cycling: cycles for hire from M. Page, rue de

l'Isle ☎ 96.41.87.71
- Golf: often crowded 18h private course suitable for beginners and juniors in a beautiful position facing the sea at Golf de Pen Guen, 22380 St-Cast-le-Guildo ☎ 96.41.91.20; and 9h private course (half-woodland, half-links) at Golf des Sables-d'Or-Les-Pins, 22240 Fréhel ☎ 96.41.42.57
- Painting: drawing and watercolour courses, both outdoor and in the studio, from Atelier de Galinée ☎ 96.41.10.28
- Riding: Centre Equestre du Bois Bras ☎ 96.41.95.01
- Sailing: school offering sailing and windsurfing tuition to beginners and improvers at the Ecole de Voile based in the port ☎ 96.41.86.42
- Tennis: 12 courts to hire at the Tennis Club ☎ 96.41.88.16
- Walking: follow the coastal paths.

 St-Malo (*Ille-et-Vilaine*)
Pop: 48,000
St-Brieuc 86 km, Paris 415 km
🚹 esplanade St-Vincent ☎ 99.56.64.48

Delightful old city of narrow, cobbled streets, once the haunt of pirates (corsairs) and magnificently situated on a rocky promontary off the mainland. Great restoration followed the massive bomb damage suffered during 1944 and, together with the closely neighbouring resorts of Paramé, St-Servan and Rothéneuf, this is now a built-up and commercialised coastline which stretches from St-Malo towards Cancale to the east and towards Val-André to the west. Casino.

- Camping: La Houbarderie ☎ 99.81.85.29 and Cité d'Aleth ☎ 99.81.60.91
- Cycling: cycles can be hired from the SNCF station.
- Golf: new 18h private course with many water hazards at St-Malo le Tronchet, 35540 Miniac Morvan ☎ 99.68.96.69
- Thalassotherapy: (open Feb-Dec) Les Thermes Marins, Grande Plage, 100 boulevard Hébert, B.P.32, 35401 St-Malo ☎ 99.56.02.56

 St-Quay-Portrieux (*Côtes-du-Nord*)
Pop: 4,000
St-Brieuc 20 km, Paris 460 km
🚹 17 bis rue Jeanne-d'Arc ☎ 96.70.40.64

Busy and popular family resort on the Côte d'Armor, with good bathing beaches and sports facilities, exhilarating cliff walks and pretty countryside nearby, perhaps best explored by bicycle.

- Beach: five safe and sandy beaches (Casino, Châtelet, Comtesse, Port and Grève Noire).
- Camping: Camping Bellevue ☎ 96.70.41.84
- Casino: ☎ 96.70.40.36
- Golf: flat 18h public course, interestingly laid out with raised greens, at Golf des Ajoncs d'Or, 22410 St-Quay-Portrieux ☎ 96.70.48.13

- Riding: Ranch des Ajoncs d'Or, Kerisago, route de Paimpol ☎ 96.20.32.54
- Sailing: and windsurfing, sea kayaking, catamaran, judo, waterskiing and other sports and activities are offered for young people aged between 13 and 20 years. Tuition is available on a weekly, fortnightly, monthly or longer basis from the CLJ (Centre des Loisirs pour les Jeunes) and is located at 10 boulevard de Gaulle, but bookable through the Tourist Office.
- Tennis: nine courts to hire.

 Trébeurden (*Côtes-du-Nord*)
Pop: 4,000
Perros-Guirec 13 km, Paris 524 km
🚹 place de Crech-Héry ☎ 96.23.51.64

The Gulf Stream brings its warm waters to this extremely pretty fishing port and seaside resort. Lovely walks along the rocky coast, with only the seabirds as company, or inland past megalithic monuments and historic old chapels, contrast with the ultra-modern white dome of the satellite communications centre at Pleumeur-Bodou.

- Beach: large sweeping sandy beach (Tresmeur) plus numerous rocky coves of fine sand stretching along the coast from Landrellec to Pors-Mabo.
- Camping: Armor Loisirs ☎ 96.23.52.31 and Camping Roz-Ar-Mor ☎ 96.23.58.12
- Golf: 18h private heathland course at Golf de St-Sansom, route de Keneroc, 22670 Pleumeur Bodou ☎ 96.23.87.34
- Riding: Relais Equestre d'Armor ☎ 96.23.63.95
- Watersports: sailing from Tresmeur beach and skin diving with the GISSACG, Bateau de Sauvetage ☎ 96.23.66.71

 Trégastel-Plage (*Côtes-du-Nord*)
Pop: 2,000
Perros-Guirec 7 km, Paris 528 km
🚹 place Ste-Anne ☎ 96.23.88.67

Small seaside resort at the very tip of the Côte de Granit Rose. The natural pink tinge to the smooth and strangely formed rocks here makes for an attractive and interesting coastline. Popular for family holidays and for sailing enthusiasts who compete in the 24-hour regatta in summer.

- Beach: two main sandy beaches (Coz-Pors and Grève Blanche) but numerous other small coves in the area.
- Camping: Le Golven ☎ 96.23.87.77 and Tourony Camping ☎ 96.23.86.61
- Golf: see Perros-Guirec.
- Riding: Poney-Club, route de Woas-Wen ☎ 96.23.85.29 and Club Hippique, route du Calvaire ☎ 96.23.86.14
- Sailing: Club Nautique school at Plage du Coz-Pors ☎ 96.23.45.05
- Tennis: 12 courts to hire.

La Trinité-sur-Mer *(Morbihan)*
Pop: 2,000
Vannes 30 km, Paris 485 km
cours des Quais ☎ 97.55.72.21

An attractive little fishing port on the River Crach which specialises in oysters. Traditionally a centre for open-sea racing, there is mooring here for pleasure boats.

● Camping: Camping de la Baie ☎ 97.55.73.42

Château de Chambord

CENTRE

Administrative
Centre: Orléans
Population: 2,152,500
Area: 39,061 sq km

Départements:
18 Cher
28 Eure-et-Loir
36 Indre
37 Indre-et-Loire
41 Loir-et-Cher
45 Loiret

Anyone who wants to taste good wine and savour the rich history of France could do no better than to visit Centre with its châteaux, cathedrals and world-famous vineyards. As its name proclaims, somewhere in this region is to be found the very centre of France. This is not in the vast wheatfields to the north in the Eure-et-Loir, nor in the three *départements* which see the glory of the great River Loire and of the châteaux on its banks, but in Berry, to the south of Bourges and its marvellous cathedral.

The novelist George Sand (1808-1976) described the cathedral of St-Etienne at Bourges as 'a blend of the delicate and the colossal'. Many consider that its intricate west front and the splendid Gothic and Romanesque carvings there, its stained glass and the proportions of its tall interior make it the equal of Chartres, Rouen or Amiens. To her home in Nohant George Sand attracted the great artists of the day: Chopin, Balzac, Delacroix, Flaubert and Turgenev. At Chapelle-d'Anguillon, in the sporting acres of the Solognes, there is a museum in honour of Alain Fournier, author of the modern classic novel *Le Grand Meaulnes.* Near Chartres, secular pilgrims make their way to Illiers-Combray to recapture the sounds, scents and tastes of another great novel whose spiritual setting was Combray – *A la Récherche du Temps Perdus*, by Marcel Proust (1871-1922).

Chartres soars up above the surrounding wheatfields, its twin spires visible for miles above the low horizon, broken only by dwarf silos and tiny windmills. It was originally a ninth-century pilgrim church, the relic and point of pilgrimage being the *chemise* of the Virgin Mary. The twelfth-century façade marks the movement in religious architecture from the Romanesque to the Gothic. The twelfth-century windows of the portal and the deepest 'Chartres blue' of the stained glass, seen from within the cathedral, are unforgettable.

Pilgrims of another sort, tourists with a taste for sleeping, dining and wining in a series of châteaux, can follow another course, *La Route Jacques Coeur.* Jacques Coeur was a flourishing financier in the fifteenth century, whose wealth and skill secured him the post of treasurer to King Charles V. From his own purse he was able to back the French king in his fight against the English in the Hundred Years War. Today, the châteaux on the *Route Jacques Coeur* are privately owned and, in many cases, still lived in by the owners. Some of the costs of their upkeep can be offset by 'paying guests', staying, at least for a day or two, at one of the châteaux of Berry: the Château Meneton Salon (nineteenth century), Château Maupas (fourteenth century), Château de Meillant (fifteenth century), Château de Culan (thirteenth century) or the Renaissance Château d'Ainay-le-Vieil, many of them near to the pleasant market town of St-Amand-Montrond.

The châteaux on the Loire itself, or its tributaries, are on an altogether grander scale than anything else in France. Within the watershed cut out by the Loire, the Indre and Cher, running down through Orléans, Touraine, Anjou and out into the Atlantic beyond Nantes, there is a rich variety of castle landscape. The château as ruin, the château as medieval fortress or fortified keep, the château as 'fairy-tale' palace, the château as decorated Renaissance grouping with terraces, mannered stairways and bridges, lawns and lakes; finally, the château as *son-et-lumière* spectacular, illustrating these earlier historic phases, and as a showpiece for today's visitors.

This was, roughly, the land Henry Plantagenet inherited from his father, to which he added, through his marriage to Eleanor, all of Aquitaine. Two years later he succeeded to the throne of England as Henry II and for 300 warring years the whole of western France was English territory, until the English were finally driven out by Joan of Arc in the fifteenth century.

In May each year, at Orléans, a *fête* celebrates Joan's triumphant entry into the city after expelling the English. There are few other authentic reminders of the Maid of Orleans. However, in a single abbey, Fontevraud, the English Angevin dynasty has left the bones of two of its kings, Henry II and Richard the Lionheart, and of two queens, Eleanor of Aquitaine and Isabel of Angoulême, wife of King John.

French literature has always had strong links with the Loire valley through the romantic verses of Villon, first heard in Charles d'Orléans's court in Blois, Ronsard from the Loir valley, the full-blooded irreverence of Rabelais, native of Chinon, and the cool analysis of Descartes. In the later centuries further bonds were tied in the *Comédie Humaine* novels of Balzac, born in Tours, and of de Vigny, Proust and Fournier. French art has largely skirted round the region, but foreign Renaissance influences in architecture came with the fourteenth century and the châteaux were suddenly alive with Italian masons and craftsmen. For the last three years of his life, Leonardo da Vinci was the guest of François I at Amboise.

Over the years domestic architecture has used the local white limestone, *tufa*, dug from the riverbeds. Today, as in the past, it is used to make the cool, cave-like shelters for the local wines, Vouvray, Chinon or Bourgeuil, as well as for the growing of mushrooms, and building homes for the people. At Amboise houses fronting the cliffs can be seen, their rooms carved deep within its stone, the homes of latter-day troglodytes.

Some of the fortresses are ruined reminders of the Hundred Years War. The elegance of bridge span and tower are silent witnesses to the splendid days of the 'Ladies of Chenonceaux' (the home first of Henry II's mistress, Diane de Poitiers, and then of his wife, Catherine de Médici). Some things remain unchanged, undamaged, ageless: beyond the *tufa* walls of a small village, past the vineyards, under ancient keeps and winding through the château lawns, a lovely river runs – the Loire.

PRACTICAL TOURIST INFORMATION

General information on the region can be obtained by telephoning or writing to the Comité Régional du Tourisme (CRT) office, while specific booklets are produced detailing camping, hotel and self-catering gîte *accommodation. These can be obtained by writing to the tourist board office for the* département *(CDT) of your choice:*

Regional Tourist Board
Comité Régional du Tourisme (CRT) Centre – Val de Loire, 9 rue Pierre-Lentin, 45041 ORLEANS Cedex ☎ 38.62.68.48

Départements
Cher (18): Comité Départemental du Tourisme (CDT), 21 rue Victor-Hugo, B.P.145, 18003 BOURGES Cedex ☎ 48.24.75.33
Eure-et-Loir (28): Comité Départemental du Tourisme (CDT), place de la Cathédrale, B.P.289,

CHARTRES Cedex ☎ 37.21.54.03
Indre (36): Comité Départemental du Tourisme (CDT), place de la Gare, 36000 CHATEAUROUX ☎ 54.34.10.74
Indre-et-Loire (37): Comité Départemental du Tourisme (CDT), place Maréchal-Leclerc, 37042 TOURS Cedex ☎ 46.05.58.08
Loir-et-Cher (41): Comité Départemental du Tourisme (CDT), Pavillon Anne-de-Bretagne, 3 avenue Jean-Laigret, 41000 BLOIS ☎ 54.74.06.49
Loiret (45): Comité Départemental du Tourisme (CDT), Carré St-Vincent, boulevard Aristide-Briant, 45000 ORLEANS ☎ 38.53.05.95

SELF-CATERING ACCOMMODATION

The following British operators offer self-catering accommodation in the area:

AA Motoring Holidays, P.O. Box 100, Fanum

House, Halesowen B63 3BT ☎ 021-550 7401
Allez France, 27 West Street, Storrington,
Pulborough RH20 4DZ ☎ 09066 2345
Arblaster & Clarke, 104 Church Road, Steep,
Petersfield GU32 2DD ☎ 0730 66883
Billington Travel, 2a White Hart Parade,
Riverhead, Sevenoaks TN13 2BJ ☎ 0732 460666
Bowhills Ltd, Swanmore, Southampton SO3 2QW
☎ 0489 877627
Brittany Ferries, The Brittany Centre, Wharf
Road, Portsmouth PO2 8RU ☎ 0705 827701
Carasol Holidays, 6 Hayes Avenue, Bournemouth
BH7 7AD ☎ 0202 33398
Chapter Travel, 126 St John's Wood High Street,
London NW8 7ST ☎ 01-586 9451
Dominique's Villas, 2 Peterborough Mews,
London SW6 3BL ☎ 01-736 1664
French Villa Centre, 175 Selsdon Park Road,
Croydon CR2 8JJ ☎ 01-651 1231
Gîtes de France, 178 Piccadilly, London W1V 9DB
☎ 01-493 3480
Hoseasons Holidays Abroad, Sunway House,
Lowestoft NR32 3LT ☎ 0502 500555
David Newman's French Collection, P.O. Box 733,
40 Upperton Road, Eastbourne BN21 4AW
☎ 0323 410347
Prime Time Holidays, 5a Market Square,
Northampton NN1 2DL ☎ 0604 20996
SFV Holidays, Summer House, 68 Hernes Road,
Summertown, Oxford OX2 7QL ☎ 0865 57738
Slipaway Holidays, 90 Newland Road, Worthing
BN11 1LB ☎ 0903 821000
Sunvista Holidays, 5a George Street, Warminster
BA12 8QA ☎ 0985 217444
Vacances, 28 Gold Street, Saffron Walden
CB10 1EJ ☎ 0799 25101
Vacances en Campagne, Bignor, Pulborough
RH20 1QD ☎ 07987 433
VFB Holidays, 1 St Margaret's Terrace,
Cheltenham GL50 4DT ☎ 0242 526338

SPORTS AND ACTIVITIES

*For unusual and interesting holiday ideas, contact
the Loisirs Accueil office for the* département *of
your choice:*

Loisirs Accueil Cher,
10 rue de la Chappe, 18000 BOURGES
☎ 48.70.74.75
Loisirs Accueil Eure-et-Loir,
19 place des Epars, B.P.67, 28002 CHARTRES
☎ 37.21.37.22
Loisirs Accueil Indre,
rue Bordillon, 36000 CHATEAUROUX
☎ 54.22.91.20
Loisirs Accueil Indre-et-Loire,
Chambre d'Agriculture, 38 rue Augustin Fresnel,
B.P.139, 37171 CHAMBRAY-LES-TOURS
☎ 47.27.01.63
Loisirs Accueil Loir-et-Cher,
11 place du Château, 41000 BLOIS ☎ 54.78.55.50
Loisirs Accueil Loiret,
3 rue de la Bretonnerie, 45000 ORLEANS
☎ 38.62.04.88

RESORTS

Amboise *(Indre-et-Loire)*
Pop: 12,000
Tours 25 km, Paris 220 km
🚹 quai Général-de-Gaulle ☎ 47.57.09.28

The late fifteenth-century château, set high above
the Loire on a terraced spur, commands a
magnificent view over the town and valley. During
July and August a *son-et-lumière* spectacle is held,
recalling the period when François I and his court
were established here. For their entertainment
were staged a succession of brilliant festivals and
balls, tournaments and wild beast fights. Having
purchased the *Mona Lisa*, the king then
established its artist, Leonardo da Vinci, at
Amboise, where he continued to work until his
death.

Not far away is the lovely Château de
Chenonceau, astride the River Cher. As the home
of Henry II's beautiful mistress Diane de Poitiers,
fine gardens were laid down and a bridge thrown
across between château and riverbank. When
Henry died, killed in a duel, his wife Catherine de
Médici compelled Diane to surrender her beloved
Chenonceau, and further gardens and parkland
were planned, together with the construction of a
gallery to the bridge. From May to September *son-
et-lumières* are staged. Throughout this area there
are numerous *caves* offering wine-tasting.

● Art: Leonardo, artist, sculptor, architect and
engineer, spent his last years at Amboise. In
the basement of the Manoir de Clos Lucé
there is an exhibition of 50 scale models of
machines based on his drawings.
● Boat Trips: when the water level permits,
there are trips on the Cher and helicopter trips
depart from Neuvy-le-Roi ☎ 47.24.81.44 to
take visitors over the area.
● Camping: Municipal ☎ 47.57.23.23
● Cycling: cycles for hire from the SNCF station.
● Languages: Eurocentre ☎ 47.23.10.60 offers
French language study courses.

Aubigny-sur-Nère *(Cher)*
Pop: 6,000
Orléans 69 km, Paris 180 km
🚹 Hôtel de Ville ☎ 48.58.00.09

On the well-known *Jacques-Coeur* château route
and with the major châteaux of the Loire 90 km
away, this tranquil and pretty little town, and the
area around it, are a delight for the walker, artist
or cyclist. The large artificial lake, Etang du Puits,
situated 12 km north of the town, is a popular base
for the practice of most watersports and for fishing.
Also on the *Route Jacques-Coeur* is the elegant
Château de la Verrerie, thought to be that which
features in the enchanted world of Alain Fournier's
great novel *Le Grand Meaulnes*.

● Camping: L'Etang du Puits ☎ 48.58.02.37
● Fishing: category 1 fishing on the Nère river
and on the Etang du Puits lake.

- Golf: see Romorantin-Lanthenay.
- Riding: Relais Equestre Les Grands at Argent-sur-Sauldre ☎ 48.73.64.18.
- Tennis: six courts to hire.

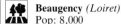

Beaugency *(Loiret)*
Pop: 8,000
Orléans 30 km, Paris 140 km
🛈 place du Martroi ☎ 38.44.54.42

The great 22-arched medieval bridge spans the Loire here, looked over by the ancient fortified town of narrow streets. The Château de Dunois, with a fine original eleventh-century keep, houses an interesting museum of everyday life, each room being dedicated to a particular theme. From this picturesque setting, the town is an excellent base for touring east of Blois.

- Camping: Municipal ☎ 38.44.50.39
- Cycling: cycles for hire from the SNCF station.
- Fishing: category 2 fishing on the Loire.
- Golf: 18h private course at Golf des Bordes, 41220 St-Lauren-Nouan ☎ 54.87.72.13; and long 18h private course at Golf de Sologne La Ferté-St-Aubin, route de Jouy-le-Potier, 45160 Ardon ☎ 38.76.57.33; and new 18h private course at Golf de Marcilly-Orléans, Domaine de la Plaine, 45240 Marcilly ☎ 38.76.11.73 (closed Tues).

Blois *(Loir-et-Cher)*
Pop: 50,000
Orléans 59 km, Paris 180 km
🛈 3 avenue Jean-Laigret ☎ 54.74.06.49

A charming town, of great artistic and historic interest, with five centuries of history embodied in the stone of the magnificent château which operates *son-et-lumière* between March and October. A short distance away (16 km), and on the opposite bank of the river, is the beautiful Château de Chambord, the largest château of the Loire valley and a masterpiece of Renaissance architecture. The forests which surround it have viewing points to enable visitors to observe the deer and wild boar in their natural habitat. Other châteaux in the area include the richly furnished, classically elegant Cheverny and Chaumont, while the small château at Talcy, north east of Blois, should also be included in excursions. Most of these châteaux can be reached easily and pleasantly by bicycle and the Tourist Office can provide maps for cyclists. A major sports complex has been created at the Lac du Loire, a short distance along the right bank, with extensive facilities.

- Boat Trips: bookable through the Tourist Office and operating between Chaumont and Amboise (Apr-Oct).
- Camping: Camping du Lac de Loire ☎ 54.78.82.05
- Cycling: cycles for hire from Cycles Leblond, 44 Levée des Tuileries ☎ 54.73.30.13 and

from the SNCF station.
- Fishing: category 2 fishing on the Loire.
- Flights: bookable through the Tourist Office and operating from the Du Brueil aerodrome, light aircraft flights of anything from 25 min to almost 2 hr give unforgettable bird's eye views of the châteaux. Helicopter flights of between 10 min and 1 hr, over the châteaux, operate from Blois-Hélistation, Pont Charles de Gaulle ☎ 54.74.35.52 (min. four passengers).
- Riding: Centre Equestre, La Chaussée-Saint-Victor ☎ 54.74.59.67
- Walking: Blois forest.
- Watersports: sailing, canoeing, waterskiing and pedalos at Lac de Loire on the right bank in the direction of Orléans.

Bourges *(Cher)*
Pop: 80,000
Orléans 106 km, Paris 238 km
🛈 21 rue Victor-Hugo ☎ 48.24.75.33

In the very centre of France, this great cathedral city abounds in art and architectural treasures, with the picturesque buildings of medieval Bourges at its very heart: le Palais Jacques Coeur built in 1443, the Renaissance Musée de l'Hôtel Lallemant, the fourteenth-century houses of the rue Bourbonnoux. There are also splendid gardens such as the roses and lawns of the Jardin de l'Ardeveche. The artificial lake, Lac du Val d'Auron, sees the sailing of yachts as well as model sailing boats. The surrounding country is famous for its Charolais cattle and for the vast fields of rape seed. Berry, today, is essentially the same mysterious, nostalgically beautiful, misty country of its novelist Alain Fournier. In April the popular festival *Printemps de Bourges* draws distinguished artists and thousands of visitors.

- Camping: Municipal ☎ 48.20.16.85
- Cycling: eight-day round trip, with accommodation and onward transportation of luggage arranged, past the historic monuments and along river and canal paths. Bookable through Loisirs Accueil Cher. Also cycles for hire from the SNCF station.
- Flights: half-day helicopter flights along the *Jacques-Coeur Route* leave from and return to Bourges, making two stops at monuments en route. Details from Loisirs Accueil Cher (min. five passengers).

Bourgueil *(Indre-et-Loire)*
Pop: 5,000
Chinon 17 km, Paris 279 km
🛈 la Mairie ☎ 47.97.70.50 (July-Sep)

A small town in vineyard country, it is indeed a wine-grower's village, with an elegant market place and its own wine museum (Cave Touristique de la Dive Bouteille) 2 km away in a cave near Chevrette, where wine tasting is a feature of the day. The climate here is ideal for the cultivation of the grape, so its famous vineyards dominate the

Loire valley and there are plenty of opportunities to taste and buy the local wines. Famous nearby châteaux include Langeais, Villandry, Ussé and Azay-le-Rideau, with Fontevraud l'Abbaye the burial place of Henry II, Eleanor of Aquitaine, Richard Coeur de Lion and Isabelle of Angoulême, wife of King John.

● Camping: La Grande Prairie ☎ 47.97.85.62

 Briare *(Loiret)*
Pop: 6,000
Orléans 77 km, Paris 155 km
🛈 place Eglise ☎ 38.31.24.51

Between 1890 and 1897 work went on to connect the Briare Canal with the Canal Latéral to the Loire, without having to cross the river. The engineer-designer of this remarkable work, a 664 m long canal-bridge, the famous *Ruban d'Eau*, was Gustave Eiffel, who had just completed the construction of a certain tower in Paris. This canal-bridge is still used for commercial traffic, and as a cruising thoroughfare it is the largest of its type in the world. Nearby, at Gien, the château includes an international hunting museum.

● Boat Hire: for week-long one-way or return cruises.
● Boat Trips: leisurely cruises; enjoy a meal as the countryside glides past.
● Camping: Le Martinet ☎ 38.31.24.51
● Fishing: category 2 fishing on the Loire.
● Tennis: seven courts to hire.

 Chartres *(Eure-et-Loir)*
Pop: 40,000
Tours 140 km, Paris 88 km
🛈 place de la Cathédrale ☎ 37.21.54.03

There are many sixteenth-century houses gathered round the cathedral in the medieval upper town, and in the lower town hump-backed bridges link riverside walks to the Pont de la Courtille where boats can be hired. In addition to the pull of the magnificent cathedral, the twin spires of which are visible for miles across thc flat agricultural land, Chartres attracts visitors for whom it can provide an excellent base for exploring the Ile de France region to the south of Paris, and the Loire valley itself.

● Ballooning: hot-air balloon flights over the Château de Maintenon including three nights' accommodation, bookable through Loisirs Accueil Eure-et-Loir.
● Camping: Les Bords de l'Eure (municipal) ☎ 37.28.79.43
● Canoeing: canoeing and kayaking courses in the Eure, Huisne, Loir and Conie valleys, including accommodation in bivouac or hotel, bookable through Loisirs Accueil Eure-et-Loir.
● Cycling: cycles for hire from the SNCF station.
● Fishing: fishing weeks at Thiron Gardais with accommodation in a nature lodge, bookable

Chartres

through Loisirs Accueil Eure-et-Loir.
● Fitness: at the Manoir du Palomino, on the banks of the Eure and 6 km from Chartres, a keep-fit course (with board) including tennis, golf, sauna, gymnasium and body care. Bookable through Loisirs Accueil Eure-et-Loir.
● Golf: 9h private course (approx 50 km distant) at Golf du Perch-Nogent-le-Rotrou, Vallée des Aulnes, 28400 Souancé-au-Perche ☎ 37.52.10.33
● Horse-drawn Travel: week or weekend trips in a four-berth gipsy caravan in the Eure valley, also two- or four-horse carriage tours of the Perche country. Both bookable through Loisirs Accueil Eure-et-Loir.

 Châteaudun *(Eure-et-Loir)*
Pop: 16,000
Chartres 45 km, Paris 131 km
🛈 1 rue de Luynes ☎ 37.45.22.46

A market town in a pretty setting on the River Loir, its tall château rising from a rocky outcrop, an austere fortress of seemingly massive strength, looking down on the meandering and languid course of the Loir. This is a rich agricultural region south of Chartres, with Châteaudun the chief market town for the area, with its small squares and overhanging sixteenth-century houses. A tree-shaded avenue above the Loir gives views reaching to the Perche hillsides.

- Camping: Municipal ☎ 37.45.05.34
- Cycling: cycles for hire from the SNCF station.
- Fishing: category 1 and 2 fishing on the Loir and its tributaries. Fly fishing along a special stretch of water, together with full board, fishing rights and packed lunches, can be booked through Loisirs Accueil Eure-et-Loir.
- Walking: the Tourist Office can provide local, short-distance itineraries.

Châteauneuf-sur-Loire (Loiret)
Pop: 6,000
Orléans 25 km, Paris 132 km
🏠 place Aristide-Briand ☎ 38.58.44.79

The shady banks of the wide and languid River Loire provide a fishing paradise for anglers, while the museum here recalls days when the river was busy with traffic. The town is neat and quite modern in parts, and leisurely walks amongst the ancient plane trees or the gorgeous rhododendrons and orange trees in the château's park garden, are a delight.

- Camping: La Maltournée ☎ 38.58.42.46
- Fishing: category 2 fishing on the Loire.
- Golf: 9h private course at Golf du Val de Loire-Orléans, Château de la Touche Donnéry, 45450 Fay-aux-Loges ☎ 38.59.25.15 (closed Tues); see also Beaugency.

Chinon (Indre-et-Loire)
Pop: 9,000
Saumur 29 km, Paris 280 km
🏠 12 rue Voltaire ☎ 47.93.17.85

This lovely old town stretches along the tree-lined banks of the Vienne, its turreted dwellings dominated by the enormous ruined defensive works high on the escarpment above. Built between the tenth and fifteenth centuries, the château is linked with names from the history books, Richard the Lionheart, Joan of Arc and Cesare Borgia. An area of great beauty, with vineyards, oak and fir-tree forests, numerous excursions are possible, and this is a particularly good region to discover on a bicycle. A medieval market is held on the first weekend in August and elegant Azay-le-Rideau, on the banks of the Indre, is close by, as is La Devinière, the childhood home of Rabelais, son of a Chinon lawyer.

- Boat Trips: 2-hr trips from Chinon to Montsoreau.
- Camping: Municipal L'Ile Auger ☎ 47.93.08.35
- Canoeing: hire and tuition available from 25 rue du Faubourg Saint-Jacques ☎ 47.93.39.59
- Cycling: cycles for hire at the SNCF station.
- Fishing: category 2 fishing on the Vienne.
- Golf: attractive 18h woodland public course at

Golf de Saint-Hilaire, Centre des Loisirs Loudun-Roiffé, 86120 Les Trois Moutiers ☎ 49.98.78.06
- Riding: carriage trips available from Centre d'Attelage du Grand-Palefroi, St-Lazaire ☎ 47.93.30.75

Loches (Indre-et-Loire)
Pop: 7,000
Tours 41 km, Paris 255 km
🏠 place de la Marne ☎ 47.59.07.98

Amidst pretty countryside this is a pleasant small town on the Indre, of great architectural and historic interest. The neat white faces of the old houses contrast with the sinister fortifications of the Château de Loches and with the dungeons and dank cells buried deep within it. The thirteenth-century tower of the château is named 'the Beautiful Agnes Tower' after Agnes Sorel, the mistress of Charles VII, who lived here. In the Great Hall, Joan of Arc met and persuaded Charles to go to Reims to be crowned, while in the Vieux Logis a copy of the proceedings of her subsequent trial is displayed. The impressive old dungeons occupy several floors below ground. From the terrace above there is a superb view.

- Camping: Municipal ☎ 47.59.05.91
- Cycling: cycles for hire from the SNCF station.

Lorris (Loiret)
Pop: 3,000
Orléans 50 km, Paris 125 km
🏠 SI ☎ 38.92.42.76

A peaceful little town on the edge of the forest of Orléans. This is, above all else, a walking and rich fishing area where large family groups, having come from Paris or Orléans for the weekend, will frequently be found enjoying the leafy walkways or the lakeside bathing area of the Lac du Bois, and, of course, playing interminable games of *boules*!

- Camping: Plage et Forêt ☎ 38.92.32.00
- Fishing: on the canal d'Orléans and in numerous pools.

Montargis (Loiret)
Pop: 18,000
Orléans 71 km, Paris 106 km
🏠 place du Pâtis ☎ 38.98.00.87

A popular and attractive town of elegant, pale, stone buildings with the River Loing running through it, and, parallel to it, the Briare Canal. A weekend tourist train service operates between June and September, travelling into Burgundy between Montargis and St-Sauveur and enabling the visitor to appreciate the lovely Puisaye countryside of châteaux, pools, woods, canals, locks and cider-apple orchards.

- Art: In the Girodet museum in rue de la Chaussée French and foreign schools are well represented (open all year except Mon and Tues).

- Camping: Municipal ☎ 38.98.00.20
- Cycling: cycles for hire from the SNCF station.
- Golf: new 18h private course at Golf de Vaugouard Montargis, Fontenay-sur-Loing, 45210 Ferrières ☎ 38.95.81.52 (water hazards).

 Romorantin-Lanthenay (Loir-et-Cher)
Pop: 19,000
Blois 40 km, Paris 180 km
☐ place de la Paix ☎ 54.76.43.89

A large and pleasant market town at the centre of the Sologne country of heathland, woods and lakes in a loop of the Loire below Orléans. Much of this land is private so it is not ideal for walkers, but there is excellent fishing in the River Sauldre which flows through the old town with its ancient houses and gardens. Lovely views of the fifteenth-century Château du Moulin from the several bridges that cross the river. An ideal centre for excursions to the châteaux of the Loire, with Cheverny (28 km), Beauregard (30 km) and Chambord (38 km), and many others on the *François 1er Route* from Sologne to Berry. Indoor and outdoor swimming pools, an indoor skating rink and an unusual motor museum.

- Camping: Tournefeuille ☎ 54.76.16.60
- Cycling: cycles for hire from the SNCF station.
- Fishing: category 2 fishing on the Sauldre.
- Golf: 9h private course at Golf de Salbris, Château de Rivaulde, 41300 Salbris ☎ 54.97.21.85

 Sully-sur-Loire (Loiret)
Pop: 6,000
Orléans 45 km, Paris 140 km
☐ place de Gaulle ☎ 38.36.23.70

One of the great moated châteaux of the Loire valley, the imposing medieval fortress faces the quiet little town of Sully-sur-Loire. Numerous excursions are possible throughout the area while local diversions include river bathing from the small beach and play area close to the château, canoeing and riding.

- Camping: Communal ☎ 38.36.23.93
- Fishing: category 2 fishing on the Loire, in choice spots along the Sange river and in Les Douves, the château's moated waters.
- Golf: 18h private course at Golf de Sully-sur-Loire, L'Ousseau, 45600 Viglain ☎ 38.36.52.08
- Riding: Centre Hippique, Domaine de l'Arlantoy ☎ 38.36.23.52
- Tennis: five courts to hire.

 Tours (Indre-et-Loire)
Pop: 136,000
Angers 109 km, Paris 234 km
☐ place Maréchal-Leclerc ☎ 47.05.58.08

Tours, the metropolis on the Loire near its junction with the Cher, is at the heart of what was once exclusively agricultural land but which has now embraced electronics, pharmaceuticals, plastics and the service industries. It is a centre for higher education; the university has 12,000 students, and there are 3,000 foreign students of the French language based here. Between the thirteenth and fifteenth centuries the Château Royal de Tours was the residence of the French Valois monarchs, later becoming a military barracks until, after World War II, it was split into three museums. Great restoration work began in 1970 and the area around the place Plumereau, the old quarter of the city near the university, came to new life with pedestrian precincts, small courtyards of fifteenth-century timbered houses and narrow streets leading to quiet gardens. Tours organises a number of concerts and exhibitions during the year, principally perhaps the Touraine Music Festival, held at the Grange de Meslay, a thirteenth-century tithe barn, at the end of June. Above all Tours is ideally situated as a centre for visits to the Loire valley châteaux which encircle it (Chinon, Azay-le-Rideau, Amboise, Chenconceau, Cheverny, Chambord and Blois), by road or from the air by helicopter and balloon.

- Camping: Municipal ☎ 47.54.11.11
- Cycling: cycles for hire from the SNCF station.
- Flights: helicopter and light aircraft flights over the chateaux, bookable through Loisirs Accueil Indre-et-Loire.
- Golf: 18h private course at Golf de Touraine, Château de la Touche, 37510 Joue-les-Tours ☎ 47.53.20.28 and 18h course at Golf de l'Ardrée, St-Antoine-du-Rocher.
- Languages: Institut d'Etudes Françaises de Touraine ☎ 47.05.76.83 offers French language study courses.
- Tennis: courses at the Club de Tours, bookable through Loisirs Accueil Indre-et-Loire.

 Vendôme (Loir-et-Cher)
Pop: 18,000
Blois 32 km, Paris 171 km
☐ 45 rue Potterie ☎ 54.77.05.07

The Loir winds sinuously through this charming town, branching off to form various tiny islands connected by bridges, across which shoppers walk to rest in quiet parks or to picnic in the shade of ancient trees. There are also attractive pedestrian walkways, like the rue du Change where the wares of the shops spill out through the doors, and surprises, like the huge waterwheel turning behind glass in the Vieux Moulin restaurant in the cours du Moulin Perrin. Surrounded by gently rolling farmland, there are lovely views from the ruined château at the top of the town.

- Camping: Municipal ☎ 54.77.00.27
- Cycling: cycles for hire from the SNCF station.

Special literature is available on a number of different planned itineraries which take motorists to many of the lesser-known châteaux, museums and churches:

Route Jacques Coeur (Loiret, Cher)
La Bussière, Gien, Blancafort, Aubigny-sur-Nère, La Verrerie, Boucard, La Chapelle d'Angillon, Maupas, Menetou-Salon, Bourges, Jussy-Champagne, Dun-sur-Auron, Meillant, Abbaye de Noirlac, Ainay-le-Vieil.
Details from: Comité Départemental du Tourisme, Hôtel du Département, 10 rue de la Chappe, 18014 BOURGES Cedex ☎ 48.70.71.72

Route François 1er Sologne-Berry (Loiret, Loir-et-Cher, Indre, Cher)
La Ferté-St-Aubin, Lamotte-Beuvron, Talcy, Blois, Chambord, Beauregard, Villesavin, Cheverny, Troussay, Fougéres-sur-Bièvre, Pontlevoy, Gué-Péan, Selles-dur-Cher, Le Moulin, Romorantin-Lanthenay, Valençay, Bouges, Levroux, Palluau, Villegongis, Chateauroux, Diors, Nohant, Chateaumeillant, Argenton-sur-Creuse, Saint-Marcel, Chateau-Guillaume, Le Bouchet.
Details from: Syndicat d'Initiative, place de la Paix, 41200 ROMORANTIN-LANTHENAY ☎ 54.76.43.89

Route Touristique de la Vallée du Loir (Eure-et-Loir, Loir-et-Cher, continuing into the Pays de la Loire)
Chartres, Châteaudun, Montigny-le-Gannelon, Cloyes, Freteval, Vendôme, Montoire, Troo, Lavardin, Couture, La Poissonnière.
Details from: Office de Tourisme-Syndicat d'Initiative, Hôtel du Bellay du Saillant, B.P.34, 45 rue Poterie, 41101 VENDOME ☎ 54.77.05.07

Route des Hauts Dignitaires (Loiret and continuing into the Ile-de-France)
Malesherbes, La Bussière, Pont-Chevron, Sully-sur-Loire, Gien.

Details from: Loisirs Accueil Loiret, 3 rue de la Bretonnerie, 45000 ORLEANS ☎ 38.62.04.88

Route des Dames de Touraine (Indre-et-Loire, Loir-et-Cher, Indre)
Amboise, Clos-Lucé, Montrichard, Montpoupon, Montresor, Pietà de Nouans-les-Fontaines, Chartreuse du Liget, Loches, Le Grand Pressigny, Azay-le-Ferron, Bouges, Valençay, Beauregard.
Details from: Direction Départementale du Tourisme, place de la Préfecture, 37032 TOURS Cedex ☎ 47.61.61.23

Route de la Vallée des Rois (Loiret, Loir-et-Cher, Indre-et-Loire)
Pont-Canal de Briare, Gien, Sully-sur-Loire, Saint-Benoit-sur-Loire, Germigny-des-Prés, Chateauneuf-sur-Loire, Orléans, Cléry-Saint-André, Meung-sur-Loire, Beaugency, Chambord, Blois, Beauregard, Chaumont, Amboise, Clos-Lucé, Grange de Meslay, Tours, Plessis-les-Tours, Prieuré-Saint-Cosmé, Villandry, Cinq-Mars, Langeais, Ussé, Les Réaux.
Details from: address at Tours as above plus: Châteaux des Réaux, le Port-Boulet, Chouzé-sur-Loire, 37140 BOURGUEIL ☎ 47.95.14.40

Route de la Vallée du Cher (Indre-et-Loire, Loir-et-Cher, Cher and continuing into the Auvergne)
Villandry, Savonnières, Plessis-les-Tours, Tours, Leugny, Nitray, Chenonceau, Montrichard, Gué-Péan, Selles-sur-Cher, Brinay, Mehun-sur-Yèvre, Bourges, Meillant, La Celle, Abbaye de Noirlac, Ainay-le-Vieil.
Details from: Expoval, Maison des Produits de la Vallée du Cher, Saint-Georges-sur-Cher, 41400 MONTRICHARD ☎ 54.32.33.77

Chemins du Roi Soleil (Eure-et-Loir and continuing into the Ile-de-France)
Anet, Chapelle Royale de Dreux, Maintenon.
Details from: Chapelle Royale, 2 square d'Aumale, 28100 DREUX ☎ 37.46.07.06

CHAMPAGNE-ARDENNE

Administrative Centre:
Châlons-sur-Marne
Population: 1,346,000
Area: 25,600 sq km

Départements:
08 Ardennes
10 Aube
51 Marne
52 Haute-Marne

Regional Parks:
Parc Naturel Régional
de la Montagne de
Reims, Maison du
Parc, Pourcy, 51160
Ay ☎ 26.59.44.44

Parc Naturel Régional
de la Forêt d'Orient,
Maison du Parc, 10220
Piney ☎ 25.41.35.57

It was at the hilltop village of Hautvillers in the Marne, late in the seventeenth century, that the steward of the abbey, the Benedictine monk Dom Pérignon crowned his life's work. He had spent years experimenting with a way to preserve, after bottling, the bubbles in the local wine which was naturally *pétillant*, or sparkling. He finally succeeded and the fruit of his work is today successfully captured in varying quantities: the magnum (2 bottles), the Jeroboam (4), the Methuselah (8), the Salmanazar (12), the Balthazar (16) and the huge Nebuchadnezzar (the equivalent of 20 bottles). He is also credited with the invention of the mushroom-shaped cork to withstand the pressure of the effervescent champagne. In Reims and Epernay, twin Champagne cities, the process has been perfected.

The vineyards of the champagne country cover 164,500 hectares and are rigorously restricted to a north-south stretch of chalky hillside some 112 km long by a kilometre or so wide. In three main zones, these are: la Montagne de Reims, la Vallée de la Marne and les Côtes des Blancs.

Three varieties of grape are used, the red Pinot Noir and Meunier, and the white Chardonnay selectively chosen and mixed. Unlike the vineyards of Burgundy or Bordeaux, however, where small villages and châteaux are at the heart of the process, in the champagne country deep underground cellars in two cities, Reims and Epernay, shelter and humour the fermenting wine at a regulated and steady 10°C (59°F).

These underground galleries, 190 km of them, are cut from the chalk beneath the great wine houses. Veuve Cliquot, Pommery and Mumm at Reims; Pol Roger and Moët et Chandon at Epernay, while at Mareuil-sur-Ay, the great vineyard of Bollinger is dominated by its eighteenth-century château. Follow the *Route du Champagne* in the *département* of Aube (indicated by the bunch of grapes symbol). The tour passes through a number of wine-producing towns and villages marked by signs 'Commune à appellation champagne'.

There is much more to the region, however, than the millions of bottles of champagne stored there. More to Reims than the Taittinger cellars, more to Epernay than the elegant avenue de Champagne or a magnum of Moët et Chandon's Dom Pérignon.

The Ardennes (originally meaning 'the heart of the forest') is walkers' country. The Forêt de l'Orient is 648 sq km of woodland, animal breeding grounds, lakes and reservoirs and the deciduous forest home for a number of protected animals – boar, stags and roe deer. Numerous pathways open it up for those who wish to visit on foot, horseback or bicycle.

The Montagne de Reims Regional Park covers 490 sq km of vineyards, forests and cultivated land and is not only a nature reserve but a conservation area for France's rural heritage. Thousand-year-old beech trees flourish in the forest-covered massif near the wine village of Verzy, where paths for walkers and motorists are signposted.

Traditionally, the kings of France were crowned at Reims cathedral, most memorable perhaps Charles VII in 1429, urged on by Joan of Arc. It ranks in splendour with Notre Dame, Chartres and Amiens, its west façade one of the glories of thirteenth-century Gothic architecture. During World War I, Reims was only a kilometre or two away from the front line. Much of the city was destroyed and the cathedral itself badly damaged. During the latter stages of World War II, General Eisenhower's Allied Headquarters were in Reims, and on 7 May 1945, in the Lycée Technique des Garçons, the Germans signed the surrrender document. The room has been kept as it was then.

Certainly war has left its deepest marks on the region. At Sedan there stands the largest fortified castle in Europe, 22 hectares in area, with its massed ramparts and bastions. Langres, at the gateway to Burgundy, shows military architecture at its most formidable, with 4 km of encircling ramparts, gates, sentry walks and ancient towers. At Fère Champenoise, the National Cemetery and War Memorial commemorate those who fell in the battle of the Marne in World War I. The advance of US troops under General Patton from Cherbourg to Bastogne, *La Voie de la Liberté*, is marked along the road leading through Epernay, Reims, St-Menehould and Verdun. At Colombey-les-Deux-Eglises, the pink granite Croix de Lorraine rises to the sky to mark the home for many years of General de Gaulle.

PRACTICAL TOURIST INFORMATION

General information on the region can be obtained by telephoning or writing to the Comité Régional du Tourisme (CRT) office, while specific booklets are produced detailing camping, hotel and self-catering gîte *accommodation. These can be obtained by writing to the tourist board office for the* département *(CDT) of your choice:*

Regional Tourist Board
Comité Régional du Tourisme (CRT), 5 rue de Jéricho, 51037 CHALONS-SUR-MARNE Cedex
☎ 26.64.35.92

Départements
Ardennes (08): Comité Départemental du Tourisme (CDT), 18 avenue Georges-Clemenceau, 08000 CHARLEVILLE-MEZIERES
☎ 24.56.06.08
Aube (10): Association Départementale de Tourisme (ADT), Hôtel du Département, B.P.394, 10026 TROYES Cedex ☎ 25.73.48.01
Marne (51): Comité Départemental du Tourisme (CDT), 2 bis, boulevard Vaubécourt, 51000 CHALONS-SUR-MARNE ☎ 26.68.37.52
Haute-Marne (52): Comité Départemental du Tourisme (CDT), B.P.509, 52011 CHAUMONT Cedex ☎ 25.32.86.70

SELF-CATERING ACCOMMODATION

The following British operators offer self-catering accommodation in the area:

Arblaster & Clarke, 104 Church Road, Steep, Petersfield GU32 2DD ☎ 0730 66883
Gîtes de France, 178 Piccadilly, London W1V 9DB

☎ 01-493 3480
VFB Holidays, 1 St Margaret's Terrace, Cheltenham GL50 4DT ☎ 0242 526338

SPORTS AND ACTIVITIES

For unusual and interesting holiday ideas, contact the Loisirs Accueil office below:

Loisirs Accueil Ardennes,
18 avenue Georges Corneau,
08000 CHARLEVILLE-MEZIERES
☎ 24.56.00.63

RESORTS

Bourbonne-les-Bains *(Haute-Marne)*
Pop: 3,000
Vesoul 56 km, Paris 310 km
🏠 place des Bains ☎ 25.90.01.71

With Roman remains in evidence, this 2,000-year-old spa is a peaceful health resort situated in the fresh, clean air of the pleasant and picturesque Val d'Apance. Surrounded by wooded hills, it is the only spa in the Champagne-Ardenne region, its facilities modern and its warm, thermal waters noted for containing as much salt per litre as human blood. There is a safari park nearby at La Bannie and pleasant walks to be taken amidst the beech trees. Casino.

- Camping: Camping le Montmorency ☎ 25.90.08.64
- Cuisine: weekend cookery courses are run at the Hotel d'Orfeuil under the tuition of its master chef. Contact the hotel at 29 rue d'Orfeuil, 52400 Bourbonne-les-Bains ☎ 25.90.05.71
- Fishing: category 1 and 2 fishing on the Apance and Amance rivers and category 2

fishing on the Saône and Meuse.
- Riding: spend two days' accompanied riding in the Pays des Sources. Contact Hôtel de Bourgogne, 66 rue Vellone ☎ 25.90.00.81
- Spa: rheumatism/bone joint damage (1 Mar-30 Nov) ☎ 25.90.07.20 alt: 270 m, climate: temperate. This spa specialises in the treatment of sports injuries and, as such, has attracted the patronage of some top-class sportsmen and women.

 Epernay *(Marne)*
Pop: 30,000
Reims 26 km, Paris 140 km
🛈 7 avenue de Champagne ☎ 26.55.33.00

In the heart of the white grape vineyards sits Epernay, the wine capital of Champagne with its famous avenue where the most prestigious champagne houses are to be found. Visits to the cellars of world-famous champagne houses such as Moët et Chandon, Dom Pérignon, Mercier and Perrier Jouët (amongst others), with their miles of tunnels and underground storerooms are guaranteed to fascinate and enlighten. The Taittinger cellars at Reims are also open to visitors. The motoring *Route du Champagne* leads to the pretty village of Hautvillers (6 km north) with beautiful views. This is where, in the seventeenth century, the monk Dom Pérignon discovered the champagne process.

- Camping: Camping Municipal ☎ 26.55.32.14

 Giffaumont-Champaubert *(Marne)*
St-Dizier 8 km, Paris 240 km
🛈 Maison du Lac ☎ 26.72.62.80

Set amidst a pretty area of half-timbered houses, this is a recent reservoir development beside the 49 sq km of Lac du Der-Chantecoq, the largest artificial lake in Europe, whose construction necessitated the destruction of three towns. This is a vast sports and leisure activity centre, providing fishing, riding, watersports and boat trips from the port of Giffaumont.

- Camping: Camping de la Plage ☎ 26.72.61.84

 Langres *(Haute-Marne)*
Pop: 12,000
Dijon 68 km, Paris 300 km
🛈 place Bel'Air ☎ 25.87.03.32

In the heart of a forest-covered massif and magnificently perched on the edge of an exposed plateau, Langres is an old cathedral city contained within 4 km of Roman ramparts. The nearby reservoir lakes of Liez, Charmes, Mouche and Vingeanne all provide good fishing and are popular for watersports.

- Camping: Camping Municipal ☎ 25.87.50.65
- Riding: (for any ability rider) weekend or longer treks around the four lakes. Contact L'Ecole d'Equitation de Melville, (stables are based at a château) St-Martin-les-Langres ☎ 25.87.39.93

 Monthermé *(Ardennes)*
Pop: 3,000
Charleville-Mézières 18 km, Paris 243 km
🛈 6 rue E.-Dolet ☎ 24.53.06.50

Close to the Belgian border in a pretty setting at the bottom of the high wooded valley where the Semoy flows into the Meuse, Monthermé is the perfect location for fishing, walking and relaxing. It is an area of outstanding natural beauty where steep towering rocks tempt the climber and enthrall the geologist, for this is the junction of two regions dating from different periods, the Cambrian and Devonian.

- Camping: Rapides de Phades ☎ 24.53.06.73 and Camping l'Echina Chez Marius ☎ 24.53.05.56
- Cycling: accompanied cycling and walking trips, bookable at the Tourist Office.
- Fishing: category 2 fishing on the Meuse and Semoy rivers.
- Golf: 9h private course at Golf des Ardennes, Charleville-Mézières, Les Poursaudes Villers-le-Tilleul, 08430 Poix Terron ☎ 24.37.31.98

CORSE

Administrative
Centre: Ajaccio
Population: 289,000
Area: 8,681 sq km

Départements:
20A Corse-du-Sud
20B Haute-Corse

Regional Park:
Parc de la Corse
(1,000,750 hectares)
4, rue Fiorella, B.P.
417, 20184 Ajaccio
☎ 95.21.56.54

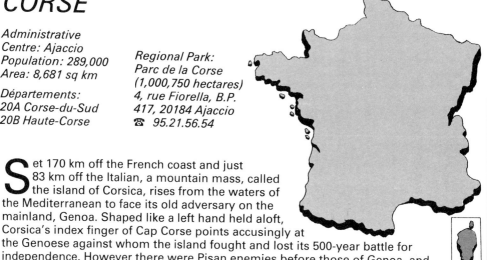

Set 170 km off the French coast and just 83 km off the Italian, a mountain mass, called the island of Corsica, rises from the waters of the Mediterranean to face its old adversary on the mainland, Genoa. Shaped like a left hand held aloft, Corsica's index finger of Cap Corse points accusingly at the Genoese against whom the island fought and lost its 500-year battle for independence. However there were Pisan enemies before those of Genoa, and earlier still Phoenician invaders and colonisers, followed by Greeks, Etruscans and Romans and later the English and the French.

In 1768 Corsica became French. In the following year, its most famous son, Napoléon Bonaparte, was born in Ajaccio. Within 30 years France dominated the continent of Europe from Spain to Russia. Paris remained its capital, but the nation state was now led by, and subject to the will of, an islander from Ajaccio, the Emperor Napoléon.

Eighty km across and 160 km from north to south, the island is unspoilt, at times quite wild and mountainous. To the north west lies the steepest country (Monte Cinto 2,700 m), with less fierce peaks on the south-east side as they descend to the east-coast plains and the Bonifacio cliffs. Hikers can follow the GR20 (*Sentier de la Corse*), travelling high into the mountainous interior. Be advised, however, not to go alone or without adequate bad-weather clothing.

Fantastic horseback rides are possible on the island, both in the interior and along the dramatic cliff tops, and accompanied trips can be arranged from any of a dozen centres. Boar-hunting is very popular here, too, as is fishing, with a season running between the third Sunday in February and the last Monday in September. Permits are available from local fishing tackle suppliers. Leisurely, but impressive, is the charming railway route which runs north between Ajaccio and Calvi, taking in Corte, Bastia and L'Ile-Rousse, winding its way through the mountains along 230 km of unforgettable scenery.

The coastline, all 1,000 km of it, presents more dramatic contrasts. There are small sheltered coves and fishing harbours, beautiful, long sandy beaches along the east coast, with clear, inviting waters, and the hair-raising road along the west coast with sheer cliff drops to tiny beaches accessible only from the sea. These are landscapes designed to captivate.

Maquis is the Corsican word to describe the small jungle of tangled undergrowth which, over the centuries, has offered safe hiding to independence fighters, patriots defying Napoléon's troops, and Resistance fighters defying Mussolini and Hitler. The island has had a violent history and the ancient village homes testify to the harshness of life for a people subjected to recurrent raids and invasions sweeping in from the eastern coast. Yet today *maquis* means only a blossom's perfume drifting out to sea, for enough blood has been spilled in this beautiful and scented isle.

PRACTICAL TOURIST INFORMATION

General information on the island can be obtained by telephoning or writing to the Agence Régionale du Tourisme office who will also provide a comprehensive guide to hotels and camp sites of all categories and in all locations. It is important to pre-book hotel accommodation in high season. Be warned that heavy fines are imposed in Corsica for camping away from the organised sites or by the waterfront. The locals may take exception as there is a constant and serious risk of fire on the island.

Regional Tourist Board
Agence Régionale du Tourisme et des Loisirs, 22 cours Grandval, B.P.19, 20176 AJACCIO ☎ 95.51.00.22
For information on self-catering gîte accommodation:
Relais Régionale des Gîtes Ruraux, 24 boulevard Paoli, 20090 AJACCIO ☎ 95.20.51.34

Départements
Corse-du-Sud (20A) and Haute-Corse (20B): Fédération Régionale des Offices du Tourisme, 1 place Foch, B.P.21, 20176 AJACCIO Cedex ☎ 95.21.40.87

SELF-CATERING ACCOMMODATION
The following British operators offer self-catering accommodation on the island:

Allegro Holidays, 15a Church Street, Reigate RH2 0AA ☎ 0737 221323
Angel Travel, 47 High Street, Central Chambers, Tonbridge TN9 1SD ☎ 0732 361115
Beach Villas, 8 Market Passage, Cambridge CB2 3QR ☎ 0223 311113
The Corsican Connection, 91 Wembley Park Drive, Wembley Park, Middx HA9 8HF ☎ 01-903 6322
Dieppe Ferries Holidays, Weymouth Quay, Weymouth DT4 8DY ☎ 0305 777444
Euro-Express, 227 Shepherds Bush Road, London W6 7AS ☎ 01-748 2607
Falcon Holidays, 33 Notting Hill Gate, London W11 3JQ ☎ 01-221 6298
France Voyages, 145 Oxford Street, London W1R 1TB ☎ 01-494 3155
French Affair, 34 Lillie Road, London SW6 1TU ☎ 01-799 1077
French Travel Service, Georgian House, 69 Boston Manor Road, Brentford TW8 0JQ ☎ 01-568 8442
Interhome, 383 Richmond Road, Twickenham TW1 2EF ☎ 01-891 1294
Island Sun, Island House, Church Road, Lowfield Heath, Crawley RH11 0PQ ☎ 0293 547300
Meon Villas, Meon House, College Street, Petersfield GU32 3JN ☎ 0730 68411
Solmer Travel, 10 Berwyn Road, Richmond TW10 5BS ☎ 01-876 1331
Stallard Holidays, Stallard House, 29 Stoke Newington Road, London N16 8BL ☎ 01-254 6444

Vacances en Campagne, Bignor, Pulborough
RH20 1QD ☎ 07987 433

SPORTS AND ACTIVITIES
For unusual and interesting holiday ideas, contact the Loisirs Accueil office below:

Loisirs Accueil Corse,
24 boulevard Paoli, 20090 AJACCIO
☎ 95.22.70.79

RESORTS

 Ajaccio *(Corse-du-Sud)*
Pop: 55,000
Calvi 159 km
🚻 1 place Foch ☎ 95.21.40.87

The birthplace of Napoléon Bonaparte, Corsica's greatest son, Ajaccio is also the capital of Corsica. Set in a magnificent bay, this is a city of white houses with red tiled roofs and terracotta façades, of tree-lined avenues whose names reflect the memory of Napoléon, and of the old French citadel, raised against the Genoese enemy, standing out against a more modern skyline. Three-hour boat trips, to the Iles Sanguinaires in the Golfe d'Ajaccio, take visitors past reefs and small islands, the homes of gulls and cormorants. Here, as elsewhere in Corsica, the scent of the *maquis* is always present: scrub that is a mixed growth of heather, arbutus, lavender, rosemary, myrtle, juniper and broom and which colours the landscape deep purple.

● Boat Trips: leave for Nice, Toulon and Marseille, the journey taking between 5 and 10 hr. Bookable through SNCM Ajaccio ☎ 95.21.90.70
● Camping: Barbicaja ☎ 95.52.01.17
● Casino: boulevard Lantivy ☎ 95.21.41.44
● Riding: Cercle Hippique, route de Campo-dell'Oro ☎ 95.22.16.22 and Poney-Club d'Ajaccio, route de Sartène ☎ 95.23.03.10
● Thalassotherapy: Centre de Thalassothérapie (at Porticcio) ☎ 95.25.00.95
● Watersports: the climate is favourable between April and the end of October for diving and water-borne activities; equipment can be hired from the Base Nautique en Corse, Thalassa-Corse, Tahiti Plage, route du Ricanto, 20000 Ajaccio ☎ 95.22.01.58

 Bastia *(Haute-Corse)*
Pop: 45,000
Calvi 93 km, Ajaccio 153 km
🚻 33 boulevard Paoli ☎ 95.31.02.04

Bastia is at the foot of the Cap Corse peninsula in the north, and marks the start of the long plain down to the east coast. It is perhaps the least Corsican of all the towns on the island; if anything it is Italian in style and atmosphere. A busy port, there are regular boat services to France, Italy and Sardinia as well as shorter island excursions. The sea approach, with the citadel silhouetted against and above the promontory, is very beautiful. There is considerable life in the old town, particularly around the picturesque *vieux port*. The place St-Nicholas is at the centre of the night life, with cafés, restaurants and excellent shops, and the huge beach within the vast bay is busy with watersports of all description.

● Camping: Le Bois de Saint Damiano ☎ 95.33.53.08
● Riding: Société Hippique Urbaine de Bastia ☎ 95.33.53.08 and Centre Equestre de la Marana ☎ 95.33.16.76

 Calvi *(Haute-Corse)*
Pop: 4,000
Bastia 93 km, Ajaccio 159 km
🚻 chemin de la Plage ☎ 95.65.05.87

Calvi is one of the most popular resorts. It has a broad and shallow beach of sand bordered by pine trees, a busy marina set amongst palms and a backdrop of the Cinto Massif, tipped with snow as late as the early summer. The town boasts a ruined citadel and ramparts and is the alleged birthplace of Christopher Columbus. It is also the headquarters of the French Foreign Legion. Lined with hotels, there is virtually no limit to the holiday activities on offer, and the night life tends to be at once noisy and charming. Full-day boat trips are available to the gulfs of Girolata and Porto and there are wine tasting opportunities at the local vineyards.

● Camping: Bella Vista ☎ 95.65.11.76 and La Pinède ☎ 95.65.17.80
● Riding: La Jument Pie, route de Calvi ☎ 95.60.74.40
● Sailing: Calvi Nautic Club, plage de la Roya ☎ 95.37.00.61

L'Ile-Rousse *(Haute-Corse)*
Pop: 3,000
Calvi 24 km, Ajaccio 155 km
🚻 place Paoli ☎ 95.60.04.35 (Apr-Sep)

A very popular holiday resort with French visitors, it takes its name from the colour of the red granite rocks of the promontory on which the jetty stands. Originally an old Roman settlement, it is today a busy, lively port and yachting harbour which hosts regattas in September. The climate is very mild throughout the year and there are beautiful white sandy beaches. Casino.

Porto *(Corse-du-Sud)*
Calvi 76 km, Ajaccio 83 km
🚻 9 route de la Marine ☎ 95.26.10.55

Perhaps the Golfe de Porto is the most beautiful part of all Corsica. The minute village clusters in the fold of the valley, surrounded by eucalyptus trees and on the very edge of the pebbled beach. Ideal for sea or mountain holidays, exploring the

Regional Park on foot or the coastline by boat. Hotels and restaurants deep in the bay offer evenings filled with music and dancing.

● Camping: Les Oliviers ☎ 95.26.14.48

 Porto-Vecchio *(Corse-du-Sud)*
Pop: 8,000
Sartène 63 km, Ajaccio 131 km
🄳 place Hôtel de Ville ☎ 95.70.09.58

This is the third largest port on the island. A town of old streets and Genoese fortifications, it was founded by the Greeks, and is at the centre of an area rich in prehistoric sites. To the south east of the island, along the rocky coast between Bonifacio and Solenzara, sudden bays of white sand and emerald green waters open up, amongst them the Golfe de Porto-Vecchio. Olive groves surround the port, busy with its export trade in timber and cork. However, the chief trade today is tourism. Within a few miles of Porto-Vecchio lies a stretch of the finest beaches in Corsica, such as the plage de Palombaggia, its white sand and dunes sheltered by parasol pine trees. The *Grande Randonnée* 20 runs from nearby Conca across the Aiguilles de Bavella peaks to Calenzana, a testing but exhilarating long-distance walk, and there are excursion trails through the forest of Ospedale and the Bavella Needles. There is mooring for 450 boats in the marina.

● Camping: U Stabbiaciu ☎ 95.70.37.70 and Golfo di Sogna ☎ 95.70.08.98. Naturist camping at La Chiappa ☎ 95.70.00.31
● Riding: Ranch du Stabbiaciu ☎ 95.70.17.30
● Sailing: Centre Nautique des Fauvettes ☎ 95.70.00.56

 Propriano *(Corse-du-Sud)*
Pop: 3,000

Sartène 13 km, Ajaccio 73 km
🄳 17 rue Général-de-Gaulle ☎ 95.76.01.49

Set on a hillside above the sea, Propriano occupies a spectacular position and is very popular with British visitors. The calm seas are suitable for children's bathing and there are many sandy beaches along the gulf of Valinco. The little port is full of atmosphere, and the cliff road above the bay leads towards a lovely rural hinterland. Watersports include diving, snorkelling, waterskiing, sailing, windsurfing, underwater sea fishing and speedboat racing. The marina has moorings for 460 boats and a car-ferry service operates to mainland France, to the ports of Nice, Toulon and Marseille.

● Camping: Colomba ☎ 95.76.06.42
● Riding: Le Voyage à Cheval, Centre Equestre de Baracci ☎ 95.76.08.02
● Sailing: Centre Nautique du Valinco ☎ 95.76.03.52

 St-Florent *(Haute-Corse)*
Pop: 1,500
Calvi 70 km, Ajaccio 176 km
🄳 Immeuble de Ste-Anne ☎ 95.37.06.04

At the base of the Cap Corse peninsula, in the Golfe de St-Florent, St-Florent sits in a bay that might grace the front cover of a travel brochure. The pebbled beach is sheltered by the encircling mountains and bordered by vineyards and olive groves. Steps wind down between tall houses to the central square at the heart of the old streets and narrow alleys. The ancient Genoese citadel looks down on the long jetty, pretty fishing harbour and berthside for pleasure craft (moorings for 550). An excellent resort for watersports, particularly for underwater diving.

● Camping: Campo d'Olzo ☎ 95.37.03.34
● Riding: Ranch de St-Florent ☎ 95.37.03.06

FRANCHE-COMTE

*Administrative
Centre: Besançon
Population: 1,060,300
Area: 16,189 sq km*

Départements:
25 Doubs
39 Jura
70 Haute-Saône
90 Territoire-de-
    Belfort

*Regional Park:
Parc Naturel Régional
du Haut-Jura, Maison
du Haut-Jura, Lajoux,
39310 Septmoncel*
☎ *84.41.20.37*

Franche-Comté (the Free Country) reflects a hardy people's defiance, over many years, of invasion threats from the east. The Territoire de Belfort, the smallest of all France's *départements*, fills the inviting gap between the Vosges and the Jura mountains.

In the Franco-Prussian war of 1870, a handful of troops within the Vauban fort of Belfort held out for 103 days under siege by 40,000 Germans. Their heroic resistance ensured that, at the later peace conferences, Belfort was allowed to remain French. To honour this defiance, the city's symbol, the enormous *Lion de Belfort*, in pink Vosges sandstone, was carved by Frédéric Bartholdi, the sculptor of the Statue of Liberty.

A dozen miles away, at Ronchamp, the great Swiss architect, le Corbusier, replaced a war-damaged chapel by a contemporary work of art – the church of Notre-Dame-du-Haut, a concrete and glass ship in full sail.

The Jura mountains form a 240-km curve, an afforested range separating France from Switzerland, with great plateaux, river gorges, wide and narrow ravines, and everywhere dark forests flanking mountains rising to 1,800 m. This is magnificent country for walking, cycling or riding – 1,000 km to explore. It is also excellent country for fishing, in the River Doubs or the lakes of Jura – Maclu, Marlay and Chalain. There are ideal camping areas around the attractive villages of Clairvaux-les-Lacs and Doucier. Lake Vouglans is a centre for canoeing and kayaking, sports to which the geography of the region readily lends itself. Beginners can learn at several bases – Malsaucy, Ornans, Villersexel, Montbozon, Morteau, Montbarrey, La Roche and La Pesse.

Walkers will head for the showpiece spectaculars: the sensational 28 waterfalls making up the *Cascades du Hérisson*, or, at Morteau, the breath-taking waterfalls of the *Saut du Doubs*. The *Gouffre de Poudrey* is an underground cavern 20 km from Besançon, the largest of its kind in Europe. There are also *randonnées*, taking in the mountain peaks of the Jura, and the *Route des Sapins*, between Levier and Champignole, a pine trail of some 128 km. In the snow months, keen skiers can take *La Grande Traversée du Jura (GTJ)*, the very popular cross-country ski trail.

There is downhill and cross-country skiing at Métabief. Morez, in the Gorges de la Bienne area, is also a good winter sports resort for family groups. From the ski resort of Les Rousses the Swiss and French Alps can be seen across the waters of Lake Geneva.

The River Doubs rises in the southern Jura, runs north to form the border with Switzerland, dips into that country and then returns to France, now emboldened and navigable, deep and strong, to head west and south through Montbeliard, looping round Besançon and joining the Saône beyond Dôle.

Dôle is an ideal centre for cruising on either the Saône or the Doubs, in trips of two days to a week or more. Dôle itself is charming, its old houses and narrow streets clustered round the sixteenth-century church of Notre-Dame. The place des

Summer forest scene in the Haut Jura

Fleurs gives a charming view of the old town where Louis Pasteur was born.

The painter Gustave Courbet was born in another attractive old town, Ornans, on the River Loue, a tourist centre in the valley. Here the river is overhung by the balconies of the old houses, and it is no surprise that Courbet drew inspiration from the lyrical scenes around him. There are spas at Luxeuil-les-Bains and at Salins-les-Bains, both having the additional attraction of a casino.

Comté cheese is highly regarded. Less holey than its close relatives, Emmenthal and Gruyère, it has an agreeable nutty flavour. The Jura wines of the region are to be found in the south around Arbois and Lons-le-Saunier, a thermal spa and the birthplace of Rouget de Lisle, the composer of the *Marseillaise*, the French national anthem. Château Chalon produces the pair of golden wines: *le vin jaune de garde*, which spends six years maturing in barrels prior to bottling, and *le vin de paille*, a dessert wine whose grapes are allowed to over-ripen on straw mats in the sun.

The Citadel of Besançon overlooks the entire city from a rock base 118 m high. The Doubs winds around the city in the shape of the Greek capital letter omega. Besançon has been the heart of the French watch-making industry for many years. With the coming of quartz mechanisms, the city has adapted its skills to precision engineering. La Grande Rue, a pedestrian mall, is the lively centre of the old quarter, birthplace not only of Victor Hugo but also of the Lumière brothers, inventors of cinematography, whose effect on the world was possibly even greater.

Kirsch and plum brandy are distilled in Franche-Comté, and that famous milky aniseed drink, Pernod, clinking in ice-filled glasses in the bistros of every region in France, is made in Besançon, the capital.

PRACTICAL TOURIST INFORMATION

General information on the region can be obtained by telephoning or writing to the Comité Régionale du Tourisme (CRT) office, while specific booklets are produced detailing camping, hotel and self-catering gîte accommodation. These can be obtained by writing to the tourist board office for the département (CDT) of your choice:

Regional Tourist Board
Comité Régionale du Tourisme (CRT),
32 Charles-Nodier, 25000 BESANCON Cedex
☎ 81.83.50.47

Départements
Doubs (25): Association Départementale du
Tourisme (ADT), Hôtel du Département, avenue
de la Gare d'Eau, 25035 BESANCON Cedex
☎ 81.81.80.80
Jura (39): Comité Départemental du Tourisme
(CDT), Préfecture, 39021 LONS-LE-SAUNIER
☎ 84.24.19.64
Haute-Saône (70): Comité Départemental du
Tourisme (CDT), rue des Bains, 70000 VESOUL
☎ 84.75.43.66
Territoire-de-Belfort (90): Association
Départementale du Tourisme (ADT), Hôtel du
Département, rue de l'Ancien Théâtre, 90020
BELFORT ☎ 84.21.27.95

SELF-CATERING
ACCOMMODATION

*The following British operators offer self-catering
accommodation in the area:*

Gîtes de France, 178 Piccadilly, London W1V 9DB
☎ 01-493 3480
Interhome, 383 Richmond Road, Twickenham
TW1 2EF ☎ 01-891 1294
Vacances en Campagne, Bignor, Pulborough
RH20 1QD ☎ 07987 433
VFB Holidays, 1 St Margaret's Terrace,
Cheltenham GL50 4DT ☎ 0242 526338

SPORTS AND ACTIVITIES

*For unusual and interesting holiday ideas, contact
the Loisirs Accueil office for the area of your
choice:*

Loisirs Accueil Doubs,
Immeuble 'Les Eaux Vives', 15 avenue Edouard
Droz, 25000 BESANCON ☎ 81.80.38.18
Loisirs Accueil Jura,
B.P.652, 8 avenue du 44e. RI, 39021 LONS-LE-
SAUNIER Cedex ☎ 84.24.19.64
Loisirs Accueil Haute-Saône/Belfort, rue des
Bains, 70000 VESOUL ☎ 84.75.43.66

RESORTS

Clairvaux-les-Lacs *(Jura)*
Pop: 1,500
Lons-le-Saunier 22 km, Paris 415 km
⌂ rue du Lac ☎ 84.25.82.66

Superb scenery and attractive countryside make
this a lovely holiday area, with walks to vantage
points, waterfalls (Cascades du Hérisson) and lots
to see. There are two lakes, the smaller Petit Lac
(18 hectares) and the popular Grand Lac (64
hectares) which offer lakeside bathing, sailing,
windsurfing and boat and pedalo hire. Riding,
canoeing and cycle hire are also available locally.

● Camping: Camping en Fayolan and Camping
Le Grand Lac.
● Canoeing: ☎ 45.64.31.52
● Fishing: category 1 fishing on the Drouvenant
and Ain rivers.

Gray *(Haute-Saône)*
Pop: 8,000
Vesoul 55 km, Paris 360 km
⌂ Pavillon du Tourisme, Ile Sauzay
☎ 84.65.14.24

On the banks of the Saône, this is a peaceful town
of old houses and pretty streets set amidst an area
of pleasant walks and good outdoor recreation
opportunities. Gray is one of the principal boat-
hire bases in the area and also a centre for the
popular sport of canoe-kayaking.

● Boat Hire: Connoisseur Cruisers
☎ 84.65.44.62
● Boat Trips: day cruises bookable through the
Tourist Office.
● Camping: Longue Rive ☎ 84.65.16.85
● Canoeing: Sports Nautiques Gray-Saône has
summertime activities and canoe hire.
● Fishing: category 2 fishing on the Saône river.
● Riding: Club Hippique, route de Noiron
☎ 84.65.42.28

Lons-le-Saunier *(Jura)*
Pop: 25,000
Besançon 85 km, Paris 390 km
⌂ 1 rue Pasteur ☎ 84.24.20.63

Pleasant and popular spa town (with casino) and
health resort at the foot of the Jura plateau and
close to the famous Burgundian wine-growing area
of the Côte d'Or.

● Camping: La Marjorie ☎ 84.24.26.94
● Spa: respiratory/lymphatic disorders (1 Jun-
31 Oct) ☎ 84.24.20.34 alt: 255 m, climate:
temperate.

Luxeuil-les-Bains *(Haute-Saône)*
Pop: 10,000
Vittel 70 km, Paris 370 km
⌂ Maison du Tourisme ☎ 84.40.06.41

Modern, well-equipped health resort situated in a
fine historic town set at the heart of forests, a
perfect location for those needing rest and
recuperation, and popular with Parisians, for
whom Luxeuil is only eight hours away by train.

● Camping: Camping du Stade ☎ 84.40.02.39
● Casino: rue des Thermes.
● Cycling: cycles can be hired from the SNCF
station.
● Fishing: category 1 fishing on the Breuchin,
Lanterne and Semouse rivers.
● Golf: (approx. 40 km distant) 18h private
course at Golf de Prunéville-Montbéliard,
Ferme des Petits Bans, 25420 Dampierre-sur-
le-Doubs ☎ 81.98.11.77. Set between the

Vosges and the Jura mountains at 107 m above sea level, this course was built by the Peugeot family in 1961 and has spectacular views (closed mid-Nov-Mar).

- Lace-making: beginners or improvers' courses are held at the Conservatoire de la Dentelle, 1 rue des Thermes (May-Oct)
- Spa: gynaecological conditions (Apr-Oct) ☎ 84.40.44.22 alt: 300 m, climate: fresh.
- Tennis: nine courts to hire.

 Malbuisson *(Doubs)*
Pop: 400
Pontarlier 15 km, Paris 450 km
🆘 Grande-Rue ☎ 81.89.31.21

High-altitude village overlooking the large Lac de Saint-Point, ever busy with those enjoying its sailing and lakeside bathing. There is also tennis, pedalo hire and numerous signed walks to follow through the forests with waterfalls and caves to discover along the 20 km *Route des Sapins*.

- Camping: Camping des Fuvettes.
- Fishing: category 1 and 2 fishing on the river Doubs.
- Winter Sports: cross-country resorts of Métabief and Les Hôpitaux-Neufs 5 km away.

 Ornans *(Doubs)*
Pop: 4,000
Besançon 25 km, Paris 440 km
🆘 la Mairie ☎ 81.62.15.05

The old houses of this pleasant little town range along the banks of the River Loue, their wooden balconies jutting out over the water. This was the birthplace of the artist Gustave Courbet and is today a popular tourist centre and excursion base for visiting the Loue and Lison river valleys and the Royal Saltworks at Arc-et-Senans. Surounded by woodland, hikers can follow the *Grande Randonnée* routes, GR 590 and 595, with other small villages in the area, such as Montgesoye, Vuillafans, Lods and Mouthier-Haute-Pierre, offering hotel and camp-site accommodation.

- Camping: Camping du Chanet ☎ 81.62.23.44
- Fishing: category 1 fishing on the Loue.
- Golf: 18h private course in a lovely densely wooded area at Golf de Besançon, La Chevillotte, 25660 Saône ☎ 81.55.73.54

 Pontarlier *(Doubs)*
Pop: 20,000
Lons-le-Saunier 75 km, Paris 452 km
🆘 SI ☎ 81.46.48.33

Situated between the Doubs river, with its canoeing and fishing attractions, and the Swiss frontier, Pontarlier is an ideal excursion base for those seeking an active, outdoor holiday in the upper Doubs area.

- Cycling: cycles can be hired from the SNCF station.
- Fishing: category 1 and 2 fishing on the River Doubs.
- Winter Sports: resorts of Métabief and Les Hôpitaux-Neufs are nearby.

 Les Rousses *(Jura)*
Pop: 3,000
Lons-le-Saunier 65 km, Paris 465 km
🆘 Office de Tourisme ☎ 84.60.02.55

A winter sports resort for both alpine and cross-country skiing, close to the Swiss border and at the foot of the Dôle (1,680 m). It is made up of four small villages: Les Rousses, Prémanon, Lamoura and Bois d'Amont. There is summer bathing in the Lac des Rousses (94 hectares), which, in winter, provides the setting for the unique sport known in French as *le snowing* (or ice-sailing). Pleasant signposted walks follow part of the long-distance routes GR5 and GR9, which cross this area. Other diversions include a golf course, ice-skating rink and a herd of reindeer from Lapland (at Prémanon) where children can enjoy sledge rides.

- Fishing: category 1 fishing on the Orbe, Biennette and Chaille rivers.
- Riding: Centre Equestre, route du Noirmont ☎ 84.60.04.09

 Salins-les-Bains *(Jura)*
Pop: 5,000
Besançon 45 km, Paris 410 km
🆘 Office de Tourisme ☎ 84.73.01.34

A picturesque little spa town in a valley, with some fine town houses and encircled by woodlands and pasture. The minerals in the salty water are reputed to be effective tonics for those suffering from rheumatism. Local activities include tennis, riding and hang gliding and there is a casino and disco for evening entertainment.

- Spa: respiratory/lymphatic disorders (Feb-Nov) ☎ 84.73.04.63 alt: 354 m, climate: temperate.

 Vesoul *(Haute-Saône)*
Pop: 20,000
Belfort 60 km, Paris 375 km
🆘 rue des Bains ☎ 84.75.43.66

With the pretty, old quarter at its heart, and set on the gentle slopes of La Motte, Vesoul has developed greatly since the arrival of the Peugeot factories, its economy and population growing with the increase in other modern industry. A large lakeside recreation area is attractive for sailing, windsurfing, fishing and summer bathing, and the Tourist Office can provide details of cycling routes, riding and walking trails and flights over the local châteaux and villages.

ILE DE FRANCE

Administrative
Centre: Paris
Population: 9,808,500
Area: 16,189 sq km

Départements:
75 Ville de Paris
77 Seine-et-Marne
78 Yvelines
91 Essonne
92 Hauts-de-Seine
93 Seine-St-Denis
94 Val-de-Marne
95 Val d'Oise

Regional Park:
Parc Naturel Régional
de la Haute-Vallée de
Chevreuse, 13 Grande
Rue, 78720
Dampierre-en-
Yvelines
☎ 30.52.54.65

N otre-Dame on the Ile de la Cité is the heart of Paris. Immediately surrounding it are the 20 spiralling *arrondissements*, while outside the gates of the city, and encircling it, there is the royal green belt of the Ile de France.

A ring of forests, Paris's *poumons verts* (green lungs), Fontainebleau, Compiègne, Rambouillet, Chantilly, St-Germain-en-Laye, L'Isle Adam, owe their survival to the French kings' enthusiasm for hunting. The green lungs continue to work for the health of Paris today. At weekends, the villages, streams, forests and lakes are popular spots for family excursions. Alternative, or even second homes have been sought in a preserved countryside which is still within a few kilometres of the frenetic metropolis.

Constant warfare with Maine, Touraine and Aquitaine in days gone by led to the building of a chain of fortresses, keeps and strongholds, and the location of the French court in the châteaux of the Loire. With the ending of the Hundred Years War and the final withdrawal from France of foreign armies, came the king's wish to return once more to his capital.

In 1510, François I began the conversion of his ancient hunting lodge at Fontainebleau into a Renaissance palace, calling on the skills of Italian artists and masons. Where the king went, court and courtiers followed. Other humbler, but still great, homes sprang up. Succeeding kings developed and decorated what had been begun earlier.

In 1661 Louis XIV had started work on a vast enterprise at Versailles. The aim was to combine the administration of the kingdom with the pleasure of the hunt.
Louis XV and Louis XVI were to pursue the same course, and by the early nineteenth century a new force emerged that would help to ensure that the country would be preserved for yet another hundred years, if not forever.

In 1830, Jean Baptiste Corot came to live in the tiny village of Barbizon. He painted the country and lakes around Ville-d'Avray and Mortefontaine and was joined here by a handful of painters, among them Millet and Théodore Rousseau, all influenced by the work of the Englishmen, Constable and Turner. Corot persuaded his fellow artists to leave their studios and work out of doors, a revolutionary step. This *Ecole Barbizon*, as it was later called, had strong links with the Forest of Fontainebleau. It also found its patron, for the artists would meet at the *Auberge du Père Ganne*, an inn now preserved as a museum.

The work of the school spread over 40 years and passed on its skill and its fascination with the representation of light to its artistic successors, the Impressionists. They too were drawn to the Ile de France.

In 1863, at the Salon des Réfusés, works rejected by the official Salon were shown. By 1871, Cézanne and Pissarro were painting at Pontoise; Renoir, Monet, Sisley and Dégas at Louveciennes, Argenteuil or Marly-le-Roi. In 1872, a work of Monet's, *Impression: Sunrise*, earned for the group what was intended as an abusive title – Impressionist. A period of intense activity in landscape painting followed, and by 1881 the painters had gone their various ways. Cézanne to Provence, Monet to Giverny, Renoir to Algeria then Italy, and Sisley to Moret-sur-Loing near Fontainebleau, soon to become almost a second Barbizon.

Both Barbizon and Moret-sur-Loing are celebrated by visitors anxious to trace the tracks of the Barbizon School and the Impressionists. There are museums of Millet's works and of those of Rousseau in Barbizon. In Moret-sur-Loing there is a *son-et-lumière* celebration of Sisley's work.

Visitors in their millions are also drawn by the royal châteaux. Versailles is fourth in the popularity league for visits (after Paris itself, Mont-St-Michel and Rocamadour), with an estimated three million each year. Many roads are closed to traffic in the area of Chantilly, St-Germain-en-Laye and Compiègne, but walkers are well catered for. *Grande Randonnée* trails help to pierce the forests and explore the past.

Louis XIV, the 'Sun King', was 23 when he started his huge building enterprise, with the assistance of the triumvirate Le Vau (architect), Le Brun (interiors) and Le Nôtre (gardens), and it was far from completed when he moved in 21 years later. Indeed, there were still 36,000 workmen on the site! Within the castle buildings, in addition to the Bourbon family, 1,000 courtiers were accommodated. The work had involved the draining of marshes and the laying-on of water to feed the 1,400 fountains in the 685-hectare gardens. The cost today is such that the fountains only play on a limited number of Sundays during the summer months, *Les Grands Eaux*, and at the floodlit and firework demonstrations, *Les Fêtes de Nuit*.

In 1687, the baroque pleasure palace of the Grand Trianon was added at Louis XIV's direction, and Louis XV continued the embellishments, adding, for the particular pleasure of Madame de Pompadour, the Petit Trianon.

When Louis XVI, the last of the Bourbon kings, came to the throne, he lived in the Petit Trianon, and Marie Antoinette in the rustic village (L'Hameau) which Louis had provided for her. Perhaps the most famous room in the palace is the 75-m-long *Galerie des Glaces*, scene of the signing of the Treaty of Versailles in 1919. The Château de Vaux-le-Vicomte, an elaborate moated palace which was the property of Louis XIV's finance minister, Fouquet, was so splendid that it threatened to eclipse Versailles. Louis's solution to this battle of pride was to banish Fouquet and confiscate his château and lands.

Chantilly, another 'fairy-tale' Renaissance château in a park that hosts fashionable horse races, including the Prix de l'Arc de Triomphe, has enormous eighteenth-century stables, originally servicing stag and boar hunts in Chantilly Forest, now housing the Musée Vivant de Cheval.

Is there a special magic about the Ile de France that kings should renounce the Loire in its favour? A power that makes artists leave their studios to paint the woods and the sunlight beside the river? A pull that persuades Debussy to make his home at St-Germain-en-Laye, Jean Cocteau at Milly-la-Forêt, Ravel at Montfort-l'Amaury?

In June 1986, President Mitterand, at a sensitive, indeed critical, moment in negotiations among the ten members of the European Community, played host to the heads of government at an inn in Barbizon. Apparently the after-dinner atmosphere was euphoric; somehow a crisis had been averted. 'La Dame de Fer' (Prime Minister Thatcher) softened enough to admit to possessing a Corot canvas. Had the Ile de France magic worked once again, as when, a hundred years earlier, at the same hostelry, a lodger called Robert Louis Stevenson wrote *Treasure Island* for the enchantment of the world?

PRACTICAL TOURIST INFORMATION

General information on the region can be obtained by telephoning or writing to the Comité Régional du Tourisme (CRT) office, while specific booklets are produced detailing camping, hotel and self-catering gîte *accommodation. These can be obtained by writing to the tourist board office for the* département *(CDT) of your choice:*

Regional Tourist Board
Comité Régional du Tourisme (CRT), 137 rue de l'Université, 75007 PARIS ☎ 47.53.79.93

Départements
Ville de Paris (75): Office du Tourisme de Paris, 127 avenue des Champs-Elysées, 75008 PARIS ☎ 17.23.61.72
Seine-et-Marne (77): Comité Départemental du Tourisme (CDT), Maison du Tourisme, Château Soubiras, 77190 DAMMARIE-LES-LYS ☎ 64.37.19.36
Yvelines (78): Comité Départemental du Tourisme (CDT), Hôtel du Département, 78000 VERSAILLES ☎ 19.51.82.00
Essonne (91): Comité Départemental du Tourisme (CDT), 4 rue de l'Arche, 91100 CORBEIL-ESSONNES ☎ 10.89.31.32
Hauts-de-Seine (92): Comité Départemental du Tourisme (CDT), 4 avenue Jean-Jaurès, 92140 CLAMART ☎ 16.42.17.95
Seine-St-Denis (93): Comité Départemental du Tourisme (CDT), 2 avenue Gabriel-Péri, 93100 MONTREUIL ☎ 12.87.38.09
Val-de-Marne (94): Comité Départemental du Tourisme (CDT), 11 avenue de Nogent, 94300 VINCENNES ☎ 18.08.13.00
Val-d'Oise (95): Comité Départemental du Tourisme (CDT), Hôtel du Département, 2 le Campus, 95032 CERGY-PONTOISE Cedex ☎ 10.30.92.60

SELF-CATERING ACCOMMODATION

The following British operators offer self-catering accommodation in the area:

Angel Travel, 47 High Street, Central Chambers, Tonbridge TN9 1SD ☎ 0732 361115
Bowhills Ltd, Swanmore, Southampton SO3 2QW ☎ 0489 877627
Chapter Travel, 126 St John's Wood High Street, London NW8 7ST ☎ 01-586 9451
France Directe, 2 Church Street, Warwick CV34 4AB ☎ 0926 497989
Freedom in France, Meadows, Poughill, Bude, Cornwall EX23 9EN ☎ 0288 55591
French Travel Service, Georgian House, 69 Boston Manor Road, Brentford TW8 0JQ ☎ 01-568 8442
Gîtes de France, 178 Piccadilly, London M1V 9DB ☎ 01-493 3480
Hoseasons Holidays Abroad, Sunway House, Lowestoft NR32 3LT ☎ 0502 500555

Interhome, 383 Richmond Road, Twickenham TW1 2EF ☎ 01-891 1294
Lagrange Vacances, 16/20 New Boroadway, London W5 2XA ☎ 01-579 7311
David Newman's French Collection, P.O. Box 733, 40 Upperton Road, Eastbourne BN21 4AW ☎ 0323 410347
Quo Vadis, 243 Euston Road, London NW1 2BT ☎ 01-583 8383
Slipaway Holidays, 90 Newland Road, Worthing BN11 1LB ☎ 0903 821000
Vacances en Campagne, Bignor, Pulborough RH20 1QD ☎ 07987 433
Vacations, 60 Charles Street, Leicester LE1 1FB ☎ 0533 537758
Villa France, 15 Winchcombe Road, Frampton Cotterell, Bristol BS17 2AG ☎ 0454 772410

SPORTS AND ACTIVITIES

For unusual and interesting holiday ideas, contact the Loisirs Accueil office for the area of your choice:

Loisirs Accueil Seine-et-Marne, 170 avenue Henri Barbusse, 77190 DAMMARIE-LES-LYS ☎ 64.37.19.36
Loisirs Accueil Val d'Oise, Hôtel du Département, 2 le Campus, 95032 CERGY-PONTOISE Cedex ☎ 34.43.32.52

RESORTS

Barbizon *(Seine-et-Marne)*
Pop: 1,500
Fontainebleau 10 km, Paris 60 km
🛈 41 Grande Rue ☎ 60.66.41.87

Set on the edge of the forest of Fontainebleau, and surrounded by farmland, this attractive village was the focal point for members of the Barbizon School of painters, Millet, Corot and Rousseau. Barbizon has considerable style and has been able to handle her weekend influx of visitors with ease and unspoiled grace. The town is primarily a fashionable eating place and many of the old houses have been converted into restaurants.

● Art: Barbizon School Museum in Rousseau's home ☎ 60.66.22.38 (closed Tues), and Auberge du Père Ganne (Apr-Oct, closed Tues).

Enghien-les-Bains *(Val d'Oise)*
Pop: 10,000
Pontoise 20 km, Paris 18 km
🛈 boulevard Cotte ☎ 34.12.41.15

A lakeside resort, spa and casino, on the doorstep of Paris, Enghien was in vogue at the end of the nineteenth century as its sulphur baths were the nearest available for Parisians. This is Impressionist country. Argenteuil was a frequent subject for the painters and Pontoise saw Pissarro at work along the river. Good riverbank walks with fishing and boating.

- Casino: avenue de Ceinture ☎ 34.12.90.00
- Golf: hilly 18h private course in Montmorency Forest at Golf de Domont, route de Montmorency, 95330 Domont ☎ 39.91.07.50 (quite hard to find but worth it).
- Spa: respiratory/lymphatic disorders (open all year) ☎ 34.12.70.00 alt: 50 m, climate: sedative.

 Fontainebleau *(Seine-et-Marne)*
Pop: 19,000
Melun 16 km, Paris 60 km
🛈 31 place Napoléon-Bonaparte
☎ 64.22.25.68

To what was originally a hunting lodge, François I and his successors added greater and greater decoration: Henri II's ballroom, the rich apartments of the three queens, Louis XIII's throne room, Madame de Maintenon's apartments, Marie-Antoinette's boudoir . . . The most illustrious occupant, Napoléon, preferred Fontainebleau to Versailles and it was from here, when not campaigning, that he presided over an empire that stretched from Portugal to the Russian frontier. There are formal as well as English gardens, and beyond, in the forest of Fontainebleau, woods of beech, hornbeam, oak, alder and pine, with paths marked for walkers. There are also orientation marks for climbers, a popular sport here, as is golf. There is a fine golf course, its fairways springy between avenues of oak and pine trees.

- Cycling: cycles for hire from the SNCF station.
- Golf: fine 18h private course at Golf de Fontainebleau, route d'Orléans, 77300 Fontainebleau ☎ 64.22.22.95

 L'Isle-Adam *(Val d'Oise)*
Pop: 10,000
Pontoise 13 km, Paris 32 km
🛈 1 avenue de Paris ☎ 34.69.09.76

A pleasant recreation resort on the banks of the Oise, with fishing, canoe and pedalo hire and boat trips to Pontoise and Beaumont. At nearby Auvers, Van Gogh died (1890) in the Café Ravoux, now called Chez Van Gogh.

- Camping: Les Trois Sources ☎ 34.69.08.80
- Golf: see Mantes-la-Jolie.
- Riding: Les Grands Ecuries ☎ 34.69.42.13

 Mantes-la-Jolie *(Yvelines)*
Pop: 44,000
Versailles 44 km, Paris 60 km
🛈 place Jean XXIII ☎ 34.77.10.30

Historically important as a bridge across the Seine, at a point separating Normandie from the Ile de France, Mantes was originally a beautiful setting which attracted artists like Turner, Corot, Monet and Braque. All the main thoroughfares west of Paris, road, rail and river, now converge here. There was great damage during the war and much rebuilding and growth have taken place, with a loss, in the process, of the town's early charm. There are attractive river cruises to Les Andelys, site of Richard the Lionheart's Château Gaillard, or to La Roche-Guyon, and an 'Impressionist's cruise' taking in places beloved of the artists, as far as Monet's home in Giverny.

- Boat Trips: as detailed above, bookable through the Tourist Office.
- Camping: Camping Canada (at Epône) ☎ 30.42.61.76
- Cycling: cycles for hire from the SNCF station.
- Golf: 18h private château course at Golf de Villarceaux Chaussy, 95710 Bray-et-Lu ☎ 34.67.73.83; and 18h private course (in a sports complex including swimming and tennis) at Golf de Seraincourt, Gaillonnet, 95450 Vigny ☎ 34.75.47.28; 18h private course at 78910 Civry-la-Forêt ☎ 34.87.62.29
- Riding: discover the Vexin region on horseback with La Cavale, rue du Moulin, Brueil-en-Vexin ☎ 34.75.39.32
- Sailing: Club Nautique du Mantois ☎ 30.92.63.40
- Zoo: 20 km south is a safari park in the grounds of Thoiry Château.

 Moret-sur-Loing *(Seine-et-Marne)*
Pop: 4,000
Fontainebleau 10 km, Paris 70 km
🛈 place de Samois ☎ 60.70.41.66

On the edge of the forest of Fontainebleau, an old fortified town looks south towards Burgundy. An old bridge, a watermill hidden in the willow trees and Renaissance-style houses delight both artists and fishermen today. The twelfth-century castle keep settles comfortably into this lively and animated town where, in summer, the river banks are floodlit with *son-et-lumière* illustrations of life along Sisley's favourite river.

- Fishing: on the Loing and Orvanne rivers.

 Nemours *(Seine-et-Marne)*
Pop: 12,000
Melun 32 km, Paris 77 km
🛈 41 quai Victor-Hugo ☎ 64.28.03.95

A riverside town, originally built on an island in the Loing, with a twelfth-century castle. Fine walking country in the forest of Fontainebleau and good local fishing opportunities on the pretty river. Unfortunately, the town's location leads to severe traffic congestion.

- Camping: Les Doyers ☎ 64.28.10.62
- Fishing: category 2 fishing in the Loing river and in the Nemours lake.

LANGUEDOC-ROUSSILLON

Administrative
Centre: Montpellier
Population: 1,789,200
Area: 27,448 sq km

Départements:
11 Aude
30 Gard
34 Hérault
48 Lozère
66 Pyrénées-
    Orientales

National Park:
Parc National des
Cévennes, B.P.4,
48400 Florac,
☎ 66.45.01.75

Regional Park:
Parc Naturel Régional
du Haut-Languedoc,
13, rue du Cloitre,
B.P.9, 34220
Saint-Pons
☎ 67.97.02.10

From the Cerdagne heights and Mont Canigou, the highest peak in Roussillon, the Pyrénées sweep down through the ski slopes of Font-Romeu to the peach and apricot orchards around Prades, thence to the Côte Vermeille. Inland the vast plain of Roussillon and Languedoc opens up, with its vineyards and olive fields filled with the sound of cicadas.

French Catalonia, or Roussillon, was ceded to France by Spain a mere 300 years ago, and Catalan culture lives on. The composer Pablo Casals lived in Prades for many years and an annual music festival is held in his name. In Perpignan many street signs are in both Catalan and French.

Perpignan and Montpellier are the wine centres for a region which accounts for three-fifths of France's entire wine production: the red Corbières of Hérault, the white Narbonne, the sparkling white *blanquette* of Limoux, the apéritif wine of Banyuls.

Along the *via Domitia* coastal route from Rome to Spain, stand the ancient cities of Montpellier, a lively university town with a famous medical school, Béziers and tree-lined Narbonne. Inland are Carcassonne and heretical Albi, birthplace of Toulouse Lautrec, all of them breeding grounds, like so many Basque, Gascon and Languedoc cities, of swift and fierce rugby talent.

Along this coast extends a long sweep of almost uninterrupted *plage* development; new resorts designed by different architects to avoid uniformity, but sharing the same end result, massive accommodation complexes and sports facilities for the active summer sun-worshippers. Modern yachting harbours stretch all along this coastline between the Côte d'Azur and Spain, with moorings and facilities available for 15,000 pleasure boats. The port and seaside resort of Sète is the second most important Mediterranean port after Marseille. Paul Valéry, the poet, and Georges Brassens, the *chanteur*, have written and sung in praise of Sète and both lie buried there. For two weeks in August Sète celebrates *les joutes*, knockabout water-jousting.

Closer to the Spanish frontier lies the older resort of Collioure, an early retreat of Picasso, Matisse, Dali and Dufy, its church retaining the unmistakable outline of the lighthouse it once was, and within it a fine Catalan baroque altar-piece.

It was in the Languedoc that Albigensian heresy flourished in the thirteenth-century and here that Simon de Montfort cruelly put the Cathars, holders of the new belief, to fire and the sword. In the massacre of 1209 the church of la Madeleine in Béziers was the Cathars' hopeless refuge. The Cathar Memorial Museum at Minerve (ruined castle) marks the murderous passage of de Montfort through the region in 1210. At Montségur, in 1244, the capture of the Cathars' last stronghold was marked by the burning alive of 210 men and women who refused to renounce their 'heresy'.

Between the Rhône valley and the curved hills of the Auvergne, are the Cévennes

The highly individual La Grande Motte

of Lozère. It is wild and beautiful country of rocky hills and deep ridges, head-high heather and scrub and undergrowth in abundance. Ideal for the walker, the nature lover and the observer, as Robert Louis Stevenson demonstrated in his classic *Travels with a Donkey in the Cévennes*. His and Modestine's 12-day route can be followed today: Le Monastier-sur-Gazeille to Goudet, Pradelles, Langogne, La Bastide, Pont de Montvert, Florac, St-Jean-du-Gard and so to Alès. Virtually nothing has changed here, nor in the 48 km of the Gorges du Tarn, hollowed out of the *causses* by the torrents of the river.

Nîmes was for many years defiant of the rule of Paris. It was also the centre of Protestant resistance during the religious wars of the sixteenth and seventeenth centuries. The Romans knew it too and left their mark there: in the arena, built to seat 20,000, in Agrippa's Maison Carrée, and, a few kilometres away, in the magnificent 270-m-long, three-tiered aqueduct at Pont du Gard (built 19 BC). In more recent years Nîmes, a leader in the wool and silk industries, supposedly supplied the denim material (de Nîmes) to make the original blue jeans.

The vast delta of the Rhône spreads over 770 square km of marshland, some recovered land now grazing sheep or growing rice, some made up of lagoons and a nature reserve for plants, flowers, birds and animals. Private ranches rear herds of the famous white horses of the Camargue and the black bulls are trained to play their part in the local *courses à la cocarde*. In these, unlike the real, killing *corridas* of Catalan Spain, where the prize is the ear or tail of the slaughtered beast, all that is at stake and at hazard is a coloured cockade pulled from the horns of the live bull.

PRACTICAL TOURIST INFORMATION

General information on the region can be obtained by telephoning or writing to the Comité Régional du Tourisme (CRT) office, while specific booklets are produced detailing camping, hotel and self-catering gîte *accommodation. These can be obtained by writing to the tourist board office of the* département *(CDT) of your choice:*

Regional Tourist Board
Comité Régional du Tourisme (CRT), 12 rue Foch, 34000 MONTPELLIER ☎ 67.60.55.42

Départements
Aude (11): Comité Départemental du Tourisme (CDT), 39 boulevard Barbès, B.P.173, 11000 CARCASSONNE Cedex ☎ 68.71.30.09
Gard (30): Comité Départemental de Tourisme (CDT), 3 place des Arènes, B.P.122, 30011 NIMES ☎ 66.21.02.51
Hérault (34): Comité Départemental du Tourisme (CDT), 1 place Marcel-Godechot, 34000 MONTPELLIER ☎ 67.58.00.03
Lozère (48): Comité Départemental de Tourisme (CDT), place Urbain-V, B.P.4, 48002 MENDE ☎ 66.65.34.55.
Pyrénées-Orientales (66): Comité Départemental du Tourisme (CDT), Maison de Tourisme, 66005 PERPIGNAN ☎ 68.34.29.84

SELF-CATERING ACCOMMODATION

The following British operators offer self-catering accommodation in the area:

AA Motoring Holidays, P.O. Box 100, Fanum House, Halesowen B63 3BT ☎ 021-550 7401
Air France Holidays, 69 Boston Manor Road, Brentford TW8 9JQ ☎ 01-568 6981
Allez France, 27 West Street, Storrington, Pulborough RH20 4DZ ☎ 09066 2345
Angel Travel, 47 High Street, Central Chambers, Tonbridge TN9 1SD ☎ 0732 361115
Avon Europe, Lower Quinton, Stratford-upon-Avon, Warks CV37 8SG ☎ 0789 720130
Barberousse Holidays, 11 Hatherley Lane, Cheltenham GL51 6PN ☎ 0242 222129
Belvedere Holiday Apartments, 5 Bartholomews, Brighton BN1 1HG ☎ 0273 23404
Blakes Holidays, Wroxham, Norwich NR12 8DH ☎ 0603 784131
Bowhills Ltd, Swanmore, Southampton SO3 2QW ☎ 0489 877627
Brittany Ferries, The Brittany Centre, Wharf Road, Portsmouth PO2 8RU ☎ 0705 827701
Club Holidays, 35 Balmoral Drive, Mansfield NG19 7HW ☎ 0623 517888
Cosmos Motoring Holidays, Tourama House, 17 Homesdale Road, Bromley BR2 9LX ☎ 01-464 3121
Cresta Holidays, 32 Victoria Street, Altrincham WA14 1ET ☎ 0345 056511
Crystal Holidays, The Courtyard, Arlington Road, Surbiton KT6 6BW ☎ 01-399 5144
Flaine Information, 128a Hamlet Court Road, Westcliff on Sea SS0 7LN ☎ 0702 343381
Four Seasons, Springfield, Farsley, Pudsey LS28 5UT ☎ 0532 564374
La France des Villages, Model Farm, Rattlesden, Bury St Edmunds IP30 0SY ☎ 044 93 7664
France Directe, 2 Church Street, Warwick CV34 4AB ☎ 0926 497989
Freedom in France, Meadows, Poughill, Bude, Cornwall EX23 9EN ☎ 0288 55591
French Travel Service, Georgian House, 69 Boston Manor Road, Brentford TW8 0JQ ☎ 01-568 8442

French Villa Centre, 175 Selsdon Park Road, Croydon CR2 8JJ ☎ 01-651 1231
Gîtes de France, 178 Piccadilly, London W1V 9DB ☎ 01-493 3480
Hoverspeed Ltd, Maybrook House, Queens Gardens, Dover CT17 9UQ ☎ 0304 240241
Intasun France, Intasun House, Cromwell Avenue, Bromley BR2 9AQ ☎ 01-290 1900
Interhome, 383 Richmond Road, Twickenham TW1 2EF ☎ 01-891 1294
Just France, 1 Belmont, Lansdown Road, Bath BA1 5DZ ☎ 0225 446328
Lagrange Vacances, 16/20 New Broadway, London W5 2XA ☎ 01-579 7311
Miss France Holidays, 132 Anson Road, London NW2 6AP ☎ 01-452 7409
David Newman's French Collection, P.O. Box 733, 40 Upperton Road, Eastbourne BN21 4AW ☎ 0323 410347
Pleasurewood Holidays, Somerset House, Gordon Road, Lowestoft NR32 1PZ ☎ 0502 517271
Quo Vadis, 243 Euston Road, London NW1 2BT ☎ 01-583 8383
Rendez-Vous France, Holiday House, 146/148 London Road, St Albans AL1 1PQ ☎ 0727 45400
Riviera Sailing Holidays, 45 Bath Road, Emsworth PO10 7ER ☎ 0243 374376
Sally Tours, Argyle Centre, York Street, Ramsgate CT11 9DS ☎ 0843 595566
Slipaway Holidays, 90 Newland Road, Worthing BN11 1LB ☎ 0903 821000
Sturge, Martin, 3 Lower Camden Place, Bath BA1 5JJ ☎ 0225 310623
Sun France, 3 Beaufort Gardens, London SW16 3BP ☎ 01-679 4562
Sunrose Holidays, 30 Callington Road, Saltash PL12 6DY ☎ 07555 2616
Sunscene Holidays, 40 Market Place South, Leicester LE1 5HB ☎ 0533 20644
Tourarc UK, 197b Brompton Road, London SW3 1LA ☎ 01-589 1918
Vacances, 28 Gold Street, Saffron Walden CB10 1EJ ☎ 0799 25101
Vacances en Campagne, Bignor, Pulborough RH20 1QD ☎ 07987 433
Vacations, 60 Charles Street, Leicester LE1 1FB ☎ 0533 537758
VFB Holidays, 1 St Margaret's Terrace, Cheltenham GL50 4DT ☎ 0242 526338
Villa France, 15 Winchcombe Road, Frampton Cotterell, Bristol BS17 2AG ☎ 0454 772410

SPORTS AND ACTIVITIES

For unusual and interesting holiday ideas, contact the Loisirs Accueil office for the area of your choice:

Loisirs Accueil Aude,
B.P.173, 39 boulevard Barbès, 11004 CARCASSONNE Cedex ☎ 68.47.09.06
Loisirs Accueil Lozère,
B.P.4, 48002 MENDE Cedex ☎ 66.65.34.55

Maison de la Lozère,
4 rue Hautefeuille, 75006 PARIS ☎ 43.54.26.64

RESORTS

 Aigues-Mortes (*Gard*)
Pop: 5,000
Vichy 28 km, Paris 750 km
🄸 place St-Louis ☎ 66.53.73.00

Traditionally an agricultural town, cultivating its
own local wine and exporting asparagus, Aigues-
Mortes is chiefly known for its salt production,
collected from the salt marshes on this vast coastal
plain, an area as large as that occupied by the city
of Paris. Medieval fortifications enclose the town
which attracts summer visitors in great numbers
partly for the wide, flat landscapes of the area,
partly also, perhaps, for the bullfight displays held
every Wednesday and Friday night in high season
and partly because here there is the opportunity to
ride those small, white Camargue horses.

● Boat Hire: houseboats are available to hire at
  the port base from Locaboat Plaisance
  ☎ 66.53.94.50
● Boat Trips: several operators offer canal
  cruises.
● Camping: La Petite Camargue ☎ 66.53.84.77
● Fishing: night fishing trips along the canals
  with Pescalune ☎ 66.53.79.47
● Golf: 18h private course at Golf Club de
  Campagne, route de St-Gilles, 30000 Nîmes
  ☎ 66.70.17.37
● Riding: Mas du Daladel ☎ 66.53.63.65 and
  L'Allegro ☎ 66.53.80.48

 Alès (*Gard*)
Pop: 45,000
Nîmes 44 km, Paris 708 km
🄸 place Gabriel-Péri ☎ 66.52.32.15

At the foot of the Cévennes, in a loop of the River
Gardon, Alès, with its terraced hills, is a large,
modern town of wide avenues and smart shops.
Long, winding and tiring roads lead from here up
into the Cévennes and towards the Tarn gorges. In
winter, the nearby resort of Mas-de-la-Barque is
noted for its cross-country skiing, and north east of
the town, at Méjannes-le-Clap, is a country holiday
resort entirely dedicated to sport and outdoor
pursuits, with every sort of activity offered, from
archery to potholing.

● Camping: Les Châtaigniers ☎ 66.52.53.57
● Cycling: cycles for hire from the SNCF station.
● Golf: 9h private course at Golf de
  Bombequiols, St-André-de-Buèges, 34190
  Ganges ☎ 67.73.72.67
● Riding: Mas Chambon, avenue de Croupillac
  ☎ 66.86.01.18

Alet-les-Bains (*Aude*)
Pop: 600
Carcassonne 33 km, Paris 937 km
🄸 rue de l'Ancienne Mairie ☎ 68.69.92.94

An ancient and picturesque spa village on the
banks of the Aude.

● Canoeing: hire and tuition available
  ☎ 68.69.90.70
● Fishing: category 1 fishing on the Aude.
● Spa: digestive organs (10 May-30 Sep)
  ☎ 68.69.90.27 alt: 206 m, climate: temperate.
● Walking: in the Gorges d'Alet, with wonderful
  views of the Pyrénées and Cévennes from St-
  Salvayre.

 Amélie-les-Bains (*Pyrénées-Orientales*)
Pop: 4,000
Le Boulou 16 km, Paris 860 km
🄸 avenue du Roussillon ☎ 68.39.01.98

Small and pretty riverside spa resort which caters
for a wide range of sporting and leisure interests,
including shooting, moto-cross and fishing.

● Casino: Casino Municipal (open all year)
  ☎ 68.39.06.06
● Golf: see St-Cyprien.
● Riding: at Montbolo.
● Spa: rheumatism/bone joint damage (15 Jan-
  23 Dec) ☎ 68.39.01.00 alt: 230 m, climate:
  temperate.
● Tennis: five courts to hire.

 Les Angles (*Gard*)
Pop: 500
Alt: 1600-2400m
Perpignan 92 km, Paris 1,002 km
🄸 Office de Tourisme ☎ 68.04.42.04

A winter sports resort based in a pretty village on
the Capcir plateau, with a spectacular backdrop of
mountains and lake. A new sports centre provides
an ice-skating rink, indoor pool, bowling and a
fitness centre. All levels of skiing ability are
catered for with 24 pistes, one of which is of
competition standard, and this is also a good base
for cross-country enthusiasts. In summer the Lac
de Matemale offers sailing, windsurfing and pedalo
fun amidst wonderful scenery.

 Argelès-sur-Mer (*Pyrénées-Orientales*)
Pop: 6,000
Perpignan 21 km, Paris 928 km
🄸 place des Arènes ☎ 68.81.15.85

Young, lively and commercial seaside resort with,
at its heart, the tiny old walled town of Argelès.
Sheltered by its backdrop of snow-capped Pyrénées
in the spring, and close enough to Catalan Spain
for shopping excursions by bus, the town has much
to offer as a family resort in an attractive setting.
With its 60 camp sites, the summer population
swells to 300,000. Seemingly limitless attractions
for the holidaymaker include the supervised fun
water park, Aquaglisse, with shops, restaurants
and picnic areas.

● Beach: extensive beach of fine sand with full
  beach and watersports facilities (waterskiing,

paragliding and pedalos, etc). Multi-activity tickets are available from the Tourist Office and offer up to 20 per cent discount – a good idea for those who plan to make full use of the leisure and sports facilities. Also on the beach, and for 13-21 year olds, is the CLJ (Centre de Loisirs pour les Jeunes) Youth Centre, manned by six police instructors, who will help you to master a new watersport safely.

● Camping: Le Soleil ☎ 68.81.14.48 and Prairies St-Rémy ☎ 68.81.02.33
● Casino: at allée des Pins, Argelès-Plage (Jun-Sep) ☎ 68.81.14.27
● Climbing: CLJ, Camping Roussillonnais ☎ 68.81.34.87
● Cycling: bicycle hire from Costa Rêve shopping arcade ☎ 68.81.45.46 and from the SNCF station.
● Diving: deep-sea diving facilities from Antares, avenue de la Gare ☎ 68.81.46.30
● Fishing: morning or night sea-fishing trips ☎ 68.88.36.33
● Riding: Eperon d'Argent, route de Collioure ☎ 68.81.20.87 and Kentucky Ranch, Plage Nord ☎ 68.81.32.68
● Sailing: tuition for beginners from Bateau-Ecole ☎ 68.81.27.03
● Tennis: Garden Tennis Club, chemin de Charlemagne ☎ 68.81.00.28 offers five-day courses every week in season; Tennis Club Argelèsien ☎ 68.81.33.29 has 11 courts set amongst pine woods.
● Walking: with nature reserves on either side of Argelès, the varied coastline offers bird and wildlife interest.

 Bagnols-les-Bains (*Lozère*)
Pop: 250
Mende 20 km, Paris 596 km
🛈 la Mairie ☎ 66.47.64.79

North of the Cévennes mountains, Mont Lozère juts upwards above the peat bog country, a granite crag of 1,600 m where the River Tarn has its source. Bagnols-les-Bains is a tiny rural spa resort on the River Lot, an excellent base for a number of excursions. The *Grandes Randonnées* 7 and 72 almost encircle the Mont Lozère region. At the Col des Tribes (1,100 m) you can see the separation of the water courses of the River Allier, heading for the Mediterranean in the Bouches-du-Rhône, and the Lot, seeking the Atlantic at Bordeaux. The spa buildings bear an eighteenth-century façade, witness to the age-old reputation of its waters' healing powers.

● Camping: Municipal ☎ 66.47.64.79
● Fishing: category 1 fishing in the Lot river, also bathing and canoeing.
● Spa: circulatory disorders (25 Apr-25 Oct) ☎ 66.47.60.02 alt: 910 m, climate: invigorating.

 Bagnols-sur-Cèze (*Gard*)
Pop: 18,000
Avignon 33 km, Paris 657 km
🛈 esplanade du Mont-Cotton ☎ 66.89.54.61

A traditional southern French agricultural town whose population has trebled since the Atomic Energy Commission built installations at Marcoule. There are many attractions close by, with leisurely walks through the sunny villages of the Cèze valley, river swimming or fishing and, of course, the Côtes du Rhône wines of the region to discover.

● Art: gallery of contemporary art houses some fine works by Renoir, Matisse, Bonnard, Monet and others, donated, it must be added, by the artists themselves after the original gallery was accidentally destroyed by fire during over-exuberant merry-making by the town's firemen who were celebrating their saint's day!
● Camping: Les Genets d'Or ☎ 66.89.58.67
● Cycling: cycles for hire from La Roue Libre, avenue Léon Blum ☎ 66.89.91.79
● Fishing: category 2 fishing in the Cèze and Rhône, category 1 fishing in the Tave and the Vionne rivers.
● Spa: nearby at Fumades-les-Bains – respiratory/lymphatic disorders (1 Apr-30 Nov) ☎ 66.24.81.19 alt: 200 m, climate: dry.
● Vineyards: there are opportunities for tastings all along the motorist's *Route des Vins*.

Banyuls-sur-Mer (*Pyrénées-Orientales*)
Pop: 5,000
Perpignan 37 km, Paris 941 km
🛈 avenue de la République ☎ 68.88.31.58

A small fishing port situated in a magnificent natural bay right at the centre of the rocky Côte Vermeille where the Pyrénées meet the sea. A yachting base with 300 berths, good watersports facilities, its proximity to Spain, to where shopping excursions can easily be made, and the notable lack of pollution make this a pleasant and popular seaside resort.

● Beach: pebbly. The nature of the coastline means that there are numerous small rocky coves which are sometimes difficult to reach but well worth the scramble. The clear water here proves irresistible to divers. Small shingle beach a little way down the coast at the frontier railway town of Cerbère.
● Camping: Municipal ☎ 68.88.32.13
● Fishing: half-day sea-fishing trips ☎ 68.88.50.56
● Sailing: and windsurfing tuition at the Yachting Club ☎ 68.88.33.16
● Tennis: Country Catalan Club has five courts to hire amongst other facilities ☎ 68.88.11.11
● Vineyards: this area is noted for the sweet wine produced from its steep vineyards.

Béziers *(Hérault)*
Pop: 80,000
Montpellier 67 km, Paris 822 km
🖪 27 rue du Quatre-Septembre
☎ 67.49.24.19

A large and attractive city, centre of the wine-producing Languedoc, with a fortified cathedral impressively sited on a rocky outcrop above the old bridge crossing the Orb river. A city where traditional festivals include Spanish-style bullfights in the spectacular Roman arena (Mar-Sep). Elegant shaded walkways called allées Paul Riquet, commemorate the seventeenth-century native-born engineer whose achievement it was to connect the country coast to coast (Atlantic to Mediterranean) by creating the Canal du Midi, still an important attribute of the city today.

● Boat Hire: cruise the Canal du Midi. Boats available from town bases from Vacances 3, B.P.6, Villeneuve-les-Béziers ☎ 67.39.66.74 and Midi-Marine, Poilhes-la-Romaine, 34310 Capestang ☎ 67.93.39.32
● Boat Trips: C.A.N.A.L., 63 avenue Jean Moulin, Abeilhan ☎ 67.39.24.44
● Cycling: cycles can be hired from the SNCF station.
● Golf: 9h private course at Golf de Saint Thomas Bèziers, route de Pezenas, 34290 Servian ☎ 67.98.62.01
● Horse-drawn Travel: spend a day travelling by horse-drawn caravan with Vacances 3, rue Jean Laures, Villeneuve-les-Béziers ☎ 67.39.66.74

 Le Boulou *(Pyrénées-Orientales)*
Pop: 4,500
Perpignan 24 km, Paris 929 km
🖪 rue des Ecoles ☎ 68.83.36.32

The mountain air and summer sun combine to give the small spa town and health resort of le Boulou a climate for all seasons, and a vegetation to match it, with olive fields, palm trees and mimosa. It is at once close to the seaside resorts of the Côte Vermeille, Collioure, Argelès and Banyuls, and to the Pyrénées mountains along the high Spanish border.

● Camping: Le Mas Llinas ☎ 68.83.25.46
● Casino: route de Perthus (open all year) ☎ 68.83.01.20
● Fishing: category 1 fishing in the River Tech.
● Riding: Le Fer à Cheval ☎ 68.21.63.82
● Spa: digestive organs (15 Jan-22 Dec) ☎ 68.83.01.17 alt: 90 m, climate: temperate.

Canet-Plage *(Pyrénées-Orientales)*
Perpignan 13 km, Paris 908 km
🖪 place de la Méditerranée ☎ 68.80.20.65

Perpignan's modern seaside and pleasure boat resort (berths for 1,500) where, it is reputed, Father Christmas (*Père Noël*) lives for 364 days of the year! The museum here celebrates this fact with an exhibition of 4,000 years of toys, dolls and games, some of which can be hired to play with. Close to another major resort, St-Cyprien, Canet offers a wide variety of watersports and leisure activities, including boat excursions along the coast to Spain.

● Beach: beautiful 9 km gently shelving fine sand beach.
● Boat Hire: motor boats and sailing boats to hire from Europ'Mer, Port de Canet ☎ 68.80.41.77
● Camping: Le Brasilia ☎ 68.80.23.82 and Miami ☎ 68.80.37.71
● Casino: (open Apr-Oct) ☎ 68.80.32.25
● Cycling: tours with Zublena Cycles ☎ 68.80.41.91 and bicycle hire from Opération 1000 Vélos ☎ 68.80.34.07
● Fishing: whole day tuna fishing trips with Thon Club de Canet-Plage ☎ 68.80.20.66
● Golf: new 18h course.
● Riding: Canet Stables ☎ 68.80.46.12
● Sailing: I.N.V. Sailing School, Port de Canet ☎ 68.80.47.71 and UDSIS Sailing School (Harbour Master's Office) ☎ 68.80.20.66 and Club de Voile ☎ 68.80.20.66
● Tennis: courts to hire ☎ 68.80.29.60
● Windsurfing: Tobago Club, Plage Port.

 Cap d'Agde *(Hérault)*
Pop: 14,000
Béziers 22 km, Paris 809 km
🖪 avenue des Sergents ☎ 67.26.00.30 and ☎ 67.26.38.58

Large modern purpose-built seaside resort – a paradise for sports and leisure enthusiasts and for those who demand plenty of night life! There's holiday accommodation for 20,000 and an extraordinary 19-hectare leisure pool complex, Aqualand, with huge water-slides, adventure pool, wave pool, hill slide, shops and fun for all the family. It's worth exploring inland though to remind yourself of the real France . . . while those exponents of the delights of naturism have their own famous holiday district here.

● Beach: immense sandy beach.
● Camping: Camping Municipal de la Clape ☎ 67.26.16.33 and (for the naturist district) Centre Helio-Marin ☎ 67.26.32.89
● Cycling: numerous outlets hire bicycles including one on avenue des Sergents.
● Deep-sea Diving: both for beginners and those with previous experience at the Centre Nautique de Cap d'Agde, Ile de Loisirs ☎ 67.26.81.83
● Fishing: day and night fishing trips bookable from the Centre de Pêche Sportive Amateur, Bassin 4, Quai Ouest, avenue de Pasteur Chaillies ☎ 67.26.30.99
● Languages: courses for beginners and advanced students in German, English and French are offered all year round at Centre d'Etude de Langues International d'Agde et

The lavender-fragrant Lower Cévennes

du Cap (C.E.L.I.A.C.), Pinède de la Clape ☎ 67.26.45.65
- Naturism: self-catering, camping or hotel accommodation is available. The Central Council for British Naturism can provide details: 35-41 Hazelwood Road, Northampton NN1 1LL ☎ 0604 20361
- Riding: Poney Club les Cadières, route de Marseillan ☎ 67.21.26.99
- Sailing: and windsurfing schools are numerous. Try Bune-Club, plage de la Roquille ☎ 67.26.28.65 and Centre Nautique du Cap d'Agde, Ile aux Loisirs, plage Richelieu ☎ 67.26.81.93
- Tennis: exceptional facilities consist of 62 courts (some floodlit) at Tennis Club Pierre Barthes, avenue de la Vigne ☎ 67.26.00.06
- Thalassotherapy: (Feb-Nov) Thalacap Institut de Thalassothérapie, place de la Falaise ☎ 67.26.14.80

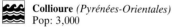 **Collioure** *(Pyrénées-Orientales)*
Pop: 3,000
Port Vendres 4 km, Paris 930 km
🛈 place du 18 Juin ☎ 68.82.15.47

Very attractive fishing village resort with an old castle and ramparts (as well as modern buildings), and more than a hint of the influence of neighbouring Spain. Eternally popular with artists, attracted by the picturesque setting, Collioure is close enough to the Spanish border for shopping excursions by bus, and provides regular summer activities and diversions (bullfights and fireworks in particular). If the summers are too hot and busy, consider February when the surrounding hillsides are a mass of white almond blossom and the cork-oaks stand leafy and green, and share the inspiration that drew the great artists here – Matisse, Picasso, Dérain and Dufy amongst others.

- Beach: six small sand and shingle beaches in

pretty rocky bays.
- Camping: Les Amandiers-L'Ouille ☎ 68.81.14.69 and La Girelle ☎ 68.81.25.56
- Fishing: morning or night sea-fishing trips ☎ 68.82.07.16
- Sailing: tuition for children (10-15 years) during July and August ☎ 68.82.00.28. Also windsurfing, diving and sailing for adults. The marina has berths for 80 pleasure boats.

 Font-Romeu *(Pyrénées-Orientales)*
Pop: 3,000
Perpignan 88 km, Paris 998 km
🛈 avenue Emmanuel-Brousse ☎ 68.30.02.74

Winter Olympic training centre with 37 km of slopes (27 pistes) and cross-country routes. The modern facilities include ice rink, swimming pool, aerobics, weight training, archery, indoor squash and tennis courts and are open throughout the year. There also exists the unique opportunity to experience travel behind a team of Siberian Huskies as they pull your sledge away into the snowy distance. With holiday accommodation for 19,000, sports and activity facilities spilling over into spring and summer (fishing, climbing, riding, golf, canoeing and walking), and the attractions of the pure mountain air, this is truly an all-year resort.

- Casino: open all summer ☎ 68.30.01.11
- Climbing: Rocher d'Escalade. Enquire at Bureau de la Montagne, rue Emmanuel-Brousse ☎ 68.30.03.28
- Golf: 9h public course at Golf de Font-Romeu, avenue Jean Paul, 66120 Font-Romeu ☎ 68.30.21.67
- Husky Travel: Chiens de Traineau organise day trips ☎ 61.87.99.96
- Riding: Ecole d'Equitation, Lycée Climatique ☎ 68.30.11.52

 **Frontignan** *(Hérault)*
Pop: 15,000
Montpellier 22 km, Paris 782 km
🛈 Rond-Point de l'Esplanade ☎ 67.48.33.94

A recently created port (600 berths) and seaside resort where the arid Massif de la Gardiole vineyard area, producing very fine muscat wine, meets the sea. Together with Balaruc-les-Bains, this industrial area offers sea fishing trips, colourful summer festivities and walks in the hills beyond.

- Beach: fine sand.
- Camping: Le Miami ☎ 67.48.76.32
- Cycling: cycles to hire from Cycles Vincent, boulevard Gambetta ☎ 67.48.15.98 and from the SNCF station.
- Sailing: two-day sailing trips (night spent berthed in a resort) bookable from the Ecole de Croisière 'Grand Large', 2 rue Massane, Montpellier ☎ 67.52.89.52

La Grande Motte *(Hérault)*
Pop: 4,000
Montpellier 20 km, Paris 754 km
🛈 place 1er Octobre-1974 ☎ 67.56.62.62

Once virtually uninhabited mosquito-infested marshland on the fringe of the Camargue National Park, this much publicised and innovative resort was the first to be developed to exploit this important stretch of coastline. Pyramid-like apartment blocks, of a design reminiscent of terraced hillsides, provide self-catering accommodation interspersed with lawns and pine trees. The rest of the town is devoted to the needs of the holidaymaker, with almost unlimited opportunity to attempt or master the watersport or other leisure activity of choice. Complemented by lively '*après plage*', this is a modern and fun resort for the young, whose population in summer rises to 40,000.

● Beach: 7 km, sandy and gently shelving.
● Boat Hire: departing from the nearby base at Carnon, Camargue Plaisance, allées des Goélands, La Grande Motte ☎ 67.50.77.00
● Camping: (total camp site accommodation for 15,000) Camping de l'Or ☎ 67.56.52.10 and Camping Lous Pibols ☎ 67.56.50.08
● Casino: open all year ☎ 67.56.54.03
● Golf: 18h public course at Golf de la Grande Motte, 34280 La Grande Motte ☎ 67.56.05.00
● Thalassotherapy: Institut de Thalassothérapie ☎ 67.85.39.71

 Le Grau-du-Roi *(Gard)*
Pop: 4,000
Arles 53 km, Paris 755 km
🛈 boulevard Front-de-Mer ☎ 66.51.67.70

Small and popular fishing village and port adjacent to the modern purpose-built sailing resort of Port-Camargue with its massive yachting marina (4,000 berths), sailing centre and good watersports. Casino.

● Camping: L'Abri de Camargue ☎ 66.51.54.83 and Bon Séjour ☎ 66.51.47.11
● Cycling: cycles for hire from the SNCF station.
● Naturism: plage des Baronnêts.
● Riding: boulevard du Boucanet.
● Sailing: cruising and ocean-racing courses are held at the Ecole de Mer ☎ 66.51.47.92, also dinghy sailing and windsurfing.

 Gruissan *(Aude)*
Pop: 2,000
Narbonne 14 km, Paris 855 km
🛈 Office de Tourisme ☎ 68.49.03.25

This is a relatively new resort, a charming fishing village on a peninsula pushing out into the lagoons. Behind are the pine-wooded slopes of the Massif de la Clape, encircling the Barbarossa Tower. The layout of this little resort is circular in design, with the yachting marina at its heart. Some of the weekend houses on Gruissan beach are mounted on stilts to resist the force of the tidal waters. The resort has everything a visitor could wish for: sailing and fishing trips, riding, watersports and a casino. Fishing is the local livelihood and in late June the townspeople celebrate with a Fête des Pecheurs.

● Boat Hire: Nauti d'Oc ☎ 68.49.06.45
● Camping: Les Ayguades ☎ 68.49.81.59
● Casino: ☎ 68.49.02.52
● Riding: Centre Hippique ☎ 68.49.00.02 and Riding Ranch at Ste-Hélène ☎ 68.49.83.44

 Montpellier *(Hérault)*
Pop: 200,000
Nîmes 52 km, Paris 759 km
🛈 6 rue Maguelone ☎ 67.58.26.04

Capital of the Languedoc-Roussillon region, this is a great historic and cultural centre close to the coast. It has all the charms of sunny, outdoor southern France, plus the always lively atmosphere of a university city, with the theatre, opera and busy street cafés. An excellent base for further excursions, the seaside resorts of Palavas-les-Flots and La Grande Motte are nearby.

● Camping: Les 4 Seigneurs ☎ 67.63.47.48
● Climbing: first-timers can attempt the Rocher de Cazevieille with L'Air Sud ☎ 67.64.31.76
● Cycling: cycles for hire at the SNCF station.
● Golf: 9h private course at Golf de Coulondres Montpellier, 4 rue des Erables, 34980 St-Gély-du-Fesc ☎ 67.84.13.75

 Narbonne-Plage *(Aude)*
Pop: 2,000
Béziers 20 km, Paris 848 km
🛈 Office de Tourisme ☎ 68.49.84.86

Not far from Narbonne (20 km), at the foot of the hills of the Massif de la Clape, the fine, white sands of the big beaches, the purity of the air and the tang of the pine trees are reminiscent of the Atlantic coast resorts. The local honey is richly prized, as are its Corbières red wines, and the market at Narbonne-Plage is held on the seafront itself, along the promenade. In the harbour there are moorings for over 500 pleasure craft, and there are good watersports facilities.

● Camping: La Falaise ☎ 68.49.80.77
● Cycling: cycles for hire from the SNCF station.

Palavas-les-Flots *(Hérault)*
Pop: 4,000
Montpellier 12 km, Paris 767 km
🛈 Hôtel de Ville ☎ 67.68.02.34

A short distance from Montpellier, this is essentially the seaside resort and fishing port for the city. Situated between the lagoons and the sea, with canalside restaurants and a lively night life, there is a large pleasure boat marina (1,000 berths) plus facilities for all watersports.

- Camping: Eden Camping ☎ 67.68.29.68
- Casino: Casino de Palavas ☎ 67.68.00.01
- Cycling: cycles to hire from Palavas Sport, Horizon 2000 ☎ 67.68.36.93
- Riding: Promenade à Cheval St-Pierre, route de Montpellier.
- Tennis: 13 courts to hire plus lessons available from the Zone Sportive ☎ 67.68.08.18

 Port-Barcarès *(Aude)*
Pop: 3,000
Perpignan 21 km, Paris 895 km
🅱 Front-de-Mer ☎ 68.86.16.56 and
☎ 68.86.18.23

Expansive and highly modern Mediterranean resort which claims to meet every need of those whose chief concern is achieving or maintaining personal physical fitness. As a result this resort has been developed as a pilot for a particular lifestyle and the organised sporting activities are virtually unlimited. The large lagoon (Lac Leucate) provides an extensive tuition, practice and competition area for catamarans, sailing dinghies, waterskiing and windsurfing; there are conger eel and tuna fishing trips on the open sea; early morning gallops along the beach for the proficient rider; intensive tennis coaching and judo courses and competitions. Four-wheel drive enthusiasts are catered for, too, with their own school and large trail close to the lagoon's shore. The marina has berths for 200 and the resort is divided into six districts, with accommodation in seafront hotels, small villas with gardens, 3,000 modern complex apartments and 13 camp sites.

- Beach: 8-km-long sandy beach.
- Camping: Camping Floride/Embouchure ☎ 68.86.11.75
- Casino: at Port-Barcarès (on board beached Greek ferry *Lydia*) ☎ 68.86.07.13 (open all summer).
- Cycling: bicycle hire from numerous outlets.
- Golf: 9h private course at Golf de la Pinède, 11370 Port Leucate ☎ 68.40.00.62
- Naturism: the naturist village of Aphrodite is here and details are available from the Central Council for British Naturism, 35-41 Hazelwood Road, Northampton NN1 1LL ☎ 0604 20361
- Riding: Centre Hippique Le Mas-de-la-Grèle ☎ 68.86.07.82 and L'Oxer-Catalan, chemin de l'Hourton ☎ 68.86.81.21
- Sailing: tuition from the Centre Nautique de Barcarès ☎ 68.86.07.28
- Tennis: 27 courts to hire, 14 of which are floodlit, at La Coudalère Clubhouse. Intensive courses for children and beginners are available, using combined instructor and video techniques.
- Thalassotherapy: Institut Thalassa offers

treatment by the day, week or longer and can be combined with personal dietary and beauty consultations ☎ 68.86.30.90

 Port-Vendres *(Pyrénées-Orientales)*
Pop: 6,000
Perpignan 30 km, Paris 935 km
🅱 quai Pierre Forgas ☎ 68.82.07.54

Close to the major Costa Brava route to Spain, Port-Vendres, or Portus Veneris as the Romans named the town, has had a turbulent past typical of this part of the Mediterranean. A natural deep-water commercial and fishing port on the Côte Vermeille with a yachting marina (250 berths), this is the nearest port serving North Africa. There is much here for the holidaymaker interested in exploring the area, while the colour and spectacle of the returning fishing fleet and the ensuing fish auction at 5 p.m. every afternoon should not be missed.

- Beach: Plage de Paulilles (3 km south) is a pretty sandy beach offering windsurfing and pedalo hire. Only 2 km from Collioure and 6 km from Banyuls-sur-Mer with all their associated facilities.
- Camping: Camping de la Presqu'Ile ☎ 68.82.11.40
- Fishing: morning and night sea-fishing trips ☎ 68.82.00.88

 Pyrénées 2000 *(Pyrénées-Orientales)*
Alt: 1,800-2,250 m
Perpignan 89, Paris 1,000 km
🅱 Office de Tourisme ☎ 68.30.12.42

A popular winter sports resort, closely linked with Font-Romeu, on the Serrat de l'Ours plain in Cerdagne country. There is downhill as well as cross-country skiing and ice hockey, with snow surfing for children. Night skiing on floodlit pistes is a speciality for adults. This is a very attractive valley with marvellous views of a superb mountain range. A little mountain train service runs from Mont Louis to La Tour-de-Carol on the Spanish frontier. Accommodation is in hamlets of cabins or in chalets and villas, and during the summer months there is very good fishing as well as riding, tennis and golf.

- Golf: see Font-Romeu.

 St-Cyprien-Plage *(Pyrénées-Orientales)*
Pop: 4,500
Perpignan 15 km, Paris 915 km
🅱 parking Nord du Port ☎ 68.21.01.33

Built around the little fishing harbour in the foothills of the Pyrénées, this modern resort was designed with an emphasis on sports and fitness activities. Thus a wide range of facilities is offered by the 'Grand Stade', whose director is French footballer Michel Platini. The large marina has 2,200 moorings, and eternally popular with children is the water fun park, Aquacity.

- Camping: Cala Gogo ☎ 68.21.07.12 and Camping Municipal Laurent Baudru ☎ 68.21.00.20
- Casino: (open all summer) ☎ 68.21.13.78
- Cycling: hire bicycles from Le Mini Cycle, carrefour Maillol ☎ 68.21.10.00
- Fishing: tuna fishing day trips available ☎ 68.21.16.07
- Football: during school holidays, full or half-board week-long children's courses (8-16) from Football Michel Platini, Grand Stade, B.P.61, St-Cyprien-Plage ☎ 68.21.24.21
- Golf: 27h private course at Golf de St-Cyprien, 66750 St-Cyprien ☎ 68.21.01.71
- Riding: hourly rides and half-day courses at U.D.S.I.S.T. Equestrian Centre ☎ 68.21.24.21 (July/Aug).
- Sailing: and windsurfing courses available all year round for beginners and improvers from U.D.S.I.S.T Marine Sports Centre, St-Cyprien-Plage ☎ 68.21.11.53
- Tennis: 17 outdoor (eight floodlit) and seven indoor courts for hire. Children's courses (8-16) full or half-board from Tennis Bernard Fritz at Grand Stade (address above).

Ste-Enimie *(Lozère)*
Pop: 500

Mende 28 km, Paris 600 km
🛈 la Mairie ☎ 66.48.50.09

Between Florac and Millau, the winding, tortuous course of the Tarn cuts through steep cliffs and fertile valleys. The beautiful little medieval village of Ste-Enimie, circled by steep terraced cliffs, sits at one of the most scenic sections of the gorges. Climbers and canoeists challenge the great natural geography of the area, while walkers hike from one great vista to another.

- Camping: Camping de Couderc.
- Fishing: category 1 fishing on the Tarn river.
- Golf: 9h private course at Golf du Sabot, 48000 La Canourgue ☎ 66.32.81.49

Sète *(Hérault)*
Pop: 42,000

Montpellier 34 km, Paris 789 km
🛈 60 Grand'Rue Mario Roustan ☎ 67.74.73.00

Nicknamed 'the Venice of Languedoc', the panorama from the hill behind this large, important commercial and industrial port reveals a fishing harbour, a maze of canals and a large lagoon (Lake Thau) stretching out into the Golfe du Lion. Regular ferry trips connect Sète with Tangiers, Oran, Algiers, Palma and Ibiza, and this is also a lively family seaside resort with all the familiar beach and waterside activities plus the unusual and entertaining water-borne jousting tournament in August.

- Beach: 15 km beach of fine sand.
- Camping: Camping des Quilles ☎ 67.53.10.25
- Cycling: cycles can be hired from the SNCF station.
- Riding: night-time rides along the banks of Lake Thau on white Camargue horses with Promenades à Cheval du Camping du Castellas, Manade Listel ☎ 67.53.26.24
- Spa: close by at Balaruc-les-Bains – rheumatism/bone joint damage (28 Feb-17 Dec) ☎ 67.48.51.02 alt: 0 m, climate: sea air.

Valras-Plage *(Hérault)*
Pop: 3,000

Béziers 15 km, Paris 827 km
🛈 place R.-Cassin ☎ 67.32.36.04

Close to Béziers, where the River Orb meets the sea, this is a typical fishing port and resort combined, with good sports and sailing facilities.

- Beach: 8 km, fine sand.
- Camping: Central ☎ 67.32.10.78
- Fishing: for a real night out, try conger-eel fishing trips, leaving 9 p.m., returning 6 a.m. (breakfast served on board). Bookable from 12 Impasse Yves Nat ☎ 67.37.30.30

LIMOUSIN

Administrative
Centre: Limoges
Population: 738,700
Area: 16,932? sq km

Départements:
19 Corrèze
23 Creuse
87 Haute-Vienne

The Limousin has never aimed to cater for the fashionable tourist; this is not the country of chic watering places and casinos. Instead it passes on to the visitor those essential gifts nature has granted it: soft countryside; water in torrents, as in the valley of the Dordogne, or as placid as the vast Vassivière lake; the fingerprints of history in châteaux and strongholds; and human skill in the arts of enamelling, porcelain work and embroidery.

Where there's water in the Limousin, there is boating, swimming, fishing and, above all perhaps, canoeing. Numerous rivers and lakes mean that the area offers splendid opportunities to practise this sport. The Dordogne, one of the longest rivers in France, may also be its most beautiful, while the Creuse winds through spectacular gorges. Argentan on the Dordogne, and Saillant d'Allassac on the Vézère, are excellent canoeing bases, offering tuition and easy water for beginners. Above Tulle, the expert is set some stiff canoeing tests on the racing Corrèze.

Fish in streams, rivers and lakes. Try the Plateau de Millevaches (freshwater springs) in the south east of Limousin; or fish for trout along the Creuse or Vézère rivers. With over 67,700 hectares of lakes and ponds in the area there are plenty of alternatives and a fishing licence can be obtained from any fishing tackle shop.

Where there are fields and rounded hills there are paths to be walked and peaceful country roads to be explored by bicycle or on horseback. The beautiful Limousin scenery invites all categories of walker. Try the unspoilt Massif of Monédières or the Creuse valley. Signed routes (Grande Randonnée) are: GR4 Aubusson to Angoulême; GR44 Bort-les-Orgues to Vassivière; GR46 Aubusson to Uzerche via Treignac.

There are many beautiful châteaux, but the modest houses of the old towns also boast interesting architectural features − pepperpot chimneys, corbels and small turrets − which make of them Limousin châteaux in their own right.

Limoges, the capital, is known throughout the world for its fine porcelain. The white kaolin clay was dug from the ground in 1765 at St-Yrieux-la-Perche and the earliest Limoges porcelain dates from six years later. Limousin enamelling skills have been known and respected since the twelfth century, thanks in part to the oxides of the local soil, to which they owe their typically vivid colouring. The museum at Guéret has a fine collection of enamelware.

The tapestry tradition came to the region when, following a dynastic marriage, Flanders weavers settled in Aubusson and Pelletin, bringing with them their craft. Centuries later, Graham Sutherland's massive tapestry for Coventry Cathedral was woven at Pelletin too.

The beautiful focal point of the country lies in the valley of the Dordogne. Dammed at Bort-les-Orgues, the river forms an artificial lake, the Lac de Bort, 18 km in length with the multi-towered medieval fortress of the fifteenth-century Château de Val, once perched high above the Dordogne, now standing on its own island in the lake. From here the river links half a dozen more lakes above Argentan, ideal for waterskiing, windsurfing and sailing.

The 45 km of shoreline around the artificial Lake Vassivière offer beaches and great stretches of water for every possible water activity and for all ages. It is the

family holiday area par excellence, unspoilt and uncommercialised.

Brive-la-Gaillarde, near the Perigord border, is the fruit (and truffle) market of the region, its central streets radiating out to the surrounding tree-lined boulevards. The recent past of Brive is recorded in the Edmond Michelet Museum to Resistance and Deportation in World War II. There is another such museum at picturesque Tulle, and at Gentioux, near the St-Pardoux lake, there is a war memorial in the form of a small child shaking its fist at the very idea of war. A few kilometres to the north west of Limoges, the village of Oradour-sur-Glane stands as it did that fell Saturday of 10 June 1944 when its entire population of 642 (247 of them children) were massacred by a Nazi SS unit and their homes burned. The charred remains of the village are today a point of pilgrimage, their significance marked in notices by the solemn admonition *'Recueillez-vous'*.

Ironically, within a handful of kilometres from this scene of horror, near St-Junien in the valley of the Glane, is the lyrical riverside setting, the *site de Corot* where the great landscape painter (1796-1875) came for peace and inspiration.

The land is studded with châteaux: Chenerailles and Rochechouart, Boussac-Chatelus where Richard Coeur de Lion was mortally wounded, the 'fairy-tale' Château Jumilhac, the ruined Turenne and the moated fifteenth-century Château de Pompadour, now a famous *haras* (stud farm) for Arab horses.

The pilgrim route to Santiago de Compostela once passed through the township of Collonges-la-Rouge. Now pilgrims visit the charming village for its own sake. No cars are allowed here. There are no overhead cables or wires. The houses date from the fifteenth century and are built in red sandstone with the Limousin pepperpots, turrets and roofs of stone tiles. Wealthy people have now bought these charming homes and visitors come from far and wide to walk the peaceful streets, for here they are in the heart of the Limousin.

PRACTICAL TOURIST INFORMATION

General information on the region can be obtained by telephoning or writing to the Comité Régional du Tourisme (CRT) office, while specific booklets are produced detailing camping, hotel and self-catering gîte accommodation. These can be obtained by writing to the tourist board office for the département (CDT) of your choice:

Regional Tourist Board
Comité Régional du Tourisme (CRT), 8 cours Bugeaud, 87039 LIMOGES Cedex ☎ 55.79.57.12

Départements
Corrèze (19): Comité Départemental du Tourisme (CDT), quai Baluze, 19000 TULLE
☎ 55.26.46.88
Creuse (23): Creuse Expansion Tourisme, 43 place Bonnyaud, 23000 GUERET ☎ 55.52.33.00
Haute-Vienne (87): Comité D partemental du Tourisme (CDT), 41 boulevard Carnot, 87000 LIMOGES ☎ 55.77.58.21

SELF-CATERING ACCOMMODATION

The following British operators offer self-catering accommodation in the area:

Bowhills Ltd, Swanmore, Southampton SO3 2QW
☎ 0489 877627
Brittany Ferries, The Brittany Centre, Wharf Road, Portsmouth PO2 8RU ☎ 0705 827701
Gîtes de France, 178 Piccadilly, London W1V 9DB
☎ 01-493 3480
Hoseasons Holidays Abroad, Sunway House, Lowestoft NR32 3LT ☎ 0502 500555
David Newman's French Collection, P.O. Box 733, 40 Upperton Road, Eastbourne BN21 4AW
☎ 0323 410347
Sturge, Martin, 3 Lower Camden Place, Bath BA1 5JJ ☎ 0225 310623
VFB Holidays, 1 St Margaret's Terrace, Cheltenham GL50 4DT ☎ 0242 526338

SPORTS AND ACTIVITIES

For unusual and interesting holiday ideas, contact the Loisirs Accueil office for the area of your choice:

Loisirs Accueil Corrèze,
Maison du Tourisme, Quai Baluze, 19000 TULLE
☎ 55.26.46.88
Loisirs Accueil Creuse,
43 place Bonnyaud, 23000 GUERET
☎ 55.52.87.50
Loisirs Accueil Haute-Vienne,
4 place Denis Dussoubs, 87000 LIMOGES
☎ 55.79.04.04
Maison du Limousin,
18 boulevard Haussmann, 75009 PARIS
☎ 47.70.32.63

RESORTS

 Argentat *(Corrèze)*
Pop: 4,000
Tulle 30 km, Paris 513 km
🛈 avenue Pasteur ☎ 55.28.10.91 (Jun-Sep)

A charming old town in the Dordogne valley, formerly a lightermen's port, with picturesque sixteenth- and seventeenth-century houses along the river, showing stone-tiled roofs and a profusion of turrets. The 713-hectare lake, Le Sablier, offers superb watersports and fishing facilities and there are numerous walks and excursions in the area.

● Beach: safe for bathing.
● Camping: Le Longour ☎ 55.28.13.84
● Canoeing: Argentat-Brivezac international canoeing rally (first Sunday in July).
● Fishing: category 2 fishing on the Dordogne and category 1 fishing on the Maronne, Doustre and Souvigne rivers.
● Tennis: four outdoor and two indoor courts for hire ☎ 55.28.02.66
● Walking: in the Gorges de la Dordogne.

 Beaulieu-sur-Dordogne *(Corrèze)*
Pop: 2,000
Tulle 39 km, Paris 522 km
🛈 place Marbot ☎ 55.91.09.94 (Jul-Sep)

This tiny town is situated on the right bank of the beautiful Dordogne. There is a 33-hectare lake, Les Aubarèdes, for fishing and canoeing, and numerous walks and excursions in the area. The Feast of the Holy Relics is held the first weekend in September.

● Camping: Camping du Pont ☎ 55.91.11.31
● Canoeing: centre with hire available.
● Fishing: category 2 fishing on the Dordogne and category 1 fishing on the Ménoire.
● Tennis: two courts for hire ☎ 55.91.02.03
● Walking: in the Gorges de la Cère.

 Bort-les-Orgues *(Corrèze)*
Pop: 5,000
Ussel 31 km, Paris 468 km
🛈 place Marmontel ☎ 55.96.02.49

The town stretches along the right bank of the Dordogne, near the point where it is joined by the Rhue. The huge artificial lake, Lac de Bort (9,870 hectares), provides full watersports facilities including waterskiing and windsurfing. Boat trips leave from the dam or ancient Château de Val, now standing on an island in the lake. The 'Orgues' are organ-pipe-shaped columns of weathered volcanic rock. An international folk dance festival is held in early August.

● Beach: safe bathing in lake.
● Camping: Beau Soleil ☎ 55.96.00.31
● Fishing: category 1 fishing on the Rhue and in numerous streams and category 2 fishing on the Dordogne.
● Tennis: four outdoor and one indoor court to hire ☎ 55.96.05.12
● Walking: to Saint-Nazaire promontory with a fine view over the gorges of the Dordogne and Diège.

 Brive-la-Gaillarde *(Corrèze)*
Pop: 55,000
Limoges 91 km, Paris 486 km
🛈 place 14-Juillet ☎ 55.24.08.80

A base for trade and industry with an historic centre and tree-lined boulevards. The river valley is agriculturally productive; a melon fair is held on the last Sunday in August and a walnut fair in late September.

- Camping: Camping des Iles ☎ 55.24.34.74
- Caving: swallowhole at Noailles (Le Gouffre de la Fage).
- Golf: 18h public course at Golf d'Aubazine, Ass. Corrèzienne de Golf Complexe Touristique du Coiroux, 19190 Beynat ☎ 55.27.25.66
- Skating Rink: open Sep-May.
- Squash: three courts at the Gymnase Club, boulevard Michelet Pont de Buy ☎ 55.23.50.83
- Tennis: numerous facilities include eight courts at the Stade Municipal ☎ 55.24.34.70; ten courts at the Plaine des Jeux de Tujac ☎ 55.74.32.35

 Limoges *(Haute-Vienne)*
Pop: 145,000
Poitiers 119 km, Paris 396 km
🇮 boulevard de Fleurus ☎ 55.34.46.87

Pleasant, modern city and administrative capital of the Limousin, now the centre of two major industries – porcelain and enamelling. Although heavily built up and with a large population, Limoges remains one of the great centres for the traditional craft of enamelling, which is continued in small workshops, some of which are open to the public. The steep narrow streets of the old lower town lead down to the Vienne and its ancient river bridge and there are garden walks beneath the fine Gothic cathedral of St-Etienne. The city is surrounded by lush pastureland and pretty hillside meadows where cattle graze.

- Art: birthplace of Renoir (two of his paintings are in the Municipal Museum near the cathedral). He began his career here as a porcelain painter.
- Golf: 18h public course at Golf de Limoges, Saint-Lazare avenue du Golf, 87000 Limoges ☎ 55.30.28.01

 Neuvic-d'Ussel *(Corrèze)*
Pop: 2,500
Ussel 21 km, Paris 459 km
🇮 rue de la Poste ☎ 55.95.88.78

The artificial lake, Lac de la Triouzoune (2,770 hectares), is perfectly situated and offers full watersports facilities including waterskiing, windsurfing and sailing. This is an attractive tourist centre.

Lac Vassivière

- Beach: safe for bathing.
- Camping: Camping Municipal de la Plage ☎ 55.95.85.48
- Fishing: category 1 fishing on the Triouzoune and Vianon rivers and category 2 fishing on the Dordogne and lakes.
- Golf: 9h course, especially for beginners, at Lycée Agricole ☎ 55.95.80.02
- Tennis: facilities available.

 **Vassivière-en-Limousin** *(Haute-Vienne)*
Limoges 60 km, Paris 370 km
🇮 SYMIVA, B.P.1, 23460 Royère-de-Vassivière ☎ 55.69.20.45

This large artificial lake, Lac Vassivière (7,450 hectares) with its 45 km of shore framed by hills, is most attractive to holidaymakers between June and September for its great watersports potential. There are five sailing clubs and regattas are held every Sunday in summer.

- Beach: several beaches are supervised and safe for bathing.
- Boating: trips by large passenger boat.
- Camping: ten or more sites surround the lake, one of which is Les Peyrades d'Auphelle ☎ 55.69.41.32
- Tennis: 12 courts available to hire.
- Walking: 300 km of signed footpaths to follow in the gently sloping wooded Limousin hills.

MIDI-PYRENEES

Administrative
Centre: Toulouse
Population: 2,268,200
Area: 45,382 sq km

Départements:
09 Ariège
12 Aveyron
31 Haute-Garonne
32 Gers
46 Lot
65 Hautes-Pyrénées
81 Tarn
82 Tarn-et-Garonne

National Park: Parc
National des Pyrénées
Occidentales, B.P.300,
65000 Tarbes
☎ 62.93.30.60

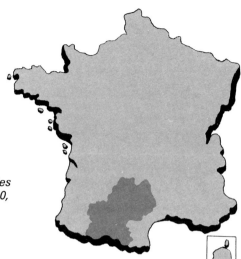

The Midi-Pyrénées is by far the largest region in France, with eight *départements* reaching from the spectacular granite cliffs of the Cirque de Gavarnie to the ruined stronghold of Montségur set almost in the sky, across to Rocamadour in the Lot, to Bonaguil in Quercy, and to Aveyron and the staggering Gorges du Tarn. There are forests and limestone *causses* (plateaux), rivers in torrent, vineyards and fertile valleys, medieval cities, châteaux and market towns and, at the heart of the region, the rich metropolis of its capital, Toulouse.

For many years visitors have been drawn to the health spas of the Hautes-Pyrénées. There are now 17 of them, all with up-to-date facilities and providing excellent holiday centres, often in magnificent locations.

Visitors are also drawn to the châteaux of the region. Of all the châteaux of the Midi-Pyrénées two vie most for attention: the ruin of beleaguered Montségur, scene of slaughter in the high Pyrénées, and that masterpiece of military architecture, high on a rocky outcrop between wooded valleys and built to withstand any assault, the breath-taking Bonaguil. Undamaged throughout six centuries, it remains as perfect today as when newly built.

The Midi-Pyrénées comprises the largest skiing area in the mountain range, with 23 resorts, some close to the Spanish frontier, offering 320 km of cross-country ski trails and 480 km of downhill slopes for skiers of all abilities. When the winter sports season ends, the network of cross-country trails become hiking paths, with Cauterets, for example, as the centre for hiking through the national park.

The orthodox Catholic faith and Lourdes now welcome three million pilgrims annually to the world-famous shrine of Ste-Bernadette, whose chief day of pilgrimage is 15 August.

West of the Upper Garonne, as it semi-circles its course to Bordeaux through plains of sunflower and rape seed, orchards and vineyards, old Gascony yields up its prize product of Armagnac. Distilled from an indifferent white wine, its golden glow comes from the oak barrels in which it matures over three, sometimes ten, years. Auch, with its medieval network of narrow, sloping streets, is the Armagnac centre, as well as the birthplace of that most famous of Gascons, the fourth musketeer, d'Artagnan.

The place du Capitole, ancient heart of Toulouse, is built of glowing rose brick. Formerly a stopping place for pilgrims making for Santiago de Compostela, it is now the city of Concorde and the Airbus. The plains around Toulouse modulate into the gentle fields and terraces of the Tarn-et-Garonne. The orchards of Moissac, with its fine Romanesque abbey church, the beautiful village of Auvillar on the Garonne, Montauban, a *bastide* in pink brick on the banks of the Tarn, all share the pastoral

peace that is riven suddenly by the racing waters of the Gorges de l'Aveyron.

Albi's huge fortified cathedral of Ste-Cecile, dominating the Gothic bridge over the Tarn, is regarded as a red-brick masterpiece of Languedoc Gothic. Toulouse-Lautrec was born here and a museum exhibits many of his paintings. Réalmont, a *bastide* town and once a Cathar refuge, is now a tourist resort. Cordes, another Middle Ages *bastide*, perches on a hilltop overlooking the Cérou river valley.

The Tarn races down from the Cévennes, splits open a canyon between the limestone *causses* and forms, along a 48-km stretch of the river, the spectacular Gorges du Tarn. Millau is a good centre from which to explore the area, discovering, not many kilometres away, at Roquefort-sur-Soulzon, the secret of blue-cheese-making from ewes' milk, its maturing done in *causse* caves at a constant temperature, its rate of manufacture 16,000 tonnes per annum. Millau also hosts a famous road marathon race over 100 km, which draws competitors from all over Europe.

Aveyron is a countryside of cruel rock; hard land from which to wrest a living.

Traditionally, sheep were driven from the Camargue or the coasts of the Languedoc to graze on the wind-swept pastures here. Today they are more often trucked-in to their summer feeding grounds. History surrounds them. This is country on the Santiago de Compostela route, the church of Ste-Foy at Conques being one of the great Romanesque churches built to comfort and protect the pilgrims.

Villefranche-de-Rouergue and Sauveterre-de-Rouergue are perfect examples of thirteenth-century *bastide* town design. The ruined stronghold of Najac, destroyed during the Cathar Crusade, rears its massive keep 137 m high on a promontory above the winding river and the single street of medieval houses. Floodlit at night, it is an impressive sight.

There are sheep too on the *causses* of the Lot or Quercy (*quercus*, an oak), fields of lavender and, where the river valleys run, vineyards that fruit the rich, dark wine of Cahors. Truffles may be found in the Limogne and Lalbenque areas, and visits can be made to the hilltop township of Gourdon, the lively medieval town of Figeac and the matchless, vertiginous pilgrim site, Rocamadour.

PRACTICAL TOURIST INFORMATION

General information on the region can be obtained by telephoning or writing to the Comité Régional du Tourisme (CRT) office, while specific booklets are produced detailing camping, hotel and self-catering gîte accommodation. These can be obtained by writing to the tourist board office for the département (CDT) of your choice:

Regional Tourist Board
Comité Régional du Tourisme (CRT), 12 rue Salambo, B.P.2166, 31022 TOULOUSE Cedex
☎ 61.47.11.12

Départements
Ariège (09): Comité Départemental du Tourisme (CDT), 14 rue Lazéma, 09000 FOIX
☎ 61.65.29.00
Aveyron (12): Comité Départemental du Tourisme (CDT), 33 avenue Victor-Hugo, 12000 RODEZ
☎ 65.68.11.43
Haute-Garonne (31): Comité Départemental du Tourisme (CDT), 63 boulevard Carnot, 31000 TOULOUSE ☎ 61.23.52.52
Gers (32): Comité Départemental du Tourisme (CDT), 9 rue d'Espagne, 32000 AUCH
☎ 62.05.37.02
Lot (46): Comité Départemental du Tourisme (CDT), 107 quai Cavaignac, B.P.79, 46002 CAHORS Cedex ☎ 65.35.07.09
Hautes-Pyrénées (65): Comité Départemental du Tourisme (CDT), 6 rue Eugène-Ténot, 65000 TARBES ☎ 62.93.03.30
Tarn (81): Comité Départemental du Tourisme (CDT), 4 rue Augustin-Malraux, 81000 ALBI Cedex ☎ 63.45.64.64
Tarn-et-Garonne (82): Office Départementale du Tourisme (ODT), Hôtel des Intendants, place du Maréchal-Foch, 82000 MONTAUBAN
☎ 63.63.31.40

SELF-CATERING ACCOMMODATION

The following British operators offer self-catering accommodation in the area:

AA Motoring Holidays, P.O. Box 100, Fanum House, Halesowen B63 3BT ☎ 021-550 7401
Agencefrance Holidays, Lansdowne Place, 17 Holdenhurst Road, Bournemouth BH8 8EH
☎ 0202 299534
Avon Europe, Lower Quinton, Stratford-upon-Avon, Warks CV37 8SG ☎ 0789 720130
Billington Travel, 2a White Hart Parade, Riverhead, Sevenoaks TN13 2BJ ☎ 0732 460666
Bowhills Ltd, Swanmore, Southampton SO3 2QW
☎ 0489 877627
Brittany Ferries, The Brittany Centre, Wharf Road, Portsmouth PO2 8RU ☎ 0705 827701
French Affair, 34 Lillie Road, London SW6 1TU
☎ 01-791 1077
French Villa Centre, 175 Selsdon Park Road, Croydon CR2 8JJ ☎ 01-651 1231
Gîtes de France, 178 Piccadilly, London W1V 9DB
☎ 01-493 3480
Hoseasons Holidays Abroad, Sunway House, Lowestoft NR32 3LT ☎ 0502 500555
Just France, 1 Belmont, Lansdown Road, Bath BA1 5DZ ☎ 0225 446328
David Newman's French Collection, P.O. Box 733, 40 Upperton Road, Eastbourne BN21 4AW
☎ 0323 410347
Pleasurewood Holidays, Somerset House, Gordon Road, Lowestoft NR32 1PZ ☎ 0502 517271
Prime Time Holidays, 5a Market Square, Northampton NN1 2DL ☎ 0604 20996
Les Propriétaires de l'Ouest, Malton House, 24 Hampshire Terrace, Portsmouth PO1 2QE
☎ 0705 755715
Sally Tours, Argyle Centre, York Street, Ramsgate CT11 9DS ☎ 0843 595566
Sturge, Martin, 3 Lower Camden Place, Bath BA1 5JJ ☎ 0225 310623
Vacances en Campagne, Bignor, Pulborough RH20 1QD ☎ 07987 433
VFB Holidays, 1 St Margaret's Terrace,

Cheltenham GL50 4DT ☎ 0242 526338
Villa France, 15 Winchcombe Road, Frampton
Cotterell, Bristol BS17 2AG ☎ 0454 772410

SPORTS AND ACTIVITIES

*For unusual and interesting holiday ideas, contact
the Loisirs Accueil office for the area of your
choice:*

Loisirs Accueil Ariège-Pyrénées,
14 rue Lazéma, 09000 FOIX ☎ 61.65.01.15
Loisirs Accueil Haute-Garonne,
18 place Dupuy, 31000 TOULOUSE
☎ 61.62.42.62
Loisirs Accueil Gers,
route des Tarbes, B.P.99, 32003 AUCH Cedex
☎ 62.63.16.55
Maison du Gers et de l'Armagnac,
16 boulevard Haussmann, 75009 PARIS
☎ 42.46.91.39
Loisirs Accueil Lot,
B.P.109, 430 avenue Jean Jaurès, 46004 CAHORS
Cedex ☎ 65.22.19.20
Loisirs Accueil Hautes-Pyrénées,
6 rue Eugène Tenot, 65000 TARBES
☎ 62.93.03.30
Loisirs Accueil Tarn,
4 rue Porta, 81000 ALBI ☎ 63.47.56.50
Maison du Tarn,
34 avenue du Villiers, 75017 PARIS
☎ 47.63.06.26
Loisirs Accueil Tarn-et-Garonne,
place Maréchal Foch, 82000 MONTAUBAN
☎ 63.63.31.40
Maison des Pyrénées,
15 rue St-Augustin, 75002 PARIS ☎ 42.61.58.18

RESORTS

 Albi *(Tarn)*
Pop: 50,000
Toulouse 76 km, Paris 700 km
🛈 place Ste-Cécile ☎ 63.54.22.30

Capital of the Tarn region, Albi has a rich artistic
and architectural heritage; the rose-pink-brick Ste-
Cécile cathedral is a masterpiece of Gothic
architecture towering above the ancient bridge
which spans the Tarn and the old houses which rise
steeply from it. As a cultural centre, Albi hosts
theatre, music and film festivals during the
summer, and the birthplace of the artist Toulouse-
Lautrec can be visited in the old part of the city.

● Art: the largest collection in the world of
  Toulouse-Lautrec's paintings is housed in the
  Palais de la Berbie museum, together with a
  notable contemporary collection which
  includes works by Dufy, Bonnard, Matisse and
  Utrillo.
● Camping: Le Caussels ☎ 63.54.38.87
● Cycling: cycles can be hired from the SNCF
  station.
● Golf: new 9h private course at Golf des Etangs
  de Fiac, Braziz, 81500 Lavaur ☎ 63.70.64.70

 Aragnouet-Piau-Engaly *(Hautes-Pyrénées)*
Alt: 1,900-2,450 m
Lannemezan 50 km, Paris 820 km
🛈 SI ☎ 62.39.61.69

A newly created winter sports centre right on the
Spanish frontier, which boasts a very good snow
record, and is primarily for accomplished skiers. If
the days aren't long enough, try the unforgettable
experience of night skiing as well. Modern,
innovative, even futuristic, accommodation (for
4,000) is protected by the Campbieilh peak. In
summer quiet, family holidays are catered for and
there are beautiful pasture walks.

 Argelès-Gazost *(Hautes-Pyrénées)*
Pop: 4,000
Lourdes 13 km, Paris 815 km
🛈 Grande Terrasse ☎ 62.97.00.25

A pleasant summer spa resort in a pretty valley,
enjoying a good climate and offering a wide variety
of activity options. In the magnificent natural
setting of ruined Beaucens Castle, public
demonstrations of eagles, hawks and kites at
liberty and in flight, complement the rugged
landscape.

● Camping: Les Trois Vallées ☎ 62.90.35.47
● Canoeing: and white-water rafting on the fast-
  running Pyrenean rivers. Contact Club Sportif
  d'Isaby, Lycée, 65400 Argelès-Gazost
  ☎ 62.90.32.19
● Cycling: cycles can be hired from the SNCF
  station.
● Spa: circulatory disorders (1 Jun-30 Sep)
  ☎ 62.97.03.24 alt: 460 m, climate: temperate.
● Walking: guided group walks on assorted
  themes, every Wednesday (Jul-Sep) from rue
  des Moulins.

 Ax-les-Thermes *(Ariège)*
Pop: 2,000
Foix 42 km, Paris 825 km
🛈 place du Breilh ☎ 61.64.60.60

Small spa town nestling in a sunny valley sheltered
from the wind. In winter this becomes a modest
winter sports resort with 55 km of pistes at
Bonascre (1,400-2,400 m). Pleasant for healthy
outdoor holidays throughout the year, particularly
for rambling and fishing, there is holiday
accommodation for 8,600. Casino.

● Camping: Malazéou ☎ 61.64.22.21
● Fishing: category 1 fishing on the Lauze river.
● Spa: rheumatism/bone joint damage (4 Feb-
  31 Dec) ☎ 61.64.24.83 alt: 720 m, climate:
  Mediterranean.

 Bagnères-de-Bigorre *(Hautes-Pyrénées)*
Pop: 10,000
Lourdes 22 km, Paris 810 km
🛈 21 rue des Thermes ☎ 62.95.50.71

Situated at the foot of the Pyrénées and close to

Lourdes, this is principally a summer spa resort where walks in the surrounding countryside, combined with numerous other outdoor activities, offer relaxing and healthy holiday stays. The subterranean river Grottes de Médous are worth exploring by boat, while in winter the ski resort of La Mongie is close by.

- Camping: Les Fruitiers ☎ 62.95.25.97
- Casino: Municipal ☎ 62.95.20.42
- Climbing: for beginners and improvers with the Bureau des Guides (Jun-Sep). Bookable through the Tourist Office.
- Cycling: accompanied tours are available, enquire at Tourist Office. Cycles can be hired from the SNCF station.
- Fishing: extensive possibilities.
- Golf: flat 18h private course at Golf de Lannemezan, La Demi-Lune, 65300 Lannemezan ☎ 62.98.01.01 (closed Tues).
- Hang Gliding: bookable from 2 place Ramond ☎ 62.95.04.83
- Riding: Centre Equestre de Bagnères ☎ 62.95.00.05
- Spa: nervous system (7 May-20 Oct) ☎ 62.95.00.23 alt: 550 m, climate: sedative. Also at nearby Capvern-les-Bains, kidneys/urinary organs (2 May-15 Oct) ☎ 62.39.00.02 alt: 450 m, climate: fresh.
- Tennis: seven courts for hire at the Club Bagnerais ☎ 62.95.07.35

Barèges *(Hautes-Pyrénées)*
Pop: 400
Alt: 1,250-2,350 m

Lourdes 39 km, Paris 840 km
🛈 Office de Tourisme ☎ 62.92.68.19

Renowned as much for its modern winter sports facilities as for its charming old summer spa, Barèges is a village resort connected to the largest skiing area in the Pyrénées, and it provides excellent skiing, with links to La Mongie. The resort has holiday accommodation for 4,200.

- Camping: La Ribère ☎ 62.92.67.91
- Helicopter Flights: over the Lac Bleu bookable through Tourist Office.
- Spa: rheumatism/bone joint damage (1 Jun-30 Sep) ☎ 62.92.68.02 alt: 1,240 m, climate: fresh.
- Tennis: two courts for hire.
- Walking: 50 km of signed footpaths and plenty of mountain lakes to discover.

Cahors *(Lot)*
Pop: 21,000
Toulouse 100 km, Paris 590 km
🛈 place Aristide-Briand ☎ 65.35.09.56

Capital of the ancient province of Quercy, Cahors is a picturesque old town situated on a loop of the river where the beautiful fortified Valentré bridge spans the Lot. The beauty and tranquillity of this river valley will delight walkers, painters and fishermen alike, while canoeists can enjoy the pleasures of the setting from the river itself. Rich in architectural and artistic treasures, Cahors is a popular tourist centre and, because of its agreeably mild winters, a pleasant rural resort throughout the year. The lower valley of the River Lot is a renowned red wine region.

The Valentré bridge at Cahors

- Camping: Municipal Saint Georges
  ☎ 65.35.04.64
- Canoeing: locally at Lot-Célé Canoë-kayak,
  camping de la Plage Saint-Cirq-Lapopie
  ☎ 65.30.29.51 and at Les Amis du Célé, Le
  Liazu ☎ 65.31.26.73
- Cycling: cycles can be hired from the SNCF
  station.
- Horse-drawn Travel: various types of caravan
  can be hired for leisurely travel through the
  countryside from La Taillade, Duravel, 46700
  Puy-l'Evêque ☎ 65.36.53.53 (open all year).
- Riding: Etrier de Bégoux, route de
  Villefranche ☎ 65.22.00.59
- Walking: GR65.

 Cauterets *(Hautes-Pyrénées)*
Pop: 1,500
Alt: 1,350-2,350 m
Lourdes 30 km, Paris 832 km
🖫 place Clemenceau ☎ 62.92.50.27

Top-rated family ski resort at the heart of the
national park at the confluence of four valleys,
with varied skiing for all levels, some of it strictly
for the accomplished or with guides. Its spa lends
the town an Edwardian turn-of-the-century charm
in this area of great natural beauty which is ideal
for walkers. The resort has holiday accommodation
for 16,000. Casino.

- Camping: Vignemale ☎ 62.92.52.08
- Climbing: between June and September (for
  beginners and improvers) with the Bureau des
  Guides ☎ 62.92.58.16
- Spa: respiratory/lymphatic disorders (open all
  year) ☎ 62.92.51.60 alt: 1,000 m climate:
  sedative.

 Eauze *(Gers)*
Pop: 5,000
Agen 70 km, Paris 718 km
🖫 Hôtel de Ville ☎ 62.09.85.62

Rural resort famed as being the Armagnac (gently
aromatic brandy) capital with a market, *la Bourse
de l'Armagnac*, taking place each Thursday by the
church. Made only in this area of France,
Armagnac production is strictly controlled by law
and its casks are hand-made of oak from the local
forest of Monlezun, prior to the important ageing
process. Other local specialities of the area include
goose-liver pâté and pigeon stew.

- Camping: Camping du Pouy-Plage
  ☎ 62.09.86.00
- Fishing: category 2 fishing on the Gélise river.
- Golf: 9h private course at Golf de Guinlet,
  32800 Eauze ☎ 62.09.80.84
- Spa: nearby at Barbotan-les-Thermes –
  circulatory disorders (1 Feb-20 Dec)
  ☎ 62.69.52.09 alt: 130 m, climate: temperate.
  Also nearby, Castéra-Verduzan,
  kidneys/urinary organs (2 May-15 Oct)
  ☎ 62.68.13.41

 Espalion *(Aveyron)*
Pop: 5,000
Rodez 33 km, Paris 580 km
🖫 la Mairie ☎ 65.44.10.63

The River Lot races through an impressive gorge
between Espalion and Entraygues. There are a
number of châteaux worth a visit, vineyards
producing rosé wines, and old villages whose
houses feature outside staircases and large, steeply
pitched roofs. Espalion is settled in a broad valley
with the old tanners' houses by the river's edge,
and there is pleasant bathing in the river, excellent
fishing, and attractive rolling countryside to walk.

- Camping: Camping du Roc-de-l'Arche
  ☎ 65.44.02.49
- Fishing: category 2 fishing on the Lot river and
  category 1 fishing on the Boraldes, Coussane
  and Astruges rivers.

Foix *(Ariège)*
Pop: 10,000
Toulouse 84 km, Paris 785 km
🖫 45 cours G.-Fauré ☎ 61.65.12.12

A medieval town on the rushing, gushing Ariège
which sees, each summer, a reconstruction of
Middle Ages life played joyfully through its streets.
In attractive rocky countryside, with the old castle
towering over the town, and with a splendid choice
of mountain or water scenery to discover, there are
plenty of sporting pursuits to enjoy, with the
Mediterranean coast, Spain and Andorra all close
by. The largest cave in Europe is at Lombrives
near Ussat-les-Bains.

- Camping: Lac de Labarre ☎ 61.65.11.58
- Cycling: cycles can be hired from the SNCF
  station.
- Golf: 9h public course at Golf Club de
  l'Ariège, 09240 La Bastide-de-Sérou
  ☎ 61.64.56.78
- Spa: Ussat-les-Bains – nervous system (1 Apr-
  31 Oct) ☎ 61.05.74.74 alt: 485 m, climate:
  fine. Also at Aulus-les-Bains – kidneys/urinary
  disorders (9 Jun-30 Sep) ☎ 61.96.01.46 alt:
  780 m, climate: invigorating.

Gavarnie *(Hautes-Pyrénées)*
Pop: 200
Lourdes 50 km, Paris 853 km
🖫 SI ☎ 62.92.49.10

An ideal village base (holiday accommodation for
700) from which to explore and enjoy the
surrounding mountains, with the Cirque de
Gavarnie, a deep and majestic natural
amphitheatre, the most visited spot in the
Pyrénées. In the words of Victor Hugo: 'the most
mysterious edifice by the most mysterious of
architects'. Access to the site is by foot, donkey or
horseback, and the views which reward the visitor,
of steep rock walls, pillars of snow, the great
waterfall and the iced lake of Mont Perdu, are
indeed staggering. The conditions for skiing here

(1,350-2,090 m) have been likened to those of Colorado in North America.

● Camping: Le Pain de Sucre ☎ 62.92.47.48
● Flights: helicopter flights over the Cirque de Gavarnie area are bookable through the Tourist Office at Gèdre ☎ 62.92.48.05

 Lourdes *(Hautes-Pyrénées)*
Pop: 20,000
Pau 40 km, Paris 800 km
🛈 place du Champ-Commun ☎ 62.94.15.64

A world-famous centre of pilgrimage, three million tourists and pilgrims annually visit the holy sites and gather during the summer months for the many ceremonies and processions which take place. With 400 hotels, Lourdes is the third most visited city in France, after Paris and Nice. This is a good excursion point for the Pyrénées.

● Camping: Plein Soleil ☎ 62.94.40.93
● Cycling: cycles can be hired from the SNCF station.
● Fishing: on the Lac de Lourdes (3 km), also boating.
● Golf: 9h public course at Golf de Laloubère-Tarbes, 65310 Laloubère ☎ 62.96.06.22
● Watersports: adventure activities including canoeing, white-water rafting, climbing and potholing are all organised (from a half-day tuition basis to week-long trips) and are bookable through the Base Départementale de Plein Air de St-Pé-de-Bigorre, Impasse du Stade, 65270 St-Pé-de-Bigorre ☎ 62.41.81.48

 Luchon *(Haute-Garonne)*
Pop: 4,000
Tarbes 89 km, Paris 880 km
🛈 18 allées Etigny ☎ 61.79.21.21

Situated at the foot of the highest peaks of the central Pyrénées and amidst beautiful forests, Luchon is a most lively and fashionable spa town with elegant shops and hotels. Over 80 mountain springs supply the thermal waters. Close by is the tiny winter skiing resort of Les Agudes which, in summer, becomes an ideal place to relax within a village atmosphere, while the larger winter and summer resort of Superbagnères, high above, provides marvellous views over the town. Casino.

● Camping: Le Beauregard ☎ 61.79.30.74
● Cycling: cycles can be hired from the SNCF station.
● Golf: 9h private parkland course at Golf de Luchon, route de Montauban, 31110 Luchon ☎ 61.79.03.27
● Spa: Bagnères-de-Luchon – respiratory/lymphatic disorders (1 Apr-20 Oct) ☎ 61.79.03.88 alt: 630 m, climate: temperate.
● Walking: in the valley of Oô.

 Luz-St-Sauveur *(Hautes-Pyrénées)*
Pop: 2,000

Cauterets 22 km, Paris 833 km
🛈 place 8-Mai ☎ 62.92.81.60

During the summer months this attractive valley village is a busy spa with plenty of sports and leisure activities, including archery, hang gliding, hunting, lake fishing, riding and, of course, spectacular walking and climbing. The winter sports resort of Luz-Ardiden (1,700-2,400 m) has 30 km of pistes and village-based holiday accommodation for 5,000.

● Camping: Cascades ☎ 62.92.85.85
● Climbing: courses bookable through the Bureau des Guides ☎ 62.92.91.94
● Spa: gynaecological conditions (15 May-30 Sep) ☎ 62.92.81.58 alt: 730 m, climate: mild.
● Walking: accompanied by experienced guides and according to various themes (flora and fauna, photography, etc.), some with overnight stops in refuges. Bookable through the Bureau des Guides ☎ 62.92.91.94 whose members also accompany climbers.

 Mazamet *(Tarn)*
Pop: 14,000
Albi 60 km, Paris 747 km
🛈 rue des Casernes ☎ 63.61.27.07

A pretty flower-filled town in the foothills of the Montagne Noire on the River Arnette, Mazamet is a dairy centre and busy market town at the entrance to the Haut-Languedoc nature reserve. In the surrounding area are the Banquet gorges and the lakes of St-Peyres.

● Camping: La Lauze ☎ 63.61.24.69
● Golf: 9h private parkland course at Golf de la Barouge, Pont de l'Arn, 81660 Mazamet ☎ 63.61.06.72

 Millau *(Aveyron)*
Pop: 23,000
Albi 113 km, Paris 633 km
🛈 avenue Alfred-Merle ☎ 65.60.02.42

A medieval town near the junction of the Rivers Tarn and Dourbie, surrounded by the familiar Midi olive groves and vineyards. Noted for its leather craft, particularly gloves, Millau is an attractive and bustling little town. Some quarters have pedestrianised arcades with galleries and fountains. The town is internationally famous for its annual 100 km marathon, attracting over a thousand runners. Nearby, at the Chaos of Montpellier-le-Vieux, the River Dourbie tears its way through a narrow canyon between grotesquely twisted rocks. A few kilometres to the south is the small town of Roquefort where the famous cheese is still made from ewes' milk. Visitors may see the vast *caves* with their own chimneys and air ducts.

● Camping: Municipal de Millau-Plage ☎ 65.60.10.97

● Cycling: cycles can be hired from the SNCF station.
● Fishing: excellent salmon and trout fishing throughout the Aveyron.
● Walking: in the Tarn gorges.

 La Mongie *(Hautes-Pyrénées)*
Alt: 1,800-2,500 m
Bagnères-de-Bigorre 25 km, Paris 836 km
🅱 SI ☎ 62.91.94.15

A purpose-built winter sports resort with superb skiing, this is the highest and biggest resort in the Pyrénées. With links to Barèges, it is very much a domain of the accomplished skiier and offers holiday accommodation for 11,500.

 Montauban *(Tarn-et-Garonne)*
Pop: 54,000
Cahors 61 km, Paris 652 km
🅱 rue du Collège ☎ 63.63.60.60

This spacious city sits on the banks of the River Tarn which is crossed by one of the finest and oldest bridges in France. The city's past prosperity as a centre of weaving is evidenced by the many fine red-brick mansions.

● Art: large collection of paintings and drawings by Ingres (born here in 1780) housed in the former Bishop's Palace.
● Camping: at Moissac – Ile du Bidounet ☎ 63.32.29.96
● Cycling: cycles for hire from Gury, avenue Gambetta ☎ 63.63.19.10
● Golf: 9h public course at Golf d'Espalais, 82400 Valence-d'Agen ☎ 63.29.04.56; also 9h private course at Golf des Roucous-Sauveterre, 82110 Lauzerte ☎ 63.95.83.70
● Riding: Poney-Club Les Allègres ☎ 63.66.34.74
● Watersports: along the river at Moissac, where the Tarn joins the Garonne, a lake has been created to cater for all watersports.

 Najac *(Aveyron)*
Pop: 900
Albi 54 km, Paris 644 km
🅱 la Mairie ☎ 65.65.80.94

The ruined medieval fortress is in a stunning position, 150 m high on a rocky spur above the single street of this ancient village and the twisting, turning River Aveyron. In summer the castle is floodlit and stands silhouetted against the sky and the grey Gothic houses below. A little to the south of Najac is Cordes, a well-preserved fortified village built in 1222 with, to the west and flanking the Gresigne forest, a group of hilltop villages which demand a visit. This is marvellous cycling and walking country, excellent also for fishing.

● Camping: Municipal ☎ 65.65.72.06 and Le Paysseyrou ☎ 65.65.80.94

● Cycling: cycles can be hired from the SNCF station.

 Naucelle *(Aveyron)*
Pop: 2,500
Rodez 32 km, Paris 620 km
🅱 Hôtel de Ville ☎ 65.47.04.32

A rural resort offering fishing, walking, riding and cycling.

● Camping: Camping du Lac de Bonnefon ☎ 65.47.00.67
● Fishing: category 1 fishing on the Viaur, Lézert, Céor and Giffou rivers.

 Pont-de-Salars *(Aveyron)*
Pop: 900
Rodez 33 km, Paris 642 km
🅱 la Mairie ☎ 65.46.84.27

This village in the Viaur valley is a lakeside resort at the centre of the vast area of reservoirs (Salars, Bage, Pareloup and Villefranche). Fine sailing facilities, good fishing, cycling and walking country. Salars hosts a folk festival in August.

● Camping: Le Lac et La Source ☎ 65.46.84.86

 Rocamadour *(Lot)*
Pop: 800
Cahors 60 km, Paris 540 km
🅱 Hôtel de Ville ☎ 65.33.62.59

A remarkable setting draws visitors in their thousands to this medieval pilgrim town, perched precariously on the cliff face. Floodlit at night between April and October, it is a truly magnificent sight, and views from the high château ramparts over the winding river valley below are impressive. The natural conditions of this rocky site lend themselves admirably to the Rocher des Aigles (eagles) conservation centre here, and daily displays of birds of prey in flight are a popular spectacle. The subterranean rivers at Padirac and the Lacave caves at Souillac are worth exploring.

● Camping: Le Relais du Campeur ☎ 65.33.63.28
● Cycling: cycles can be hired from the SNCF station.
● Golf: 9h private course at Golf du Mas del Teil, La Chapelle Auzac, 46200 Souillac ☎ 65.37.01.48
● Riding: La Grelotière, Lafage ☎ 65.33.67.16

 Rodez *(Aveyron)*
Pop: 27,000
Albi 78 km, Paris 609 km
🅱 place Foch ☎ 65.68.02.27

A predominantly modern and busy market town with, from the top of the bell tower, a panoramic view over the maze of streets below the fortress-like and impressive pink sandstone cathedral of Notre-Dame, and towards the Massif Central. To the east lies the Palange forest and close by, beside a waterfall, the lovely village of Salles-la-Source. The vast area of Lévezou lakes (Salars, Bage, Pareloup and Villefranche) to the south offer good fishing and water sports generally.

- Camping: Municipal ☎ 65.67.09.52
- Cycling: cycles can be hired from the SNCF station.
- Fishing: the authority for this region (FDAAPP) is based at Rodez at 52 rue de l'Embergue ☎ 65.42.56.03

 St-Gaudens (*Haute-Garonne*)
Pop: 13,000
Tarbes 65 km, Paris 780 km
🛈 Mas. St-Pierre ☎ 61.89.15.99

Set on a hillside overlooking the Garonne and with magnificent views across the central Pyrénées, this is a good outdoor sports centre for riding, canoeing, caving, fishing and shooting.

- Camping: Le Belvédère des Pyrénées ☎ 61.89.15.76
- Fishing: category 2 fishing on the Garonne river.
- Spa: nearby at Barbazan, digestive organs (10 May-30 Sep) ☎ 61.88.38.18 alt: 450 m, climate: temperate.

 St-Lary-Soulan (*Hautes-Pyrénées*)
Pop: 1,000
Alt: 1,600-2,450 m
Luchon 44 km, Paris 860 km
🛈 Office de Tourisme ☎ 62.39.50.81

This is a real village community in the Aure valley, unspoilt by all the trappings of a modern developing ski resort. A new spa centre combined with a wide choice of sporting activities (archery, canoeing, hang gliding, mountaineering), makes this a lively and popular spot for enjoying a healthy outdoor holiday at any season, and there is extensive holiday accommodation for 21,000. For the non-mountaineer, gentle summer outings, accompanied by members of the Bureau des Guides, lead high into the calm and solitude of the mountains on the Spanish frontier.

- Camping: Municipal ☎ 62.39.40.17
- Riding: Club des Sports et des Loisirs (Jul-Sep) ☎ 62.39.41.11

 Salies-du-Salat (*Haute-Garonne*)
Pop: 1,000
St-Gaudens 24 km, Paris 785 km
🛈 Office de Tourisme ☎ 61.90.53.93

A small spa town in the Salat valley noted for the high mineral content of its waters. Indeed, rock salt is mined here.

- Camping: Municipal ☎ 61.90.53.26
- Spa: respiratory/lymphatic disorders (2 May-

20 Oct) ☎ 61.90.56.41 alt: 300 m, climate: mild.

 Salles-Curan (*Aveyron*)
Pop: 1,500
Millau 36 km, Paris 620 km
🛈 SI ☎ 65.46.31.73

Like Pont-de-Salars, the pretty town of Salles-Curan is making the most of its location close to the reservoirs. The Lac de Pareloup, with 107 km of bank, offers good lake bathing, fishing, sailing, waterskiing and windsurfing. Organised cycling and walking trips are also very popular. The one-time fifteenth-century stronghold above the lake is now a twentieth-century hotel and the village houses are surrounded by heathland grazed by sheep.

- Camping: Beau Rivage ☎ 65.46.36.33 and Camping de la Base Nautique Pareloup ☎ 65.46.36.74
- Cycling: cycles can be hired here. Enquire at the Tourist Office.

 Superbagnères (*Haute-Garonne*)
Alt: 1,440-2,260 m
St-Gaudens 50 km, Paris 800 km
🛈 Office de Tourisme ☎ 61.79.36.36

Sharing many of the facilities of the town of Luchon below, including the unique underground sauna whose temperature is governed by the mountain itself, Superbagnères is a winter sports centre with 35 km of pistes and magnificent views towards the Spanish Pyrénées. There is holiday accommodation for 5,000 and a very popular hang gliding base.

- Riding: Centre Equestre, route d'Antignac ☎ 61.79.06.64
- Walking: in the lovely lake setting of the Oô valley.

 Villefranche-de-Rouergue (*Aveyron*)
Pop: 14,000
Albi 72 km, Paris 620 km
🛈 Pavillon de Tourisme ☎ 65.45.13.18

A thirteenth-century *bastide* town with a fine central square, Villefranche is a very active centre on the banks of the Aveyron at the point where it heads south for the magnificent Gorges de l'Aveyron, a first-class canoeing and kayaking stretch of turbulent, challenging water. The town dates from 1252 and its layout is a chess-board plan of narrow lanes and arcades. To the north east is the spa of Cransac.

- Camping: Municipal le Teulel ☎ 65.45.16.24
- Cycling: seven-day cycling tours of the Aveyron can be made using Villefranche as a base. Details from the Tourist Office.
- Fishing: good salmon and trout fishing locally.
- Spa: at Cransac – rheumatism/bone joint damage (1 Apr-31 Oct) ☎ 65.63.09.83 alt: 290 m, climate: sedative.

NORD – PAS-DE-CALAIS

*Administrative
Centre: Lille
Population: 3,913,800
Area: 12,378 sq km*

*Départements:
59 Nord
62 Pas-de-Calais*

*Regional Park:
Parc Naturel Régional
Nord – Pas-de-Calais,
Espace Naturel
Régional, 19 rue Jean-
Roisin, 59800 Lille
☎ 20.57.30.27*

Opposite Cap Gris-Nez, the closest point to England, the North Sea suddenly becomes the Channel. Along cliffs and past sandy beaches, the corniche of the Côte Opale winds its way between Boulogne and Calais, two of the great ferry ports of France. Here, at Sangatte, the Channel Tunnel is expected to emerge, and already there are British customers bidding for small properties near the coast of France.

Off the route of the great motorways, as they plunge deep into Europe, the coasts and countryside of Nord and of Pas-de-Calais are gentle and pleasant. The region may lack the glamour of the Côte d'Azur or the Côte Basque, it may not be able to boast quite so much burning sun, but it has long beaches where the sea breezes whirl sand yachts exhilaratingly fast, and where small children, abroad maybe for the first time, come to form their earliest memories of holidays in France.

Beyond Dunkerque, third in importance and most northerly of the ferry ports, lie the sandhills of Bray-Dunes. From this Flemish-French coastline of sea buckthorn and blue thistle and home of the golden oriole, where dunes and *pannes* (depressions) alternate, the *Grande Randonnée* coastal trail (*le littoral*) runs to Berck, thence along the entire French coastline to Menton on the Italian border.

The three ports of Calais, Dunkerque and Boulogne are commonly linked with bland statistics relating to passenger usage per annum. Three million passengers pass through Calais each year. In 1940, however, Dunkerque was the scene of a more dramatic embarkation, despatching to the safety of Britain 350,000 troops encircled by the armies of the German Third Reich. Inland, in the valley of the River Canche, lovely medieval towns like Montreuil are too often bypassed by holidaymakers racing south to the sun. The township is perched on a small hill with an eighteenth-century citadel and ramparts overlooking a cluster of twelfth-century dwellings.

Between Guînes and Ardres, south of Calais, is the site of the Field of the Cloth of Gold where, in 1520, Henry VIII and François I met for a scene of great pageantry but very little achievement. If history disappoints, the fishing in the lake of Ardres will not, and at Guînes a column marks the landing place of the first balloon to cross the Channel, in 1795.

The coastal resorts range from the chic and cosmopolitan, like Le Touquet, with its three golf courses, two casinos, racecourse, pretty yacht harbour and, some claim, the finest beach in all France, to Berck-sur-Mer, an all-year-round spa where the European sand yachting competitions are held each September along the 13-km beach, and Hardelot, a fashionable *plage* resort specialising in villas which are not so much for holiday hire as for second, seaside homes.

The region, being so narrowly divided from England, has been the scene of many conflicts between the two countries. The visitor today can reflect upon the greatest of would-be invaders, Napoléon. When he planned the invasion of England in 1803, he selected Boulogne as his headquarters, but Nelson's naval victories ensured that the invasion never took place. Today the 53-m Colonne de la Grande Armée, with Napoléon at its top, gazes across the Channel at the unattainable English coast.

PRACTICAL TOURIST INFORMATION

General information on the region can be obtained by telephoning or writing to the Comité Régional du Tourisme (CRT) office, while specific booklets are produced detailing camping, hotel and self-catering gîte *accommodation. These can be obtained by writing to the tourist board office for the* département *(CDT) of your choice:*

Regional Tourist Board
Comité Régional du Tourisme (CRT), 26 place Rihour, 59800 LILLE ☎ 20.57.40.04

Départements
Nord (59): Comité Départemental du Tourisme (CDT), 15-17 rue de Nouveau-Siècle, 59800 LILLE ☎ 20.57.00.61
Pas-de-Calais (62): Comité Départemental du Tourisme (CDT), 44 Grande Rue, 62200 BOULOGNE-SUR-MER ☎ 21.31.98.58

SELF-CATERING ACCOMMODATION

The following British operators offer self-catering accommodation in the area:

AA Motoring Holidays, P.O. Box 100, Fanum House, Halesowen B63 3BT ☎ 021-550 7401
Angel Travel, 47 High Street, Central Chambers, Tonbridge TN9 1SD ☎ 0732 884109
Bowhills Ltd, Swanmore, Southampton SO3 2QW ☎ 0489 877627
Chalets de France, Travel House, Pandy, Nr Abergavenny NP7 8DH ☎ 0873 890770
Cresta Holidays, 32 Victoria Street, Altrincham WA14 1ET ☎ 0345 056511
France Directe, 2 Church Street, Warwick CV34 4AB ☎ 0926 497989
Gîtes de France, 178 Piccadilly, London W1V 9DB ☎ 01-493 3480
Hoseasons Holidays Abroad, Sunway House, Lowestoft NR32 3LT ☎ 0502 500555
Hoverspeed Ltd, Maybrook House, Queens Gardens, Dover CT17 9UQ ☎ 0304 240241
David Newman's French Collection, P.O. Box 733, 40 Upperton Road, Eastbourne BN21 4AW ☎ 0323 410347
VFB Holidays, 1 St Margaret's Terrace, Cheltenham GL50 4DT ☎ 0242 526338

SPORTS AND ACTIVITIES

For unusual and interesting holiday ideas, contact the Loisirs Accueil office for the département of your choice:

Loisirs Accueil Nord,
15-17 rue du Nouveau Siècle, B.P.135, 59027 LILLE Cedex ☎ 20.57.00.61

Loisirs Accueil Pas-de-Calais,
44 Grand-Rue, 62200 BOULOGNE-SUR-MER ☎ 21.31.66.80
Maison Nord – Pas-de-Calais,
18 boulevard Haussmann, 75009 PARIS ☎ 47.70.59.62

RESORTS

Boulogne-sur-Mer *(Pas-de-Calais)*
Pop: 50,000
Calais 34 km, Paris 244 km
🚩 Pont Marguet ☎ 21.31.68.38

Only 40 km from England, this is France's principal fishing port and major cross-Channel ferry port (second only to Calais). Fleets of colourful trawlers, trailed by seagulls and loaded with sole, turbot, crab and lobster destined for restaurant cooking pots, make this a favourite with day-trippers who can also enjoy the good supermarkets and department stores (Prisunic in rue de la Lampe, Nouvelles Galeries in rue Thiers, and Champion), the cheeses and pâtés from the morning markets (Wed and Sat), and the numerous *boulangeries* and *charcuteries*. The historic town itself and the sleepy countryside inland, green and cultivated, give a taste of the real France without having travelled very far.

● Beach: spacious expanses of sand, ideal for sandyachting and riding.
● Camping: Camping Moulin Wibert ☎ 21.31.40.29
● Casino: rue Félix Adam.
● Cycling: cycles can be hired from the SNCF station.
● Riding: Club Hippique du Boulonnais at la Capelle ☎ 21.83.32.38
● Sailing: marina has 275 berths.
● Shopping: the Boulogne Shopper's Club offers discounts to British shoppers at restaurants, shops and hotels dispaying the Union Jack sign, on presentation of the Privilege Card. Apply for this card to: Boulogne Shoppper's Club, 24 rue Nationale, F-62200 Boulogne-sur-Mer (enclosing an SAE).

Calais *(Pas-de-Calais)*
Pop: 75,000
Boulogne-sur-Mer 34 km, Paris 292 km
🚩 12 boulevard Clemenceau ☎ 21.96.62.40

The fastest port of exchange between Britain and the continent of Europe, Calais looks out across the Channel. With its constant movement of cross-Channel ferries, this is the densest shipping lane in the world. Now the site of the massive Euro Tunnel works, destined to link Calais with Folkestone in 1993, this town has always been a favourite port of call for day-trippers attracted by the busy but pleasant boulevard shopping, while for those who travel a little further, whether along the splendid coast or inland, there is much attractive countryside.

- Beach: enormous sandy beach.
- Camping: Municipal ☎ 21.97.99.00
- Casino: rue Royale ☎ 21.34.64.18
- Cycling: cycles can be hired from the SNCF station.

 Dunkerque *(Nord)*
Pop: 74,000
Calais 43 km, Paris 290 km
🛈 place du Beffroi ☎ 28.66.79.21

Commercial and fishing port, the third largest in France, and a busy cross-Channel ferry port, this is also a popular seaside resort, offering a wide choice of watersports. Close to the Belgian border and with three hypermarkets just outside the town and regular open-air markets (Wed and Sat), Dunkerque provides a flavour of France for the day-tripper or a good base for further exploration. Casino.

- Art: seventeenth- and eighteenth-century paintings in the Musée des Beaux Arts, plus a fascinating section entitled 'Dunkerque at War'.
- Beach: Bray-les-Dunes is a 4 km sandy beach (5 km from the eastern end of the harbour), also Malo-les-Bains.
- Camping: Camping du Perroquet Plage, Bray-les-Dunes ☎ 28.26.50.40
- Fishing: sea-fishing trips are available.
- Golf: new 9h public course at Golf Public de Dunkerque, Fort Vallières ☎ 28.61.07.43
- Sand Yachting: weekend courses for all abilities (min. age 16) on the flat, hard sands of Malo-les-Bains. Bookable through the Tourist Office.

 Fourmies *(Nord)*
Pop: 16,000
Lille 110 km, Paris 225 km
🛈 place Verte ☎ 27.60.40.97

A pleasant small town in the heart of the Avesnois country, its hills and hedges watered by the tributaries of the Sambre and, to the north, by the lakes and marshes of the Helpe valley. There are good, marked walks in the nearby Forêt de Mormal and excellent fishing and canoeing on the pools and lakes.

- Camping: les Etangs des Moines ☎ 27.60.04.32
- Canoeing: on the Etangs des Moines ☎ 27.60.38.38
- Cycling: cycles can be hired from the SNCF station.

 Neufchâtel-Hardelot *(Pas-de-Calais)*
Pop: 3,000
Boulogne-sur-Mer 15 km, Paris 233 km
🛈 23 avenue de la Concorde ☎ 21.83.51.02

Hardelot is an elegant resort at the edge of undulating pine forest surrounded by dunes and with a calm, residential atmosphere. Pleasant villas testify to the long-standing appeal of this spot, which offers a good range of watersports, horse racing and, looking like a kind of beach ballet, sand-yachting races along its vast beach. There is a jazz and classical music festival in July and August.

- Beach: 10-km safe sandy beach.
- Cycling: cycles for hire from Léo, avenue François 1er ☎ 21.91.85.51
- Golf: 18h private course at Golf d'Hardelot, avenue du Golf, 62152 Neufchâtel-Hardelot ☎ 21.83.73.10. This is one of France's top courses, set amidst a conifer forest.
- Parascending: Para-Club UNP offers weekend courses (12 years upwards) ☎ 21.91.81.96
- Riding: Eperon d'Hardelot, avenue François 1er ☎ 21.83.71.78 and Poney-Club, avenue Charlemagne ☎ 21.91.83.77
- Sand Yachting: Club des Drakkars ☎ 21.91.81.96 hires out equipment.

 St-Amand-les-Eaux *(Nord)*
Pop: 1,500
Lille 37 km, Paris 226 km
🛈 Office de Tourisme ☎ 27.48.67.09

Near Valenciennes, on the edge of the large Forêt de Raismes, now a nature reserve and bird sanctuary. Excellent riding country with marked trails, the township is also a thermal spa complete with casino.

- Camping: Campéoles/Mont de Bruyères, rue Basly ☎ 27.48.56.87
- Casino: ☎ 27.48.50.37
- Cycling: cycles can be hired from the SNCF station.
- Golf: see Valenciennes.
- Riding: le Centre du Parc Naturel Régional ☎ 27.48.56.62
- Spa: rheumatism/bone joint damage (1 Mar-15 Dec) ☎ 27.48.50.37 alt: 17 m, climate: temperate.

 Le Touquet *(Pas-de-Calais)*
Pop: 6,000
Boulogne-sur-Mer 32 km, Paris 220 km
🛈 place de l'Hermitage ☎ 21.05.21.65

Created at the end of the last century, Le Touquet, or Paris-Plage as it was known, was for long popular with the Parisian and British smart set. It has a delightful pine-wood setting, an attractive promenade along the seafront and good sports facilities, with international horse racing, polo and tennis championships staged here. Musical events, nightclubs and casinos continue this trend, making Le Touquet a lively and cosmopolitan resort.

- Beach: 12 km long, with firm sand stretching down the coast as far as Berck-Plage.

- Camping: Camping de la Canche ☎ 21.05.09.24
- Casinos: Casino de la Forêt, place de l'Hermitage ☎ 21.05.08.76 and Casino des 4 Saisons, rue St-Jean ☎ 21.05.15.53
- Cycling: cycles can be hired from the SNCF station at Etaples.
- Flying: the Aéro-Club provides pilot tuition or tourist flights ☎ 21.05.03.99
- Golf: 54h private course at Golf du Touquet, avenue du Golf, 62520 Le Touquet ☎ 21.05.68.47. Amongst France's top courses with fine sea views and sand dunes.
- Riding: Centre Equestre, avenue de la Dune aux Loups ☎ 21.05.15.25
- Sailing: and windsurfing bases of the Centre Nautique de Touquet are at two locations – one at Baie de Canche ☎ 21.05.12.77 and the other at the south end of the beach ☎ 21.05.33.51. Because of the nature of the sand and the frequently very windy conditions, sand yachting is a popular sport here.
- Tennis: 36 courts.
- Thalassotherapy: Thalamer Institut de Thalassothérapie, 62520 Le Touquet ☎ 21.05.10.67

 Valenciennes *(Nord)*
Pop: 41,000
Lille 50 km, Paris 205 km
🛈 rue Askièvre ☎ 27.46.22.99

At the heart of the Escaut valley, not far from the Belgian border, Valenciennes has always seemed an industrial prize on the easiest invasion route to France. It has also taken on some of the colour of its Flemish and Dutch neighbours, while wars have swirled round the city and then receded like a tide. There is a fine art gallery and good canoeing on the Etang de Trith, as well as fishing, sailing and golf.

- Art: the Musée des Beaux Arts houses a fine collection of Flemish paintings and has a Rubens and Van Dyck room. There are also works by Watteau, a native of Valenciennes.
- Boat Hire: on the canals of the Escaut and Scarpe rivers ☎ 27.46.82.88
- Golf: 9h private course at Golf de Valenciennes, chemin Vert, 59770 Marly-les-Valenciennes ☎ 27.46.30.10

 Wimereux *(Pas-de-Calais)*
Pop: 7,000
Calais 31 km, Paris 250 km
🛈 place du Roi Albert 1er ☎ 21.83.27.17

The jagged coastline reveals this charming turn-of-the-century seaside town, tucked into the large Baie de St-Jean between two headlands. Little changing cabins along the seafront look out over one of the best French beaches and away to the British coastline, visible on a clear day.

- Ballooning: in mid-June the base here hosts the Festival Aérien, a hot-air balloon show with model aeroplanes and an aerial acrobatic display.
- Beach: at high tide the sea crashes in large waves and spray close to the sea wall while low tide reveals a good sand and pebble beach, safe for children.
- Camping: Camping du Baston ☎ 21.32.51.19
- Golf: 18h private links course with some difficult holes at Golf de Wimereux, route d'Ambleteuse, 62930 Wimereux ☎ 21.32.43.20
- Sailing: and windsurfing equipment to hire on the beach.
- Tennis: 11 courts to hire.
- Walking: cliff-top walks at Cap Blanc Nez and Cap Gris-Nez (excellent observation point for bird migration) as well as the Boulonnais Regional Park.

NORMANDIE

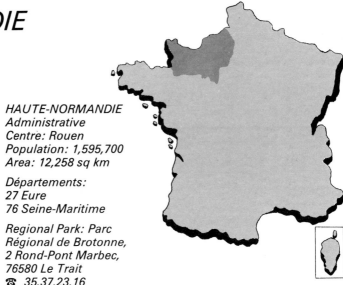

BASSE-NORMANDIE
*Administrative
Centre: Caen
Population: 1,306,200
Area: 17,583 sq km*

*Départements:
14 Calvados
50 Manche
61 Orne*

*Regional Park:
Parc Régional
Normandie-Maine,
Maison du Parc, B.P.
5, 61320 Carrouges*
☎ *33.27.21.15*

HAUTE-NORMANDIE
*Administrative
Centre: Rouen
Population: 1,595,700
Area: 12,258 sq km*

*Départements:
27 Eure
76 Seine-Maritime*

*Regional Park: Parc
Régional de Brotonne,
2 Rond-Pont Marbec,
76580 Le Trait*
☎ *35.37.23.16*

Normandy's 640 km of Channel coastline covers an equivalent English stretch from Kent to Dorset, with a similar mix inland of orchard, woodland, pasture and lush river valley and, along the coast itself, sand or pebble beaches and lofty white chalk cliffs. The Seine, rising in the Côte-d'Or in far-off Burgundy, pours its waters through Paris to Rouen and out into the huge estuary at France's second most important port, Le Havre.

Normandy is a country rich in ancient abbeys – the ruined seventh-century Jumièges, St-Wandrille, Mont-St-Michel and Caen of the thirteenth century; and of magnificent cathedrals, at Bayeux and Rouen. The Norman past is told in the Bayeux tapestry, and there are traces of Vikings in the fishing villages along the Cotentin peninsula. This is the land where figures from school history books lived their lives: William the Conqueror, whose tomb is in Caen; at Rouen, where Joan of Arc was burned at the stake; at Les Andelys, towering above a curve in the river, sits the ruined hilltop Château Gaillard, once the stronghold of Richard the Lionheart.

In June 1944, however, with 'Operation Overlord', the Allied invasion of the mainland of Europe, a more recent and bloodier history imposed itself on these fields and beaches. On the five landing beaches of Sword, Juno, Gold, Omaha and Utah (an 80-km stretch of sands between Quineville and Ouistreham), British, American, Canadian and French forces began the final phase of the overthrow of Hitler's Germany. D-Day and afterwards are remembered at the Café Gondres at Bénouville, the first house to be liberated; at Courseulles-sur-Mer, landing point of General de Gaulle returning to establish the French provisional government of the fourth Republic; at Ver-sur-Mer, where there remain fragments of the German Atlantic Wall; at Arromanches, where can be seen the hulks of the Mulberry Harbour from which one million troops landed from 400 ships. Guided tours of the region, from bases at Caen and Bayeux, feature monuments, working models and battle museums, while the price paid in war dead is visible at the British cemetery at Ranville-sur-Mer, the Canadian at Reviers, the American at St-Laurent-sur-Mer and the German at La Cambe.

In the world of letters, art and music, Normandy means the *Madame Bovary* of Flaubert, the short stories of Guy de Maupassant, and Proust of Cabourg (Balbec in *A l'Ombre des Jeunes Filles en Fleur*). It means, too, Claude Monet's *Water Lilies* at Giverny (once his home, now a museum), Orbec for Claude Debussy, Lyons for Maurice Ravel and Honfleur for Erik Satie.

Honfleur harbour

The crowds pour in by ferry, year after year, to Cherbourg, Le Havre and Dieppe. They make pilgrimages to the landing beaches, bask in the sun on those same beaches, idle an evening away in the casinos at Trouville or Deauville, and explore the monastic past of Mont-St-Michel. Then less precise pleasures will tempt them. They may explore the countryside itself with its *etangs* (small fishing ponds), strong stone manor houses and rural farmsteads where logs are piled up against the onset of winter. Because Normandy is a country of farms and orchards, they may taste the produce – butter and cheese (Camembert, Pont l'Evêque and pungent Livaroc), cider from the farmhouses along the *Route du Cidre* displaying the 'Cru de Cambremer' signs and, of course, the fierce apple brandy, Calvados.

PRACTICAL TOURIST INFORMATION

General information on the region can be obtained by telephoning or writing to the Comité Régional du Tourisme (CRT) office, while specific booklets are produced detailing camping, hotel and self-catering gîte *accommodation. These can be obtained by writing to the tourist board office of the* département *(CDT) of your choice:*

Regional Tourist Board
Comité Régional du Tourisme (CRT), 46 avenue Foch, 27000 EVREUX ☎ 32.31.05.89

Départements
Calvados (14): Comité Départemental du Tourisme (CDT), place du Canada, 14000 CAEN ☎ 31.86.53.30
Eure (27): Comité Départemental du Tourisme (CDT), 35 rue du Dr.-Oursel, 27000 EVREUX ☎ 32.38.21.61
Manche (50): Office Départemental du Tourisme (ODT), Préfecture, B.P.419, 50009 ST-LO ☎ 33.57.52.80
Orne (61): Comité Départemental du Tourisme (CDT), 60 rue St-Blaise, B.P.50, 61002 ALENCON Cedex ☎ 33.26.18.71
Seine-Maritime (76): Comité Départemental du Tourisme (CDT), B.P.666, 76008 ROUEN Cedex ☎ 35.88.61.32

SELF-CATERING ACCOMMODATION

The following British operators offer self-catering accommodation in the area:

AA Motoring Holidays, P.O. Box 100, Fanum House, Halesowen B63 3BT ☎ 021-550 7401

Agencefrance Holidays, Landsowne Place, 17 Holdenhurst Road, Bournemouth BH8 8EH ☎ 0202 299534

Allez France, 27 West Street, Storrington, Pulborough RH20 4DZ ☎ 09066 2345

Angel Travel, 47 High Street, Central Chambers, Tonbridge TN9 1SD ☎ 0732 884109

Avon Europe, Lower Quinton, Stratford-upon-Avon, Warks CV37 8SG ☎ 0789 720130

Billington Travel, 2a White Hart Parade, Riverhead, Sevenoaks TN13 2BJ ☎ 0732 460666

Blakes Holidays, Wroxham, Norwich NR12 8DH ☎ 0603 784131

Bowhills Ltd, Swanmore, Southampton SO3 2QW ☎ 0489 877627

Brittany Ferries, The Brittany Centre, Wharf Road, Portsmouth PO2 8RU ☎ 0705 827701

Carasol Holidays, 6 Hayes Avenue, Bournemouth BH7 7AD ☎ 0202 33398

Chapter Travel, 126 St John's Wood High Street, London NW8 7ST ☎ 01-586 9451

Cresta Holidays, 32 Victoria Street, Altrincham WA14 1ET ☎ 0345 056511

Dieppe Ferries Holidays, Weymouth Quay, Weymouth DT4 8DY ☎ 0305 777444

La France des Villages, Model Farm, Rattlesden, Bury St Edmunds IP30 0SY ☎ 044 93 7664

France Directe, 2 Church Street, Warwick CV34 4AB ☎ 0926 497989

French Life Motoring Holidays, 26 Church Road, Horsforth, Leeds LS18 5LG ☎ 0532 390077

French Villa Centre, 175 Selsdon Park Road, Croydon CR2 8JJ ☎ 01-651 1231

Gîtes de France, 178 Piccadilly, London W1V 9DB ☎ 01-493 3480

Hoseasons Holidays Abroad, Sunway House, Lowestoft NR32 3LT ☎ 0502 500555

Hoverspeed Ltd, Maybrook House, Queens Gardens, Dover CT17 9UQ ☎ 0304 240241

Interhome, 383 Richmond Road, Twickenham TW1 2EF ☎ 01-891 1294

Just France, 1 Belmont, Lansdown Road, Bath BA1 5DZ ☎ 0225 446328

Lagrange Vacances, 16/20 New Broadway, London W5 2XA ☎ 01-579 7311

David Newman's French Collection, P.O. Box 733, 40 Upperton Road, Eastbourne BN21 4AW ☎ 0323 410347

Normandy Country Holidays, 113 Sutton Road, Walsall W35 3AG ☎ 0922 20278

Par-tee Tours, Riverside House, 53 Uxbridge Road, Rickmansworth WD3 2DH ☎ 0923 721565

Pleasurewood Holidays, Somerset House, Gordon Road, Lowestoft NR32 1PZ ☎ 0502 517271

Prime Time Holidays, 5a Market Square, Northampton NN1 2DL ☎ 0604 20996

Quo Vadis, 243 Euston Road, London NW1 2BT ☎ 01-583 8383

Rendez-Vous France, Holiday House, 146/148 London Road, St. Albans AL1 1PQ ☎ 0727 45400

Sealink Holidays, Charter House, Park Street, Ashford TN2 8EX ☎ 0233 47033

Slipaway Holidays, 90 Newland Road, Worthing BN11 1LB ☎ 0903 821000

Vacances, 28 Gold Street, Saffron Walden CB10 1EJ ☎ 0799 25101

Vacances en Campagne, Bignor, Pulborough RH20 1QD ☎ 07987 433

Vacances France, 14 Bowthorpe Road, Wisbech PE13 2DX ☎ 0945 587830

VFB Holidays, 1 St Margaret's Terrace, Cheltenham GL50 4DT ☎ 0242 526338

RESORTS

 Agon-Coutainville *(Manche)*
Pop: 2,000
Cherbourg 77 km, Paris 343 km
🅸 place 28 Juillet 1944 ☎ 33.47.01.46 (Jun-Sep)

Popular and lively family resort with all modern tourist amenities, but where simple pleasures, like children discovering tiny crabs in pools left by the ebbing tide, are also possible. Oyster and mussel farming provide a living for many of the locals along this stretch of coast and low tide reveals the curious method of cultivation whereby the farmers 'grow' the mussels on rows of oak stakes embedded in the sand and, when the sea retreats its 7 or 8 km, employ tractors to cull their harvest. To the north lie other smaller and similar family resorts, such as Blainville-sur-Mer, Gouville-sur-Mer, Anneville, Pirou, Créances, St-Germain-sur-Ay and to the south Régnéville, Montmartin and Hauteville-sur-Mer.

- Beach: 8-km pretty beach with fine sand.
- Camping: le Marais ☎ 33.47.25.72 and le Martinet ☎ 33.47.05.20
- Casino: (Easter-Sep) ☎ 33.47.06.88
- Fishing: on the calm waters of the Mare de l'Essay reservoir.
- Golf: private 9h course at Golf de Coutainville, 50230 Agon ☎ 33.47.03.31
- Riding: Centre Equestre et Poney-Club ☎ 33.47.00.42
- Sailing: Club Nautique de Coutainville offers week-long courses for beginners ☎ 33.47.14.81
- Tennis: instruction and nine courts to hire at the Club de la Jeune France, stade du Dr.-Marquez ☎ 33.47.04.14
- Walking: in the nearby Seine valley countryside.

 Alençon *(Orne)*
Pop: 33,000
Le Mans 49 km, Paris 190 km
🅸 Maison d'Ozé ☎ 33.26.11.36

A busy and historic market town traditionally famed for its lace, Alençon is situated on the River Sarthe and on the edge of the Normandie-Maine Regional Park, an ideal centre from which to explore. Restoration of the town has left it with quiet pedestrian precincts amongst the old houses. The Perseigne Forest is a good and popular centre for walking and riding and deer can be spotted in the Ecouves Forest.

- Camping: Camping de Guéramé ☎ 33.26.34.95
- Cycling: cycles for hire from Sodiac, place du Général de Gaulle ☎ 33.29.05.50 and from the SNCF station.
- Riding: Etrier de Chauvigny, St-Germain-du-Corbéis ☎ 33.26.09.99
- Walking: in the Ecouves and Perseigne Forests.

 Les Andelys *(Eure)*
Pop: 8,000
Rouen 40 km, Paris 92 km
🄸 rue Philippe-Auguste ☎ 32.54.41.93

Spectacular natural setting at the base of steep chalk cliffs on a loop on the Seine. The formidable ruined Château Gaillard, once the home of Richard the Lionheart, towers over the river below and affords memorable views.

- Art: museum in rue Ste-Clothilde houses a major work by Nicolas Poussin (closed Mon).
- Camping: Ile des Trois Rois ☎ 32.54.23.79
- Fishing: category 2 fishing on the River Seine.
- Golf: 18h private course at Golf de Vaudreuil Louviers, 27100 Le Vaudreuil ☎ 32.59.02.60; also difficult and popular 18h private course with thirteenth-century château clubhouse at Golf de Chaumont-en-Vexin, Château de Bertichère, 60240 Chaumont-en-Vexin ☎ 44.49.00.81
- Sailing: Yacht Club des Andelys, rue des Falaises ☎ 32.54.13.19
- Watersports: a little further up the river at Poses, there is a great recreational area offering climbing, tennis, canoeing, waterskiing, windsurfing, etc.

 Arromanches-les-Bains *(Calvados)*
Pop: 400
Bayeux 10 km, Paris 250 km
🄸 rue du Maréchal-Joffre ☎ 31.21.47.56

Small and popular seaside resort and fishing harbour. Here, off Arromanches, on 7 June 1944, more than a million Allied soldiers landed on the huge man-made floating harbour called Mulberry B. The little town houses an impressive exhibition of the invasion days at the Musée du Débarquement, Normandy Landings museum.

- Camping: Camping Municipal ☎ 31.22.36.78
- Tennis: six courts to hire.

 Bagnoles-de-l'Orne *(Orne)*
Pop: 800
Alençon 48 km, Paris 238 km
🄸 place de la Gare ☎ 33.37.85.66 (Mar-Sep)

Together with Tessé-la-Madeleine, this forms one of France's principal spas. Attractively set in 46,600 hectares of woodland in the Vée valley, it has its own boating lake, casino and full sports and recreation facilities, and its centre has been barred to the heaviest traffic. There are mushroom-gathering weekends in the autumn in the Ferté-Macé district nearby, and an annual festival commemorating the Arthurian legend of Sir Lancelot of the Lake (believed in fable to have been born here), held between May and September and comprising concerts, theatre and ballet.

- Camping: Camping de la Vée ☎ 33.37.87.87
- Casino: Casino du Lac ☎ 33.37.01.88
- Cycling: cycles for hire from the SNCF station.
- Golf: 9h public course at Andaine Golf Club, route de Domfront, 61140 Bagnoles de l'Orne ☎ 33.37.81.42
- Riding: horse-drawn mail-coach tours and forest rides available from Le Village du Cheval, St-Michel-des-Andaines ☎ 33.37.12.79, who also run weekend competition driving courses.
- Spa: circulatory disorders ☎ 33.30.82.31 (1 Apr-30 Sep) alt: 220 m, climate: temperate.
- Tennis: indoor coaching is available throughout the year from Tennis Etudes ☎ 33.38.05.02
- Walking: in the Andaine Forest within the Normandie-Maine Regional Park and the rocky gorges of the Vée Valley.

 Barfleur *(Manche)*
Pop: 650
Cherbourg 27 km, Paris 358 km
🄸 quai H. Chardon ☎ 33.54.02.48 (Jul/Aug)

Small picturesque fishing port and yachting harbour.

- Camping: Les Tamaris ☎ 33.54.01.58
- Golf: 9h private course at Golf de Fontenay en Cotentin, Fontenay-sur-Mer, 50310 Montebourg ☎ 33.21.44.27
- Walking: along the coastal paths.

 Barneville-Carteret *(Manche)*
Pop: 2,500
Cherbourg 37 km, Paris 353 km
🄸 place Dr. Auvret ☎ 33.04.90.58

On the west coast of the Cotentin peninsula, Barneville is a well-known seaside resort with adjacent Carteret, a tiny fishing port and marina, offering regular trips to the Channel Islands.

- Beach: two broad clean sandy beaches sheltered by headland.
- Camping: Les Bosquets ☎ 33.04.73.62
- Walking: unspoilt and windswept cliff paths around the Cap de Carteret.

 Bayeux *(Calvados)*
Pop: 15,000
St-Lô 35 km, Paris 268 km
🄸 1 rue des Cuisiniers ☎ 31.92.16.26

The date 1066 is forever etched in every British schoolchild's memory as a landmark in history. More recently, Bayeux, the ancient cathedral city famed for its eleventh-century tapestry depicting the Battle of Hastings, made history again when it became the first town to be liberated by the Allied armies on 7 June 1944. As the inscription on the memorial, erected here to the memory of the British who fell, reminds us, it was the British who came to the help of their former conquerors, the Normans. A fine historic centre in an area of unspoilt countryside.

● Camping: Camping Municipal ☎ 31.92.08.43
● Cycling: cycles for hire from the SNCF station.
● Golf: fairly recent 18h private course at Golf de Bayeux Omaha Beach, 14520 Port-en-Bessin ☎ 31.21.72.94

 Cabourg *(Calvados)*
Pop: 3,500
Caen 24 km, Paris 225 km
🛈 Jardins du Casino ☎ 31.91.01.09

Elegant and popular seaside resort whose style dates from the turn of the century, and whose character is quiet and residential.

● Beach: fine sandy beach.
● Camping: Camping Plage ☎ 31.91.05.75 and Camping de la Prairie ☎ 31.91.03.35
● Casino: ☎ 31.91.11.75
● Golf: 9h public course at Golf Public de Cabourg, avenue de l'Hippodrome, 14390 Cabourg ☎ 31.91.70.53; and short 18h private course at Golf de Cabourg, route de Sallenelles, 14390 Le Home Varaville ☎ 31.91.25.26
● Riding: La Sablonnière, route de Caen ☎ 31.91.58.01
● Sailing: and windsurfing tuition, plus equipment for hire from the beach opposite the Grand Hotel.
● Tennis: Garden Tennis Club, rue Charles de Gaulle has 20 courts to hire ☎ 31.91.31.88

 Caen *(Calvados)*
Pop: 120,000
Alençon 102 km, Paris 240 km
🛈 place St-Pierre ☎ 31.86.27.65

World War II brought ruin to the old city, but subsequent rebuilding has made it a prosperous, modern, deep-water inland port. Flat and industrial outskirts belie the attractiveness of the centre with its avenues of neatly pollarded trees and the lively atmosphere characteristic of a university city. From the terraces of William the Conqueror's ruined castle there are good views. Also recommended is the impressive new Museum for Peace memorial building (open every day) where audio-visual and computer presentations leave the visitor reflecting on the fragility of our world.

● Boat Trips: departing from the Bassin St-Pierre, travel the length of the canal from Caen to the coast at Ouistreham.
● Camping: Camping Municipal ☎ 31.73.60.92
● Cycling: cycles for hire from the SNCF station.

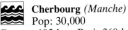 **Cherbourg** *(Manche)*
Pop: 30,000
Rennes 195 km, Paris 360 km
🛈 Office de Tourisme ☎ 33.43.52.02

For millions of cross-Channel travellers, Cherbourg is the first contact with France en route to more distant parts. Others use it as their port of call for a day-trip shopping excursion to explore the large hypermarket and buy inexpensive food and wine to take home. Cherbourg is a typical French town with tempting boulangeries, pâtisseries and charcuteries, large department store (Printemps), colourful markets (Tuesdays, Thursdays and Saturdays) and good restaurants, and makes a good starting point for excursions along the Seine valley and the northern Cotentin peninsula.

● Casino: ☎ 33.43.00.56
● Golf: 9h private course at Golf de Cherbourg, Domaines des Roches, Village de l'Eglise, 50470 La Glacerie ☎ 33.44.45.48
● Riding: L'Etrier Cherbourgeois, La Brûlette at Brix ☎ 33.41.94.03

 Courseulles-sur-Mer *(Calvados)*
Pop: 3,000
Bayeux 20 km, Paris 258 km
🛈 54 rue de la Mer ☎ 31.37.46.80

Churchill, de Gaulle and King George V came ashore near Courseulles within a week of the D-day landings to review progress. Today this modest resort has shed its humility and is growing into a popular family centre with apartment blocks to accommodate the new generation of visitors. Plenty of activity surrounds the marina (800 berths), and there is also a race course, casino and opportunities for sea fishing trips.

● Beach: fine sandy beach.
● Camping: Le Champ de Course ☎ 31.37.99.26
● Cycling: cycles can be hired from Garage du Port ☎ 31.97.97.21
● Riding: Club Hippique des Trois Vallées ☎ 31.97.99.26

 Coutances *(Manche)*
Pop: 14,000
Cherbourg 75 km, Paris 330 km
🛈 2 rue Quesnel-Morinière ☎ 33.45.17.79

Towards the west coast of the Cotentin peninsula and never more than 10 minutes away from the sea, Coutances is the religious capital of the region, with a very fine cathedral and a beautiful public garden in the style of the seventeenth-century. Lively in summer and worth exploring on foot.

● Beach: fine sandy beaches (13 km) at Hauteville-sur-Mer and Montmartin-sur-Mer. Also Agon-Coutainville (12 km).
● Camping: Les Vignettes ☎ 33.45.43.13
● Cycling: cycles can be hired from the SNCF station.
● Fishing: good salmon fishing in the area.

 Deauville (*Calvados*)
Pop: 5,000
Caen 47 km, Paris 207 km
🛈 place Mairie ☎ 31.88.21.43

Smart seaside resort which continues to attract an elegant and wealthy international clientele. The famous boardwalk, the promenade des Planches, extends along the entire 3 km seafront, the casinos are open all year, and there is a yachting marina for those who attend the regattas and ocean races. The polo playing fraternity hold their annual world championship here and horse races (*Grand Prix* last Sunday in August), and the yearling sales (August and November) are an important part of the fashionable calendar of events.

● Camping: Camping de Clairefontaine ☎ 31.88.14.06
● Casinos: Casino d'été, rue E.-Blanc ☎ 31.88.29.55 and Casino d'hiver, rue E.-Nicolas ☎ 31.88.29.91
● Cycling: cycles can be hired from the SNCF station.
● Golf: 27h private course at Golf de Deauville, 14800 St-Arnoult ☎ 31.88.20.53. This course is frequently crowded, particularly in mid-summer. New 18h private course at Golf de St-Gatien ☎ 31.65.19.99
● Riding: Centre Equestre de l'Oxer, route de Clairefontaine ☎ 31.88.99.51 and Poney-Club, boulevard de la Mer ☎ 31.98.56.24
● Sailing: all types of equipment for hire from the Centre Nautique on the promenade ☎ 31.98.11.33
● Tennis: Sporting-Club de Deauville has 23 courts and offers five-day summer courses (1 hr per day) for children and adults ☎ 31.88.02.26
● Thalassotherapy: Centre de Thalasso-Esthétique de Pointe, Bord de Mer ☎ 31.98.48.11
● Walking: GR 26.

 Dieppe (*Seine-Maritime*)
Pop: 35,000
Rouen 61 km, Paris 169 km
🛈 boulevard Général-de-Gaulle ☎ 35.84.11.77

Traditional northern fishing port and the longest established of the French seaside resorts, Dieppe is besieged during the summer by English day-trippers, for whom it provides good shopping and

beach fun. There's a distinctly English air, with lawns stretching along the seafront.

● Beach: 1.5-km sand and shingle beach.
● Camping: Les Vitamines ☎ 35.82.47.43
● Casino: Municipal, boulevard de Verdun ☎ 35.82.33.60 (open all year).
● Cycling: cycles can be hired from the SNCF station.
● Golf: good 18h private course at Golf de Dieppe, route de Pourville, 76200 Dieppe ☎ 35.84.25.05
● Walking: GR 21.

 Etretat (*Seine-Maritime*)
Pop: 2,000
Le Havre 28 km, Paris 200 km
🛈 place Hôtel de Ville ☎ 35.27.05.21 (Jun-Sep)

Popular and pleasant small resort with two huge cliffs at either end of the long shingle beach which have been carved into extraordinary shapes by the effect of the sea.

● Camping: Camping Municipal ☎ 35.27.07.67
● Casino: open all year ☎ 35.27.00.54
● Golf: windy 18h private course with a cliff-top setting at Golf d'Etretat, route du Havre, 76790 Étretat ☎ 35.27.04.89
● Tennis: six courts to hire.
● Walking: numerous coastal and inland walks.

 Falaise (*Calvados*)
Pop: 9,000
Caen 34 km, Paris 223 km
🛈 32 rue Georges-Clemenceau ☎ 31.90.17.26

Small market town in lower Normandy, the birthplace of William the Conqueror and, several centuries later, the scene of heavy fighting in 1944. There is good fishing and golf locally and delightful countryside to the west, between Falaise and Vire, in the area known as Suisse Normandie: small river valleys, wooded hills and pastureland, but not as dramatic as the name might suggest.

● Camping: Camping du Château ☎ 31.90.16.55
● Fishing: for trout in the Baise and Trainefeuille rivers.
● Flying: at the Léon Bathiat aerodrome (5 km) flying instruction at the weekends.
● Golf: 9h private course at Golf de Clécy-Cantelou, Manoir de Cantelou, 14570 Clécy ☎ 31.69.72.72

 Fécamp (*Seine-Maritime*)
Pop: 25,000
Le Havre 40 km, Paris 205 km
🛈 place Bellet ☎ 35.28.20.51

The bracing sea air of this busy cod-fishing port and seaside resort combines well with the lovely château-dotted countryside which surrounds it. In one of these châteaux the short-story writer Guy de Maupassant was born. The church of La

Trinité, formerly a Benedictine monastery, has the great girth of a cathedral, but the departed monks have left another memorial in the liqueur they invented, Benedictine, still manufactured here at the Distillery, where there is the opportunity both to visit and taste. Casino.

- Camping: Camping de Rennéville ☎ 35.28.20.97
- Cycling: cycles can be hired from the SNCF station.
- Golf: see Etretat.
- Riding: Société Hippique ☎ 35.28.31.71

 Forges-les-Eaux *(Seine-Maritime)*
Pop: 4,000
Rouen 42 km, Paris 116 km
🇧 parc de l'Hôtel de Ville ☎ 35.90.52.10

A lively holiday spa in elegant wooded parkland surroundings. In the heart of the Bray countryside of hedged and wooded farmland, this is a pleasant rural resort offering plenty of leisure amenities.

- Camping: La Minière ☎ 35.90.53.91
- Casino: avenue des Sources ☎ 35.90.52.67
- Fishing: category 1 fishing in the Andelle and Epte rivers.
- Golf: new 9h private course at Golf de Saint-Saëns, Domaine de Vaudichon, 76680 Saint-Saëns ☎ 35.34.25.24
- Spa: circulatory disorders ☎ 35.90.52.67 (open all year) alt: 175 m, climate: temperate.

Granville *(Manche)*
Pop: 15,000
Coutances 29 km, Paris 347 km
🇧 15 rue Georges-Clemenceau ☎ 33.50.02.67

A seaside and health resort, but also a busy fishing port, with the highest tides in Europe. Known in the 1930s as the 'Monaco of the North', the old upper town's fortifications and historic buildings are set high in the granite rock, while below, at its feet, the town's good beach, casino and large yachting marina (1,000 berths) make this a lively and modern tourist resort. Regular connections with Jersey and Chausey Islands and a large winter carnival (mid-Feb) and summer carnival (mid-Aug) add to the atmosphere.

- Beach: sandy beach at Plage du Plat-Gousset. Similar family seaside resorts to the north at St-Martin-de-Bréhal, Coudeville, Bréville and Donville-sur-Mer (these last two have sand yachting at low tide). To the south is the fine sandy beach at St-Pair-sur-Mer, a long-established seaside resort.
- Camping: La Vague ☎ 33.50.29.97
- Casino: place du Maréchal-Foch ☎ 33.50.00.79
- Cycling: cycles can be hired from the SNCF station.
- Fishing: river fishing on the Sienne, Thar, Bosq and Seilles.

- Golf: 18h public links course at Golf de Bréhal, 50290 Bréhal ☎ 33.51.58.88 and 18h private course at Golf de Granville, Bréville, 50290 Bréhal ☎ 33.50.23.06
- Riding: Club Hippique, Bréville, 50290 Bréhal ☎ 33.50.22.16
- Sailing: the Centre Régional de Nautisme (B.P.140, 50401 Granville) offer beginners' tuition during the school holidays, of one or two weeks' duration, with accommodation ☎ 33.50.18.95
- Tennis: nine courts to hire at La Falaise ☎ 33.50.10.57
- Thalassotherapy: Centre de Cures Marines de Granville ☎ 33.50.34.34

 Le Havre *(Seine-Maritime)*
Pop: 200,000
Rouen 87 km, Paris 203 km
🇧 place de l'Hôtel de Ville ☎ 35.21.22.88

France's second largest port (after Marseille), situated at the mouth of the Seine, the port boasts an industrial and harbour complex covering over 8,000 hectares, including the largest lock in the world accessible to supertanker-sized ships. Linked via the impressive Tancarville Bridge to all points south, Le Havre is one of the most popular cross-Channel ferry routes.

- Beach: curving sand and shingle beach which, at low tide, stretches round the La Hève cape to Ste-Adresse, with splendid views.
- Boat Trips: trips round the port and cruises up the River Seine from Salamandre, quai de la Marine ☎ 35.42.01.31
- Camping: Forêt de Montgeon ☎ 35.46.52.39
- Golf: undemanding 18h private course at Golf du Havre, Hameau Saint Supplix, 76930 Octeville-sur-Mer ☎ 35.46.36.50
- Walking: in the Montgeon Forest.

Honfleur *(Calvados)*
Pop: 9,000
Caen 63 km, Paris 199 km
🇧 33 cours Fossés ☎ 31.89.23.30

Ancient and pretty fishing and commercial port situated on the Seine estuary, and long patronised by the British. Renowned as the cradle of Impressionism, Honfleur was the favourite haunt of artists, writers and musicians (Erik Satie was born here). Today this trend continues; artists work along the colourful and attractive quaysides of the old harbour.

- Art: Musée Boudin contains works by the native Boudin as well as by Corot, Monet and Courbet, amongst others.
- Boat Trips: short trips up the Seine estuary leave from the quai des Passagers.
- Camping: Camping du Phare ☎ 31.89.10.26
- Painting: details of courses held here from Hôtel du Cheval Blanc, quai des Passagers ☎ 31.89.13.49

- Riding: Centre Equestre du Ramier
  ☎ 31.89.04.20
- Tennis: nine courts to hire at boulevard
  Charles V ☎ 31.89.06.03
- Walking: from the Notre-Dame-de-Grâce
  chapel views extend toward Le Havre across
  the Baie de Seine.

 Houlgate (*Calvados*)
Pop: 2,000
Caen 28 km, Paris 219 km
🖪 boulevard des Belges ☎ 31.91.33.09

Fashionable resort amidst hilly countryside and
with magnificent cliff-top walks and views.

- Beach: large sandy beach.
- Camping: Camping de la Vallée
  ☎ 31.24.40.69
- Casino: ☎ 31.91.60.94
- Golf: 9h private coastal course at Golf de Clair
  Vallon, 14510 Houlgate ☎ 31.91.06.97
- Hang Gliding: at Gonneville-sur-Mer off the
  Vaches Noires cliffs.
- Riding: Centre Equestre des Chevaliers
  ☎ 31.91.18.06
- Tennis: 14 courts to hire at Sporting Club,
  place de Docteur Rouget ☎ 31.91.22.85
- Windsurfing: Oasis Plage ☎ 31.91.47.10

 Jullouville (*Manche*)
Pop: 2,000
Granville 8 km, Paris 350 km
🖪 SI ☎ 33.61.82.48

A pleasant seaside resort with a fine beach, which,
together with similar resorts of Carolles and St-
Michel-des-Loup in the vast Baie de Mont-St-
Michel, offers long pine-fringed sandy beaches and
walks along coastal paths.

- Camping: La Chaussée ☎ 33.61.80.18

 Lisieux (*Calvados*)
Pop: 26,000
Caen 49 km, Paris 174 km
🖪 11 rue Alençon ☎ 31.62.08.41

Ideal as a base for excursions into the Pays d'Auge
(north, south and west of here), a pretty region of
lush green pastures, apple orchards, manor houses
and châteaux.

- Camping: Municipal ☎ 31.62.00.40
- Cycling: cycles for hire from Cycles Pasquier,
  boulevard Ste-Anne ☎ 31.31.32.03 and from
  the SNCF station.

 Mont-St-Michel (*Manche*)
Pop: 80
St-Malo 52 km, Paris 325 km
🖪 Corps de Garde des Bourgeois ☎ 33.60.14.30
(Mar-Oct)

A major tourist and historic site, the eighth-
century monastic abbey church crowns the peak of

this great granite rock in a marvellous silhouette.
Totally surrounded by the sea at high tide, and
connected to the mainland by a causeway, it is at
the mercy of spectacular tides, the startling speed
of which make walking round the sands at low tide
quite dangerous. Tidal movements can result in
variations of 15 m on certain days in March and
September, and, as one of the strongest and fastest
tides in the world (advancing across the sands at
over 10 kmph), it is capable of overtaking even the
fastest of runners! A cluster of old buildings flank
the rock, providing restaurant and hotel
accommodation, but with only one road and some
tiny alleyways through this medieval fortress,
summer visitors are virtually cheek by jowl all the
way up and all the way down.

- Camping: Camping du Mont-St-Michel
  ☎ 33.60.09.33
- Riding: La Gourmette du Mont-St-Michel
  ☎ 33.60.27.73

 Neufchâtel-en-Bray (*Seine-Maritime*)
Pop: 6,000
Rouen 45 km, Paris 133 km
🖪 6 place Notre-Dame ☎ 35.93.22.96

In the luscious green dairy-farming countryside,
this little town, on Paris's doorstep, has given its
name to one of the great Normandy cheeses. A
holiday resort for those seeking relaxation.

- Camping: Sainte-Claire ☎ 35.93.03.93
- Cycling: cycles can be hired from the SNCF
  station.
- Fishing: category 1 fishing in the Béthune
  river.
- Golf: see Forges-les-Eaux.
- Walking: in the Eu and Eawy Forests.

 Ouistreham Riva-Bella (*Calvados*)
Pop: 7,000
Caen 13 km, Paris 230 km
🖪 Jardin du Casino ☎ 31.97.18.63

Popular yachting port (650 berths), fishing harbour
and quiet family resort (Riva-Bella) where the
canal waterway to Caen meets the Channel. The
ships used for the invasion of England by William
the Conqueror were constructed here. The town's
maritime importance has recently been revived as,
since 1986, the huge cross-Channel ferries have
docked and disgorged their loads of cars and
passengers. There is a small D-day landings
exhibition here, for this is where, on Sword beach,
the spearhead of the 4th Commandos landed. This
is flat Normandy country, perfect for cycling and
walking holidays, and there are good watersports
facilities and areas perfect for birdwatching.

- Beach: fine sandy wide beach.
- Boat Hire: from Serra Marine, Port de
  Plaisance ☎ 31.97.17.41 and Ship Sélection,
  boulevard Maritime ☎ 31.96.57.12
- Camping: Camping des Pommiers

☎ 31.97.12.66
- Casino: ☎ 31.97.18.54
- Cycling: cycles for hire from Vérel, 77 avenue Foch ☎ 31.97.19.04
- Sailing: and windsurfing ☎ 31.97.13.05
- Tennis: six courts to hire at Tennis Club, avenue de la Plage ☎ 31.97.15.38
- Thalassotherapy: Institut de Thalassothérapie, avenue Kieffer offers fitness and relaxation packages.

 Rouen *(Seine-Maritime)*
Pop: 105,000
Le Havre 87 km, Paris 139 km
🛈 25 place Cathédrale ☎ 35.71.41.77

France's fourth largest port, this city has restored its old buildings. Banked by timber-clad houses, pedestrian malls now thread through the old quarters of the city, linking together the Place du Vieux Marché, where Joan of Arc was burnt at the stake in 1431, the house where Pierre Corneille, the dramatist, was born, the flamboyant twelfth-century Gothic cathedral and the Fine Arts Museum, with works by Caravaggio, Velasquez, Ingres, Delacroix and the Impressionists. Good shopping in the chic modern stores vies for attention with the ancient clock in the rue du Gros Horloge. Not far from the city centre, at Croisset, is Flaubert's house, where he wrote *Madame Bovary*.

- Camping: Municipal ☎ 35.74.07.59
- Golf: 18h private course set in a wooded valley at Golf de Rouen, chemin des Communaux, 76130 Mont-St-Aignan ☎ 35.76.38.65

 St-Aubin-sur-Mer *(Calvados)*
Pop: 1,500
Caen 17 km, Paris 240 km
🛈 Digue Favreau ☎ 31.97.30.41

Small seaside resort where the fresh sea air and the charming outlying countryside combine to give a restful stay.

- Beach: sand and pebble – one of the landing beaches of June 1944.
- Camping: Municipal ☎ 31.97.30.24
- Casino: rue Pasteur ☎ 31.96.65.36
- Riding: L'Etrier St-Aubinnais, route de Tailleville ☎ 31.96.22.88
- Sailing: and windsurfing ☎ 31.97.01.63
- Tennis: seven courts to hire at rue Jean Mermoz ☎ 31.47.33.04

 St-Lô *(Manche)*
Pop: 25,000
Caen 63 km, Paris 303 km
🛈 2 rue Havin ☎ 33.05.02.09

St-Lô was the most severely damaged Normandy town in the 1944 invasion fighting. The church of Notre-Dame has been left a ruin as a symbol of those terrible times. The town has been rebuilt around its historic centre and there are now lovely gardens along the old ramparts. The town is set on rock overlooking the valley of the Vire, a river which cuts through escarpments to the south and offers very good trout fishing upstream. St-Lô's national stud farm (Haras National) is famous as the largest horse-breeding centre in France. Visits can be made and, in summer, there are demonstrations on Thursday mornings.

- Cycling: cycles can be hired from the SNCF station.
- Riding: La Gourmette Saint-Loise, rue des Ecuyers ☎ 33.57.27.06

 St-Valéry-en-Caux *(Seine-Maritime)*
Pop: 6,000
Dieppe 32 km, Paris 198 km
🛈 place Hôtel de Ville ☎ 35.97.00.63 (May-Sep)

A string of small resorts dot the coast betwen Dieppe and Fécamp, with St-Valéry-en-Caux the central attraction. Its extensive pleasure-boat harbour (600 berths), set far back into the town, with magnificent cliffs surrounding it, attracts cross-Channel sailors. There's a nuclear power station at Paluel, near Conteville, 7 km to the west. Casino.

- Beach: sand and shingle.
- Camping: Municipal ☎ 35.97.05.07

 Le Tréport *(Seine-Maritime)*
Pop: 7,000
Dieppe 30 km, Paris 170 km
🛈 esplanade de la Plage ☎ 35.86.05.69

Charming fishing port and seaside resort at the foot of high cliffs. Easily accessible from Paris, it is popular with weekend out-of-towners. Casino.

- Beach: sand and shingle beach separated from that of Mers-les-Bains by the the Bresle river.
- Camping: Les Boucaniers ☎ 35.86.35.47 and Le Golf ☎ 35.86.33.80
- Cycling: cycles can be hired from the SNCF station.
- Fishing: on the Basse-Bresle river (permit required); also sea fishing trips.
- Riding: Centre Equestre, 104 rue André Dumont at Mers-les-Bains ☎ 35.50.35.67 takes riders through the forested grounds of the Château d'Eu.

 Trouville-sur-Mer *(Calvados)*
Pop: 6,000
Caen 43 km, Paris 206 km
🛈 32-36 boulevard Fernand-Moureaux
☎ 31.88.36.19

An enormous beach of fine sand, fully geared to the entertainment requirements of the young and not-so-young, together with elegant seafront hotels, gives this resort all-round appeal. Sea fishing trips, picture postcard villages to discover inland and the proximity of larger and more elegant Deauville make this area ever popular.

- Camping: Camping Hamel ☎ 31.88.15.55 and Le Chant des Oiseaux ☎ 31.88.06.42
- Canoeing: Canoë-kayak Club de Trouville, Complexe Nautique de Front de Mer ☎ 31.88.81.69
- Casino: ☎ 31.88.76.09
- Cycling: cycles can be hired from the SNCF station.
- Golf: see Deauville.
- Sailing: and windsurfing offered by the Club Nautique de Trouville-Hennequeville ☎ 31.88.13.59
- Tennis: seven courts near the beach ☎ 31.88.91.62
- Thalassotherapy: Cures Marines de Trouville, promenade des Planches ☎ 31.88.10.35

Vernon (Eure)
Pop: 24,000
Rouen 63 km, Paris 82 km
🅘 passage Pasteur ☎ 32.51.39.60

Midway between Paris and Rouen, along the winding valleys of the River Seine, lies Vernon, capital of the Vexin region of Normandy and a town of artistic and historical interest. There are several medieval buidings in the town and a charming and ancient bridge with a tiny half-timbered house on top of it. Just outside is the sumptuous Italianate Château de Bizy, with its stables inspired by those at Versailles. Master Impressionist Claude Monet's house and wonderful gardens are close by at Giverny.

- Art: at Giverny is Claude Monet's house and gardens (closed Mon).
- Camping: Les Fosses Rouges in St-Marcel ☎ 32.51.59.86
- Cycling: cycles can be hired from the SNCF station.
- Sailing: school for beginners at Yacht Club de Vernon ☎ 32.51.22.08
- Walking: lovely walks in the Seine, Eure and Epte river valleys.

Villers-sur-Mer (Calvados)
Pop: 2,000
Caen 35 km, Paris 214 km
🅘 place Mermoz ☎ 31.87.01.18

Pretty little seaside town situated on a woody hillside with pleasant parks and gardens and the great fossil-bearing Vaches Noires cliffs.

- Beach: long sandy beach backed by promenades.
- Camping: le Drakkar ☎ 31.87.52.41
- Casino: place Fanneau ☎ 31.87.01.07

- Golf: see Deauville and Houlgate.
- Riding: Centre Equestre de la Villedieu ☎ 31.87.51.59
- Sailing: Cercle Nautique sailing school ☎ 31.87.00.30
- Tennis: 20 courts to hire.

Vimoutiers (Orne)
Pop: 5,000
Caen 56 km, Paris 182 km
🅘 10 avenue du Général-de-Gaulle ☎ 33.39.30.29

Rural and picturesque town in the Pays d'Auge where pretty river valleys, their waters full of trout, flow past hillside orchards, full of spring-time apple blossom, and half-timbered country houses decorated with rose-coloured tiles. This is Camembert country, with Vimoutiers an important agricultural market centre. A visit to the prestigious private stud of Mézeray, close by, is a reminder that the National Stud (le Pin-au-Haras) is situated south of here. There carriage-driving displays and the chance to admire some of the finest stallions at close quarters, all within the magnificent grounds of a house known as 'the Versailles for horses', are very popular. The region stretching from L'Aigle to Argentan is a famous stud-farm district, where the soil and climate have consistently proved the most favourable for horse breeding.

- Camping: La Campière ☎ 33.39.18.86
- Fishing: category 1 fishing on the Vie and Touques rivers.
- Watersports: outdoor recreation area at Vitou.

Vire (Calvados)
Pop: 14,000
St-Lô 39 km, Paris 300 km
🅘 square de la Résistance ☎ 31.68.00.05

Pleasant country town in a lovely position above the Vire river valley and in the middle of the attractive Bocage Virois area. Follow the picturesque, signed Route du Granit and the circuit through the Gorges de la Vire, or fish in the peaceful river valleys of the Vire and Virène. Not far outside the town is an expanse of water (La Dathée) where sailing, windsurfing and canoeing take place.

- Camping: Municipal ☎ 31.68.00.94
- Cycling: cycles for hire from MJC ☎ 31.68.08.04 and from the SNCF station.
- Golf: see Falaise.
- Tennis: 11 courts to hire at stade Pierre Compte, route de Caen ☎ 31.68.06.34

PAYS DE LA LOIRE

*Administrative
Centre: Nantes
Population: 2,767,200
Area: 32,126 sq km*

Départements:
44 Loire-Atlantique
49 Maine-et-Loire
53 Mayenne
72 Sarthe
85 Vendée

Regional Park:
*Parc de Brière, 180 Ile
de Fédrun, 44720
Saint-Joachim*
☎ *40.88.42.72*

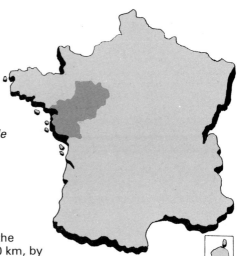

France's longest river, the Loire, rises in the Cévennes, runs north and west for 1,000 km, by Nevers and Orléans, through the château country of Blois, Amboise and Tours and the vineyards of Ancenis and Nantes, before reaching the Atlantic at St-Nazaire.

The region is filled with the river valleys of the dominant Loire and its tributaries, the Loir, Mayenne and Sarthe. There are coastal resorts along the Vendée and the Loire Atlantique coastline between La Baule and Les Sables-d'Olonne. It is a region steeped in the early histories of both France and England. Here the Plantagenet dynasty was founded when the divorced Queen of France, Eleanor of Aquitaine, married Henry, Count of Anjou-Maine at Fontevraud. Their sons, first Richard Coeur de Lion, then John Lackland, came to the throne of an England whose territories in France stretched the length of the country from Normandy and Brittany down through the ancient provinces of Maine, Touraine, Anjou, Aquitaine and Gascony. The Plantagenets held their early courts behind the massive defence works of the Château d'Angers, girdled by 17 solid and daunting towers. Chinon Castle saw the warring disputes of Henry II and his sons, Richard and John. A bridge over the River Vienne at Chinon was intended as a symbol of their reconciliation, as was a market place built at Saumur.

Today, at Fontevraud Abbey, there lie the tombs of these great lords and ladies: Henry II and Queen Eleanor, Richard the Lionheart and King John's wife, Isabelle of Angoulême. For many years a prison, the abbey is an important historic monument, currently undergoing archaeological excavation, and part of it is in use as a convention centre.

Over the centuries since the skirmishes of the Plantagenets, war has passed across the land: the Hundred Years War, the Wars of Religion and the Vendéen War against the revolutionaries in Paris. There are even sombre echoes of World War II at the German submarine pens at St-Nazaire.

Along the Vendée coast the ocean is gentler. Les Sables-d'Olonne, always a popular family resort, has now established itself as a fine yachting centre. There is a good marina at St-Gilles-Croix-de-Vie and pretty beach resorts up and down the coast at St-Jean-des-Monts, La Tranche-sur-Mer and Jard-sur-Mer.

To the north, on the Loire-Atlantique coast, La Baule is very much a resort of today. Fashionable and sophisticated, but with a history reaching back almost a hundred years, it boasts a splendid 8-km crescent beach. Nearby are the fishing ports and marinas of Pornic and Le Croisic, inland the Brière nature park and within it, at Missillac, the superb setting of the Golf de la Bretesche, a lakeside château with an 18-hole course.

Inland, too, lie the vineyards of the region: offering Muscadet wine from south of Nantes, as well as in the Vendée and the Maine-et-Loire, full-bodied white *crus de Layon* from the left bank of the Loire below Angers, and the dry and vigorous *côteaux*

Château Lassay

de Savennières from the right bank. The *Rosé d'Anjou* is lively, the *Cabernet d'Anjou* fine and delicate. The white *Côte de Saumur* is a dry, slightly perfumed wine.

The châteaux of the lower Loire, and of its tributary the Loir, running almost parallel with it, are not all military in origin. In the meadows of Mayenne stands the 'fairy-tale' medieval Château de Lassay, and at Craon a lovely late-eighteenth-century château in white stone. The Château de Montgeoffroy in the Loire-et-Maine is a perfectly decorated house of the *ancien régime*.

In the midst of the dairy pasture bordering the Loir, the Château de Bazouges, once an embattled fortress, is today an elegant residence. At the Château de Lude, again on the banks of the Loir, a *son-et-lumière* is presented, more spectacular than most, with some 350 'actors' recapturing French history on the lawns and among the 300 fountains in the grounds of this Renaissance château.

Outside Saumur, the château of Montreuil-Bellay, overlooking the Thouet river, was built in 1025 and beseiged by the Plantagenets. During the fifteenth century the fortress became a superb country house. Other châteaux well worth a visit are those at Courstanvaux (sixteenth century), Montsabert, mirroring the Monsoreau on the Loire, the fifteenth-century Château de Brissac, seven storeys tall and with 150 rooms, and the fifteenth-century Château d'Ancenis surrounded by its vineyards.

The region is full of historical association. Le Mans, with its Gothic cathedral of St-Julien is also the setting for the 24-hour motor car race, 4,800 km day and night around a 13-km lap. It was in the Sarthe that Wilbur Wright made the first flight from French soil – a trip of 125 km and a flight of over two hours. At Laval, Henri 'Douanier' Rousseau was born, founder of the *naif* school of art. At Angers, just beyond the brooding shadow of those 17 defence towers of the château, the orange-flavoured liqueur, Cointreau, is made.

There are balloon bases at Angers, nearby at the fifteenth-century Château Le Plessis Boure, a moated country mansion, and at the Château Brissac. From above you can look down on the Benedictine abbey of Solemnes on the Sarthe river, where the singing of Gregorian chants is world-renowned. Or, if the wind should drift the balloon towards the Vendée, it will sail high above a 'fairy-tale' castle straight from the works of Charles Perrault, the ruined twelfth-century Château Tiffauges. The castle once belonged to Gilles de Retz, the gallant companion-in-arms of Joan of Arc in her campaigns against the English. With the passage of the years, a change seems to have taken place in the character of Gilles de Retz. He acquired an evil reputation that endures today in a story of once-upon-a-time . . . for Tiffauges became the model for the gruesome legend of Bluebeard.

PRACTICAL TOURIST INFORMATION

General information on the region can be obtained by telephoning or writing to the Comité Régional du Tourisme (CRT) office, while specific booklets are produced detailing camping, hotel and self-catering gîte *accommodation. These can be obtained by writing to the tourist board office of the* département *(CDT) of your choice:*

Regional Tourist Board
Comité Régional du Tourisme (CRT), 3 place Saint-Pierre, 44000 NANTES ☎ 40.48.24.20

Départements
Loire-Atlantique (44): Comité Départemental du Tourisme (CDT), 34 rue de Strasbourg, 44000 NANTES ☎ 40.89.50.77
Maine-et-Loire (49): Comité Départemental du Tourisme (CDT), B.P.2148, 49021 ANGERS ☎ 41.88.23.85
Mayenne (53): Comité Départemental du Tourisme (CDT), 84 avenue Robert-Buron, 53000 LAVAL ☎ 43.49.35.40
Sarthe (72): Comité Départemental du Tourisme (CDT), 72000 LE MANS ☎ 43.81.72.72
Vendée (85): Comité Départemental du Tourisme (CDT), 8 place Napoléon, 85000 LA ROCHE-SUR-YON ☎ 51.05.45.28

SELF-CATERING ACCOMMODATION

The following British operators offer self-catering accommodation in the area:

Agencefrance Holidays, Lansdowne Place, 17 Holdenhurst Road, Bournemouth BH8 8EH ☎ 0202 299534
Allez France, 27 West Street, Storrington, Pulborough RH20 4DZ ☎ 09066 2345
Angel Travel, 47 High Street, Central Chamber, Tonbridge TN9 1SD ☎ 0732 361115
Avon Europe, Lower Quinton, Stratford-upon-Avon, Warks CV37 8SG ☎ 0789 720130
Bowhills Ltd, Swanmore, Southampton SO3 2QW ☎ 0489 877627
Brittany Ferries, The Brittany Centre, Wharf Road, Portsmouth PO2 8RU ☎ 0705 827701
Chalets de France, Travel House, Pandy, Nr Abergavenny NP7 8DH ☎ 0873 890770
Cosmos Motoring Holidays, Tourama House, 17 Homesdale Road, Bromley BR2 9LX ☎ 01-464 3121
Cresta Holidays, 32 Victoria Street, Altrincham

WA14 1ET ☎ 0345 056511
Crystal Holidays, The Courtyard, Arlington Road, Surbiton KT6 6BW ☎ 01-399 5144
Dominique's Villas, 2 Peterborough Mews, London SW6 3BL ☎ 01-736 1664
France Directe, 2 Church Street, Warwick CV34 4AB ☎ 0926 497989
France Individuelle, 22 High Street, Billingshurst, West Sussex RH14 8EP ☎ 040 381 5166
French Life Motoring Holidays, 26 Church Road, Horsforth, Leeds LS18 5LG ☎ 0532 390077
French Villa Centre, 175 Selsdon Park Road, Croydon CR2 8JJ ☎ 01-651 1231
Gîtes de France, 178 Piccadilly, London W1V 9DB ☎ 01-493 3480
Hoseasons Holidays Abroad, Sunway House, Lowestoft NR32 3LT ☎ 0502 500555
Hoverspeed Ltd, Maybrook House, Queens Gardens, Dover CT17 9UQ ☎ 0304 240241
Interhome, 383 Richmond Road, Twickenham TW1 2EF ☎ 01-891 1294
Just France, 1 Belmont, Lansdown Road, Bath BA1 5DZ ☎ 0225 446328
Lagrange Vacances, 16/20 New Broadway, London W5 2XA ☎ 01-579 7311
David Newman's French Collection, P.O. Box 733, 40 Upperton Road, Eastbourne BN21 4AW ☎ 0323 410347
Par-Tee Tours, Riverside House, 53 Uxbridge Road, Rickmansworth WD3 2DH ☎ 0923 721565
Pleasurewood Holidays, Somerset House, Gordon Road, Lowestoft NR32 1PZ ☎ 0502 517271
Rendez-Vous France, Holiday House, 146/148 London Road, St Albans AL1 1PQ ☎ 0727 45400
Rentavilla, 27 High Street, Chesterton, Cambridge CB4 1NB ☎ 0223 323414
Sealink Holidays, Charter House, Park Street, Ashford TN24 8EX ☎ 0233 47033
SFV Holidays, Summer House, 68 Hernes Road, Summertown, Oxford OX2 7QL ☎ 0865 57738
Slipaway Holidays, 90 Newland Road, Worthing BN11 1LB ☎ 0903 821000
Starvillas, 25 High Street, Chesterton, Cambridge CB4 1ND ☎ 0223 311990
Sturge, Martin, 3 Lower Camden Place, Bath BA1 5JJ ☎ 0225 310623
Sun France, 3 Beaufort Gardens, London SW16 3BP ☎ 01-679 4562
Sunvista Holidays, 5a George Street, Warminster BA12 8QA ☎ 0985 217444
Vacances France, 14 Bowthorpe Road, Wisbech PE13 2DX ☎ 0945 587830
Vacations, 60 Charles Street, Leicester LE1 1FB

☎ 0533 537758
VFB Holidays, 1 St Margaret's Terrace,
Cheltenham GL50 4DT ☎ 0242 526338
Villa France, 15 Winchcombe Road, Frampton
Cotterell, Bristol BS17 2AG ☎ 0454 772410

SPORTS AND ACTIVITIES

*For unusual and interesting holiday ideas, contact
the Loisirs Accueil office for the area of your
choice:*

Loisirs Accueil Loire-Atlantique,
Maison du Tourisme, place du Commerce, 44000
NANTES ☎ 40.89.50.77
Loisirs Accueil Mayenne,
B.P.343, 84 avenue Robert-Buron, 53018 LAVAL
Cedex ☎ 43.53.18.18
Loisirs Accueil Vendée,
8 place Napoléon, 85000 LA ROCHE-SUR-YON
☎ 51.62.08.24

RESORTS

 Angers *(Maine-et-Loire)*
Pop: 185,000
Tours 109 km, Paris 294 km
🛈 place Kennedy ☎ 41.88.69.93 and place de la
Gare ☎ 41.87.72.50

An elegant city rich in museums and treasures,
Angers stands on the River Maine, the 17-towered
military fortress built first to dominate the Loire
valley and in later centuries converted to more
domestic use as royal apartments for the Dukes of
Anjou and their court. With all the attractions of a
large city, Angers is an ideal base from which to
visit the châteaux of Anjou or, only five minutes
out of the city, to enjoy the fishing and watersports
facilities offered on the Lac de Maine.

● Ballooning: (Apr-Oct) min. six passengers.
  Enquire at the Tourist Office.
● Boat Hire: cabin cruisers to hire here and at
  Grez-Neuville.
● Camping: Lac de Maine ☎ 41.73.05.03
● Cycling: cycles can be hired from the SNCF
  station.
● Golf: 18h private course at Golf d'Angers,
  Moulin de Pistrait, St-Jean-des-Mauvrets,
  49320 Brissac Quince ☎ 41.91.96.56

 La Baule *(Loire-Atlantique)*
Pop: 15,000
Nantes 74 km, Paris 450 km
🛈 8 place Victoire ☎ 40.24.34.44

A smart and colourful seaside town on the Côte
d'Amour, with the lively fishing port of Le
Pouliguen sharing the long, sweeping bay.
Pavement cafés, tree-lined avenues, chic shops,
extensive watersports facilities, a championship
golf course and nearby horse racing (at Pornichet)
give this resort international appeal and attract
around 100,000 visitors each summer.

● Beach: vast curved safe and sandy beach.

● Camping: La Roseraie ☎ 40.60.46.66 and Les
  Ajoncs d'Or ☎ 40.60.33.29
● Casino: ☎ 40.60.20.23
● Cycling: cycles can be hired from the SNCF
  station.
● Golf: 18h private course at Golf d la Baule,
  Domaine de St-Denac, 44117 St-André-des-
  Eaux ☎ 40.60.46.18. This is a championship
  course with very fine greens (closed Tues in
  winter).
● Riding: Centre Equestre de La Baule
  ☎ 40.60.39.29
● Sailing: numerous sailing and waterskiing
  schools. Club de Voile Jean-Yves Derrien
  ☎ 40.60.63.76 and Centre de Voile Pajot
  ☎ 40.24.34.85
● Tennis: 24 courts at Country Club, 113 avenue
  de Lattre ☎ 40.60.23.44 and 18 courts at
  Sporting Club, avenue de l'Etoile
  ☎ 40.60.28.73
● Thalassotherapy: La-Baule-les-Pins,
  28 boulevard de l'Océan ☎ 40.24.30.97
● Walking: follow the 'sentiers de Douaniers'
  along the rocky coastline.

 Jard-sur-Mer *(Vendée)*
Pop: 2,000
Les Sables d'Olonne 20 km, Paris 480 km
🛈 place de la Liberté ☎ 51.33.40.47

Small seaside resort on the Côte de Lumière
backed by extensive pine and oak forest. The
atmosphere here is much quieter than at the larger
resorts along this Vendée coast, ideal for those
who wish to enjoy the calmer pursuits of walking,
cycling and fishing. There is a small pleasure-boat
harbour and the beaches are popular with
windsurfers.

● Beach: dune-fringed sand, shingle and rock.
● Camping: Les Ecureuils ☎ 51.90.44.38 and
  L'Océon d'Or ☎ 51.90.36.05

 Laval *(Mayenne)*
Pop: 55,000
Angers 74 km, Paris 300 km
🛈 place du 11 Novembre ☎ 43.53.09.39

Attractive and historic town built on both banks of
the River Mayenne and crossed by a beautiful
thirteenth-century hump-backed bridge.
Considered the father of the *naïf* school of art, the
artist Henri Rousseau (known as the *Douanier* or
Customs Officer) was born here. Today two of his
paintings are exhibited within the château, the
medieval home of the Counts of Laval. The
winding river valley offers peaceful fishing and
boat excursions, while the old town and garden
(Bout du Monde) of nearby Château-Gontier are
well worth exploring.

● Boat Hire: houseboats to hire here on the
  Mayenne river.
● Camping: Camping du Potier ☎ 43.53.68.8
● Golf: 9h private course overlooking the river

at Golf de Laval, Le Jariel, 53000 Change les Laval ☎ 43.53.16.03
- Riding: Club Hippique, Bois de l'Huisserie.

 Longeville-sur-Mer *(Vendée)*
Pop: 2,000
La Roche-sur-Yon 28, Paris 448 km
🄸 rue Georges-Clemenceau ☎ 51.33.34.64 (Jun-Sep)

Like Jard-sur-Mer, this is a small, quiet resort which has grown up between the pine and oak forests and the sea. Windsurfing is popular here and there are also facilities for tennis, canoeing and riding.

- Beach: 7-km sand and pebble beach with dunes.
- Camping: Les Dunes ☎ 51.33.32.93

 Mamers *(Sarthe)*
Pop: 7,000
Alençon 25 km, Paris 183 km
🄸 place de la République ☎ 43.97.60.63

Close to the Normandie-Maine Regional Park, Mamers can provide all the pleasures of a rural holiday combined with the usual facilities of a small town. An area with a rich and historical past as well as great pastoral beauty (every tree seems full of mistletoe), the artist, walker or cyclist will find much to appeal. An annual marathon is held here in June, an event which attracts over 1,000 amateur runners. Its name, incidentally, derives from a Roman soldier, Mamertus, who had some local connections, long forgotten, and the final letter 's' is pronounced.

- Camping: La Grille ☎ 43.97.68.30
- Cycling: bicycles to hire from 2 boulevard Victor-Hugo ☎ 43.97.60.26
- Fishing: category 1 fishing in the Bienne and category 2 in the Orne and Dive rivers.
- Golf: new 21h golf course at Golf de Bellême St-Martin, St-Martin du Vieux Bellême, 61130 Bellême ☎ 33.73.15.35
- Micro-lighting: or, as they term it in France, ULM (Ultra-Léger-Motorisé), is practised 5 km out of Mamers at Commerveil.
- Riding: Club Hippique du Saosnois ☎ 43.97.63.23 offers treks through the Perseigne national forest.
- Tennis: three courts to hire at Tennis Club (complexe de loisirs) ☎ 43.97.93.68
- Walking: literature detailing short-distance walks in the Saosnois area (between the Bellème and Perseigne forests) is available from the Tourist Office.

 Le Mans *(Sarthe)*
Pop: 160,000
Tours 82 km, Paris 202 km
🄸 38 place de la République ☎ 43.28.17.22

Since the turn of the century Le Mans has owed its notoriety to the fact that the 24-hour endurance race is held here each June. However, this is first and foremost a river town, with great artistic and historic treasures – cathedral, museums and old town undergoing careful restoration. The artificial lakes at Tuffé and Saint-Calais offer canoeing, bathing and fishing amongst other amenities, and short or extended boat trips along the Sarthe, Oudon and Mayenne rivers allow for leisurely appreciation of the magnificent countryside.

- Boat Trips: leave Le Mans regularly for short trips including a meal, or there are two-eight berth cruisers to hire for longer trips, available from Sarthe Plaisance, quai A. Lalande ☎ 43.28.82.00
- Camping: Camping La Chataigneraie at Yvre-l'Eveque ☎ 43.89.60.68 where there is also a children's activity and amusement park 'Papea' close by, with play area, pony rides, pedalos, etc.
- Golf: 18h private course at Golf du Mans, route de Tours, Mulsanne, 72230 Arnage ☎ 43.42.00.36
- Horse-drawn Travel: horse-drawn caravans leave from Laigné-en-Belin ☎ 43.21.51.44

 Nantes *(Loire-Atlantique)*
Pop: 430,000
Angers 89 km, Paris 383 km
🄸 place du Commerce ☎ 40.47.04.51

Large university and cathedral city on the Loire and a busy commercial and economic centre. The city's oldest sections are worth exploring as is the Château des Ducs de Bretagne which contains three museums. The opera, theatre, concerts and museums make Nantes a great cultural centre, while the attractions of the coast and seaside are within easy reach, with the popular resort of La Baule or the small fishing ports of Croisic and La Turballe as options.

- Boat Trips: travel in glass-sided futuristic boats on luxury gastronomic cruises up the River Erdre, passing manor houses and châteaux along the banks. Bookable from Grands Bateaux de l'Erdre, quai de Versailles ☎ 40.20.24.50
- Golf: 18h private course at Golf de Nantes, 44360 Vigneux de Bretagne ☎ 40.63.25.82

 Noirmoutier, Ile de *(Vendée)*
Pop: 5,000
Nantes 82 km, Paris 470 km
🄸 Office de Tourisme ☎ 51.39.80.71

Attractive small island just offshore from Fromentine and accessible either at low tide (three hours every day) across the Gois causeway, or by toll bridge (open 24 hours a day). For the casual visitor, the island is also served by boats from Pornic directly onto the plage des Dames, one of the many lovely sandy beaches. Salt flats cover the interior of the island, in complete contrast to the pretty pine-sheltered inlets which dot the coast. Sea-fishing trips, riding along the beaches, tennis (27 courts), archery, sailing (seven schools) and windsurfing are all available for the active holidaymaker.

● Camping: (in Noirmoutier-en-l'Ile) Le Clair Matin ☎ 51.39.05.56, (in Barbatre) Les Onchères ☎ 51.39.81.31 and (in La Guerinière) La Sourderie ☎ 51.39.81.76

 Pornic (*Loire-Atlantique*)
Pop: 3,000
Nantes 50 km, Paris 433 km
🏠 place du Môle ☎ 40.82.04.40

A small and picturesque fishing port and resort which is traditional in character. Lying on the Côte de Jade, a name taken from the colour of the sea, there are numerous small sandy beaches and rocky coves and regular boat trips to the Ile de Noirmoutier.

● Camping: La Madrague ☎ 40.82.06.73
● Casino: le Môle.
● Golf: 9h private course at Golf de Pornic, 49 bis boulevard de l'Ocean, Ste-Marie-sur-Mer, 44210 Pornic ☎ 40.82.06.69 (closed Tues – low green fees).

 Sablé-sur-Sarthe (*Sarthe*)
Pop: 12,000
Le Mans 48 km, Paris 251 km
🏠 place Raphaël-Elizé ☎ 43.95.00.60

A pleasant town situated on both banks of the Sarthe river, and an ideal spot from which to explore by car, foot, balloon, horse or boat. Picturesque old villages, such as Asnières-sur-Vègre, follow the meandering course of the river.

● Balloon Flights: Club Aérostat de Solesmes ☎ 43.95.09.93 offer early morning or late afternoon flights.
● Boat Hire: cabin cruisers to hire at the port from France-Anjou Navigation ☎ 43.95.14.42, to travel along the Maine basin.
● Camping: La Prairie du Château ☎ 43.95.42.61
● Cycling: cycles can be hired from the SNCF station.
● Fishing: category 2 river fishing.
● Riding: accompanied riding trips at Sillé-le-Guillaume ☎ 43.20.11.91 (weekends and every day in August). Horse-drawn vehicles can be hired by the week for slow and leisurely travel through the countryside from La Farfollière ☎ 43.95.00.31
● Tennis: eight courts to hire ☎ 43.95.02.02

 Les Sables-d'Olonne (*Vendée*)
Pop: 17,000
La-Roche-sur-Yon 36 km, Paris 453 km
🏠 rue du Maréchal-Leclerc ☎ 51.32.03.28

Probably the most popular family seaside resort on the Vendée coast, Les Sables-d'Olonne is literally 'action-packed', with a long, south-facing beach, activities and entertainments, yacht marina and fishing port, zoo and aquarium. Its magnificent sandy beach and exceptionally sunny climate, on a par with that enjoyed in the south of France, mean that its season extends virtually all year round.

● Camping: Les Roses ☎ 51.21.16.50 and Les Dunes ☎ 51.32.31.21
● Casinos: Casino de la Plage and Casino des Sports.
● Cycling: cycles can be hired from the SNCF station.
● Languages: French language study courses are held here. Details from Paris Langue International ☎ 45.08.03.20

 St-Brévin-les-Pins (*Loire-Atlantique*)
Pop: 9,000
Pornic 17 km, Paris 444 km
🏠 10 rue de l'Eglise ☎ 40.27.24.32

Up-and-coming resort, putting great effort into the sports and activities it is able to offer. There are vast expanses of forest and spacious stretches of sandy beach, plus a lively night life with casino and discos. Impressive connecting bridge with St-Nazaire.

● Beach: 8-km fine sandy beach interspersed with large rocks.
● Camping: La Courance ☎ 40.27.22.91 and Les Pierres Couchées ☎ 40.27.85.64
● Casino: boulevard de l'Océan ☎ 40.27.21.51 (Jun-Sep).
● Fishing: sea and freshwater fishing. Particularly popular here is shrimping, 1 hour before and after low tide.
● Cycling: hire from Cycl Hic, allée de la Tour Carrée ☎ 40.27.34.33 and SPAD, avenue du Maréchal Foch ☎ 40.27.25.34
● Deep-sea Diving: those already holding diving certificates of competence can join exploration parties with the Club Subaquatique de la Côte de Jade, avenue Julien Grellier ☎ 40.27.20.52
● Football: a team of ex-professionals, led by Jean-Vincent, offer weekly courses for boys (8-16) who are physically fit and able to undergo structured and energetic training. Clubs are also welcome. Contact Stages Vacances Jean-Vincent, Hôtel de Ville, 44250 St-Brévin-les-Pins ☎ 40.39.04.09
● Riding: Air et Soleil, l'Ermitage ☎ 40.27.85.64 and Huchepie, allée Joëlle ☎ 40.39.96.69
● Sailing: beginners and improvers (seven years

upwards) are offered tuition with the Club Nautique de la Côte de Jade, B.P.28, 44250 St-Brévin-l'Océan ☎ 40.27.41.93 (Mar-Nov).
- Tennis: nine courts to hire at Parc Municipal des Sports de la Saulzaie ☎ 40.27.15.26
- Ultra-light: travel as a passenger and take magnificent aerial photographs with Delta-Club de la Côte de Jade, prairie de Grandville. Enquire at the Tourist Office for details.

 St-Hilaire-de-Riez-Sion (*Vendée*)
Pop: 6,000
Nantes 78 km, Paris 448 km
🆔 21 place Gaston-Pateau ☎ 51.54.31.97

Reclaimed marshland extends behind the coastal dunes here in a contrasting landscape of fields, moors and pine woods. The beaches are sandy and spacious, interspersed by rocky headlands, and the little port of Sion has anchorage for small fishing boats and is in the process of completing a pleasure boat marina. Close to the lively fishing port and modern resort of St-Gilles-Croix-de-Vie.

- Beach: sandy and supervised.
- Camping: La Plage de Riez Municipal ☎ 51.54.36.59
- Fishing: river and sea fishing.
- Riding: avenue de la Faye.
- Tennis: 14 courts to hire at Tennis Club Riez Ocean, rue de l'Atlantique ☎ 51.54.46.81

 St-Jean-de-Monts (*Vendée*)
Pop: 5,000
Nantes 76 km, Paris 456 km
🆔 67 esplanade de la Mer ☎ 51.58.00.48

Lively and highly modern seaside resort town with an excellent spacious beach which is ideal for families. There are plenty of organised sporting activities to keep everyone amused.

- Art: pottery, drawing and silk-painting classes are held every day in July and August by the Club Art et Vacances at the Palais des Congrès (adults in the morning, children in the afternoon). Between June and September children and adults can attend pottery classes in the Atelier de la Dunette, chemin des Bosses, Orouët ☎ 51.58.88.77
- Beach: wide, sandy and gently shelving.
- Camping: L'Abri des Pins ☎ 51.58.83.86 and Les Amiaux ☎ 51.58.22.22
- Casino: la Pastourelle ☎ 51.58.01.02
- Golf: 9h public course at Sporting Golf, 85160 St-Jean-de-Monts ☎ 51.58.13.06
- Riding: Club Hippique et Poney Club du Havre de Vie, route des Sables, Orouët ☎ 51.58.27.30 and Centre Equestre de la Buzelière ☎ 51.58.64.80 offer treks in the forest or along the beach.
- Sailing: Cercle Nautique Montois, avenue de l'Estacade offers tuition for beginners and improvers ☎ 51.58.01.80

- Tennis: tuition for children and beginners in both tennis and golf, available from Tennis et Golf de Marais, 48 avenue de Baisse ☎ 51.58.17.53. Eleven courts to hire at La Parée Jesus ☎ 51.58.01.54 and 12 courts at Parc des Sports ☎ 51.58.23.56

 St-Nazaire (*Loire-Atlantique*)
Pop: 69,000
La Baule 17 km, Paris 439 km
🆔 place François Blancho ☎ 40.22.40.65

This is a predominantly modern city, having been rebuilt after massive destruction during the last war. Here some of the world's largest ships are constructed in the enormous estuary shipyards, within sight of the impressive toll bridge which crosses the Loire at this point, thus providing swift connection with St-Brévin-les-Pins and the coast beyond. Good shopping and busy markets, fishermen's auctions on the quayside, and the submarine base, scene of a daring and spectacular Anglo-Canadian raid against the German U-boat base on 28 March 1942. The strange and ancient megaliths in the surrounding countryside offer a direct contrast with the modern city.

- Beach: good coastal bathing at numerous beaches and creeks nearby, particularly at Saint-Marc-sur-Mer.
- Boat Trips: fascinating 1 hr 30 min trips around the massive port installations and beneath the elegant new road bridge, and visiting the submarine basin where the French polar submarine *l'Espadon* is open to the public. Trips are also possible (by bus) around the shipyard wharves, to observe the construction work in progress. These trips are bookable through the Tourist Office. Numerous outlets offer guided trips through the Brière Regional Park. Good places to start from are St-Joachim and St-Lyphard, small villages typical of the area.
- Camping: Camping de l'Eve ☎ 40.91.90.65 and, at St-Marc-sur-Mer, Camping les Jaunais ☎ 40.91.90.60
- Canoeing: on the stretch of water known as the Etang du Bois Joalland which is also a pleasant walking area.
- Cycling: cycles can be hired from the SNCF station.
- Golf: 18h private course in the Regional Park (Parc de Brière) at Golf de la Bretesche Missillac, 44160 Pontchâteau ☎ 40.88.30.03
- Riding: La Chaussée Neuve, St-André-des-Eaux ☎ 40.01.24.64 and at Les Parcs, St-Lyphard ☎ 40.91.32.06
- Walking: follow the Sentiers de Douanier along the coast and discover the 20 or so beaches and secluded creeks.

Saumur *(Maine-et-Loire)*
Pop: 34,000
Angers 45 km, Paris 293 km
🛈 25 rue Beaurepaire ☎ 41.51.03.06

Unique in France, and renowned world-wide for its Cadre Noir cavalry school, the old equestrian traditions are still maintained at the National Riding School where visitors can watch the horses being schooled. Noted also for the fine white wine produced in the surrounding vineyards, Saumur is a beautiful château town (twinned with Warwick in England), with some fine stone buildings and a massive bridge across the Loire. Ideal as a base for exploring the great and innumerable châteaux in the region.

- Camping: L'Ile d'Offard ☎ 41.67.45.00
- Cycling: cycles can be hired from the SNCF station.
- Fishing: category 2 fishing on the Loire.
- Riding: Centre de Tourisme Equestre, La Métairie, Trèves-Cunault ☎ 41.67.92.43

La Tranche-sur-Mer *(Vendée)*
Pop: 2,000
La Roche-sur-Yon 40 km, Paris 456 km
🛈 place Liberté ☎ 51.30.33.96

A small and pleasant family seaside resort which, like others along this Vendée coast, is backed by oak and pine tree forests. A popular rendezvous with the windsurfing fraternity, the beach is wide and south-facing and has, in the past, been commended for its quality by an award of the official Ruban Bleu. Long days of summer sunshine and mild springs mean that millions of tulips, crocuses and daffodils bloom in the Floralies Park in the town, providing a riot of colour in March and April.

- Beach: large, pine-backed and gently shelving.
- Camping: Camping le Jard ☎ 51.30.48.79 and Les Préveils ☎ 51.30.30.52
- Fishing: canal, river and sea fishing.
- Micro-lighting: beginners can attempt this sport at U.L.M. Côte de Lumière, Ecole de Pilotage, route des Angles ☎ 51.27.40.97
- Tennis: 12 courts to hire.
- Watersports: numerous outlets for hiring equipment on the beach.

PICARDIE

Administrative
Centre: Amiens
Population: 1,678,600
Area: 19,411 sq km

Départements:
02 Aisne
60 Oise
80 Somme

The most familiar image of Picardy is of long country roads, flanked by tall poplars, leading across gentle farmland; of low horizons, flat pasture and a minor river with a name of infamy, the Somme.

At small villages, sometimes a mere group of homes at a crossroads, real life stopped three-quarters of a century ago with the slaughter, in millions, of the youth of Europe – villages like Beaumont-Hamel, whose name joins with melancholy pride those of Crécy and Agincourt. The poplars were grown to hide the movements of infantry and cavalry forces from enemy eyes. The poppies of Picardy, and of Flanders to the east, had no such military purpose. They just happened to lift their heads in those summertime fields of 1916 and 1917 when a million men of 30 nations laid down theirs in death. Today the Somme links together small lakes, and men come here to fish for trout, pike and eels. The Bay of the Somme runs from the sand hills of Marquenterre to the mouth of the Authie, land recovered from the sea, and now, with its marshes and lakes, a fine refuge for birdlife.

The coast of Picardy features long stretches of sand, ideal at Fort-Mahon-Plage and Quend-Plage for sand yachting and windsurfing, as it is all along the 20 km of Marquenterre coast. There are small, attractive yachting harbours and fishing ports at St-Valéry-sur-Somme and Le Crotoy and it is possible to sail the Somme in barges from a base at Amiens. The market gardens (*les hortillonages*) of the canal stretch through the city and can be toured and visited by *bateau à cornet*.

Picardy is rich in cathedrals – Senlis, Beauvais, Noyon, Soissons and Laon, the ancient capital of Carolingian (Charlemagne's) France – but pride of place must go to the thirteenth-century Gothic cathedral of Notre-Dame at Amiens, the largest in France and amongst the most beautiful in the world.

There is fine walking country in the forest of Crécy where, in 1346, the English longbow defeated the French archers, in the Marne champagne vineyards by Château Thierry, once the battlefields of World War I, and amongst pretty villages. The Remembrance Route tours the 120 war museums and cemeteries – French, British, Australian, German, Canadian – some vast, some modest and restrained, all of them sad.

For those whose schooldays left them remembering only one date in history, the small harbour of St-Valéry-sur-Somme will have special significance. For it was from here that William the Conqueror set sail in 1066 and fundamentally altered the course of history for both England and France.

PRACTICAL TOURIST INFORMATION

General information on the region can be obtained by telephoning or writing to the Comité Régional du Tourisme (CRT) office, while specific booklets are produced detailing camping, hotels and self-catering gîte accommodation. These can be obtained by writing to the tourist board office for the département (CDT) of your choice:

Regional Tourist Board
Comité Régional du Tourisme (CRT), 11 Mail Albert 1er, 80000 AMIENS ☎ 22.97.37.37

Départements
Aisne (02): Comité Départemental du Tourisme (CDT), 1 rue Saint-Martin, 02000 LAON ☎ 23.20.45.54
Oise (60): Comité Départemental du Tourisme (CDT), 1 rue Villiers-de-l'Ile-Adam, B.P.222,

60008 BEAUVAIS Cedex ☎ 44.45.82.12
Somme (80): Comité Départemental du Tourisme
(CDT), 21 rue Ernest-Cauvin, 80000 AMIENS
☎ 22.92.26.39

SELF-CATERING ACCOMMODATION

The following British operators offer self-catering accommodation in the area:

Angel Travel, 47 High Street, Central Chambers, Tonbridge TN9 1SD ☎ 0732 361115
Gîtes de France, 178 Piccadilly, London W1V 9DB ☎ 01-493 3480
Hoseasons Holidays Abroad, Sunway House, Lowestoft NR32 3LT ☎ 0502 500555
David Newman's French Collection, P.O. Box 73,

40 Upperton Road, Eastbourne BN21 4AW ☎ 0323 410347
Vacances en Campagne, Bignor, Pulborough RH20 1QD ☎ 07987 433
VFB Holidays, 1 St Margaret's Terrace, Cheltenham GL50 4DT ☎ 0242 526338

SPORTS AND ACTIVITIES

For interesting holiday ideas, contact the Loisirs Accueil office for the area of your choice:

Loisirs Accueil Aisne,
B.P.116, 1 rue Saint-Martin, 02006 LAON Cedex ☎ 23.20.45.54
Loisirs Accueil Somme,
21 rue Ernest-Cauvin, 80000 AMIENS ☎ 22.92.26.39

RESORTS

 Beauvais *(Oise)*
Pop: 55,000
Amiens 60 km, Paris 75 km
🏠 rue Malherbe ☎ 44.45.08.18

Beauvais is at the centre of a great agricultural spread of fields. Above them the Gothic cathedral of St-Pierre, whose choir vault is the highest in the world, rises to view from every side. The medieval city was gravely damaged during World War II and the famous tapestry works, established in the seventeenth century, were evacuated at the outbreak of war to the Gobelin factory in Paris. The National Gallery of Tapestry, next to the cathedral, displays the techniques of the craft and some superb finished works.

- Camping: Municipal ☎ 44.02.00.22
- Cycling: cycles can be hired from the SNCF station.
- Golf: 9h private course at Golf du Val Secret, Ferme de Farsoy, 02400 Bresles
  ☎ 23.69.01.80

 Cayeux-sur-Mer *(Somme)*
Pop: 2,000
St-Valéry-sur-Somme 13 km, Paris 190 km
🏠 boulevard du Général-Sizaire ☎ 22.26.61.15

A lively fishing port and family seaside resort offering sailing, sand yachting and sea fishing trips as well as riding, tennis, and archery.

- Beach: pebbly, but sandy at low tide with a long boardwalk fronting the pleasant little changing cabins.
- Camping: Camping de Brighton
  ☎ 22.26.71.04 and Le Canal ☎ 22.26.62.84
- Casino: ☎ 22.26.60.06
- Riding: Ferme de la Vieille Eglise, route d'Eu
  ☎ 22.26.63.23 and Poney Vert, Centre de Loisirs, rue du Général-Leclerc
  ☎ 22.26.62.36
- Sailing: Centre de Loisirs Permanent, rue du Maréchal-Leclerc ☎ 22.26.62.36 offers all-year-round one-week courses for children (under 12) and adults. Windsurfing classes are given for beginners or improvers.

Chantilly *(Oise)*
Pop: 10,000
Beauvais 43 km, Paris 50 km
🏠 avenue du Maréchal Joffré ☎ 44.57.08.58

Chantilly is a very chic race course, perhaps the only one to have a 'fairy-tale' château overlooking the track and swans gracing its sides. This is where Thoroughbreds are bred, trained and raced for such trophies as the Prix du Jockey Club, and the vast eighteenth-century stables now form a museum devoted to the horse, the Musée Vivant du Cheval. Bridle paths thread their way through the elegant town, past smart homes and across broad avenues. In Chantilly Forest, originally laid

out as a deer park, there are lovely walks along the *Grande Randonnée* trails where, in spring, the richly fragrant *muguet* (lily of the valley) grows wild. Very close to Paris, there is an excellent choice of golf courses and good cycling terrain.

- Cycling: cycles can be hired from the SNCF station.
- Golf: very good 27h private course at Golf de Chantilly, 60500 Vineuil Saint Firmin
  ☎ 44.57.04.43; also 36h private course at Golf de l'Icl Lamorlaye, Rond Point du Gd Cerf Lys-Chantilly, 60260 Lamorlaye
  ☎ 44.21.26.00; very good 18h private course where internationals are played, at Golf de Morfontaine, 60520 La Chapelle-en-Serval
  ☎ 44.54.68.27

 Compiègne *(Oise)*
Pop: 43,000
Beauvais 57 km, Paris 82 km
🏠 place Hôtel de Ville ☎ 44.40.01.00

The Compiègne Forest, favourite hunting territory for successive French monarchs, is just as popular today with those looking for the peace of the countryside. Buried in the woods are small hotels ready to cater for their needs. *Grande Randonnée* trails lead the visitor through the beautiful woodlands, broken here by narrow gorges, there by streams with linking ponds, the whole area skirted by a ridge of hills. Oak, beech, pine and lime trees flourish and, as in the forest of Chantilly, the lily of the valley grows wild, an event celebrated in May by the Lily of the Valley Festival. This is a fine centre from which to explore *la douce France*.

- Boat Trips: half-day barge cruises go from here to Rethondes where, in a clearing in the forest, a railway carriage stands, the site of the signing of armistice papers for both world wars. There are also full day trips to Noyon.
- Camping: Hippodrome ☎ 44.20.28.58
- Cycling: cycles can be hired from the SNCF station.
- Golf: fairly flat 18h private course established in 1895, at Golf de Compiègne, avenue Royale, 60200 Compiègne ☎ 44.40.15.73

 Le Crotoy *(Somme)*
Pop: 2,500
Abbeville 21 km, Paris 184 km
🏠 Office de Tourisme ☎ 22.27.81.97

Le Crotoy and St-Valéry face each other across the Somme estuary, two busy little fishing harbours and seaside resorts. A small steam railway connects them both for the benefit of visitors. This is essentially bird country. Migrating birds rest here before their long flights, and the nearby Marquenterre ornithological park (Apr-Nov) is an important bird sanctuary. The waters, and often the quays and jetties, are alive with cockles, eels, crustaceans and prawns and the long, sandy beaches might have been as purpose-made for sand yachting as the dunes seem for riding.

- Camping: Le Pré Fleuri ☎ 22.27.81.53
- Casino: ☎ 22.27.05.73
- Riding: ☎ 22.27.80.80
- Sailing: Centre Nautique de la Baie de la Somme ☎ 22.27.83.11

 Fort-Mahon-Plage (*Somme*)
Pop: 1,000
Abbeville 35 km, Paris 200 km
🖼 Office de Tourisme ☎ 22.27.70.75

The beach here, like that of the neighbouring resort of Quend-Plage-les-Pins, offers spacious sandy expanses which are ideal for sand yachting, the speciality of this part of Picardie. Dunes and pine trees are extensive and attract walkers and ornithologists, while both children and adults will find that Aqualand, the indoor water fun park, has great appeal on cooler days.

- Beach: sandy and safe.
- Camping: Le Royon ☎ 22.23.40.30 and Le Soleil ☎ 22.27.70.06
- Casino: ☎ 22.23.36.37
- Golf: 18h private course at Golf de Nampont-Saint-Martin, 80120 Rue ☎ 22.25.00.20
- Riding: Centre Equestre l'Etrier, rue de l'Authie ☎ 22.27.45.58 offers rides along the beach and through the countryside.
- Sailing: and windsurfing school at Association Fort-Mahonnaise Activités Nautiques (AFMAN) ☎ 22.27.75.78
- Sand Yachting: hire possible on both beaches.

 Noyon (*Oise*)
Pop: 14,000
Laon 54 km, Paris 105 km
🖼 place de l'Hôtel de Ville ☎ 44.44.21.88

The large cathedral dominates Noyon, a town of some interest historically, for it was the birthplace of Calvin (1509) the Protestant reformer. The surrounding country is noted for its cherries and gooseberries and, early in July each year, the town celebrates this abundance with a *Fête des Fruits Rouges*. Standing between the canals that run parallel with the River Oise, and much rebuilt

since the war, this is a quiet little town, although nearby there is the busy and popular Ailette nautical park, a public recreation area for watersports and golf.

- Boat Trips: barge cruises to Compiègne.
- Golf: north towards St-Quentin, 9h private course at Golf du Mesnil-St-Laurent, 02720 Homblières ☎ 23.68.19.48; also 9h public course at Golf de l'Ailette, 02000 Laon ☎ 23.24.83.99

 Poix-de-Picardie (*Somme*)
Pop: 2,000
Amiens 28 km, Paris 120 km
🖼 rue St-Denis ☎ 22.90.08.25

A rural resort to the south west of Amiens with pleasant signposted walks which make a tourist circuit of the wooded Evoissons valley.

- Camping: Bois des Pecheurs ☎ 22.90.11.71
- Fishing: category 1 fishing on the Poix.
- Golf: flat 18h private course at Golf d'Amiens, 80115 Querrieu ☎ 22.91.02.04

 St-Valéry-sur-Somme (*Somme*)
Pop: 1,500
Abbeville 19 km, Paris 185 km
🖼 23 rue de la Ferté ☎ 22.60.93.50

Unspoilt small harbour at the mouth of the Somme from which William the Conqueror sailed in 1066, a fact celebrated annually by the town in June. St-Valéry has maintained many of its historical sites and has a pleasant tree-lined esplanade which looks out over the bay dotted with fishing boats and yachts. A steam train operates tours around the Baie de Somme between Le Crotoy and Cayeux-sur-Mer and the Tourist Office can supply maps to follow for theme walks.

- Camping: La Croix l'Abbé ☎ 22.60.81.46
- Canoeing: beginners can learn on the canal and on the sea with Sport Nautique Valéricain ☎ 22.26.91.64; also sailing classes.
- Cycling: cycles can be hired here. Enquire at the Tourist Office.
- Fishing: salt and freshwater fishing.
- Walking: GR125 towards the Basque coast.

POITOU-CHARENTES

*Administrative
Centre: Poitiers
Population: 1,528,100
Area: 25,790 sq km*

*Départements:
16 Charente
17 Charente-Maritime
79 Deux-Sèvres
86 Vienne*

*Regional Park:
Parc Naturel Régional
du Marais-Poitevin –
Val de Sèvre et
Vendée, Maison du
Parc, La Ronde, 17170
Courcon
☎ 46.27.82.44*

While the long arm of the Ile de Ré reaches out into the Atlantic, the Ile d'Oléron almost completes the protective encirclement of the big bay of La Rochelle, where low white houses are bleached in the sun, green shutters shade the windows and pink and red hollyhocks stand on sentry duty.

Inshore, what was once sea is now reclaimed land. The one-time Gulf of Poitou has been drained and banked against the sea, then gridded with canals to become the Charente-Maritime of today. At its coastal heart stands the ancient port of La Rochelle, always an important port but now, with its massive yachting harbour of Les Minimes (3,000 berths), one of Europe's largest marinas. After the reclamation, beaches appeared and with them, under sunshine as sustained and hot as that of the Côte d'Azur, came seaside resorts, both fashionable as at Royan, and for all the family as at La Palmyre.

The sand dunes have been tamed in their wild flight by pine plantations. The salt marshes are now friendly breeding grounds for the Portuguese oyster, most famous from the Ile de Ré, the Ile d'Oléron and Marennes. The region yields 40,000 tonnes of oysters each year and provides a living for 25,000 people. The *bouchots* (wooden stakes) of the mussel farmers now stud the coastline of the Ile d'Oléron and offshore at Fouras, Brouage and Esnandes.

There are 480 km of Atlantic coast here, and the beaches, flanked by dunes and pines, are bathed in over 2,000 hours of sun each year, Such is the climate that, in St-Trojan, a Mimosa Festival is held as early as February to celebrate the beauty of the golden wattle. In summer, the village markets display Charentais melons, goats' milk and cheese, grapes, apricots and honey and, at Niort, the candied stems of angelica.

History has left its mark on the area. At Saintes, on the Charente, once the Roman capital of western Gaul, stand the ruins of an amphitheatre and the triumphal Arc de Germanicus, erected in AD 19 in honour of the Emperor Tiberius. At Sanxay there is a second-century Roman temple and baths as well as an amphitheatre to seat 8,000.

In the eleventh century, the Christian armies were engaged in reconquering Spain from the Muslims. In homage to St-Jacques (Santiago in Spanish), patron saint of these crusading armies, pilgrims from all over Europe made the long march to Compostela de Santiago in northern Spain, along well-defined routes, the most frequented of these being that from the north east through Châtellerault, Poitiers, Aulnay, Saintes and Pons, thence to Bordeaux and across the Pyrénées into Spain. During the 200 years of this religious migration, half a million pilgrims passed each way through the Saintes region, and to succour these travellers some 300 churches and convents were built. The Romanesque architecture of Niort, Angoulême, Chauvigny, Parthenay, Aulnay, Confolens and Poitiers stands witness to the medieval act of Christian pilgrimage.

Since the Middle Ages, but for the most part during the seventeenth and eighteenth centuries, the work of draining and reclaiming the former bay of Poitou, to the north of Niort, has recovered 411,170 hectares in what is now the Val-de-Sèvre Regional Park. Within it rests that unique and fascinating stretch of Poitou fens called the Marais Poitevin. A network of meadows at either side of the Sèvre-Niortaise river, ribboned with canals and bordered by willows and poplars, ash and alder, gives it its nickname 'Green Venice'. The farmers here work their land from *plates* (flat-bottomed punts), and carry their produce and livestock with them on board these shallow craft through peaceful canals both wide (*rigoles*) and narrow *(conches)*. The visitor can share this idyllic scene with heron, plover and woodcock, oriole, jay and kingfisher, for boats are for hire at the villages of Arçais, Coulon, Damvix and La Garette. To the south there are river cruises on the Charente between Rochefort and Angoulême, and day cruises between Saintes and Jarnac pass through the cognac country.

The region has always been a prosperous one. The distilling of a relatively mediocre local wine into a magnificent brandy has contributed much to the wealth of the countryside. Over 250 million bottles of cognac are produced here every year. The apéritif, Pineau de Charente, is made by mixing fresh grape must with cognac, and is drunk chilled.

In addition to the thirteenth-century château at Cognac, now used as a storage cellar, there are many other fine châteaux to be visited or admired from a distance: the Château du Chilleau at Sanxay, the magnificent Château de Verteuil near Ruffec, Château Echire near Niort, Oiron, St-Loup-sur-Thouet, the medieval château at Dampierre-sur-Boutonne, and the châteaux at Touffu and St-Medard.

A rich area indeed in history and architecture; rich too in its seaside sands, dunes and pines. Perhaps the richest pleasure of all, however, is the memory of a pastoral scene – gentle water beneath a curtaining of trees, a flat-bottomed punt being poled from one field to another under a quiet sky and, standing in the bow of the vessel, a goat looking with interest towards the approaching bank.

PRACTICAL TOURIST INFORMATION

General information on the region can be obtained by telephoning or writing to the Comité Régional du Tourisme (CRT) office, while specific booklets are produced detailing camping, hotel and self-catering gîte *accommodation. These can be obtained by writing to the tourist board office of the* département *(CDT) of your choice:*

Regional Tourist Board
Comité Régional du Tourisme (CRT), B.P.56, 86002 POITIERS Cedex ☎ 49.88.38.94

Départements
Charente (16): Office Départemental du Tourisme (ODT), place de la Gare, 16000 ANGOULEME ☎ 45.92.27.57
Charente-Maritime (17): Comité Départemental du Tourisme (CDT), 11 bis, rue des Augustins, B.P.1152, 17008 LA ROCHELLE ☎ 46.41.43.33
Deux-Sèvres (79): Office Départemental du Tourisme (ODT), 74 rue Alsace-Lorraine, 79000 NIORT ☎ 49.24.76.79
Vienne (86): Office Départemental du Tourisme (ODT), B.P.287, 11 rue Victor-Hugo, 86007 POITIERS Cedex ☎ 49.41.58.22

SELF-CATERING ACCOMMODATION

The following British operators offer self-catering accommodation in the area:

AA Motoring Holidays, P.O. Box 100, Fanum House, Halesowen B63 3BT ☎ 021-550 7401
Agencefrance Holidays, Lansdowne Place, 17 Holdenhurst Road, Bournemouth BH8 8EH ☎ 0202 299534
Allez France, 27 West Stret, Storrington, Pulborough RH20 4DZ ☎ 09066 2345
Angel Travel, 47 High Street, Central Chambers, Tonbridge TN9 1SD ☎ 0732 361115
Avon Europe, Lower Quinton, Stratford-upon-Avon, Warks CV37 8SG ☎ 0789 720130
Blakes Holidays, Wroxham, Norwich NR12 8DH ☎ 0603 784131
Bowhills Ltd, Swanmore, Southampton SO3 2QW ☎ 0489 877627
Brittany Ferries, The Brittany Centre, Wharf Road, Portsmouth PO2 8RU ☎ 0705 827701
Cosmos Motoring Holidays, Tourama House, 17 Homesdale Road, Bromley BR2 9LX ☎ 01-464 3121
Cresta Holidays, 32 Victoria Street, Altrincham WA14 1ET ☎ 0345 056511
Crystal Holidays, The Courtyard, Arlington Road, Surbiton KT6 6BW ☎ 01-399 5144
Dieppe Ferries Holidays, Weymouth Quay, Weymouth DT4 8DY ☎ 0305 777444

France Directe, 2 Church Street, Warwick CV34 4AB ☎ 0926 497989
France Voyages, 145 Oxford Street, London W1R 1TB ☎ 01-494 3155
Francophile Holidays, 9 Sheaf Street, Daventry NN1 4AA ☎ 0327 78103
French Life Motoring Holidays, 26 Church Road, Horsforth, Leeds LS18 5LG ☎ 0532 390077
French Travel Service, Georgian House, 69 Boston Manor Road, Brentford TW8 0JQ ☎ 01-568 8442
Gîtes de France, 178 Piccadilly, London W1V 9DB ☎ 01-493 3480
Hoseasons Holidays Abroad, Sunway House, Lowestoft NR32 3LT ☎ 0502 500555
Interhome, 383 Richmond Road, Twickenham TW1 2EF ☎ 01-891 1294
Kingsland Holidays, 1 Pounds Park Road, Plymouth PL3 4QP ☎ 0752 766822
Lagrange Vacances, 16/20 New Broadway, London W5 2XA ☎ 01-579 7311
Prime Time Holidays, 5a Market Square, Northampton NN1 2DL ☎ 0604 20996
Rendez-Vous France, Holiday House, 146/148 London Road, St Albans AL1 1PQ ☎ 0727 45400
Rentavilla, 27 High Street, Chesterton, Cambridge CB4 1NB ☎ 0223 323414
Sally Tours, Argyle Centre, York Street, Ramsgate CT11 9DS ☎ 0843 595566
SFV Holidays, Summer House, 68 Hernes Road, Summertown, Oxford OX2 7QL ☎ 0865 57738
Slipaway Holidays, 90 Newland Road, Worthing BN11 1LB ☎ 0903 821000
Starvillas, 25 High Street, Chesterton, Cambridge CB4 1ND ☎ 0223 311990
Sturge, Martin, 3 Lower Camden Place, Bath BA1 5JJ ☎ 0225 310623
Sun France, 3 Beaufort Gardens, London SW16 3BP ☎ 01-679 4562
Sunvista Holidays, 5a George Street, Warminster BA12 8QA ☎ 0985 217444
Vacances, 28 Gold Street, Saffron Walden CB10 1EJ ☎ 0799 25101
Vacances en Campagne, Bignor, Pulborough RH20 1QD ☎ 07987 433
Vacances France, 14 Bowthorpe Road, Wisbech PE13 2DX ☎ 0945 587830
Vacations, 60 Charles Street, Leicester LE1 1FB ☎ 0533 537758
VFB Holidays, 1 St Margaret's Terrace, Cheltenham GL50 4DT ☎ 0242 526338
Villa France, 15 Winchcombe Road, Frampton Cotterell, Bristol BS17 2AG ☎ 0454 772410

SPORTS AND ACTIVITIES

For unusual and interesting holiday ideas, contact the Loisirs Accueil office for the area of your choice:

Loisirs Accueil Charente
place Bouillaud, 16021 ANGOULEME
☎ 45.92.24.43
Loisirs Accueil Charente-Maritime,

11 bis, rue des Augustins, 17008 LA ROCHELLE
☎ 46.41.43.33
Loisirs Accueil Vienne
B.P.287, 11 rue Victor-Hugo, 86007 POITIERS
Cedex ☎ 49.41.58.22
Maison Poitou-Charentes,
68-70 rue du Cherche-Midi, 75006 PARIS
☎ 42.22.83.74

RESORTS

Châteauneuf-sur-Charente (*Charente*)
Pop: 4,000
Angoulême 20 km, Paris 430 km
🛈 la Mairie ☎ 45.97.12.42

Despite its name, Châteauneuf is an old town prettily situated in the Charente river valley, and with a very fine Romanesque church. In the tranquil and peaceful undulating countryside the orderly rows of vineyards are a reminder that this is cognac-producing country. Here pleasant walks and riverside pursuits attract those seeking to holiday in the heart of rural France. It makes ideal cycling country too.

● Camping: Le Bain des Dames ☎ 45.97.12.42
● Cycling: cycles can be hired from Garage Devige, rue du Général de Gaulle.
● Fishing: category 2 fishing on the Charente; also bathing.
● Golf: 9h private course at Golf d'Angoulême l'Hirondelle, Champfleuri, 16000 Angoulême ☎ 45.61.16.94 (closed Tues).

Châtelaillon (*Charente-Maritime*)
Pop: 6,000
La Rochelle 12 km, Paris 477 km
🛈 allée du Stade ☎ 46.56.26.97

A small port and, with Angoulins, a pleasant and popular family seaside resort, sharing 4 km of very good beach. At low tide the oyster beds and farms of the *boucholeurs* (mussel breeders) can be visited by means of tractors across the soft sand. There are summertime regattas in the little port and regular cruises to the isles of Ré, Aix and Oléron. The racecourse here holds afternoon and evening meetings during August and September.

● Beach: sandy and safe.
● Camping: Le Clos des Rivages ☎ 46.56.26.09 and L'Abbaye ☎ 46.56.42.19
● Casino: ☎ 46.56.26.24

Cognac (*Charente*)
Pop: 22,000
Angoulême 44 km, Paris 480 km
🛈 16 rue du XIV Juillet ☎ 45.82.10.71

Cognac is renowned the world over for its famous *eau-de-vie* ageing in cellars (*les chais*) along the banks of the Charente river. Hennessy, Martell and Rémy-Martin have their distilleries here and visits can be made to the cellars where the brandy is prepared with great care. A championship golf course, built by the Martell family, is close by, and, for those who are interested, the International Detective Film Festival is held here in April.

- Boat Trips: short or long trips, with or without meals on board, are bookable through the Tourist Office.
- Camping: Le Bain des Dames ☎ 45.82.67.33
- Cognac Houses: the following cognac houses welcome visitors, details of opening times available from the Tourist Office:
  Biscuit: Domaine de Lignères, 16170 Rouillac ☎ 45.21.88.88; Camus: 29 rue Marguerite de Navarre, 16100 Cognac ☎ 45.32.28.28; Hennessy: 1 rue de la Richonne, 16100 Cognac ☎ 45.82.52.22; Martell: place Edouard Martell, 16100 Cognac ☎ 45.82.44.44; Otard: Château de Cognac, 16100 Cognac ☎ 45.82.40.00; Polignac, pavillon du Laubaret ☎ 45.32.13.85
- Golf: undulating 18h public course at Golf du Cognac, St-Brice, 16100 Cognac ☎ 45.32.18.17 (closed Tues).

Confolens (Charente)
Pop: 4,000
Poitiers 72 km, Paris 414 km
🛈 place des Marronniers ☎ 45.84.00.77

A small town beautifully situated on the Vienne river with a multi-arched stone bridge, medieval streets and half-timbered houses. The watery landscapes, old churches and peaceful river valleys are a pleasure for walkers and painters alike. For ten days in August each year, however, the town takes on a very festive air as the impressive Folklore Festival is staged here. High-quality presentations of street theatre, dancing and music from nations all over the world bring sudden colour and vivacity to this otherwise sleepy town.

- Camping: Les Ribières ☎ 45.84.01.97
- Fishing: category 2 fishing and bathing in the River Vienne.

Coulon (Deux-Sèvres)
Pop: 2,000
Niort 11 km, Paris 415 km
🛈 place de l'Eglise ☎ 49.35.99.29

The *Marais Poitevin* (Poitou fens) is an area of strange watery landscapes where flat-bottomed boats called *plates*, laden with animals or crops, are steered by the farmers with long poles. Travel between fields and villages, via these canals, is enclosed within the slow and peaceful world of vegetation and birdlife. Typical of the marshland is this small, pretty holiday village from where trips can be made throughout the year, although the best time to visit is between May and October.

- Boat Trips: several operators offer guided tours. Accompanied trips are also available from St-Hilaire-la-Palud, La Garette and Arçais.

- Camping: La Venise Verte ☎ 49.35.90.36
- Canoeing: two-seater Indian-style canoes can be hired from a base at La Ronde for from two-day to one-week circuits, with tent, cooking equipment, maps, etc. provided. This adventure can be booked from Bateaux Jacques Renaud, Z.I. du Port, 17230 Marans ☎ 46.01.17.16
- Fishing: category 2 fishing in the Sèvre-Niortaise river.
- Golf: 18h public course at Golf de Mazières-en-Gatine, 79130 Mazières-en-Gatine ☎ 49.63.28.33 (fine undulating parkland course – handicap required).

 Fouras *(Charente-Maritime)*
Pop: 3,000
La Rochelle 27 km, Paris 485 km
🛈 Le Sémaphore ☎ 46.84.60.69

Picturesquely situated on a narrow peninsula facing the small island of Aix, Fouras is both a seaside resort and fishing port, with many sports activities on offer as well as visits to oyster farms and the essential tastings! Cruises are available to all three offshore islands, Ré, Aix and Oléron (the largest French island after Corsica), for a change of scenery and beach fun.

- Beach: safe, sheltered and sandy.
- Camping: Municipal Le Cadoret ☎ 46.84.02.84 and L'Esperance ☎ 46.84.24.18
- Casino: place Bugeau ☎ 46.84.63.16

Jarnac (Charente)
Pop: 5,000
Cognac 15 km, Paris 452 km
🛈 place du Château ☎ 45.81.09.30

Between Cognac and Jarnac the vineyards stretch over the horizon, dotted with farmhouses and large manors. Here, on certain evenings in July, during the Val du Charente Festival, symphony orchestras play beside a beautiful stretch of the river. This country holiday resort, the home town of President Mitterand, is also the home of Courvoisier cognac, their massive and elegant building dominating the main square. Life revolves around the pretty Charente, with bathing, canoeing and fishing.

- Boat Trips: by the hour or day (with or without meals) and week-long river cruises on the Charente, bookable through the Tourist Office.
- Camping: L'Ile Madame ☎ 45.81.18.54
- Fishing: category 2 fishing on the Charente.
- Golf: see Cognac.

Jonzac (Charente-Maritime)
Pop: 5,000
Saintes 49 km, Paris 613 km
🛈 Office de Tourisme ☎ 46.48.49.29

An impressive fifteenth-century castle looks down on the narrow streets in the valley of the Seugne. The town has examples of houses which still survive from the old Santiago de Compostela pilgrim route. Now an important market town for cognac, Charentes butter and *pineau*, the local apéritif, Jonzac is also a newly created spa resort.

- Camping: Les Megisseries ☎ 46.48.41.05
- Riding: Air de Loisirs du Mail de la Seugne ☎ 46.48.30.76
- Spa: rheumatism/bone joint damage treated at Thermes de Jonzac ☎ 46.48.42.18

Montbron *(Charente)*
Pop: 3,000
Angoulême 30 km, Paris 457 km
🇫 SI ☎ 45.23.60.09

A pleasant country holiday resort on the River Tardoire, with a medieval château. Good fishing and, in its livelier stretches, excellent canoeing. The open-air recreation base at Lake Chambon is close by and has extensive sports facilities.

- Camping: La Piscine ☎ 45.70.70.21
- Canoeing: (July/Aug) canoe hire available. Base du Plein Air du Chambon (6 km) ☎ 45.70.70.42 runs trips down the Tardoire as far as La Rochefoucauld.
- Fishing: category 1 fishing in the Tardoire river.
- Tennis: three courts to hire ☎ 45.23.63.88

Montendre *(Charente-Maritime)*
Pop: 3,000
Saintes 62 km, Paris 518 km
🇫 Maison du Tourisme ☎ 46.49.46.45

A family holiday resort in parkland surrounding the ruins of a twelfth-century keep in a region of heath and pine trees near the spa resorts of Jonzac and Pons. Activities include walking and riding *randonnées* in the vast Coubre Forest, and fishing and sailing on the Lac du Baron.

- Camping: Rencontres La Forêt ☎ 46.49.20.17
- Riding: Centre Equestre, route de St-Pierre ☎ 46.49.48.66

Montignac-sur-Charente *(Charente)*
Pop: 800
Angoulême 16 km, Paris 430 km
🇫 la Mairie ☎ 45.39.70.09

The peaceful natural beauty and simple country pleasures of this small riverside village are complemented by the proximity of the busy town of Angoulême which offers shopping and excursions.

- Camping: Les Platanes ☎ 45.39.89.16
- Canoeing: canoes for hire for half or full days during the summer ☎ 45.39.70.49
- Fishing: category 2 fishing in the Charente.

Also bathing and boating.
- Riding: nearby at the Ecole d'Equitation de Xambes ☎ 45.39.74.47

La Palmyre *(Charente-Maritime)*
Pop: 3,000
Royan 17 km, Paris 520 km
🇫 Les Mathes-La Palmyre ☎ 46.22.48.72

This is a young resort, already very popular for its charming setting amid forests and flowers and its sandy beach fringed with the pine trees of the Coubre Forest. Facing the island of Oléron and the ocean, there is a small harbour for pleasure boats, a racecourse and enthusiastic support for riding, cycling and walking along the forest trails. Aquatic sports take place at Bonne Anse bay and the zoo is first class, catering for the whole family in a 'Wild West' ambiance. However, the popularity of the area means that cars sometimes bottleneck the roads leading to and from the beaches.

- Camping: Palmyre-Loisirs ☎ 46.23.64.90 and La Bonne Anse ☎ 46.22.40.90
- Golf: see Royan.

Poitiers *(Vienne)*
Pop: 84,000
Tours 100 km, Paris 334 km
🇫 11 rue Victor-Hugo ☎ 49.41.58.22

This architecturally exciting city, with its large university centre, is set on a hill above the Rivers Clain and Boivre. Many visitors are drawn to the Romanesque cathedral of St-Pierre, the famous façade of the church of Notre-Dame-la-Grande, and the richly stocked museum of Ste-Croix. In addition, the newly created Futuroscope at Jaunay-Clan, a unique amusement park complex, including 3-D cinemas with 360-degree image, is also proving popular with children and adults who can enjoy a fascinating world of discovery amidst the scientific and futuristic attractions.

- Camping: Municipal ☎ 49.41.44.88
- Golf: 9h private course built by the US Army at Golf de Poitiers Golf Poitevin, Terrain des Chalons, route de Bignoux, 86000 Poitiers ☎ 49.61.23.13 (handicap necesssary); also nearby 9h public course at Golf du Haut-Poitou, Parc de Loisirs de St-Cyr, 86130 Jaunay-Clan ☎ 49.62.57.22 (closed Tues).

Rochefort-sur-Mer *(Charente-Maritime)*
Pop: 28,000
La Rochelle 35 km, Paris 465 km
🇫 avenue Sadi-Carnot ☎ 46.99.08.60

A French Airforce base, trading port, pleasure-boat harbour and well-known spa resort situated a few kilometres from the ocean on flat, open countryside. It is paradise for windsurfers as it has strong winds yet is sheltered from the Atlantic breakers by the islands. Casino.

- Boat Hire: discover the slow pace of life along

the 160-km stretch of the River Charente between Rochefort and Angoulême (21 locks), passing cognac vineyards, Romanesque churches and pretty villages. Contact Loisirs Accueil Charente.

- Camping: Le Rayonnement ☎ 46.99.14.33
- Cycling: cycles can be hired from Heline, rue Gambetta ☎ 46.99.08.56 and from the SNCF station.
- Horse-drawn Travel: Rochefort Randonnée Cagouillarde ☎ 46.84.85.87
- Spa: rheumatism/bone joint damage (open all year except Jan) ☎ 46.99.08.64 alt: 5 m, climate: sea air.

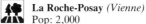 **La Rochefoucauld** *(Charente)*
Pop: 4,000
Angoulême 22 km, Paris 443 km
🏠 la Mairie ☎ 45.62.02.61

Renowned for its great architecture, La Rochefoucauld is a country holiday resort where, every weekend in July, the spectacularly situated château is brought to life in a wonderful *son-et-lumière* presentation. There is canoeing, riding and walking in the nearby Braconne Forest.

- Camping: Chemin des Flots ☎ 45.63.10.72
- Fishing: category 1 fishing in the Tardoire river.
- Tennis: five courts to hire ☎ 45.62.07.36

La Rochelle *(Charente-Maritime)*
Pop: 80,000
Niort 63 km, Paris 468 km
🏠 10 rue Fleuriau ☎ 46.41.14.68

A smart and sophisticated resort of parks and promenades, La Rochelle is well known both as an important yachting centre, with sailing events attracting international competition, and as the tenth most important fishing port in France. One of the largest marinas in Europe, there are berths for 3,000 pleasure boats in the port of Les Minimes, a virtually self-contained complex for the sailing fraternity, with a regular ferry service to the Old Port area of the town. An art and historical centre, there are several museums of interest, elegant buidings and fine cobbled streets. Horse-drawn carriages allow for leisurely sightseeing, while island excursions to the Ile de Ré (pretty) and the Ile d'Oléron (stunning beaches) are regular and recommended.

- Beach: sandy.
- Camping: Port Neuf ☎ 46.43.81.20 and Le Soleil ☎ 46.44.42.53
- Casino: allées du Mail ☎ 46.34.12.75
- Cycling: cycles can be hired from the SNCF station.
- Languages: Institut d'Etudes Françaises ☎ 46.41.17.13 offers French language study courses.

La Roche-Posay *(Vienne)*
Pop: 2,000
Poitiers 49 km, Paris 315 km
🏠 cours Pasteur ☎ 49.86.20.37

This is a small picturesque spa town set on a hill by the ruins of a twelfth-century keep, with the modern spa on a plateau at the foot. There is good fishing in the Creuse and Gartempe rivers, a racecourse and an excellent golfcourse. Casino.

- Camping: Le Riveau ☎ 49.86.21.23
- Golf: 18h private woodland course at Golf de Chatellerault, Parc du Connétable, 86270 La Roche-Posay ☎ 49.86.20.21
- Riding: La Gatinière Equitation ☎ 49.86.18.35
- Spa: skin diseases (open all year) ☎ 49.86.21.03 alt: 75 m, climate: mild.

Ronce-les-Bains (Charente-Maritime)
Pop: 2,000
Saintes 45 km, Paris 510 km
🖰 (at La Palmyre) ☎ 46.22.41.07

A sheltered seaside resort in the midst of the pines of the Coubre Forest. The fine sandy beaches of Galon d'Or are 3 km away as is the important oyster-farming centre and fishing village of La Tremblade. This is a large shallow bay at the mouth of the Seudre, where at low tide mud flats reveal the oyster stakes of the breeders. The beaches are uncrowded and the swimming sheltered. The sea is busy with windsurfers and waterskiers. Lovely hiking excursions, as well as riding and cycling paths, dot the region.

- Beach: several sandy pine-fringed beaches.
- Camping: La Pignade ☎ 46.36.25.25

Royan (Charente-Maritime)
Pop: 19,000
Saintes 38 km, Paris 500 km
🖰 Palais des Congrès ☎ 46.38.65.11

A fashionable seaside resort on the Gironde estuary where massive war damage caused the town and its cathedral to be rebuilt. As a result of the post-war building, Royan is today the largest and most modern coastal resort between Biarritz and La Baule. From the old quarter of the town at Pontaillac, the sea's waters lap around the busy sardine port and yachting marina. There is a ferry point for the crossing of the Gironde to Bordeaux country, and the promenade of the Front de Mer is lined with pink and deep-rose tamarisk flowers. To the north lie the marshy plains, commercial breeding grounds for the oyster.

- Beach: several sandy beaches extend onto both the Gironde and the ocean here and also to the north at the smaller resorts of St-Palais-sur-Mer and to the south at St-Georges-de-Didonne where there is a magnificent 3.5 km beach bordered by pines and oaks.
- Boat Trips: day cruises operate to the islands.

- Camping: Clairefontaine ☎ 46.39.08.11 and La Triloterie ☎ 46.05.26.91
- Casino: Sporting Casino de Royan Pontaillac ☎ 46.39.03.31
- Cycling: cycles can be hired from Burais, boulevard de Lattre-de-Tassigny ☎ 46.05.08.90 and from the SNCF station.
- Golf: 18h public course at Golf de la Côte de Beauté, 17420 Saint-Palais ☎ 46.23.16.24 (very popular hilly course set in the Foret de la Coubre with wonderful views; book in advance).
- Languages: CAREL ☎ 46.05.31.08 offers French language study courses.
- Riding: rides through the forests with Centre Equestre Maine-Gaudin ☎ 46.23.11.44
- Sailing: and windsurfing with Maison du Marin ☎ 46.39.20.82
- Thalassotherapy: Centre de Cures Marines, place Foch ☎ 46.05.06.36 and Royan Revitalisation who run health and beauty sessions, bookable through the Tourist Office.
- Watersports: sailing and waterskiing.

Saintes (Charente-Maritime)
Pop: 30,000
Royan 38 km, Paris 470 km
🖰 62 cours National ☎ 46.74.23.82

Built on either side of the lovely River Charente, Saintes is a busy and delightful regional market town and an important art centre. There are many superb Roman remains to be seen: the Germanicus Arch, in honour of the Emperor Tiberius, the Abbaye aux Dames and the amphitheatre. Saintes was an important resting and staging post for the pilgrims heading for the shrine of Santiago de Compostela in Spain, and the Romanesque churches of the district bear witness to this early activity. In the heart of brandy country, round trips may be made, by river or helicopter, to visit the cognac vineyards along the Charente valley, to Cognac and beyond.

- Boat Trips: between April and October, with or without meals on board, bookable through the Tourist Office.
- Camping: Municipal ☎ 46.93.08.00
- Canoeing: hire of canoes, rowing boats and pedaloes at the Base Nautique de Lucérat.
- Golf: 9h public woodland course at Golf de Saintes, Fontcouverte, 17100 Saintes ☎ 46.74.27.61 (closed Tues).
- Riding: Centre Equestre de Chantemerle ☎ 46.91.12.80
- Spa: close by at Saujon – nervous system (open all year) ☎ 46.02.97.55 alt: 7 m, climate: temperate.

PROVENCE-ALPES-COTE D'AZUR

*Administrative
Centre: Marseille
Population: 3,675,700
Area: 31,436 sq km*

*Départements:
04 Alpes-de-Haute-
    Provence
05 Hautes-Alpes
06 Alpes-Maritimes
13 Bouches-du-Rhône
83 Var
84 Vaucluse*

*National Parks:
Parc des Ecrins
(600,450 hectares)
7 rue du
Colonel-Roux, 05000
Gap* ☎ *92.51.40.71*

*Parc du Mercantour
(400,300 hectares)
23 rue d'Italie, 06000
Nice* ☎ *93.87.86.10*

*Parc de Port-Cros,
(48,970 hectares)
50 avenue Gambetta,
83400 Hyères*
☎ *94.65.32.98*

*Regional Parks:
Parc de la Camargue,
Le Pont de Rousty,
13200 Arles*
☎ *90.97.10.93*

*Parc du Lubéron,
place Jean Jaurès,
B.P. 128, 84400 Apt*
☎ *90.74.08.55*

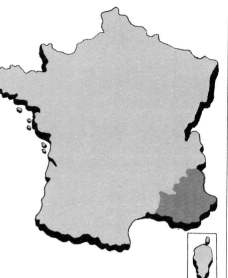

The bounds of present-day Provence (an area the size of Wales, say, or New Hampshire) are set roughly by the Alps, the Rhône, the Mediterranean coastline and the Italian frontier.

Greek traders and seamen had early on established Massalia (Marseille) as a busy port for trading with the East and with North Africa, but when Celts and Ligurians, who had settled along this coast, threatened the peace of the port, it was the Romans who, by force of arms, drove trade routes through the coastal stretch and whose names remain today: the Via Aurelia (Route Nationale 7), the coast road through Nice, Fréjus, Le Luc, Aix, Salon and Nîmes, the Via Agrippa through Arles, Avignon and Orange and the Via Domitia between Embrun, Sisteron and Apt. Arles became the granary of Rome, Massalia became Massilia and the *Provincia Romana* (Provence) was established.

Provence has spread since Roman times, embracing the mountains to the north, where winter sports flourish, the Alpes-Maritimes behind the Côte d'Azur, the flat wetlands of the Camargue, the pulsing, baking beaches of the Riviera resorts, and the hilltop inland villages, at first safety retreats or lookout points, then ruins, and now restored to house fashionable restaurants or as private retreats once more. Today, Provence takes in the cicada-chirping olive groves and the vineyards of Lower Provence, the town mansions of Aix, flanked by avenues of plane trees in the Cours Mirabeau, the neo-baroque villas and casinos of the coastal strip, and the Gothic fourteenth-century Palais des Papes at Avignon.

Greece, Rome, the French papacy, the monasteries of the tenth century, the troubadours of the twelfth, the English aristocracy of the nineteenth, have all shaped contemporary Provence. They have left their traces at Marseille and Eze-Village, at Orange, Nîmes and Pont du Gard, at Avignon, Arles and Aix, at Nice, Cannes and Antibes.

However, there are two other physical attributes which are essentially Provençal: the chill villainy of the Mistral wind whirling down the tunnel of the Rhône valley in late winter and early spring and, above all else, the sun and the quality of light that

Aix-en-Provence

drew and inspired Cézanne, Matisse, Van Gogh, Picasso, Monet, Renoir, Signac, Dérain and Chagall. It would seem that almost every village was once home to some now-treasured artist; their paintings are now displayed in small galleries and museums throughout the area. It was as difficult for them then as it is for us now to explain or describe the clarity of the light, the stunning vividness of the Midi sun, the deep, secret colours hidden in apparent shadow. The light that drew these artists to Provence, that intoxicated and enthused them there, now glows from the canvases they worked on.

PRACTICAL TOURIST INFORMATION

General information on the region can be obtained by telephoning or writing to the Conseil Régional office, while specific booklets are produced detailing camping, hotel and self-catering gîte accommodation. These can be obtained by writing to the tourist board office for the département *(CDT) of your choice:*

Regional Tourist Board
Conseil Régional Provence-Alpes-Côte d'Azur, 2 rue Henri-Barbusse, 13241 MARSEILLE Cedex
☎ 91.08.62.90

Départements
Alpes-de-Haute-Provence (04): Comité Départemental du Tourisme (CDT), 42 boulevard Victor-Hugo, B.P.170, 04000 DIGNE
☎ 92.31.57.29
Hautes-Alpes (05): Comité Départemental du Tourisme (CDT), Immeuble 'Le Relais' 5 ter, rue Capitaine de Bresson, 05002 GAP Cedex
☎ 92.53.62.00
Alpes-Maritimes (06): Comité Départemental du

Tourisme (CDT), 55 promenades des Anglais, 06000 NICE ☎ 93.44.50.59
Bouches-du-Rhône (13): Comité Départemental du Tourisme (CDT), 6 rue du Jeune-Ancharsis, 13006 MARSEILLE ☎ 91.54.92.66
Var (83): Comité Départemental du Tourisme (CDT), 1 boulevard Foch, 83300 DRAGUIGNAN
☎ 94.68.58.33
Vaucluse (84): Chambre Départementale de Tourisme, 2 rue Saint-Etienne, quartier de la Baleine, 69005 LYON ☎ 78.42.50.04

SELF-CATERING ACCOMMODATION

The following British operators offer self-catering accommodation in the area:

AA Motoring Holidays, P.O. Box 100, Fanum House, Halesowen B63 3BT ☎ 021-550 7401
Agencefrance Holidays, Lansdowne Place, 17 Holdenhurst Road, Bournemouth BH8 8EH
☎ 0202 299534
Air France Holidays, 69 Boston Manor Road, Brentford TW8 9JQ ☎ 01-568 6981
Allez France, 27 West Street, Storrington, Pulborough RH20 4DZ ☎ 09066 2345

Angel Travel, 47 High Street, Central Chambers, Tonbridge TN9 1SD ☎ 0732 361115

Avon Europe, Lower Quinton, Stratford-upon-Avon, Warks CV37 8SG ☎ 0789 720130

Beach Villas, 8 Market Passage, Cambridge CB2 3QR ☎ 0223 311113

Belvedere Holiday Apartments, 5 Bartholomews, Brighton BN1 1HG ☎ 0273 23404

Blakes Holidays, Wroxham, Norwich NR12 8DH ☎ 0603 784131

Bowhills Ltd, Swanmore, Southampton SO3 2QW ☎ 0489 877627

Brittany Ferries, The Brittany Centre, Wharf Road, Portsmouth PO2 8RU ☎ 0705 827701

Carasol Holidays, 6 Hayes Avenue, Bournemouth BH7 7AD ☎ 0202 33398

Chalets de France, Travel House, Pandy, Nr Abergavenny NP7 8DH ☎ 0873 890770

Chapter Travel, 126 St John's Wood High Street, London NW8 7ST ☎ 01-586 9451

Côte d'Azur Properties, 7 Ashbourne Mansions, Finchley Road, London NW11 0AB ☎ 01-458 9011

Cresta Holidays, 32 Victoria Street, Altrincham WA14 1ET ☎ 0345 056511

Crystal Holidays, The Courtyard, Arlington Road, Surbiton KT6 6BW ☎ 01-399 5144

Destination Provence, 3 Gallows Hill Lane, Abbotts Langley WD5 0BD ☎ 09277 62196

Dominique's Villas, 2 Peterborough Mews, London SW6 3BL ☎ 01-736 1664

Euro-Express, 227 Shepherds Bush Road, London W6 7AS ☎ 01-748 2607

Eurovillas, 36 East Street, Coggleshall, Colchester CO6 1SH ☎ 0376 561156

Fleur Holidays, 29 North Park Drive, Blackpool FY3 8LR ☎ 0253 301719

La France des Villages, Model Farm, Rattlesden, Bury St Edmunds IP30 0SY ☎ 044 93 7664

France Directe, 2 Church Street, Warwick CV34 4AB ☎ 0926 497989

France Voyages, 145 Oxford Street, London W1R 1TB ☎ 01-494 3155

Freedom in France, Meadows, Poughill, Bude, Cornwall EX23 9EN ☎ 0288 55591

French Life Motoring Holidays, 26 Church Road, Horsforth, Leeds LS18 5LG ☎ 0532 390077

French Travel Service, Georgian House, 69 Boston Manor Road, Brentford TW8 0JQ ☎ 01-568 8442

French Villa Centre, 175 Selsdon Park Road, Croydon CR2 8JJ ☎ 01-651 1231

Gîtes de France, 178 Piccadilly, London W1V 9DB ☎ 01-493 3480

Hoseasons Holidays Abroad, Sunway House, Lowestoft NR32 3LT ☎ 0502 500555

Hoverspeed Ltd, Maybrook House, Queens Gardens, Dover CT17 9UQ ☎ 0304 240241

Intasun France, Intasun House, Cromwell Avenue, Bromley BR2 9AQ ☎ 01-290 1900

Interhome, 383 Richmond Road, Twickenham TW1 2EF ☎ 01-891 1294

Just France, 1 Belmont, Lansdown Road, Bath BA1 5DZ ☎ 0225 446328

Kingsland Holidays, 1 Pounds Park Road, Plymouth PL3 4QP ☎ 0752 766822

Lagrange Vacances, 16/20 New Broadway, London W5 2XA ☎ 01-579 7311

Meon Villas, Meon House, College Street, Petersfield GU32 3JN ☎ 0730 68411

Miss France Holidays, 132 Anson Road, London NW2 6AP ☎ 01-452 7409

David Newman's French Collection, P.O. Box 733, 40 Upperton Road, Eastbourne BN21 4AW ☎ 0323 410347

NSS Riviera Holidays, 199 Marlborough Avenue, Hull HU9 5QA ☎ 0482 42240

Palmer & Parker Holidays, 63 Grosvenor Street, London W1X 0AJ ☎ 049481 5411

Par-Tee Tours, Riverside House, 53 Uxbridge Road, Rickmansworth WD3 2DH ☎ 0923 721565

La Première Quality Villas, Solva, Haverfordwest SA62 6YE ☎ 03483 7871

Quo Vadis, 243 Euston Road, London NW1 2BT ☎ 01-583 8383

Rendez-Vous France, Holiday House, 146/148 London Road, St Albans AL1 1PQ ☎ 0727 45400

Rentavilla, 27 High Street, Chesterton, Cambridge CB4 1NB ☎ 0223 323414

Riviera Sailing Holidays, 45 Bath Road, Emsworth PO10 7ER ☎ 0243 374376

Sally Tours, Argyle Centre, York Street, Ramsgate CT11 9DS ☎ 0843 595566

Sealink Holidays, Charter House, Park Street, Ashford TN24 8EX ☎ 0233 47033

Slipaway Holidays, 90 Newland Road, Worthing BN11 1LB ☎ 0903 821000

Starvillas, 25 High Street, Chesterton, Cambridge CB4 1ND ☎ 0223 311990

Sturge, Martin, 3 Lower Camden Place, Bath BA1 5JJ ☎ 0225 310623

Sun France, 3 Beaufort Gardens, London SW16 3BP ☎ 01-679 4562

Sunvista Holidays, 5a George Street, Warminster BA12 8QA ☎ 0985 217444

Tourarc UK, 197b Brompton Road, London SW3 1LA ☎ 01-589 1918

The Travel Business, 94 Dulwich Village, London SE21 7AQ ☎ 01-299 0214

Eric Turrell, Moore House, Moore Road, Bourton-on-the-Water, Cheltenham GL54 2AZ ☎ 0451 20927

Vacances, 28 Gold Street, Saffron Walden CB10 1EJ ☎ 0799 25101

Vacances en Campagne, Bignor, Pulborough RH20 1QD ☎ 07987 433

Vacances France, 14 Bowthorpe Road, Wisbech PE13 2DX ☎ 0945 587830

Vacations, 60 Charles Street, Leicester LE1 1FB ☎ 0533 537758

VFB Holidays, 1 St Margaret's Terrace, Cheltenham GL50 4DT ☎ 0242 526338

The Villa Agency, 225 Ebury Street, London SW1W 8UT ☎ 01-824 8474

Villa France, 15 Winchcombe Road, Frampton Cotterell, Bristol BS17 2AG ☎ 0454 772410

SPORTS AND ACTIVITIES

For unusual and interesting holiday ideas, contact the Loisirs Accueil office for the area of your choice:

Loisirs Accueil Hautes-Alpes,
16 rue Carnot, 05000 GAP ☎ 92.51.73.73
Loisirs Accueil Bouches-du-Rhône,
Domaine du Vergon, 13370 MALLEMORT
☎ 90.59.18.05

RESORTS

 Aix-en-Provence *(Bouches-du-Rhône)*
Pop: 125,000
Marseille 31 km, Paris 756 km
🛈 2 place Général-de-Gaulle ☎ 42.26.02.93

An unforgettable town with a genuine Provençal atmosphere – fine old houses, fountains, tree-lined avenues (notably the Cours Mirabeau) and busy pavement cafés. In high summer, when the arts festival is staged here, there is a truly cosmopolitan air and the tantalising views of Mont-Ste-Victoire, repeatedly painted by the artist Cézanne, invite closer exploration.

● Art: Granet Museum houses a notable art collection while the Pavillon Cézanne contains memorabilia of the artist.
● Camping: Arc-en-ciel ☎ 42.26.14.28 and Chantecler ☎ 42.26.12.98
● Casino: place Jeanne d'Arc ☎ 42.26.30.33
● Golf: long and flat 18h private course at Golf d'Aix-Marseille, Domaine de Riquetti, 13290 Les Milles ☎ 42.24.20.41; new and popular 18h private course at Golf de Fuveau Château l'Arc, Rousset sur l'Arc, 13790 Fuveau ☎ 42.53.28.38
● Spa: rheumatism/bone joint damage (open all year) ☎ 42.26.01.18 alt: 250 m, climate: Mediterranean.
● Walking: from Le Tholonet follow the *Route Paul Cézanne.*

 Antibes – Juan-les-Pins *(Alpes-Maritimes)*
Pop: 64,000
Cannes 11 km, Paris 914 km
🛈 11 place Général-de-Gaulle ☎ 93.33.95.64

Charming old town with pretty tiled houses in narrow streets, as well as a glistening resort of luxury villas, lush gardens and parks and millionaires' yachting marina. Cap d'Antibes, the tip of the peninsula, is a pleasure to walk, with breath-taking views. In July the World Jazz Festival is staged, with music in the streets both here and just along the coast road in Juan-les-Pins, with its fine sandy beaches and lively bars and cafés.

● Art: Picasso museum at Château Grimaldi (closed Tues).
● Beach: fine sand at plage La Garoupe.
● Camping: Camp Rossignol ☎ 93.33.56.98,

Les Embruns ☎ 93.33.33.35 and Les Frênes ☎ 93.33.36.52
● Casino: route de Grasse ☎ 93.33.23.45
● Cycling: cycles can be hired from the SNCF station.
● Golf: short 18h course at Antibes-Biot (7 km) ☎ 93.65.08.48
● Languages: Côte d'Azur Languages ☎ 93.67.77.29 and Club Riviera Langues International, Château Laval, 14 route de la Badine, Antibes ☎ 93.74.36.08. Both offer French language study courses.
● Riding: Club Hippique Saint-Georges, route de Grasse ☎ 93.20.99.64

 Arles *(Bouches-du-Rhône)*
Pop: 51,000
Avignon 37 km, Paris 728 km
🛈 35 place de la République ☎ 90.96.29.35

A large city with a delightful old town area and some of the most outstanding Roman remains in Europe. In addition to summer drama and folk festivals staged in the ancient theatre, Spanish bullfights are held in the old amphitheatre during July and September, and Provençal-style bullfights are held every weekend from Easter onwards. Arles lies at the mouth of the wild salt marshes of the Camargue, a vast nature reserve famous for its white horses and flocks of pink flamingos. Many excursions visit this area, a delight for walkers and painters, although increasingly encroached on by the spreading rice fields and vineyards. Numerous Van Gogh associations abound, for it was here that the artist lived for the last two years of his life, painting views of the area and making the name Arles famous worldwide.

- Camping: Les Rosiers ☎ 90.96.02.12 and Bienheureuse ☎ 90.98.45.28

 Auron (*Alpes-Maritimes*)
Alt: 1,600-2,450 m
St-Etienne-de-Tinée 8 km, Nice 98, Paris 800 km
🏠 At Auron – Office de Tourisme, immeuble ·La Ruade ☎ 93.23.02.66 and at St-Etienne-de-Tinée – 1 rue des Communes de France ☎ 93.02.41.96

Principal winter sports resort of the Alpes-Maritimes (the French and World Championships have been held here), situated on a high sunny plateau which, in summer, converts to a highly activity-orientated resort for young families. Furnished apartments both here and at St-Etienne-de-Tinée (highest road in Europe), provide holiday accommodation for 10,000 and the resorts of Isola and Valberg are close by.

 Avignon (*Vaucluse*)
Pop: 120,000
Aix-en-Provence 80 km, Paris 685 km
🏠 41 cours Jean-Jaurès ☎ 90.82.65.11

Ancient ramparted city on the Rhône with its legendary Pont d'Avignon (only four of the original 22 arches remain), immortalised in song. The impressive Palais des Papes (Papal Palace), acting as fortress, residence and centre of Christendom when a succession of popes held court here during the fourteenth century, makes this one of the great art cities of France. Avignon is also a major commercial and tourist centre. A small tourist train offers a choice of two circuits of interest for the foot-weary, while the Tourist Office itself boasts a marvellous high-tech aid for the dispensing of information, with its touch-sensitive audio-visual commentary box in both English and French.

- Boat Trips: dine and cruise trips on the Rhône, bookable through the Tourist Office.
- Camping: Pont ☎ 90.82.63.50 and Bagatelle ☎ 90.86.30.39
- Cycling: cycles can be hired from the SNCF station.

 Bandol (*Var*)
Pop: 6,800
Toulon 17 km, Paris 825 km
🏠 Allée Vivien ☎ 94.29.41.35

Popular and pretty seaside resort nestling beneath pine-covered hills with Bendor Island, just

offshore, linked by frequent boat trips from the large yachting marina. The children will love a visit to the zoo at Sanary where, in addition to the monkeys and llamas, there is a botanic garden of tropical plants and fantastic displays of flowering Mediterranean shrubs.

- Beach: three sandy beaches with full watersports facilities.
- Camping: de Capelan ☎ 94.29.43.92
- Casino: (open all year) rue de la République ☎ 94.29.40.88
- Cycling: cycles can be hired from the SNCF station.

 Barcelonnette (*Alpes-de-Haute-Provence*)
Pop: 3,500
Briançon 84 km, Paris 735 km
🏠 place 7 Portes ☎ 92.81.04.71

An old town surrounded by mountains and situated near the Le Sauze (1,400 m), Super-Sauze (1,700 m) and Pra-Loup (1,650-2,500 m) winter sports resorts, the latter of which offers, in summer, beautiful woodland walks and views.

- Camping: Tampico ☎ 92.81.02.55

 Beaulieu-sur-Mer (*Alpes-Maritimes*)
Pop: 4,500
Nice 10 km, Paris 940 km
🏠 place de la Gare ☎ 93.01.02.21

Popular at the turn of the century as a playground for the crowned heads of Europe, this is an enchanting resort with a palm-fringed promenade and elegant villas built into the hillsides. Narrow pebbly beaches provide limited watersports facilities. While its large and busy yachting marina (berths for 1,000) adds a touch of international wealth and style, its streets and markets remain typically Provençal.

- Casino: avenue Blundell-Maple ☎ 93.01.00.39

 Bormes-les-Mimosas (*Var*)
Pop: 3,000
St-Tropez 35 km, Paris 875 km
🏠 rue Jean Aicard ☎ 94.71.15.17 and avenue Mer (Jun-Sep) ☎ 94.64.82.57

A charming old town lying between wooded hills and the sea, its name derives from the abundance of mimosa which fills the villa gardens. Reputedly enjoying the mildest winters in France, Bormes is an ideal all-year, flower-filled resort, close enough to enjoy the sea and all the associated watersports and entertainment facilities along the coastal strip, yet far enough above sea level to maintain an air of calm. There is a large modern marina (880 berths) at the port of La Favière.

- Beach: several safe and sandy beaches in the area (La Ris, La Favière, Cabasson and L'Estagnol).

- Camping: Domaine la Favière ☎ 94.71.03.12
  and Manjastre ☎ 94.71.03.28
- Casino: rue Carnot ☎ 94.71.15.28
- Riding: Centre Equestre des Campaux
  ☎ 94.49.57.53
- Sailing: school (also for deep-sea diving).

 Briançon *(Hautes-Alpes)*
Pop: 12,000
Gap 88 km, Paris 678 km
🛈 Porte de Pignerol ☎ 92.21.08.50

The highest town in Europe (1,326 m), at the
extreme edge of Provence and the Dauphiné
region, Briançon lies at the crossroads of the four
valleys of Durance, Clarée, Guisane and
Cerveyrette. Only 2 km from the Italian border,
and ideal for cross-country enthusiasts, the town is
conveniently close to several well-known ski
centres – Montgenèvre, Serre-Chevalier and Puy-
St-Vincent. Its gentle, healthy climate, high
mountain scenery and wide, lush valleys are
popular with nature lovers.

- Camping: Municipal de la Schappe
  ☎ 92.21.04.32 and Camping Les 5 Vallées
  ☎ 92.21.06.27
- Winter Sports: the nearby resorts of
  Montgenèvre (11 km), Serre Chevalier (6 km)
  and Puy-St-Vincent (20 km).

 Cagnes-sur-Mer *(Alpes-Maritimes)*
Pop: 36,000
Antibes 10 km, Paris 920 km
🛈 6 boulevard Maréchal-Juin ☎ 93.20.61.64

Fishing port and seaside resort set against scented
woodland with an old town dominated by a castle
formerly owned by the Grimaldi family. Today,
with its annual art festival (Jun-Sep), it is an area
popular with artists.

- Art: Renoir's home at Musée Renoir de
  Souvenir (closed Tues).
- Beach: 4-km pebbly beach.
- Camping: Oasis ☎ 93.20.75.67 and
  Panoramer ☎ 93.31.16.15

 Cannes *(Alpes-Maritimes)*
Pop: 74,000
Nice 32 km, Paris 900 km
🛈 1 La Croisette ☎ 93.39.24.53

For over a century Cannes has been one of the
most popular and glamorous resorts on the French
Riviera with its exclusive shops, grand hotels and
famous palm-fringed boulevard (La Croisette).
Here beaches stretch the length of the bay and
there is a charming old town and port area where
yachts and fishing boats bob side by side. Major
international events take place here, notably the
annual Film Festival. If the gambling tables don't
attract, there is theatre, ballet and concerts,
cabarets, nightclubs and restaurants to entertain
long into the starry nights.

Cannes

- Beach: many public and private beaches, all of
  them sandy.
- Boat Hire: Agence Maritime Internationale,
  12 quai Saint-Pierre ☎ 93.39.40.44
- Boat Trips: the uniquely shaped *Nautilus*
  offers splendid underwater views on regular
  excursions to the Iles de Lérins. Trips leave
  from the Gare Maritime ☎ 93.39.42.56
- Camping: Les Lentisques ☎ 93.90.00.45
- Casinos: Municipal (Nov-May)
  ☎ 93.38.12.11, Les Fleurs (open all year)
  ☎ 93.68.00.33, and Palm Beach (Jun-Oct)
  ☎ 93.43.91.12
- Cycling: cycles can be hired from the SNCF
  station.
- Golf: very popular and quite hilly 18h
  championship course at Cannes-Mougins
  (5 km), 175 route d'Antibes, 06250 Mougins
  ☎ 93.75.79.13; well-established 27h course at
  Cannes-Mandelieu (6 km) ☎ 93.49.55.39;
  and 18h private course at Golf de Valbonne,
  06560 Valbonne ☎ 93.42.00.08
- Languages: College International de Cannes
  ☎ 93.47.42.14 offers French language study
  courses.
- Riding: Centre Hippique des Basses
  Breguières, chemin Font de Currault, 06250
  Mougins ☎ 93.45.75.81 (closed Thurs).
- Tennis: 18 courts to hire at Tennis Municipal
  de la Bastide, 230 avenue Francis Tonner
  ☎ 93.47.29.33
- Watersports: Base du Mouré Rouge offers
  tuition in sailing, windsurfing, canoeing, etc.
  9 rue Esprit Violet ☎ 93.43.83.48

 Cassis *(Bouches-du-Rhône)*
Pop: 6,500

Marseille 23 km, Paris 800 km
🛈 place Baragnon ☎ 42.01.71.17

Small, picturesque fishing port and village lying on the Calanques coast and towered over by the cliffs of Cap Canaille. Pleasure trips by mini-sub to the dramatic coves and inlets of the calanques are an adventure.

● Camping: Cigales ☎ 42.01.71.17
● Casino: avenue Lerich ☎ 42.01.78.32

 Castellane *(Alpes-de-Haute-Provence)*
Pop: 1,500
Digne 55 km, Paris 795 km
🛈 Office de Tourisme ☎ 92.83.61.14

Dominated by the huge limestone rock, this is a pretty little town and a lovely spot for a country holiday at the edge of one of the most famous natural spectacles in France, the Verdon gorges. Here there is the opportunity to canoe or even to attempt white-water rafting, while walkers can choose among numerous routes for sampling the scenery. The nearby Lac de Castillon has more watersports facilities.

● Camping: Belvedere ☎ 92.83.62.60 and Chasteuil-Provence ☎ 92.83.61.21
● Fishing: category 1 fishing in the Verdon river and lakes.
● Riding: ☎ 92.83.63.94
● Watersports: white-water rafting bookable from AN Rafting, Moulin de la Salaou ☎ 92.83.70.83

 Cavalaire-sur-Mer *(Var)*
Pop: 4,000
St-Tropez 18 km, Paris 880 km
🛈 square de Lattre-de-Tassigny ☎ 94.64.08.28

Sunny pinewood resort on the Corniche des Maures in a magnificent sweeping bay. There's so much to enjoy on this coastline at any time of year – rocky inlets (calanques) of clear, calm water, the colour of the bougainvillaea and mimosa, and, from walks in the hills behind, stunning views of the region. It is easy, too, to appreciate the vulnerability of this dry landscape of pine and bay trees, for the ever-present risk of forest fires requires great care from visitors. Mostly modern, the development here caters for family holidays, and excursions include day trips to Ventimiglia in Italy and frequent boat connections to the Iles d'Hyères (Ile du Levant, Ile de Porquerolles and Ile de Port-Cros) lying just off the coast.

● Beach: several sand and shingle beaches from which animals are strictly banned.
● Camping: Camping de la Baie ☎ 94.64.08.15 and Bonporteau ☎ 94.64.03.24

 Digne-les-Bains *(Alpes-de-Haute-Provence)*
Pop: 17,000

Cannes 135 km, Paris 742 km
🛈 le Rond-Point ☎ 92.31.42.73

Spa resort attractively situated in the mountainous pre-Alps in a sunny, sheltered valley where the olive trees meet the winter snows. Sporting activities include canoeing, riding and tennis.

● Camping: Municipal ☎ 92.31.04.87
● Spa: rheumatism/bone joint damage (Mar-Dec) ☎ 92.31.06.68 alt: 600 m, climate: dry.

 Eze-sur-Mer *(Alpes-Maritimes)*
Pop: 2,000
Monte-Carlo 8 km, Paris 944 km
🛈 la Mairie ☎ 93.41.03.03

Popular coastal resort midway between Nice and Monte-Carlo on the Basse Corniche, with sheltered beaches and spectacular headlands. High above is Eze-Village, once a medieval fortress, and, perched 427 m above Eze-sur-Mer, commanding breath-taking views as far as Corsica. This ancient village has old, traffic-free streets, a sentry walk and a fourteenth-century gateway, supplemented now, as a concession to its great popularity, with chic boutiques.

● Beach: shingle.
● Camping: Nationale ☎ 93.01.81.64

 Fontaine-de-Vaucluse *(Vaucluse)*
Pop: 600
Avignon 30 km, Paris 704 km
🛈 place de l'Eglise ☎ 90.20.32.22 (Easter-Oct)

This small village has become something of an international tourist attraction by virtue of its pleasant location and the presence here of one of the most powerful springs in the world. The spring of Vaucluse, at the mouth of a major subterranean river at the foot of a great cliff, gushes out at a dramatic rate during high water periods. The peacefulness of this place and the racing, green water cascading into waterfalls and overhung by leafy trees, once inspired the Italian poet Petrarch, and now provides the backdrop for elegant waterside restaurants and the sports of fishing and canoeing. Nearby is the larger town of L'Isle-sur-la-Sorgue, the river running through it crossed by small bridges.

● Camping: Les Prés ☎ 90.20.32.38
● Climbing: accompanied climbs in the Dentelles de Montmirail. Short courses are offered by the Monts du Vaucluse guides and enquiries should be made at the Tourist Office.

 Forcalquier *(Alpes-de-Haute-Provence)*
Pop: 4,000
Aix-en-Provence 66 km, Paris 774 km
🛈 place Bourguet ☎ 92.75.10.02

This old market town clings to the hillside of the farming uplands overlooking the Durance river.

The clarity of the atmosphere has always attracted painters to the area, and was the reason for the establishment of the Haute Provence Observatory (14 km to the west), equipped with one of Europe's most powerful telescopes.

 Fréjus *(Var)*
Pop: 33,000
Cannes 36 km, Paris 871 km
🅑 place Calvini ☎ 94.51.53.87 and Fréjus-Plage
☎ 94.51.48.42

This is vineyard country (Côtes de Provence) with a Roman past attested to by the Roman amphitheatre, arena and aqueduct. Visitors are welcome at the many glasshouses devoted to the cultivation of orchids, roses and cyclamen, as well as to the wine *caves*. There is a 54-hectare fun park, Aquatica, a zoo and a safari park 5 km away.

● Beach: long, fine-sand beach at Fréjus-plage.
● Camping: Camping de la Baume
☎ 94.52.04.08

 Gap *(Hautes-Alpes)*
Pop: 31,000
Grenoble 105 km, Paris 667 km
🅑 5 rue Carnot ☎ 92.51.57.03

Gap is the major town of the Hautes-Alpes, set at the centre of the majestic Ecrins National Park, an area perfect for cycling or walking, and with good river fishing. Its naturally beautiful setting within the encircling mountains, the water-based activities at the nearby Lac de Serre-Ponçon, and the lively atmosphere of its country markets will delight in summer. In winter the snow cover offers the cross-country enthusiast miles of trails and the choice of numerous alpine resorts close by.

● Camping: Napoléon ☎ 92.52.12.41
● Climbing: close to Gap, Gap-Céüze 2000 is a climber's paradise. Fully equipped for beginners, and boasting the most famous cliff in the Hautes-Alpes (with more than 200 approaches), it is an amazing sport, even just to watch. A guide to the paths of Céüze is available from the Tourist Office.
● Cycling: cycles can be hired from the SNCF station.
● Golf: new high-altitude course at Gap Bayard.

Grasse *(Alpes-Maritimes)*
Pop: 38,000
Cannes 17 km, Paris 908 km
🅑 3 place Foux ☎ 93.36.03.56

A charming town of terraced, red-tiled houses gathered round the twelfth-century cathedral (containing three Rubens paintings) and set high in the foothills 14 km from the sea. The old town of stepped alleyways, elegant fountains and courtyards overlooks Provence as though from a balcony, with delightful views across fields whose fragrant blossoms, treated and bottled, have

established Grasse as the perfume capital of the world. The Fragonard, Galimard and Molinard perfumeries are open to the public all year round. Casino.

● Art: the Provençal Art and History museum encompasses the heritage of eastern Provence and includes a fine collection of Provençal *santons*.
● Camping: Pont de la Paoute ☎ 93.09.11.42
● Golf: 9h private course at Golf du Val Martin, Domaine du Val Martin, 06560 Valbonne
☎ 93.42.07.98
● Riding: Poney Club de Paradenya, 42 chemin de la Mosquée, Quartier Harjes
☎ 93.36.13.23 (closed Thurs) has facilities for the handicapped.

 Gréoux-les-Bains *(Alpes-de-Haute-Provence)*
Pop: 1,600
Aix-en-Provence 55 km, Paris 860 km
🅑 place de l'Hôtel de Ville ☎ 92.78.01.08

The ideal climate and setting of this old spa town, its lavender- and thyme-scented air and the fame of its long-exploited and effective waters attract both *curistes* and tourists in great numbers. Built on the side of a rocky slope with the Verdon river winding below, Gréoux is perfect as an excursion base, with the surrounding countryside offering walkers and fishermen plenty of opportunities. A speciality of the area is lavender-flavoured honey, a perfect souvenir.

● Camping: Les Cygnes ☎ 92.78.08.08
● Gliding: Association Aéronautique Verdon/Alpilles at Vinon-sur-Verdon aerodrome (8 km).
● Sailing: on the Lac d'Esparron.
● Spa: rheumatism/bone joint damage (1 Feb-23 Dec) ☎ 92.74.22.22 alt: 400 m, climate: dry.
● Walking: in the spectacular Verdon gorges.

Grimaud *(Var)*
Pop: 3,000
St-Tropez 10 km, Paris 865 km
🅑 place des Ecoles ☎ 94.43.26.98

The well-restored medieval village of Grimaud nestles in the hills 5 km inland from the sea, backed by the chestnut and cork-oak woods of the Massif des Maures. Dominating the village is its château, commanding superb views over the lovely bay. By way of contrast, Port Grimaud, the fashionable yachting port below, with its Venetian-like maze of canals, was created in 1964 and is a highly acclaimed development of colourful houses and large marina. Designed with the yachting fraternity in mind, each house has its own mooring and it is a triumph of design. It is also popular with visitors who can take trips through the canals on small boats.

● Camping: La Plage ☎ 94.56.31.15 and Les Mûres ☎ 94.56.16.97

- Golf: see Ste-Maxime.
- Riding: Centre Hippique des Maures, Beauvallon ☎ 94.56.16.55

 Guillestre (*Hautes-Alpes*)
Pop: 2,000 Alt: 1,050 m
Barcelonnette 49 km, Paris 713 km
🛈 place Salva ☎ 92.45.04.37

An attractive mountain village, one of a group of six neighbouring villages offering winter sports accommodation. Sheltered from the severest weather by its position in the foothills, Guillestre, together with the ski resorts of Vars and Risoul, and the cross-country centre of Ceillac provide shuttle services between one another. In the summer season, the village offers a range of exhilarating activities. There is white-water rafting on the Durance river at St-Clément, rock climbing or gliding at St-Crépin and walking in the Val d'Ecrins nature reserve. The produce of the area includes rosemary honey, milky and strongly flavoured, lavender honey, golden-yellow and delicate, and pine-tree honey, deep brown and strong. Nearby, on its majestic rocky promontory, stands Montdauphin, a fortified town built by Vauban.

- Camping: La Rochette ☎ 92.45.02.15

 Hyères (*Var*)
Pop: 45,000
Toulon 18 km, Paris 855 km
🛈 Rotonde J.-Salusse, avenue de Belgique
☎ 94.65.18.55

A busy sailing and watersports resort at the southernmost tip of the Côte d'Azur with a superb sunshine record. The Romans and Greeks knew of Hyères. Here the Renaissance houses of the old town overlook the modern town with its broad streets lined with palm trees which are grown here for export. Of the three islands opposite, the Iles d'Hyères, the biggest is Porquerolles (fine beaches). The other two are Port-Cros (fishing) and l'Ile du Levant (naturist centre). There are fine sandy beaches and a sheltered yachting harbour.

- Camping: Domaine du Ceinturon
  ☎ 94.66.32.65 and Camping Rebout
  ☎ 94.66.41.21
- Languages: Ecole de Langue Française
  ☎ 94.65.03.31 offers French language study courses.
- Cycling: cycles can be hired from the SNCF station.
- Riding: Relais Equestre de la Ferme
  ☎ 94.66.41.78 and Centre Equestre
  St-Georges, Domaine de la Bravette
  ☎ 94.57.24.00

 Isola 2000 (*Alpes-Maritimes*)
Pop: 500
Nice 97 km, Paris 800 km
🛈 Office de Tourisme ☎ 93.23.15.15

High in the Alpes-Maritimes yet only 50 km from the Côte d'Azur, the winter station of Isola 2000, set in the Tinée valley with its pine and chestnut trees, and close to the Italian border, is a major resort of the southern Alps. Surrounded by mountain streams, alpine pastures and rocky waterfalls, and close to the highest mountain pass in Europe, the superb natural and sunny amphitheatre provides an ideal setting for this purpose-built resort. There are pistes for all levels of skier, plus an obvious air of fun demonstrated by weekly firework and torchlit ski descents during the season. In January each year, the *scooters des neiges* World Cup is held here. During the summer, mountaineering, riding and fishing replace the snow-based activities.

- Winter Sports: the resorts of Valberg and Auron are close by.

 Les Issambres (*Var*)
Pop: 2,000
Ste-Maxime 10 km, Paris 880 km
🛈 Parc des Loisirs ☎ 94.96.92.51

A pleasant little seaside village between the Gulfs of St-Tropez and Fréjus, set at the foot of the Massif des Maures and thus protected from the Mistral wind. Les Issambres, which claims 320 days of sunshine each year, is part of a coastal complex along 8 km of beaches and coves, with watersports for all tastes. There are good walks along the coast and on the little hillside paths, scented by laurel, mimosa, pine and eucalyptus. Sandy beaches bake in the sunshine and, from the small harbour and fishing port, excursions can be made to the nearby Iles d'Or. All the usual holiday activities are featured here, including tennis, waterskiing and fishing.

- Camping: Au Paradis des Campeurs
  ☎ 94.96.93.55

 Le Lavandou (*Var*)
Pop: 4,000
Toulon 41 km, Paris 878 km
🛈 quai Gabriel Péri ☎ 94.71.00.61

Sun, sea and sand have caused this once small fishing village to grow into a massively popular seaside resort which still retains much of its original charm. Situated at the foot of the Massif des Maures, Le Lavandou is, for those who like to know these things, recorded in the *Guinness Book of Records* for having prepared the largest ever *bouillabaisse* (fish soup)! Traditional folk festivals and customs are important here, principal amongst them, perhaps, being the *Printemps de la Mer*, a month-long springtime celebration of the sea. Every Saturday night between August and October, feverish activity and a rush to the harbour to greet the returning tuna fishermen may cause alarm to the uninitiated. The competitive weighing-in of the largest catch takes place amidst much good-natured fun and excitement.

- Beach: 10 km of fine sandy beaches plus more close by at Cavalière.
- Camping: Les Mimosas ☎ 94.05.82.94
- Marina: 850 berths.
- Sailing: and windsurfing tuition available.

 La Londe-les-Maures *(Var)*
Pop: 5,000
Toulon 20 km, Paris 858 km
🛈 avenue Albert Roux ☎ 94.66.88.22

A modern Mediterranean summer resort, much developed and extended out across the plain from the original town. The small, new marina has berths for 400 pleasure boats and the three islands opposite invite exploration.

- Beach: sandy with the naturist beach of Les Salins for sun worshippers.
- Camping: Le Pansard ☎ 94.66.83.22
- Golf: 18h private course tucked away in the hills at Golf de Valcros-Hyères, 83250 La Londe-les-Maures ☎ 94.66.81.02 (handicap required).
- Sailing: and windsurfing offered by Club Nautique Londais, Port de Miramar ☎ 94.66.82.45

 Mandelieu-la-Napoule *(Alpes-Maritimes)*
Pop: 14,000
Cannes 8 km, Paris 894 km
🛈 avenue Cannes (Mandelieu) ☎ 93.49.14.39
and rue J.-Aulas (La Napoule) ☎ 93.49.95.31

These two modern seaside, and three river, harbours provide the largest capacity on the Riviera and a full complement of watersports activities are available in the massive Golfe de la Napoule. Options range from lazing on the beach beneath the hot sun or playing golf at the well-established course, exploring the Tanneron Forest and Provençal villages inland or seeking the solitary peace of a shaded bank along the Siagne river.

- Beach: three private sandy beaches and many coves.
- Boat Trips: regular daily trips to the Iles de Lérins and around the coast.
- Camping: Le Plateau des Chasses ☎ 93.49.25.93 and L'Argentière ☎ 93.49.95.04
- Casino: Loews ☎ 93.49.90.00
- Fishing: sea and river fishing possible here.
- Golf: see Cannes.
- Riding: Poney Club San'Estello ☎ 93.93.14.18
- Skin Diving: beginners' lessons (Mar-Dec) with special courses for children (eight years upwards) during the summer months from Club Nautique d'Esterel, Port de la Rague ☎ 93.49.74.33; also from Plongée Internationale Club, Port de Cannes Marina ☎ 93.49.01.01
- Tennis: seven courts to hire at Tennis Club

Municipal d'Argentière ☎ 93.93.03.03 and 11 courts at Tennis Club San'Estello ☎ 93.49.58.41
- Sailing: and windsurfing courses during the summer months from Maison de la Mer, route du Bord de Mer ☎ 93.49.88.77

 Marseille *(Bouches-du-Rhône)*
Pop: 880,000
Toulon 64 km, Paris 776 km
🛈 4 la Canebière ☎ 91.54.91.11 and gare St-Charles ☎ 91.50.59.18

The largest port in the Mediterranean and France's second city. La Canebière, its famous street of shops, hotels, restaurants and offices, leads down to the Vieux Port, its quays crowded with commercial and pleasure craft. Leading off the Canebière is the African quarter of the cours Belsaunce and the rue d'Aix, a maze of casbah-type stalls and shops. By contrast, the fashionable streets bustle with chic bars and top fashion houses. Offshore lies the Château d'If, originally a prison and later the setting for Dumas's *Count of Monte-Cristo*. Boat trips leave from the old port for a round trip of great interest, while drives along the corniche road will reward you with fine sandy beaches.

- Art: the Musée des Beaux Arts in the Longchamp Palace has works by Rubens, David, Ingres, Corot and Watteau amongst others. This is the city of Le Corbusier's residential complex, the *Cité Radieuse*, an avant-garde experiment in architectural design (1952).
- Boat Trips: regular services to Corsica and North Africa.
- Camping: Bonneveine ☎ 91.73.26.99
- Golf: see Aix-en-Provence.
- Spa: nearby at Camoins-les-Bains – respiratory/lymphatic disorders (1 Mar-15 Dec) ☎ 91.43.02.50 alt: 130 m, climate: Mediterranean.

 Menton *(Alpes-Maritimes)*
Pop: 25,000
Nice 30 km, Paris 960 km
🛈 Palais de l'Europe, avenue Boyer ☎ 93.57.57.00

The exceptional climate here has made famous the lemon trees of Menton, which flourish all year round in the subtropical temperatures. The Fête des Limons, its floats covered with hundreds of thousands of oranges and lemons, is held on Shrove Tuesday each year. Backed by impressive mountains, Menton's old town is in a marvellous site, the last resort before the Italian border, and is graced by beautiful beaches and pleasant parks. Important art exhibitions are held here and the Chamber Music Festival in July is internationally known.

- Art: there is a fine collection of modern art at the Palais Carnolès Museum and the Jean Cocteau Museum is devoted to his works.
- Camping: Municipal ☎ 93.35.81.23
- Golf: 9h private course at Golf de Tende, 06430 Domaine de Tende ☎ 93.04.61.02
- Languages: Cours Universitaires de Langue Française ☎ 93.57.57.00 offers French language study courses.

 Montauroux *(Var)*
Pop: 2,000
Cannes 35 km, Paris 894 km
🗎 Hôtel de Ville ☎ 94.76.43.08

Betwen the sea and the mountains, with a fresh and healthy climate, Montauroux is a small agricultural village on a rocky plateau. The nearby lake of St-Cassien offers watersports.

- Camping: Les Floralies ☎ 94.76.44.03

 Monte-Carlo *(Principality of Monaco)*
Pop: 28,000
Menton 9 km, Paris 956 km
🗎 boulevard des Moulins ☎ 93.30.87.01

Monte-Carlo, the capital of the tiny principality of Monaco, with its Prince's Ruritarian Palace and guard, has always symbolised wealth, privilege and hedonism. The world-famous casino is surrounded by lovely gardens and is set on a terrace with glorious views over the surrounding villas, grand hotels, high-rise blocks and luxury shops. Throughout the season it hosts exhibitions, galas, concerts, a television festival in February, international tennis in April, a flower festival in May and floodlit displays throughout the year. The Monte-Carlo motor rally roars through the streets at the end of January on a twisting circuit of 3,145 km and, as one of the stars of the Formula 1 circuit circus, sees the staging of the Monaco Grand Prix in May. In a more peaceful corner the extraordinary exotic gardens contain some 7,000 species of rare cacti plants and flowers, living proof of Monaco's perfect climate.

- Casino: place du Casino ☎ 93.50.69.31
- Golf: 18h private course built into cliffs and with magnificent views at Golf de Monte-Carlo, La Turbie, 06320 Cap d'Ail ☎ 93.41.09.11
- Languages: Monte-Carlo Regency School of French ☎ 93.50.49.00 offers French language study courses.

 Montgenèvre *(Hautes-Alpes)*
Pop: 450
Alt: 1,800-2,700 m
Briançon 12 km, Paris 690 km
🗎 Office de Tourisme ☎ 92.21.90.22

One of Europe's greatest skiing centres, near Briançon and right on the Italian frontier, this is a large international resort which has been popular since the beginning of the century. Miles of ski runs link both French and Italian resorts. In summer there is canoeing, tennis, riding, climbing, golf and hang gliding, in addition to walkers' trails and fishing in the many mountain lakes.

- Camping: (at 7 km) Camping du Bois des Alberts ☎ 92.21.16.11
- Golf: 9h course at Golf de Gap Bayard ☎ 92.52.38.14

 Nans-les-Pins *(Var)*
Pop: 1,500
Aix-en-Provence 42 km, Paris 799 km
🗎 avenue Georges-Clemenceau ☎ 94.78.95.91

At the foot of the Massif de la Sainte-Baume, this is a quiet Provençal village at an altitude of 430 m, where lovely walks are possible.

- Camping: Camping International de la Sainte-Baume ☎ 94.78.92.68

Nice *(Alpes-Maritimes)*
Pop: 400,000
Cannes 32 km, Paris 930 km
🗎 avenue Thiers ☎ 93.87.07.07; Acropolis Esplanade Kennedy ☎ 93.92.82.82; 5 avenue Gustave-V ☎ 93.87.60.60

This beautiful university city, set between the hills and the sea, is the capital of the French Riviera. Rich in history and culture and now an international tourism and business centre (with the second largest airport after Paris), Nice offers good shopping in elegant avenues and squares or in the busy narrow backstreets of the old town. The famous promenade des Anglais, although built by the English for seafront strolling in another age, is now a palm-fringed avenue more akin to a race track, with its six lanes of traffic. There are plenty of diversions, such as sea trips to Corsica, helicopter flights over the bay, summer trotting races, the February carnival with its large, flower-covered floats, museums and art galleries, the opera and theatre. Italy is close enough for excursions – try the Friday market in Ventimiglia. The climate is exceptional, with mild autumns and winters, and its proximity to some of the alpine resorts (Auron, Valberg and Isola 2000, all within 96 km), means that a holiday combining sea and snow is an attractive possibility.

- Art: Matisse, who worked and died here, is honoured with a museum in the villa suburb of Cimiez; the Musée des Beaux Arts contains much Impressionist work amongst other schools; there is also a Marc Chagall museum and several other public and private galleries.
- Beach: 30 shingle beaches stretch over 6 km, 15 public and 15 private, offering every conceivable watersport activity.
- Boat Trips: cruises of one day or longer to Corsica from SNCM, Gare Maritime, quai du

Commerce ☎ 93.89.89.89; and to Monaco, the Lérins islands and St-Tropez from Bateaux Gallus 80, 24 quai Lunel ☎ 93.55.33.33
- Canoeing: Nice Canoë-kayak, 5 rue Francois 1er ☎ 93.87.82.11
- Casinos: Casino Ruhl, promenade des Anglais ☎ 93.87.95.87 and Casino Club, rue Sacha Guitry ☎ 93.85.67.31
- Flights: panoramic flights over the Baie des Anges (Bay of Angels), the hinterland and the Riviera are available from Air Nice, Cannes-Mandelieu airfield at Cannes-la-Bocca. ☎ 93.07.70.07 and Nice Helicopters, 30 avenue Jean Médecin ☎ 93.80.00.77
- Golf: see Antibes and Cannes.
- Hang Gliding: Nice Deltazur Club, 54 bis, rue de la Buffa ☎ 93.88.62.89
- Languages: Centre International d'Etudes Françaises ☎ 93.86.66.43 offers French language study courses.
- Riding: Club Hippique, route de Grenoble ☎ 93.29.81.10. The Côte d'Azur Hippodrome racecourse at Cagnes-sur-Mer holds daytime races (Dec-Mar) and evening races (July-Aug) ☎ 93.20.30.30
- Skin-diving: International Diving Club, 2 ruelle des Moulins ☎ 93.55.59.50
- Tennis: Ligue de la Côte d'Azur, avenue Suzanne Lenglen ☎ 93.96.92.98
- Thalassotherapy: Profils (Hotel Méridien), avenue Gustave V ☎ 93.87.73.37; and Marina Health Centre, Villeneuve Loubet ☎ 93.73.55.07

 Orange *(Vaucluse)*
Pop: 27,000
Avignon 31 km, Paris 659 km
🇧 cours Aristide-Briand ☎ 90.34.70.88

Orange, its name having Dutch rather than fruity origins, preserves two of the most prestigious monuments in France today: the amazing Roman theatre built in the first century AD, with seating for 7,000 spectators, and the highly decorated Triumphal Arch. The good acoustics of the amphitheatre allow for the staging, during July and August each year, of the *Chorégies* (opera and choral works) which attract international visitors. The coastal resorts are within two hours' drive.

 Les Orres *(Hautes-Alpes)*
Pop: 450 Alt: 2,770 m
Gap 46 km, Paris 714 km
🇧 Comité de Station ☎ 92.44.01.61

This small ski resort, an exceptionally beautiful spot amid alpine pastureland and larch forests, overlooks Lac Serre-Ponçon in the Hautes-Alpes. An old and charming alpine village, the resort offers downhill and cross-country skiing in winter, with *après ski* including aerobics, discos, games rooms and solariums. In summertime another sporting world of tennis, archery, riding and rock climbing and watersports opens up.

 Le Pradet *(Var)*
Pop: 8,000
Hyères 10 km, Paris 846 km
🇧 place Général-de-Gaulle ☎ 94.21.71.69

Close to Toulon and Hyères, this coastline is notably diverse, with rocky inlets backed by wooded hills. The tiny fishing port and pleasure-boat harbour, together with the traditional vineyards and the fresh, local produce cultivated in this pleasant temperate climate, make Le Pradet popular with winter visitors.

- Beach: Bonnettes, separated by rocky creeks with, further south, the Pointe des Ousinières, an area rich in sea-urchins.
- Camping: Mauvallon ☎ 94.21.78.28

 Puy-St-Vincent *(Hautes-Alpes)*
Pop: 300 Alt: 1,400-2,700 m
Briançon 25 km, Paris 708 km
🇧 Maison de Tourisme Bât. Communal ☎ 92.23.35.80

This small village in the Hautes-Alpes can accommodate 10,000 skiers at the height of the season. Surrounded by the Massif des Ecrins, high above the valley of the Vallouise, it is this protection that virtually guarantees little or no wind and gives good snow throughout the season. The two resorts of Puy-St-Vincent and La Vallouise offer 60 km of ski runs and long cross-country trails. Beginners and experts will find their own level here and the most up-to-date sports are also available – delta-planing, gliding, mono-skiing and snow-surfing. It is also an exceptionally sunny region which, in spring and summer, is transformed into a place of green beauty, a paradise for rockclimbers and walkers, with the famous peaks of Les Ecrins (4,102 m) and Pelvoux (3,900 m) as lofty targets. There is abundant flora and fauna, mountain goats, squirrels, marmots and chamois, beautiful butterflies and, on every side, larch trees. Additionally, centred on the Vallouise valley and around Lac Serre-Ponçon, there is canoeing, swimming and riding.

 Ramatuelle *(Var)*
Pop: 2,000
St-Tropez 10 km, Paris 879 km
🇧 place de l'Ormeau ☎ 94.79.26.04

Built into the side of a hill above the beautiful Baie de Pampelonne, this is a picturesque old fortified village of narrow streets and ramparts. The peaceful, rural surroundings of olive groves and vines are deceptive, for Ramatuelle is only a winding drive away from the cosmopolitan glitter of St-Tropez. Festivals are held throughout the season, those taking place in the ancient theatre being subject to the most extraordinary acoustics. From the Moulins de Paillas there is an unforgettable panorama of the coast and from here, Mistral permitting, it is possible to watch the sun rise over Corsica.

- Beach: 5 km of fine sandy beach spreading around the Cap Camarat, with pretty rocky inlets.
- Camping: les Tournels ☎ 94.79.80.54

St-Cyr-sur-Mer *(Var)*
Pop: 2,000
Aix-en-Provence 48 km, Paris 800 km
🏛 Maison de Tourisme ☎ 94.26.13.46

Close to La Ciotat, where there are modern naval shipyards, and sharing the same large sunny bay, this is a family resort with full watersports facilities, pleasant walks in the wooded hills to the sound of birdsong and cicadas, and three boat harbours offering pleasure and fishing trips.

- Beach: safe and sandy.
- Camping: Camping les Baumelles ☎ 94.26.21.27
- Tennis: 18 courts to hire.

St-Jean-Cap-Ferrat *(Alpes-Maritimes)*
Pop: 2,500
Nice 10 km, Paris 940 km
🏛 59 avenue D.-Semeria ☎ 93.01.36.86

Throughout the St-Jean-Cap-Ferrat peninsula, separating the two bays of Villefranche and Beaulieu, expensive and elegant villas are almost hidden from view by the luxuriant vegetation. Originally a humble fishing village, and now at the very heart of the popular Côte d'Azur, St-Jean has a charming yachting harbour and fishing port.

- Art: the Villa Museum Ile-de-France is set in magnificent gardens (French, Spanish, Florentine, Japanese and English in style), and houses an excellent collection of furniture, tapestry and carpets, as well as Impressionist paintings by Monet, Renoir and Sisley.
- Beach: the beaches facing Villefranche are of soft sand and there are good watersports facilities.

St-Paul-de-Vence *(Alpes-Maritimes)*
Pop: 3,000
Antibes 16 km, Paris 930 km
🏛 rue Grande ☎ 93.32.86.95

In a setting of oranges, olive trees and mimosa, and among fields of carnations and roses, St-Paul-de-Vence, a medieval fortified town on a hillside, perfectly exemplifies the attractions of the Provence hinterland. Away from the fierce rush of coast traffic and the press of people, the old town wall shields the clustered houses, their tiled roofs providing cool shelter from the baking sun. It is as attractive today as in the 1920s when St-Paul was 'discovered' by the artists Modigliani and Bonnard. The old houses have been restored, restaurants have appeared and, with every year, there are new members of the artistic colony, busy with antique shops, studios, workshops and galleries. The Maeght Foundation sponsors regular exhibitions and concerts, as well as showing its important

and concerts, as well as showing its important collection of twentieth-century art. The famous inn of the Auberge de la Colombe d'Or also acts as an art gallery for treasures gathered by the early patron of the great painters. In Vence itself, 3 km away, the Chapel of the Rosary was both designed and decorated by Henri Matisse.

- Camping: Domaine de la Bergerie ☎ 93.58.09.36

St-Raphaël *(Var)*
Pop: 25,000
Cannes 43 km, Paris 875 km
🏛 rue Jules-Barbier ☎ 94.95.16.87

A very popular resort at the foot of the Esterel mountains where the coastline is made up of creeks and rocky reefs. The temperate climate of radiant summers and mild winters makes this a popular all-year resort. Its cafés and shops line the broad pavements and there is a lively waterfront with a fishing port and huge modern marina (1,800 berths). Casino.

- Beach: well sheltered and sandy.
- Camping: Douce Quietude ☎ 94.95.55.50
- Cycling: cycles can be hired, for the day or longer, from the SNCF station.
- Golf: 18h private course at Golf de Valescure, route du Golf, 83700 St-Raphaël ☎ 94.82.40.46
- Walking: good walking trails into the Maures mountains.

St-Rémy-de-Provence *(Bouches-du-Rhône)*
Pop: 9,000
Arles 25 km, Paris 705 km
🏛 place Jean Jaurès ☎ 90.92.05.22

In the heart of the Provençal flower-growing and seed business, St-Rémy is the site of some spectacular Roman ruins called *Les Antiques*. This is Glanum, the ruins of a mausoleum, and a commemorative memorial arch celebrating the Roman conquest of the Gauls. Close by, in the monastery of St-Paul-de-Mausole, Vincent Van Gogh spent the last year of his life as a patient. He painted some of his most famous works in the St-Rémy area, drawn to the place by the rare quality of the light and the brilliant Provençal colouring of the surrounding countryside. There are magnificent walks amid thyme and lavender along the footpaths of the Massif Alpilles, for this is an area of many aromatic plants and flowers which can be discovered on foot, horseback or bicycle. There is also gliding and fishing and, for the benefit of the visitor, cockade racing and the traditional Release of the Bulls.

- Camping: Pegomas ☎ 90.92.01.21

St-Tropez *(Var)*
Pop: 6,000
Cannes 75 km, Paris 875 km
🏛 quai Jean Jaurès ☎ 94.97.45.21

A small fishing port with a fashionable yachting basin giving berth to cruisers which are almost larger than the buildings which line the harbour. There are narrow alleys of exclusive clothes shops and painters working at easels. Typically Provençal and set in one of the most beautiful gulfs of the Côte d'Azur, St-Tropez was a village retreat for writers and artists in the early years of this century (de Maupassant, Colette, Bonnard and Matisse). From the 1950s the literary world of Paris made annual migration here, followed by film stars, celebrities of all kinds, the sporting and artistic, politicians and those merely with money, plus their camp followers. 'St-Trop', the seaside village, had become a world name, as cosmopolitan as the Champs Elysées.

Originally named after Torpes, a Christian centurion martyred under Nero, whose headless body was washed ashore at this point on the coast, the township commemorates its patron saint for three days in the middle of May each year, with the *Bravades*, a flourish of colourful processions.

- Art: the Musée de l'Annonciade (closed Tues and Nov) concentrates its collection on modern French painters with St-Tropez connections, Matisse, Braque, Utrillo, Dufy and Rouault among them.
- Beach: the famous plage de Pampelonne is 5 km of fine sand while other good beaches nearby include La Bouillabaisse, Graniers and Tahiti.
- Riding: Club de Beauvallon ☎ 94.56.16.55
- Sailing: and windsurfing offered by Union Sportif Tropézienne ☎ 94.97.12.58

 St-Véran *(Hautes-Alpes)*
Pop: 300 Alt: 2,040 m
Briançon 51 km, Paris 730 km
🛈 SI ☎ 92.45.82.21

This is one of a beautiful little group of villages nestling in the Queyras National Park, whose seventeenth- and eighteenth-century houses are charming. The inhabitants are welcoming as well as skilled in the local craft of pine-wood carving of great delicacy (Le Queyras toys). There is a downhill skiing centre in winter and a wonderful walking region in summer, with facilities for riding and canoeing.

 Ste-Maxime *(Var)*
Pop: 7,000
Cannes 61 km, Paris 877 km
🛈 promenade Simon Lorière ☎ 94.96.19.24

Set beneath the Massif des Maures in the lovely gulf of St-Tropez, with a pretty garden-lined seafront promenade. Full watersports facilities and boat trips along the coast, as well as excellent golf, provide energetic diversions.

- Beach: gently shelving and sandy.
- Casino: (Easter-Oct) ☎ 94.96.12.96
- Golf: mature 9h private course with magnificent views over the bay at Golf de Beauvallon, 83120 Ste-Maxime ☎ 94.96.16.98
- Riding: Centre Hippique des Maures, Domaine du Bouchage, Beauvallon ☎ 94.56.16.55
- Tennis: several clubs including Tennis Club de Ste-Maxime ☎ 94.96.05.28

 Les Saintes-Maries-de-la-Mer *(Bouches-du-Rhône)*
Pop: 2,000
Arles 38 km, Paris 764 km
🛈 5 avenue Van Gogh ☎ 90.47.82.55

An ancient and picturesque fishing port steeped in the tradition and folklore of the area. There are three pilgrimages each year: on a Sunday in October and on 24 and 25 May. Then the famous Gypsy Celebrations are held, and the *Farandoles* are danced. Games with the Camargue bulls, boat trips up the River Rhône, feast days and street dancing all combine to make this a lively and colourful small town. The flat Camargue region, natural habitat for a variety of birds, particularly flamingos, is also home for white horses and bulls around whom many of the local festivities revolve. The area can best be explored on horseback.

- Beach: 19 km of fine sand (plus naturist area).
- Camping: La Brise ☎ 90.47.84.67
- Riding: numerous outlets offer accompanied treks into the area. Enquire at the Tourist Office.

 Salon-de-Provence *(Bouches-du-Rhône)*
Pop: 35,000
Aix-en-Provence 35 km, Paris 722 km
🛈 56 cours Gimon ☎ 90.56.27.60

Salon is at the heart of France's olive-growing region, set in lovely countryside heavy with the perfume of pine, thyme and lavender, with walks and rides along signposted footpaths. A traditional market town which, since 1936, has been the site of the French Air Force officers' training college, the town itself has ancient squares and fountains shaded by tall plane trees. It was here that the astrologer Nostradamus wrote his prophecies. The massive Château de l'Emperi, which dominates the small town, has a fine collection of military history from Louis XIV to the present day.

- Camping: Nostradamus ☎ 90.56.08.36
- Golf: 9h private course at Golf de l'Ecole de l'Air, 13300 Salon-de-Provence ☎ 90.53.90.90

 Sanary-sur-Mer *(Var)*
Pop: 12,000
Marseille 54 km, Paris 827 km
🛈 Pavillon de Tourisme ☎ 94.74.01.04

This is a sunny seaside resort, residential in character and with a sheltered and picturesque port (600 berths).

- Beach: four little beaches with others such as the sandy Bonne-Grâce (to the east) at Six-Fours-les-Plages.
- Boat Trips: to the Ile d'Embiez (visit the oceanographic study centre).
- Camping: Val d'Aran ☎ 94.29.98.14

 Serre-Chevalier (*Hautes-Alpes*)
Alt: 1,350-2,800 m
Briançon 6 km, Paris 665 km
🅱 Office de Tourisme Intercommunal de Serre-Chevalier based at St-Chaffrey
☎ 92.24.00.34 with bureaux also at Chantemerle
☎ 92.24.00.34, Villeneuve ☎ 92.24.71.88 and Monétier ☎ 92.24.41.98

Quite apart from the truly excellent skiing possible from the dozen or so villages which together make up the Serre-Chevalier resorts there is also an opportunity to attempt new sports such as mono-skiing, snow-surfing or mountain parachuting. Or how about heliski? This involves being dropped by helicopter close to the summit and then skiing back down. In summer, the joys of the alpine meadows attract nature lovers as well as those sports enthusiasts for whom the area now provides rock climbing, panoramic hikes, hang gliding, cycling, archery, tennis and canoeing. There is extensive holiday accommodation for 30,000.

- Cycling: cycling in groups with a choice of routes, ideal for both the tourist and for those who want something more challenging. Tours leave every Saturday morning in summer, organised by the Vélo-Club de Serre-Chevalier ☎ 92.20.37.27
- Fishing: numerous mountain lakes offer excellent trout fishing.
- Hang Gliding: magnificently situated on the slopes of the Col du Granon ☎ 92.21.29.83
- Riding: Centre Equestre de Villeneuve le Sporting ☎ 92.24.78.61
- Tennis: several courts at all three bases, with tuition available.
- Walking: the Ecrins National Park is perfect for nature lovers. Visit the Alpine Garden at Col du Lauteret and the park's centre at Casset.

 Sisteron (*Hautes-Alpes*)
Pop: 7,000
Gap 48 km, Paris 700 km
🅱 Hôtel de Ville ☎ 92.61.12.03

A picturesque old town where an ancient citadel, atop a dramatic and deeply carved rock mass, overlooks the neck of the Durance river and the valley beyond. Sunny villages perched on slopes, the sometimes rugged, sometimes wooded beauty of the surrounding countryside, and the cool, fresh summer evenings are some of the exceptional qualities of this area.

- Camping: Camping de la Baume ☎ 92.61.19.69

- Gliding: modern equipment and first-class instruction is available from the Union Aérienne Sisteron Durance, Aérodrome de Vaumeilh, 04200 Sisteron. Piloting tuition for beginners will enable you to fly through the dramatic mountain scenery and there is good camping accommodation close to the aerodrome itself ☎ 92.61.27.45
- Riding: Relais Equestre La Fenière at Peipin (6 km) ☎ 92.64.14.02 and Club Equestre at Ribiers (8 km) ☎ 92.65.14.60
- Walking: extensive short or long-distance walks are possible.

 Six-Fours-les-Plages (*Var*)
Pop: 25,000
Toulon 8 km, Paris 834 km
🅱 plage de Bonne-Grâce ☎ 94.07.02.21

An all-year watersports resort at the southernmost point of this stretch of coastline, from where there are great views. The dry air, rich in ozone, stimulates the appetite for the many seafood restaurants serving fresh local produce.

- Beach: gently shelving and sandy.

 Superdévoluy (*Hautes-Alpes*)
Alt: 1,500-2,500 m
Marseille 216 km, Paris 640 km
🅱 Office de Tourisme ☎ 92.58.82.80

A functional, family-sized resort which enjoys the best of both worlds: the northern snows and the southern sun. In winter, combined with the village resort of La-Joue-du-Loup, it provides over 96 km of ski runs, plus cross-country trails. In summer, there is basket-ball coaching, archery, riding and lovely walks.

 Vaison-la-Romaine (*Vaucluse*)
Pop: 5,000
Avignon 47 km, Paris 670 km
🅱 place du Chanoine Sautel ☎ 90.36.02.11

A pretty little medieval town with fascinating Roman remains which include street excavations complete with flagstones, baths and mosaics. Beautiful marble statues, jewellery and pottery are now gathered in the museum. The town itself is on the banks of the Ouvèze and its houses climb in tiers up to the foot of the old castle. Rocky paths lead into the hills and there are numerous delights for walkers and painters, with magnificent panoramas of the wooded hills, the vineyards on the plain below and the mountains to the north.

- Camping: le Moulin de Cesar ☎ 90.36.00.78

 Valberg (*Alpes-Maritimes*)
Alt: 1,700 m
Nice 85 km, Paris 850 km
🅱 SI ☎ 93.02.52.54

One hour by road from Nice, Valberg is a sunny and well-equipped skiing resort at the foot of the

Mercantour in the southern Alps. Popular with families, there are many sports facilities for both winter and summer, amidst lovely scenery. The very young can enjoy pony rides through the woods or the artificial toboggan run, while adults can try clay-pigeon shooting or attempt mountain parachuting down the grassy slopes, a new sport which guarantees thrills without any real danger. There is holiday accommodation for 10,000.

● Fishing: in the wild and rugged beauty of the Daluis and Cians gorges.
● Parachuting: qualified instruction for beginners and improvers is bookable at the Tourist Office and run by the Club Omnisports de Valberg.
● Tennis: the Club Omnisports de Valberg holds group and individual courses and there are seven courts for hire. Enquire at the Tourist Office.
● Walking: lovely flower-filled meadows in spring and summer.

 Vallauris-Golfe-Juan *(Alpes-Maritimes)*
Pop: 22,000
Cannes 5 km, Paris 910 km
🛈 84 avenue de la Liberté ☎ 93.63.73.12

Golfe-Juan, on the coast, and Vallauris 2.5 km from the sea and set among orange trees and mimosa, are both blessed with a gentle climate. Golfe-Juan is set at the foot of the Vallauris hills with a long sandy beach in a shallow curve. There is good anchorage and underwater fishing.

The ancient pottery tradition at Vallauris was revived by Picasso and recreated here over a period of 20 years. The international biennial exhibition of ceramic arts draws artists from all over the world, while visitors will be tempted by the ceramics and pottery which spill out from the shops onto the pavements.

● Art: the National Picasso Museum has a Picasso fresco *War and Peace*, and at the centre of the market-place of Vallauris stands the impressive bronze Picasso statue of a man carrying a sheep.
● Golf: see Cannes.
● Tennis: municipal courts to hire at avenue de la Liberté ☎ 93.63.41.23

RHONE-ALPES

Administrative
Centre: Lyon
Population: 4,780,700
Area: 43,694 sq km

Départements:
01 Ain
07 Ardèche
26 Drôme
38 Isère
42 Loire
69 Rhône
73 Savoie
74 Haute-Savoie

National Parks:
Parc National des
Ecrins, 7 rue du
Colonel-Roux, 05000
Gap ☎ *92.51.40.71*

Parc National du
Mercantour, 23 rue
d'Italie, 06000 Nice
☎ *93.87.86.10*

Parc National de la
Vanoise, 135 rue du
Docteur Julliand,
B.P.705, 73007
Chambéry
☎ *79.62.30.54*

Regional Parks:
Parc Naturel Régional
du Pilat, 2 rue Benay,
42410 Pélussin
☎ *74.87.65.24*

Parc Naturel Régional
du Vercors, chemin
des Fusillés, B.P.14,
38250
Lans-en-Vercors
☎ *76.95.40.33*

Rising in Switzerland, the River Rhône first flows west to Lyon then south towards the Mediterranean, its course defining in turn the borders of each *département* of the region, from the Savoie heights to where the racing waters of the Ardèche gorges cascade down from the Massif Central to join the Rhône in its final run to the Midi.

Not far from the source of the Rhône, Mont Blanc's peak at 4,807 m looks down and across the eight *départements*. Beneath it lie Haute Savoie and Savoie, to the west Ain, Rhône and Loire, to the south west Isère, Drôme and Ardèche – a vast region more than a third of the size of England.

From Mont Blanc a great mountain barrier stretches south, separating France from Italy and Switzerland, from the glaciers and icy peaks of the Mont Blanc range and the Savoie Alps, to the dark rocky crags of the southern Dauphiné Alps.

Beyond the region, the mountains continue their sweep down through the Hautes-Alpes, the Alpes-de-Haute-Provence, the Alpes Maritimes and finally to the *corniches* fringing the Mediterranean coastline. These great mountain peaks of snow and ice, once sparsely peopled and savage in aspect, are today the home of such international winter playgrounds as Chamonix, Megève and Val d'Isère. Each year new ski stations are constructed or developed and new winter resorts built to accompany them: Avoriaz, Les Arcs, Méribel, Flaine, Isola 2000 and La Plagne. Today, quality newspapers publish regular snow reports for the pistes, alongside the foreign rates of exchange, for the European two-car family has also become the two-holiday one, not only in summer but in winter too. These once unfriendly mountains are now 'big business', thanks in part to a handful of poets, scientists and climbers who admired, researched and explored them 200 years ago. The Swiss scientist de Saussure walked up Mont Blanc in 1787 in his search for fossils. Wordsworth visited Chamonix in 1790. The Romantic poets Byron and Shelley knew and admired Meillerie near Evian. Jean-Jacques Rousseau favoured Chambéry.

The spas of the area became fashionable after Queen Victoria bestowed her

Samoëns

patronage on Aix-les-Bains, followed by the court and the modish few.

During the nineteenth century, rock climbing in the French Alps by the rich and adventurous put English names on many of the peaks there. The name of Edward Whymper, the great English mountaineer, is on a gravestone in Chamonix.

Away from the high exhilaration of the ski slopes, gentler resorts cluster: lakeside homes and châteaux, spas and smart shops. At Aix-les-Bains on the Lac du Bourget, a popular weekend trip from Chambéry, visitors still come to take the curative waters at a rate of 50000 each year, and also to inspect the Roman baths and hot springs. On Lac Leman (Lake Geneva), Thonon-les-Bains is a picturesque old town overlooked by the Chablais foothills. Evian-les-Bains, a few kilometres closer to the Swiss frontier, has charming gardens and parks, a casino and an elegant promenade, the quai de Blonay. Recently developed as an all-year-round conference centre, Evian water is its chief product, with 300 million bottles produced annually.

Beside the deep blue waters of Lake Annecy, the beautiful fifteenth-century town of Annecy is an enchantment. Graceful homes pose on the inlets and small promontories of the lake's twisting shoreline. Castles look down on the lake and on the old town at its head. The Canal du Thiou threads its way through the old quarter beneath a series of little bridges. Arcaded lanes and quays criss-cross below the twelfth-century Château d'Annecy, its four towers silhouetted against the mountains, and past the sixteenth-century Palais de l'Isle, lying as though at a mooring in the waters of the canal.

Savoie is magnificent walking country and a notable *Grande Randonnée* is that of *le Tour de Mont Blanc*. Thônes and La Clusaz, between Annecy and Mont Blanc, are good centres for walking in the Aravis Massif. The more rugged routes are furnished with *gites d'étape* (mountain shelters). Pralognan-la-Vanoise is the best centre from which to explore the Vanoise National Park, and there are pretty villages tucked away in the mountains, in the Haute Tarentaise and in the Parc du Queyras.

In Isère, surrounding Grenoble on three sides, rise up the south-west mountain ranges of the Vercors, home and citadel of the Resistance fighters, the Oisans mountains, with all-year-round skiing at Les Deux-Alpes and Alpe d'Huez, and, between Grenoble and Chambéry, the wooded Chartreuse.

The green or golden liqueur, with its 130 secret plant and herbal ingredients – pinks, fir buds and balm, to say nothing of a little absinthe – is distilled by Carthusian monks at Voiron.

Grenoble, at the junction of the Isère and the Drac, is a lively and modern university town. Its Musée des Beaux Arts has a fine collection of paintings by Corot, Gauguin, Pissarro, Bonnard and Renoir, as well as older works by Rubens and Watteau. The road from Grenoble into the Vercors, after passsing through the attractive Pont-en-Royans, with ancient houses perched on the rockface overlooking the River Bourne, carves through La Machine Pass near St-Jean-en-Royans, clinging to the cliffside on a spectacular, if vertiginous, route above the Cholet torrent 600 m below.

The theme of the region is now taken up by the mighty Rhône as it unites the *départements* of Ain, Rhône, Loire, Drôme and Ardèche and heads south. Gex, an elevated resort in the Jura mountains, looks east across Lake Geneva to the Savoie Alps. The foothills of the Jura can be tested by excursions from Ceyzeriat, a good walking centre. Divonne-les-Bains, on the Swiss border, is a spa and casino town popular with the Swiss. Nearby, at Ferney-Voltaire, is the château where Voltaire (1694-1778) lived.

Across the boundary of the River Saône extend the great Burgundy and Beaujolais vineyards, close to the market town of Bourg-en-Bresse. The Beaujolais fête is celebrated at Villefranche every June. Thirty-two km to the south, the beautiful sixteenth-century village of Perouges, carefully restored to its original state, awaits its next call from the French cinema as a location for yet another film.

The valley of the Rhône has been the great route into France for 2,000 years. Julius Caesar established *Lugdunum* (Lyon) in 43 BC. The Roman amphitheatre dates from 15 BC and is capable of seating 10,000 spectators. Here the first Christians were martyred. At Vienne there is a first-century Corinthian temple ruin. The Renaissance quarter of Lyon features more than a hundred interconnecting covered passages *(traboules)* and their linked courtyards, together with rare wrought-iron work on doors and windows, sculptured pieces and decorated wells. Today, however, Lyon is essentially modern and busy, an industrial centre with a cuisine reputedly unmatched in France. The *Côtes du Rhône* wines come from the long stretch of river south towards Avignon; the famous Hermitage vineyards are at Tournon in the Drôme. Lyon is also a conference centre, and boasts an active theatrical and musical life; the marionettes Punch and Judy were born in Lyon under their Guignol names of Canut and Madelon. In September each year a Berlioz festival is held here; the composer was born at La Côte-St-André, some 48 km away.

The Forez Mountains, the flanks of Mont Gerbier-de-Jonc, source of France's longest river, the Loire (1,000 km), the lavender fields of the Drôme and the superb gorges of the Rivers Canse and Ardèche – all these offer fine walking country. Less strenuously, they can be drifted over soundlessly by balloon from bases at Aubenas or, appropriately enough, at Annonay where, in 1793, the first balloon flight was made by the Montgolfier brothers. Far below may be seen a sprinkling of châteaux of every age and condition: St-Just, St-Martin and Bellegarde in the Loire; the Marquise de Sévigné's Château Grignan and the medieval castle of Suze-Larousse in the Drôme; in the Ardèche, testimony to the Wars of Religion, the Château d'Alba, the Château de Ventadour, and the austere twelfth-century fortress of Aubenas.

River cruises on the Rhône link Beaujolais and Burgundy country with that of the Côtes du Rhône below Lyon and from there south to Provence. Smaller vessels, canoe and kayak, race down the 30-km Gorges de l'Ardèche from Vallon-Pont-d'Arc to swirl past St-Martin-en-Ardèche and into the waters of the Rhône at Pont-St-Esprit, along an astonishing stretch of natural and savage beauty. Steep cliff faces of chalk, racing waters, grottoes and caves and an almost Mediterranean climate make this nature reserve an ecological refuge for rare species of plant, animal and birdlife. Here, buckthorn and spurge, honeysuckle, clematis and rock rose bloom in their seasons. The red-backed shrike impails its prey on a convenient thorn. Falcons, sparrowhawks and the golden eagle survey the canyon from on high. Dippers and grey wagtails flirt with the surface of the water. The goldfinch and the kingfisher dart into sight and, higher up the cliffs, swifts and jackdaws circle. The brilliant colours of the bee-eater (*guépier d'Europe*) flash for a moment then seem to vanish, its blue body merging with the blue of the sky. Only the rolling, liquid call of its song betrays its presence.

PRACTICAL TOURIST INFORMATION

General information on the region can be obtained by telephoning or writing to the Comité Régional du Tourisme (CRT) offices (one for the Rhône valley and one for the Alps), while specific booklets are produced detailing camping, hotel and self-catering gîte *accommodation. These can be obtained by writing to the tourist board office for the* département *(CDT) of your choice:*

Regional Tourist Boards
(for the Rhône valley) Comité Régional du Tourisme (CRT), 5 place de la Baleine, 69005 LYON ☎ 78.42.50.04
(for the Alps) Comité Régional du Tourisme (CRT), 9 boulevard Wilson, 73100 AIX-LES-BAINS ☎ 79.88.23.41

Départements
Ain (01): Comité Départemental du Tourisme (CDT), 34 rue Général-Delestraint, B.P.78, 01002 BOURG-EN-BRESSE Cedex ☎ 74.21.95.00
Ardèche (07): Comité Départemental du Tourisme (CDT), 8 cours du Palais, B.P.221, 07000 PRIVAS Cedex ☎ 75.64.04.66
Drôme (26): Comité Départemental du Tourisme (CDT), 1 avenue de Romans, 26000 VALENCE ☎ 75.43.27.12
Isère (38): Syndicat d'Initiative de Vienne, cours Brillier, 38200 VIENNE ☎ 74.85.12.62
Loire (42): Comité Départemental du Tourisme (CDT), 5 place Jean-Jaurès, 42021 ST-ETIENNE Cedex ☎ 77.33.15.39
Rhône (69): Comité Départemental du Tourisme (CDT), B.P.2254, 69214 LYON Cedex ☎ 78.42.25.75
Savoie (73): Association Départementale de Tourisme (ADT), 24 boulevard de la Colonne, 73000 CHAMBERY ☎ 79.85.12.45
Haute-Savoie (74): Association Départementale de Tourisme (ADT), 56 rue Sommellier, B.P.348, 74012 ANNECY ☎ 50.51.32.31

SELF-CATERING ACCOMMODATION

The following British operators offer self-catering accommodation in the area:

AA Motoring Holidays, P.O. Box 100, Fanum House, Halesowen B63 3BT ☎ 021-550 7401
Agencefrance Holidays, Lansdowne Place, 17 Holdenhurst Road, Bournemouth BH8 8EH ☎ 0202 299534

Alpine Homes, The Red House, Garstons Close, Titchfield, Fareham, Hants PO14 4EW ☎ 0329 844405
Bowhills Ltd, Swanmore, Southampton SO3 2QW ☎ 0489 877627
Brittany Ferries, The Brittany Centre, Wharf Road, Portsmouth PO2 8RU ☎ 0705 827701
Cresta Holidays, 32 Victoria Street, Altrincham WA14 1ET ☎ 0345 056511
Flaine Information, 128a Hamlet Court Road, Westcliff-on-Sea SS0 7LN ☎ 0702 343381
Four Seasons, Springfield, Farsley, Pudsey LS28 5UT ☎ 0532 564374
French Life Motoring Holidays, 26 Church Road, Horsforth, Leeds LS18 5LG ☎ 0532 390077
Gîtes de France, 178 Piccadilly, London W1V 9DB ☎ 01-493 3480
Hoverspeed Ltd, Maybrook House, Queens Gardens, Dover CT17 9UQ ☎ 0304 240241
Inghams Travel, 10/18 Putney Hill, London SW15 6AX ☎ 01-785 7777
Intasun France, Intasun House, Cromwell Avenue, Bromley BR2 9AQ ☎ 01-290 1900
Interhome, 383 Richmond Road, Twickenham TW1 2EF ☎ 01-891 1294
Just France, 1 Belmont, Lansdown Road, Bath BA1 5DZ ☎ 0225 446328
David Newman's French Collection, P.O. Box 733, 40 Upperton Road, Eastbourne BN21 4AW ☎ 0323 410347
Pleasurewood Holidays, Somerset House, Gordon Road, Lowestoft NR32 1PZ ☎ 0502 517271
Prime Time Holidays, 5a Market Square, Northampton NN1 2DL ☎ 0604 20996
Les Propriétaires de l'Ouest, Malton House, 24 Hampshire Terrace, Portsmouth PO1 2QE ☎ 0705 755715
Rendez-Vous France, Holiday House, 146/148 London Road, St Albans AL1 1PQ ☎ 0727 45400
Sally Tours, Argyle Centre, York Street, Ramsgate CT11 9DS ☎ 0843 595566
Slipaway Holidays, 90 Newland Road, Worthing BN11 1LB ☎ 0903 821000
Sturge, Martin, 3 Lower Camden Place, Bath BA1 5JJ ☎ 0225 310623
Tourarc UK, 197b Brompton Road, London SW3 1LA ☎ 01-589 1918
Vacances, 28 Gold Street, Saffron Walden CB10 1EJ ☎ 0799 25101
Vacances en Campagne, Bignor, Pulborough RH20 1QD ☎ 07987 433
Vacations, 60 Charles Street, Leicester LE1 1FB ☎ 0533 537758

VFB Holidays, 1 St Margaret's Terrace,
Cheltenham GL50 4DT ☎ 0242 526338

SPORTS AND ACTIVITIES

*For unusual and interesting holiday ideas, contact
the Loisirs Accueil office for the area of your
choice:*

Loisirs Accueil Ardèche,
8 cours du Palais, 07000 PRIVAS ☎ 75.64.04.66
Loisirs Accueil Loire-Forez,
5 place Jean Jaurès, 42021 SAINT-ETIENNE
Cedex ☎ 77.33.15.39
Loisirs Accueil Savoie,
24 boulevard de la Colonne, 73000 CHAMBERY
☎ 79.85.01.99

RESORTS

 Aix-les-Bains *(Savoie)*
Pop: 23,000
Annecy 33 km, Paris 530 km
🛈 place Maurice Mollard ☎ 79.35.05.92

An all-year health and holiday resort in a beautiful
location between the largest lake in France and
Mont Revard. Virtually an inland sea, the Lac du
Bourget offers excellent fishing and a large variety
of watersports, as well as boat trips which operate
from the harbour. Renowned for its temperate
climate, walkers can enjoy exploring the forests
beneath the mountain as well as the delightful
lakeside and mountain villages. With Italy and
Switzerland nearby for excursions and numerous
entertainments which include an open-air theatre,
casino, nightclubs and a racecourse, Aix is perfect
for all tastes.

● Beach: sandy lakeside beach.
● Camping: Sierroz ☎ 79.61.21.43
● Cycling: cycles can be hired from the SNCF
station.
● Golf: 18h private course at Golf d'Aix-les-
Bains, avenue du Golf, 73100 Aix-les-Bains
☎ 79.61.23.35 (open all year).
● Riding: Hippodrome de Marlioz
☎ 79.88.35.67
● Spas: rheumatism/bone joint damage (open all
year) ☎ 79.35.38.50 alt: 250 m, climate:
temperate. The Institut Marlioz deals with
respiratory/lymphatic disorders ☎ 79.61.00.91
alt: 280 m, climate: temperate.

 Alpe d'Huez *(Isère)*
Alt: 1,450-3,350 m
Grenoble 62 km, Paris 620 km
🛈 place Paganon ☎ 76.80.35.41

The sharp, shining glaciers of Mont de Lans are
the backdrop to this old Alpine village, an all-year
ski resort where, from June to September, there is
summer skiing at over 3,000 m. Like its neighbour,
Les Deux Alpes, this resort is in the Oisans range,
a frozen forest of peaks, reached by a dizzying,
hairpin-bend road up a seemingly vertical valley

wall. There is holiday accommodation for 30,000 in
hotels and chalets, with a variety of activities on
offer including helicopter flights, tennis, cross-
country trails, parascending and hang gliding.

 Annecy *(Haute-Savoie)*
Pop: 52,000
Aix-les-Bains 34 km, Paris 545 km
🛈 1 rue Jean Jaurès ☎ 50.45.00.33

Capital of the Haute-Savoie region, Annecy is an
extremely attractive and lively lakeside town of
great artistic and historic interest. Well equipped
for sports in both summer and winter, its enormous
appeal rests with the pure waters of its lake (of the
same name) and the proximity of the mountains.
On the same latitude as Montreal (Canada) and
Zagreb (Yugoslavia), and an ideal base for
excursions, festivities and cultural events.

● Camping: Municipal.
● Canoeing: courses are organised at Base
Nautique des Marquisats ☎ 50.23.08.59
● Cycling: cycles can be hired from the SNCF
station.
● Fishing: the lake offers category 1 fishing.
● Golf: undulating 18h private course
overlooking the lake at Golf d'Annecy,
Echarvines, 74290 Talloires ☎ 50.60.12.89
(Mar-Nov).
● Hang Gliding: Site de la Forclaz
☎ 50.23.40.22 and para-gliding (parapente)
at Vol de Pente, 6 rue de la Cité
☎ 50.52.89.85
● Riding: La Cravache d'Annecy, boulevard du
Lycée ☎ 50.45.32.38 and Les Ecuries du Lac
☎ 50.60.14.41
● Tennis: four courts to hire at boulevard du
Fier ☎ 50.57.45.32

 Les Arcs *(Savoie)*
Alt: 1,200-3,200m
Val d'Isère 43 km, Paris 650 km
🛈 Office de Tourisme ☎ 79.07.04.92

Modern high-rise apartment blocks rather detract
from what is certainly one of France's top resorts,
for here are some of the best facilities for learning
at any age. The 'ski évolutif' method, first
pioneered here 15 years ago, and consisting of
gradual progression from short to long skis, is
foolproof and instruction is quickly followed by
competent and confident skiing. The massive ski
area includes the four valleys of Villaroger, Arc
2000, Bourg-Saint-Maurice and Peisey-Nancroix
and is really made up of three resorts (Arc 2000,
Arc 1800 and Arc 1600) inter-connected but fully
independent and offering holiday accommodation
for 22,000. The Winter Olympics of 1992 will be
held on these slopes. Non-skiing activities vary
between resorts, but include snow-plough
excursions and trips by horse-drawn sleigh,
parascending and mono-ski and, of course, if your

visit coincides with Christmas, guess who drops in by hang glider?

- Golf: 18h private course 1,520 m above sea level where the fairways are crossed by mountain streams at Golf des Arcs, 73700 Bourg-Saint-Maurice ☎ 79.07.48.00

 Avoriaz *(Haute-Savoie)*
Alt: 1,800-2,500 m
Annecy 93 km, Paris 595 km
Office de Tourisme ☎ 50.74.02.11

A modern apartment-block resort in an attractive mountainside setting with a traffic-free heart. At the centre of the Portes-du-Soleil ski area, this is a south-facing resort close to the Swiss border, with holiday accommodation for 14,500.

- Riding: bookable through the Tourist Office and run by the Centre Equestre La Doua.

 Brides-les-Bains *(Savoie)*
Pop: 600
Annecy 77 km, Paris 616 km
rue Leray ☎ 79.55.20.64

The higher reaches of the Isère form the Tarentaise region of Savoy. A glitter of famous ski resorts surrounding Tignes and Val d'Isère are still reached from Italy via the little St-Bernard pass just as when the Roman legions first headed for the Rhône valley and Gaul. The Winter Olympics of 1992 will be held on the slopes of the Tarentaise valley at Méribel, Courchevel, Les Menuires, Val Thorens, La Plagne, Pralognan, Les Arcs, Tignes and Val d'Isère. The opening and closing ceremonies will take place at Albertville and this little town will become the Olympic village, linked to Méribel by an overhead transport system.

- Camping: ☎ 79.55.22.74
- Casino: ☎ 79.55.23.07
- Spa: (Salins-les-Thermes) metabolic disorders (15 Apr-31 Oct) ☎ 79.55.23.44 alt: 600 m, climate: mild.

 Chamonix *(Haute-Savoie)*
Pop: 9,000 Alt: 1,035-3,850 m
Annecy 94 km, Paris 615 km
place du Triangle de l'Amitié ☎ 50.53.00.24

A great international resort at the foot of the Mont Blanc range, there are 80 hotels here as well as chalets and studio apartments. A popular and attractive mountaineering and skiing resort with full indoor sports facilities, casino, cabarets and cinemas – *après-ski* lasts long into the night. Not for the faint-hearted is the Aiguille du Midi cable-car trip which reaches the dizzying height of 3,800 m, providing an unforgettable view over the Chamonix valley. Extensive holiday accommodation for 37,000.

- Golf: 18h private course set in the scenic valley beneath Mont Blanc at Golf de Chamonix,

74400 Les Praz de Chamonix (May-Oct) ☎ 50.53.06.28
- Riding: Club Hippique la Guerinière ☎ 50.53.42.84

 Châtel *(Haute-Savoie)*
Pop: 1,000 Alt: 1,100-2,200 m
Morzine 50 km, Paris 570 km
☎ 50.73.22.44

On the Swiss border, in the Chablais valley, Châtel is a pretty Alpine village of chalets with flower-draped walls and balconies. Good fishing on the Dranse river which flows into Lake Geneva (Lac Leman) and over 200 km of walking trails attract summer hikers. In the Portes du Soleil skiing area, there is holiday accommodation for 16,000.

- Camping: L'Oustalet ☎ 50.73.21.97
- Fishing: category 1 fishing on the Dranse river.
- Riding: Centre Hippique du Leman ☎ 50.73.25.17

 La Clusaz *(Haute-Savoie)*
Pop: 1,500 Alt: 1,100-2,600 m
Megève 29 km, Paris 570 km
Office de Tourisme ☎ 50.02.60.92

One of the longest established winter sports resorts with very much the character of a village, La Clusaz has a large and attractive skiing area on five different mountains, closely interlinked by lift or piste and offering skiing for all standards. Here you can learn how to hang glide or parascend, use the fitness gym or slide some more on the ice rink. Sight-seeing trips by snowmobile are also available, even by moonlight. The village lies to the east of Annecy in the Col des Aravis, surrounded in summer by pasture land and vast woods of larch trees, providing magnificent walking country. An international festival of Folk Dance is held in July and there is holiday accommodation for 18,000.

- Camping: Plan du Fernuy ☎ 50.02.44.75
- Riding: Ranch le Cortibot ☎ 50.02.62.34 (Club des Sports)
- Tennis: Club des Sports offers coaching (July-Sep) over five days for adults and children (6-12 years).

 Courchevel *(Savoie)*
Alt: 1,300-2,700 m
Chambéry 97 km, Paris 635 km
La Croisette ☎ 79.08.00.29

A fashionable and select resort with the fastest and most exciting runs in Europe, this is part of the Trois Vallées ski area, together with Méribel, Les Menuires and Val Thorens. Its own snow-free airport allows twice daily flights from Paris, and its luxury hotels and piano bars, nightclub atmosphere and jet-set patronage have made it a great international resort. Host for certain events in the Winter Olympics of 1992, Courchevel has holiday accommodation for 32,000.

Les Deux Alpes *(Isère)*
Alt: 1,650-3,600 m
Grenoble 74 km, Paris 635 km
🅑 maison des Deux Alpes ☎ 76.79.22.00

Les Deux Alpes, as with its fellow resort of Alpe d'Huez, sits at a glacial point some 3,600 m high amid the Oisans range, a frieze of sharpened peaks against the Mont de Lans glacier. Popular with families, this is a large, modern ski resort whose stunning mountain scenery also attracts summer visitors to the summer skiing available here, as well as the riding and walking. Hotel and chalet accommodation for 22,000.

● Camping: Deux Alpes ☎ 76.79.20.47

 Evian-les-Bains *(Haute-Savoie)*
Pop: 6,000
Annecy 84 km, Paris 580 km
🅑 Office de Tourisme ☎ 50.75.04.26

An all-year health and holiday resort on the south shore of Lac Leman (Lake Geneva), nestling in the rocky Chablais foothills. A magnificent region of forests, mountain lakes and small villages, the immediate area invites further exploration with Switzerland and Italy as optional extras. In addition to its world-famous natural spring and thermal establishment, the town offers a full programme of entertainment possibilities, with exhibitions, festivals, tennis, riding and golf. Casino.

● Camping: Grande Rive ☎ 50.75.50.76
● Canoeing: courses combining lake and river canoeing are organised by Maison des Jeunes et de la Culture, 4 avenue Anna de Noailles, B.P.131, 74501 Evian ☎ 50.75.19.69
● Cycling: cycles can be hired from the SNCF station.
● Golf: 18h private course overlooking the lake at Golf d'Evian, Rive Sud du Lac de Genève, 74500 Evian ☎ 50.75.14.00 (closed Dec and Jan).
● Riding: Les Ecuries du Gavot ☎ 50.26.27.82
● Spa: kidneys/urinary organs (open all year) ☎ 50.75.02.30 alt: 376 m, climate: mild.
● Tennis: five-day courses for adults and children (7-13 years), of 2 hr per day, are offered by Evian Sport Tennis, Les Mateirons, 74500 Evian ☎ 50.75.30.02 (Jun-Sep) and Royal Club Evian ☎ 50.75.14.00 offers similar (Feb-Nov).

 Flaine *(Haute-Savoie)*
Alt: 1,600-2,500 m
Distances: Megève 49, Paris 605 km
🅑 Office de Tourisme ☎ 50.90.80.01

Purpose-built south-facing family skiing resort with compact accommodation for 8,000, principally in self-catering apartments and chalets. There are 8 km of cross-country trails, or you can try hang gliding, ice skating or the swimming pool. In summer the resort offers the pleasures of its scenery plus riding, tennis and golf.

● Golf: 18h private course facing Mont Blanc at Golf de Flaine les Carroz, 74300 Flaine ☎ 50.90.85.44
● Riding: Centre Equestre le Mazot ☎ 50.90.80.74 (Club des Sports).
● Tennis: intensive and semi-intensive coaching is available in Flaine during the summer and organised by Sepad Loisirs, 23 rue Cambon, 75001 Paris ☎ 42.61.55.17

 Grenoble *(Isère)*
Pop: 392,000
Lyon 106 km, Paris 550 km
🅑 14 rue de la République ☎ 76.54.34.36

A spectacular backdrop of mountains encircles this great and dynamic industrial and university centre. The capital of the Dauphiné region, this is a city that cannot fail to impress. Host to the Winter Olympics in 1968, it is literally surrounded by winter sports resorts within the mountain ranges of Belledonne, Chartreuse, Oisans and Vercors. For a panoramic view across the city and towards Mont Blanc on the horizon, enjoy the cable car trip up to the nineteenth-century Bastille, or visit Isère during the colourful autumn or summer when the cross-country trails of winter become hiking paths and the clear mountain streams and magnificent pastoral landscape attract the angler, walker, climber and naturalist. Two health spas, Allevard and Uriage, are within a short distance, the latter (plus golf course) situated at the base of the winter sports resort of Chamrousse.

● Golf: 18h private course at Golf Club de Grenoble, La Grande Grange, St-Quentin-en-Isère, B.P.8, 38210 Tullins ☎ 76.93.67.28; and 9h private course at Golf d'Uriage Grenoble, Les Alberges, Vaulnaveys-le-Haut,

Grenoble

38410 Uriage ☎ 76.89.03.47
● Spas: Allevard-les-Bains (17 May-24 Sep)
respiratory/lymphatic disorders ☎ 76.97.56.22
alt: 475 m, climate: temperate. Uriage-les-
Bains (1 Apr-24 Oct) skin diseases
☎ 76.89.10.17 alt: 410 m, climate: temperate.

 Megève *(Haute-Savoie)*
Pop: 5,000 Alt: 1,100-2,600 m
Chamonix 36 km, Paris 600 km
🛈 Office de Tourisme ☎ 50.21.27.28

A fashionable and elegant resort with, at its heart,
an old Savoy village where horse-drawn sleighs are
the only traffic. There is a challenging variety of
slopes and cross-country trails, and an Olympic-
sized ice-skating rink, heated swimming pools and
gymnasium. Skiing tuition is given. In summer,
there is the use of 16 tennis courts and a golf
course. Luxury shops, casino, nightclubs and bars
provide entertainment late into the night. Holiday
accommodation for 40,000.

● Golf: 18h private course at Golf de Megève,
Le Mont d'Arbois, 74120 Megève
☎ 50.21.31.51
● Riding: Centre Equestre des Coudrettes, route
du Crêt du Midi ☎ 50.21.16.52
● Tennis: five-day courses for beginners,
improvers and children at Espace Tennis,
Palais des Sports ☎ 50.21.15.71 (Jun-Sep).
Also intensive coaching (four hr per day) for
adults and children from Club de Tennis du
Mont d'Arbois ☎ 50.21.31.51

 Les Menuires *(Savoie)*
Alt: 1,850-3,400 m
Chambéry 100 km, Paris 637 km
🛈 Office de Tourisme ☎ 79.08.20.12

Modern apartment-block, purpose-built ski resort
with over 100 km of runs for all levels of skier.
Part of the Trois Vallées ski area, together with
Courchevel, Méribel and Val Thorens (and host
for events in the 1992 Winter Olympics), the resort
has been designed so that the skiing is close to the
accommodation and shopping areas. The annual
Rock and Blues Festival, in mid-March, attracts
famous international artistes who star during a
week of concerts and also compete in friendly
skiing competitions during the day. Very much a
young resort, the night life is lively, with bars,
discos and cinemas, and provides holiday
accommodation for 20,500.

 Méribel *(Savoie)*
Alt: 1,400-2,952 m
Annecy 89 km, Paris 628 km
🛈 Office de Tourisme ☎ 79.08.60.01

A pretty chalet and pinewood resort linked to the
village of Brides-les-Bains. At the heart of the
Trois Vallées, this is the most extensive skiing area
in the world, comprising Les Menuires, Courchevel
and Val Thorens. There are over 90 km of pistes.

For the Winter Olympics of 1992, Méribel will play
host to the women's alpine ski events and the ice-
hockey competitions. It can offer holiday
accommodation for 25,000.

● Golf: high-altitude 9h private course with
beautiful views at Golf de Méribel, 73550
Méribel Altiport ☎ 79.08.60.49

 Morzine *(Haute-Savoie)*
Pop: 3,000
Annecy 93 km, Paris 595 km
🛈 place Centrale ☎ 50.79.03.45

Part of the Portes-du-Soleil region embracing 12
French and Swiss resorts, this has become the third
largest ski resort in France. An excellent sport
centre offering holiday accommodation for 22,500.

● Canoeing: courses for children (14 years
upwards) are organised by the Auberge de
Jeunesse, les Coutterets ☎ 50.79.14.86
● Riding: Centre Equestre les Dereches
☎ 50.79.18.97
● Tennis: coaching over six days organised by
the Auberge de Jeunesse ☎ 50.79.14.86 (Jun-
Sep).

 La Plagne *(Savoie)*
Alt: 1,900-3,250 m
Chambéry 109 km, Paris 645 km
🛈 Office de Tourisme ☎ 79.09.02.01

La Plagne is a large winter sports resort of modern
apartment blocks made up, in effect, of six
'villages': Aime 2000, Plagne 1800, Plagne
Villages, Bellecôte, Belle Plagne and Plagne
Centre, with total holiday accommodation for
30,000. Extensive summer activities are offered by
the resorts, including white-water rafting and
kayaking, mountain biking, riding treks,
paragliding, fitness packages incorporating tennis,
squash, sauna and sun-bed, even music lessons and
astronomy. With Tignes and Val d'Isère, it is one
of the highest altitude resorts in France and will
host the bobsleigh and luge events in the Winter
Olympics of 1992.

 Samoëns *(Haute-Savoie)*
Pop: 2,000 Alt: 700-3,100 m
Morzine 30 km, Paris 586 km
🛈 Office de Tourisme ☎ 50.34.40.28

An attractive old village in a valley set in Mont
Blanc country, in a mixture of green woods and
high pastures with, towering above all, Mont Blanc
itself. At the head of the valley is the soaring
Cirque du Fer à Cheval, a semi-circle of limestone
cliffs with a tumble of waterfalls thundering over it.
Samoëns is the perfect centre for excursions to the
look-out point of La Rosière, to Mont Blanc itself,
6 km away, and to the spectacular waterfall. There
are some very old houses gathered around the
market place, in this traditional home of masons
and stone workers and, at the heart of the town, a

La Plagne

lime tree of ancient lineage. The Lac aux Dames forms the centre of the summer recreational activities, offering tennis, canoeing, archery and fishing. There is holiday accommodation for 16,000.

- Camping: Le Giffre Municipal ☎ 50.34.41.92 and Le Chanosset ☎ 50.34.43.54
- Canoeing: and white-water rafting on the river Giffre ☎ 50.93.63.63
- Fishing: category 1 fishing in the Clevieux river.
- Hang Gliding: and delta-planing ☎ 50.34.95.80
- Riding: Centre Equestre du Pont du Giffre. Enquire at the Tourist Office.

 Thonon-les-Bains *(Haute-Savoie)*
Pop: 30,000
Annecy 73 km, Paris 570 km
🛈 place de l'Hôtel de Ville ☎ 50.71.50.88

A spa town with pleasant gardens on the banks of Lac Leman (Lake Geneva), its flower-filled terraces overlooking the lake, and perhaps a little livelier than its neighbouring spa, Evian. There are good bathing resorts nearby and Swiss visitors make regular boat trips to the pretty township of Yvoire, along the lake shore. From Thonon's port of Rives, there is a service of boat cruises to Lausanne and Geneva in Switzerland. There is good sailing at the Plage de Ripaille.

- Boat Trips: ☎ 50.71.14.71

- Camping: Camping de Morcy ☎ 50.71.32.65
- Canoeing: courses are organised by Club de Canoë-kayak, Port des Clerges ☎ 50.71.51.72
- Cycling: cycles can be hired from the SNCF station.
- Golf: see Evian.
- Riding: Ferme des Fleysets ☎ 50.71.30.81
- Spa: kidneys/urinary organs (open all year) ☎ 50.26.17.22 alt: 430 m, climate: fresh.
- Tennis: courses offered by Tennis Club de la Grangette ☎ 50.71.29.67 and Tennis de Ripaille ☎ 50.71.29.67

 Tignes *(Savoie)*
Pop: 1,500
Val d'Isère 13 km, Paris 668 km
🛈 Office de Tourisme ☎ 79.06.15.55

Tignes, with Val d'Isère, forms one of the most famous and extensive skiing areas in the world. Indeed, its slopes will figure prominently in the Winter Olympics of 1992. In a lake setting 2,100 m up, in a bleak white bowl above the tree line, the resort sits at the foot of the Grande Motte (3,656 m). Modern apartment blocks provide holiday accommodation for 27,000, and visitors will find summer skiing and other sports facilities to be amongst the best anywhere. Also popular as a base for exploring the Vanoise National Park.

- Camping: Le Chantel ☎ 79.06.15.55
- Golf: 9h course which, at 2,300 m above sea level, is clearly competing for the 'highest course in Europe' title! ☎ 79.06.37.22

- Riding: Club des Sports ☎ 79.06.53.87 also organise white-water rafting trips.

 Val d'Isère *(Savoie)*
Pop: 2,000 Alt: 1,850-3,300 m
Chambéry 132 km, Paris 670 km
Office de Tourisme ☎ 79.06.15.55

An extensive and world-famous skiing area linked with Tignes, and providing holiday accommodation for 21,000, Val d'Isère still retains its original form, with old stone houses gathered around the Savoyard church. This is a top-level winter and summer resort which caters for a public who want all-year-round skiing, golf in the mornings and tennis matches in the afternoons, as well as canoeing and hang gliding. In the 1992 Winter Olympic Games, the men's downhill skiing competitions will take place here.

- Camping: Les Richards ☎ 79.06.00.60
- Canoeing: Club des Sports ☎ 79.06.03.49
- Riding: Centre Equestre de Val d'Isère ☎ 79.06.20.80

 Vallon Pont d'Arc *(Ardèche)*
Pop: 2,000
Alès 50 km, Paris 670 km
Office de Tourisme ☎ 75.88.04.01

The meandering course of the River Ardèche is at its most spectacular here as it cuts through the chalky cliffs, notably at the famous natural stone arch of Pont d'Arc. Shallow-bottomed boats carry visitors through this nature reserve, for this is supreme canoeing water, with 30 km of gorges to descend, over a period of days, with facilities for camping at stages along its course. Additionally, visitors are able to enjoy fishing, riding and walking in this scenic area.

- Boat Trips: bookable through the Tourist Office.
- Camping: Mondial Camping ☎ 75.88.00.44 and Le Provençal ☎ 75.88.00.48
- Canoeing: several outlets hire out canoes and kayaks and offer tuition with short, supervised descents. Ardèche Bateaux ☎ 75.37.10.07, Loulou Bateaux ☎ 75.88.01.32 and Base Nautique de Pont d'Arc ☎ 75.88.00.69

 Valmorel *(Savoie)*
Alt: 1,400 m
Chambéry 87 km, Paris 625 km
Office de Tourisme ☎ 79.09.84.44

A recently created family resort which has been designed in more traditional style, with careful use of wood and stone, offering holiday accommodation for 8,000. Floodlit piste for the excitement of night skiing.

- Hang Gliding: and parascending ☎ 79.09.85.55

 Val Thorens *(Savoie)*
Alt: 2,300-3,300 m
Chambéry 109 km, Paris 645 km
Office de Tourisme ☎ 79.00.08.08

Modern apartment blocks, providing holiday accommodation for 14,500, make up this purpose-built and traffic-free village which, at 2,300 m, is the highest resort in Europe. There is direct access to the slopes from the accommodation areas and its climate, altitude and location guarantee the best snow conditions throughout the year. This resort forms part of the Trois Vallées skiing area, together with Courchevel, Méribel and Les Menuires, and, like these others, will host events in the 1992 Winter Olympics. Summer or winter, the extensive sports complex offers tennis, squash, a swimming pool, fitness gym and golf training simulator. This is, incidentally, the only place in the world where tennis is played at such high altitude.

 Villard-de-Lans *(Isère)*
Alt: 1,050-2,170 m
Grenoble 34 km, Paris 585 km
Office de Tourisme ☎ 76.95.10.38

A summer and winter sports resort with 120 km of pistes for all levels of skier and extensive marked runs for cross-country enthusiasts. In addition, winter activities offered include Scandinavian-style weekends consisting of rides in dog sleds, accommodation in a mountain refuge with sauna, and six hours' skiing per day, with an instructor who will introduce you to trekking. Also possible is a Nordic ski trek involving the complete crossing of the Vercors, while an imaginative way to pass a weekend is to rediscover the traditions of the region by joining a weekend bread-baking course and baking your own loaves in a 200-year-old oven (Fri-Sun evening). Or how about combining learning the skills of archery with cross-country skiing through the forest? Summer reveals the glories of the town's location, with alpine meadows to walk or ride through and clear mountain streams for fishing. Tennis, riding, rock climbing, archery and mountain biking (the host of the World Championships in 1987) are some of the other sports catered for. There is holiday accommodation for 20,000.

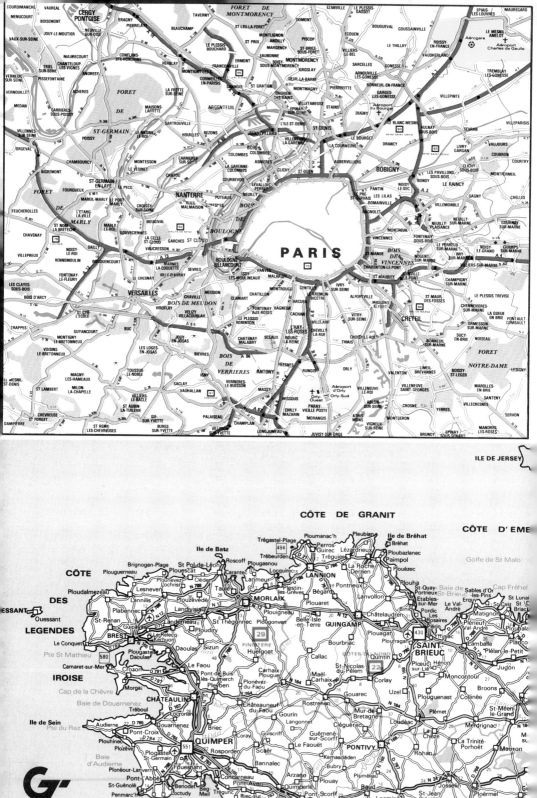

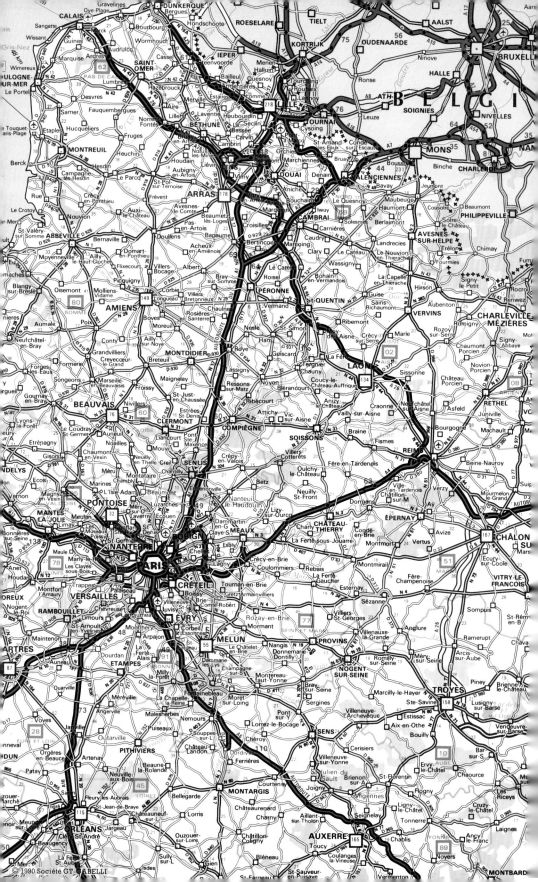

O C É A N

A T L A N T I Q U E

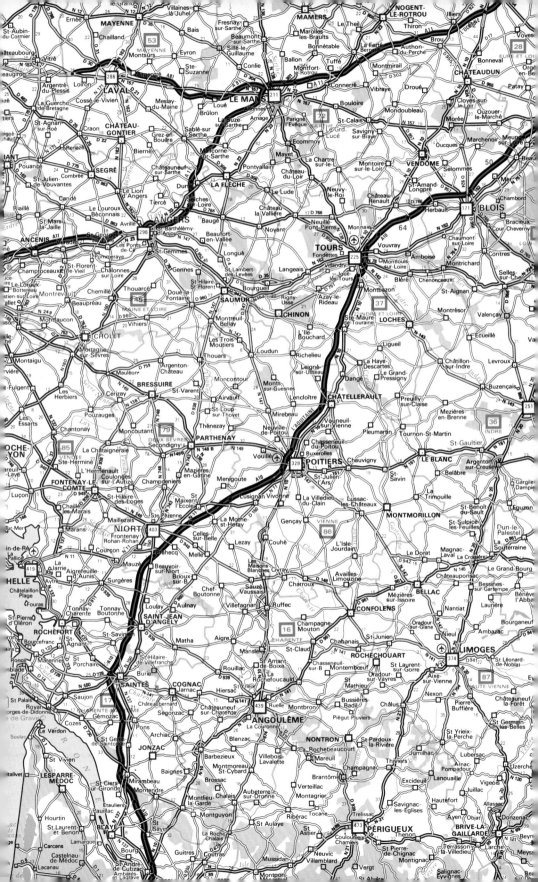

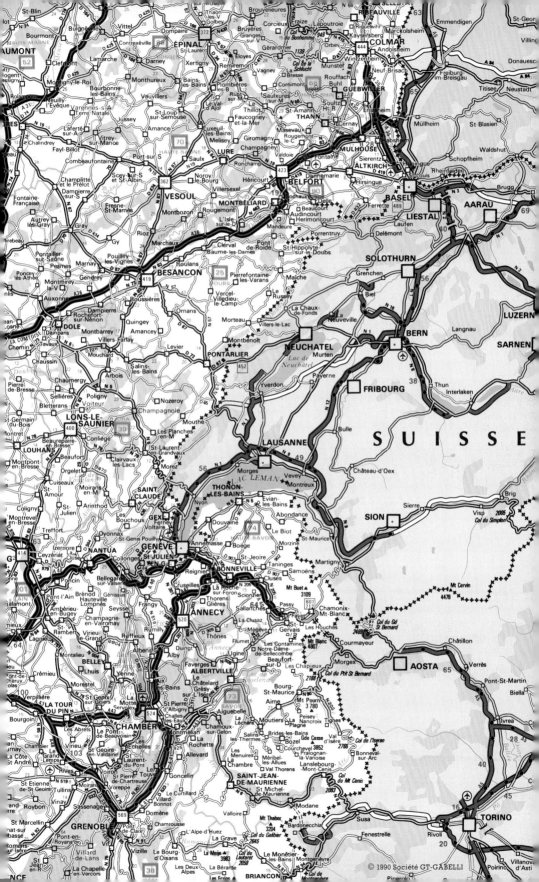

© 1990 Société GT-GABELLI

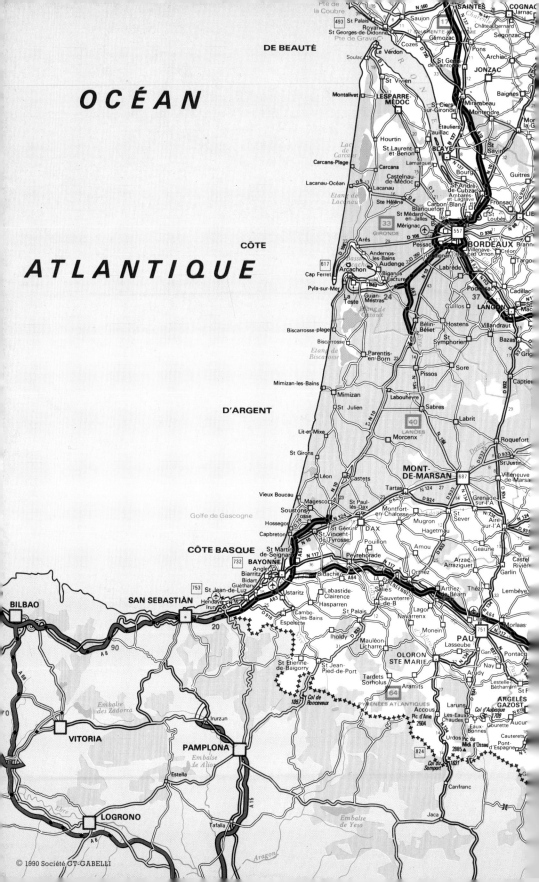